# Praise for *Little Merchants*

*"The richly textured narrative of Little Merchants explores the experiences of the boys and girls who carried papers every day. By 1980 there were nearly one million of them. Waking at 4 a.m. or racing after school, the kids delivered the papers on time (usually), even in miserable weather and sometimes to deadbeats. Illustrated with vintage photos, Little Merchants is a social history of 20th century childhood in America, told from the point of view of the youth who porched newspapers to the nation's doorsteps."*
Lorraine McConaghy Ph.D.
Senior Historian Museum of History & Industry, Seattle

*"As youth committed to deliver newspapers, they learned psychology, social interchange, integrity, and the free-enterprise economic system, while a middle-school student. Little Merchants got it right and tells it all."*
Jim Mack
Vice-President, Financial Advisor, Morgan Stanley

*"Nothing taught me more about work and dealing with people than delivering newspapers as a boy. Sandra Walker has captured that era beautifully in Little Merchants. I have this urge to bundle 100 of her books and drop one on your doorstep."*
Jim Stingl
Journalist, *Milwaukee Journal Sentinel*

*"Illuminating an era of Americana, Sandra Walker has captivated the story of youth as newspaper carriers, portraying their experiences in a compelling, often poignant chronicle. Little Merchants is a fascinating, informative and humorous read."*
Joe Forsee
Executive Director, International Circulation Managers Association (ret.)

*"As a paperboy, I developed skills in sales, service, self-discipline and time management that created an important foundation for my 40 years in the newspaper business. That strong foundation turned out to be sound."*
Bill Malone
Vice-president of circulation

# LITTLE MERCHANTS

*The golden era of youth delivering newspapers*

# LITTLE MERCHANTS

*The golden era of youth delivering newspapers*

By
Sandra Walker

Orion Wellspring, Inc.
Seattle, WA

First edition, first printing October, 2013
Copyright © 2013 by Sandra Walker. All rights reserved.
Published by Orion Wellspring, Inc., Seattle, WA 98109


ISBN-13: 978-0-9888192-0-7
ISBN: 978-0-9888192-1-4 (ebook)


9 8 7 6 5 4 3 2 1
Printed and bound in the United States of America.


Library of Congress Cataloging-in-Publication Data
Little Merchants: The golden era of youth delivering newspapers / by Sandra L. Walker
Includes Bibliography and Index
Illustrations
Personal oral histories, 1920-1970

Editor: Kathryn Gilmore
Cover Design: Mary Gogulski
Book cover: Gene Ausmus at the Wabash Railroad Depot, Centralia, Missouri, pick-up
spot for his Columbia Missourian bundles. 1944. Family photo.




Orion Wellspring, Inc.
20 Blaine St.
Seattle, WA 98109

# TABLE OF CONTENTS

# PREFACE

Legions of youngsters delivered newspapers throughout the twentieth century. This, their first steady job, impacted them financially, socially and physically. The following chapters tell the significant effect to these children, to their families, and to our country when youth managed paper routes.

A pilot project, created in Seattle with the Nearby History program at the Museum of History and Industry (MOHAI), led to an expanded study. Patterns emerged as the work spread beyond the Northwest into Colorado, Missouri, Ohio, New York, Maine, Florida, Alaska, California, and further. Hundreds of silver-haired participants, former newspaper carriers, recalled their experiences in handling a paper route during childhood. Explained from their perspective, the stories elucidate the circumstances and challenges that young carriers encountered and endured as they moved forward.

Their personal involvement is not reduced to an anonymous tabulation of statistical data, or to the typical profile of an average paperboy. Rather, the oral history collection from 1920 through 1970, exposes the tests that children faced in an adult-dominated community and adult-operated newspaper business. Amidst all the adults, the youth readily learned about many big people's antics.

In Detroit, Des Moines, Denver or any viable town in America, the reliable paperboy was held accountable, while he tried to defeat unleashed snarling dogs, dodge cars, ignore diseases, and shift from his fast, daily delivery to the slow collection ritual at the end of the week.

The same situation existed for girls, though "papergirl" never became a common label. Throughout the book, the word "paperboy" and the male pronouns he, his, and him are written since boys dominated the newspaper delivery system. In 1948, to replace the nineteenth century term of "newsie," the industry emphasized using the word "newspaperboy" as the specific identification. However, "papergirls" were every bit as capable and responsible. A chapter is devoted to the gals' exceptional ability. They too faced irritating curmudgeons and deadbeats.

Because troublesome customers---the complainer, the cheat, and the thinly clad lady---were never interviewed, their opinions are not aired. And with the opposite side of an incident excluded, the names of these customers are fictitious, but only the names are fictional. Their attitudes and actions are very real.

Noting all the responses and studying the myriad of occurrences, I began identifying common threads in the topics. For example: rising from penniless to pockets jingling with subscription coins, novice paperboys ran to a carnival or circus with their first collection money, staying until every penny was spent.

Incidences with relevant happenings in different locations, in different years, still remained less than a universal trait for all paperboys. Their behavior varied from the similar characteristics that defined the role of young newspaper carriers, such as the way a canvas bag was slung over the shoulder or the trouble of collecting always defined the job, to the unique acts that developed even stronger character and more common sense. Speaking from their decade, as individuals repeated similar occurrences, their actions demonstrated a significant effect on trying to strike a balance between behavior in childhood and that of a young businessman.

Over the years a story can grow, like a fishing tale, so I checked various statements that might be embellished. A route described as 10 miles seemed to stretch the factual distance. Traveling one described route, I crossed the paved, well-lit streets to the end of the former route and finished at 11.4 miles. When the paperboy had covered the same distance, his path was an unpaved, poorly lit road which he traversed alone. Also, on occasion, I tried rising at 4 a.m., stepping out into the quiet dark, but never covered an entire morning route on empty streets seven days a week, 52 weeks a year, for several years. I didn't pass the test.

For impatient adults who complained, "Where's that paperboy?" if the newspaper was 10 minutes late, the answer lies in the difficulties posed by sloshing through pouring rain, taking painful falls in icy ruts, and sinking into the cold waters of Puget Sound, to name just a few reasons for being late. Of course, the delivery schedule was also side-tracked by curiosity, conversations, or school detention, adding to the downward slide in meeting adult expectations.

Join the children in Catawissa, Cordova, Cottonwood, or your town. Learn from the carriers' perspective, appreciate their efforts, laugh with them about the errors, and enjoy the help offered by considerate folks. Arcing from poignant to repugnant, from hilarious to horrific, the paper carrier's routine ran from drudgery to exciting rewards. You can decide if the past decades, when newspaper delivery depended on children, were simpler, safer, and slower times. Or more complex and challenging for them, to include carriers selecting fast as the standard pace for their speedy delivery. And then slow, on the oh-so-slow collecting.

To learn more about the newspaper carrier project, visit
**www.thelittlemerchants.com** or
email the author: **papercarrierusa@msn.com**

# PART I
## STRUGGLE

### The Best Times

Run! Running in high-top shoes, too large for his small feet, Jesse's soles slapped the pavement. He'd already tightened the broken laces as best he could for a six-year-old. Run faster! Running through the sizzling afternoon heat, cola sloshing in his tummy, Jesse sprinted down the street slightly ahead of the other boys.

He veered around the corner into the alley, dodged a trash can, scared a feral cat, cleared a crate full of empty bottles, and rushed to the door. Made it. Gasping, the little rascal slipped inside the familiar back room of Duffy's Tavern. He blinked. Adjusting from the bright sunlight, only to peer into thick cigar and cigarette smoke clouding the dim interior, he coughed as he inhaled dense, stale odors. Relaxing his tight clutch on copies of The Wenatchee World, Jesse stepped close to the scarred wooden tables and held out the papers. His presence interrupted the card games.

Turning cards over next to frothy glasses of beer, the players reached into their pockets. The men knew all too well that Jesse's persistence was stronger than their resistance. Actually his innocent grin was irresistible. Best to buy his afternoon papers and send the likeable nuisance off to other taverns. However, pausing to actually read local news wasn't the card players' priority, so they handed him a quarter, some dimes, even a dollar bill and let him keep his stock.

Jesse Montoya's successful start promised another profitable afternoon. His winning strategy depended on reaching the front of a line of little merchants buying the day's edition at the newspaper office. He became adept in purchasing bundles before the other boys. Be fast. Be first. Quick was the minimum speed to guarantee the best sales location.

And he thrived on competition, especially with himself to be faster, more profitable.

It was the summer of 1946 in the hot climate of central Washington. Using a dollar of seed money that his father managed for him, the grade-schooler bought a stack of 40 Wenatchee World papers, at two for a nickel. With $1 paid, the independent merchant left in a flash headed for specific places to sell his stock in trade: Duffy's, the Shamrock, the Orondo Tavern and other community recreation rooms. Knowing that if he walked directly into the bar he'd be promptly ordered out, he scooted in back doors and conducted his sales in back rooms with agreeable customers, like today's card players.

Jesse said, "Thank you," and left the men, money jiggling in his pocket. He dashed to another convivial center carrying his stash of The Wenatchee World still intact. Tavern spots and card rooms meant income. So did hotels and high-traffic corners. Some days the scamp grabbed a corner between Mission Street and Wenatchee Avenue and started shouting, "World news!" His yells notified other sellers the corner was occupied. Paperboys recognized the turf as Jesse's, until the next day. Motivated by need not greed, his system worked because he worked.

With three older brothers, Lee, Fred and Joe, all accomplished paperboys, Jesse Montoya captured advantages through his entrepreneurial models. Lee led the way in the early 1940s by managing a morning route and then a second route in the afternoon. Before 6:00 a.m., dark most months, his papers arrived from Spokane, 171 miles to the east. Handling the morning Spokesman Review bundles, and then after school delivering the local Wenatchee Daily World to 150 customers, Lee was a leader for his brothers, and a mentor for the family's littlest salesman.

Jesse's older brother often set the small fry on the handlebars of his big bicycle and sped down the streets to the business center. Jesse, though not yet six, immediately wanted to make money and buy a bike. Bouncing on a narrow metal handlebar, balanced high like an auto hood ornament, a bug stopper, he dreamed of owning a bicycle seat and speeding on his own. He joined the Montoya boys' sales team and shortly perfected a winning style.

His balancing prowess expanded. Besides staying on the handlebars, he balanced his playtime with school and work hours. Plus, to sell papers it was crucial to figure correct change. He surged ahead in street-school math lessons, and before long he balanced his finances. He gave funds to the family, then paid the necessary seed dollar, and last Jesse paid his weekly dollar towards his most important goal: a bicycle. He did keep a few coins aside for treats or the movies. A young boy, straddling between childhood and adulthood, Jesse enjoyed carefree play and conscientious work as balance radiated from the core of his existence. Month after month, the school year continued as his newspaper sales expanded. He passed from first grade to second.

## "Congratulations! Salesman of the Year"

So on a warm May afternoon, as Jesse rushed into the newspaper office for an additional stack of papers, Mr. Rufus Woods, the publisher of The Wenatchee World, noticed the little hustler.

Mr. Woods asked, "Jesse, how many papers have you sold?"

Beaming with pride, Jesse reported his sales. He was tickled hearing his name, particularly since Mr. Woods was important. Everyone in Wenatchee and throughout central Washington knew the prominent town leader. More than a newspaper publisher, his enterprising, enthusiastic voice was even known well beyond the Washington state line for his crucial work in convincing the government to construct Grand Coulee Dam. And here he was, gently leaning down to personally ask how the boy's nascent business was progressing.

To Jesse's surprise Mr. Woods congratulated him, declaring the busy seller the "Salesman of the Year." Such an accomplishment deserved fanfare. Right there, with a natural winning pose, Jesse was photographed. He felt respected with his small fingers resting in Mr. Woods' large hand. The little paperboy joined his hand in the hand of the Northwest region's famous newspaper publisher, civic leader, a forward thinker.

The owner's genial smile spread slightly less than Jesse's wide elfin grin, showing a boy's cheerful countenance, which just couldn't be contained in his slight frame. Even if the worn clothes were tight and the scuffed shoes too big, his impish smile fit perfectly. Bright eyes and a radiating grin lit his freckles. He was aglow with happiness.

His only working clothes tripled as fishing, school and play clothes, but not his one set of clothes for Sunday mass. The single set of durable work garments, aged by fine wear, served the active, successful salesman, who was actually a sales boy.

Suspenders held his pants so he could hold on to the papers as he rushed in and out of taverns or sped along on his bike. Being sensible, he rolled up one pant leg to prevent the trouser from catching in the chain. A nasty spill would damage the bicycle and Jesse cared greatly about his new wheels. Selling papers to pay for his large 18-inch bike was the crucial drive behind the energetic orbits around his world in Wenatchee.

The child's work clothes were particularly noticeable alongside Mr. Woods' properly pressed three-piece business suit. The president of the newspaper company dressed the same as any influential businessman of his generation. And seeing the little ragamuffin, the grandfatherly gentleman must have been reminded of his early years, when he saw small street hawkers selling newspapers in their soiled knickers and newsey cap.

May, 1947, Mr. Rufus Woods, publisher of *The Wenatchee World*, recognizes Jesse Montoya's success. "Congratulations!" Photo archives of *The Wenatchee World*.

Regardless of their differing attire, Jesse felt like a partner. The company and dozens of paperboys were partners. Distinctly different yet cooperating. The publisher produced the newspaper and boys like Jesse distributed the paper. A working team with a respectful relationship, in which Mr. Woods was the key to Jesse's opportunities.

Closing in on Memorial Day and the end of the school year, his short pants showed growth with wear and tear during months of use. School mates judged his ragtag appearance but he saw himself differently because, "I didn't realize we were poor." With common sense he wasted no time contemplating or complaining about the family's finances. He just contributed to his father's limited funds, often earning $9 a day selling papers. Unrestricted in comfy clothes, his stance reflected the soil of the earth: production. The production, not appearance, mattered. And frankly, he'd be the envy of any little Lord Fauntleroy.

Hand-me-down clothes didn't stunt his growth, but to fill the large, used shoes he needed to grow. With summer activities, he'd likely sprout up stimulated by the sunshine. The month of May already registered several hot days. Such heat required additional ice blocks so he pulled his red Radio Flyer wagon along the streets to the ice storage company and brought back heavy blocks for the family's ice box. He gladly helped his busy mother. Why in a few weeks, school would close and she'd let him spend the whole day outside, on his own, capturing free fun.

## Summer: The Best of Times

Like a modern Huck Finn, Jesse and his pals spent warm sunny mornings at the river, on the river, in the river, across the river. But unlike Huck's fictional adventures on the Mississippi, Jesse's real adventures centered on the great Columbia River. The long Columbia started as a smaller winding path out of the rugged, glacier-covered Rocky Mountains of British Columbia. The water gained strength and speed as it rolled over the 1,243 miles to the Pacific Ocean. More than half of the river, 745 miles, flowed through the United States. Wenatchee prospered along the vast moving highway that provided the city and greater region with electricity and irrigation.

Not concerning themselves with the commercial benefit of the Columbia, the lively boys used it as the best playground imaginable. The sounds of water slapping rocks was no match to happy squeals and splashes. Balanced on stilts, made from thin scrap wood, they walked elevated between the wet river rocks to catch crawfish, which provided bait for fishing. When they had their fill of fishin' for salmon and with the sun warming the rocks, the mud, their skin, the gang hurried off to Bare Ass Beach, appropriately labeled.

One designated helper loaded the boys' few summer garments on his bike and rode over the bridge, hopefully not losing socks, shorts or shoes along the way. The rest of the kids soaked in laughter. Their round white bottoms smacked cold water; their short legs kicked and arms stroked as naked bodies swam across the wide sweeping Columbia. The current carried them down stream to where the bicyclist waited.

The nude rascals, their appearances equal, grabbed play clothes, now converted to work clothes and pulled them over bruises, scrapes, and sunburns. With no watches, though they didn't yet tell time on a clock, the boys still knew to split play time with work time. But all the morning activity made them hungry. Together they headed for Mission Street, drying off on their way to Tony's. The boys patronized Tony's as regularly as tavern fellows selected a liquid provider.

Jesse used both hands to hold a large, white bun steamed by a fat, tasty hot dog. His lunch special was piled with spicy chili and fresh onions. The sandwich cost him a quarter. Scurrying away to be the first to reach the newspaper office, he washed off his Coney Island with a cold sweet Coke. Summer's best time, topped with the best lunch, all for 30 cents.

Full of swimming, selling and succeeding, his summer played into autumn. Jesse moved from second grade, on to third grade, outgrowing his one set of clothes by springtime each year. He earned money after school and more on the weekends. For three years he hawked the *Wenatchee World*. His very best sales days were with the special edition dedicated to The Washington State Apple Blossom Festival, held in the proclaimed *Apple Capital of the World.*

All of Wenatchee and the surrounding region resonated with the exciting festival, that had started in 1920. For Jesse's first year, 1947, selling the huge paper, his small body with his big spirit drew buyers captivated by his easy smile. People flocked to the downtown streets for the Saturday parade that attracted 75,000. Jesse sold without covering any distance, except for his frequent runs to the newspaper office. The weight of each 144-page festival edition meant he carried only a few copies. Racing for more papers, he kept resupplying his sales spot until the buyers emptied out and his pockets filled up with money. He even tucked dollars inside his shirt. The salesboy more than tripled his usual profitable days, staying busier than the bees.

And bees in the Wenatchee region stayed busy pollinating more blossoms that created larger apple crops, as low flying airplanes crossed acres of productive orchards to spray a synthetic insecticide. Known to be an effective killer against the causes of malaria and yellow fever, the dichlorodiphenyltrichloroethane (DDT) reduced insect diseases in agriculture. The apple tonnage increased. The dedicated special edition for the Festival became a best-seller. The spraying airplanes flew and Jesse flew along the streets on his bike. His earnings increased.

# Leaving the Street Corner

Jesse's days were tempered by reality in the parameter of his large playground, as he balanced play with work. His experience aided the grade-schooler to take over his brother's route in 1950. Instead of hawking papers, he maintained a steady daily delivery. He learned the customers' names, and they were happy to have another reliable Montoya boy leave the afternoon paper conveniently at their door.

He added one more best to an expanding line of his best times. Whether the headlines were simple or striking, subscribers paid for the daily delivered paper providing Jesse a steady income. It was time to spend some savings, and with small ones waiting he'd sensibly share his used, tight pieces. Holding the money saved over the summer, he and his mother walked into town to J.C. Penney before Labor Day to purchase school clothes. Checking the price, he bought two pairs of dark trousers, ones that actually fit. Now he was decked in a set of togs for church, new ones for school, and some comfy no-worry clothes for his route.

Straddled between the best of childhood days and the additional rewards of adulthood times serving as a salesman, Jesse grew. He no longer contended with a man who asked him, laughing, "Is that bag carrying you?" He handled the canvas bag without the strap shortened, fit into large boots, reached pedals on a big boy's bike, and most of all, grew in wisdom founded on common sense and self confidence taught from his efforts on the streets.

No wonder he was oblivious to people considering him poor. Jesse was rich with a happy supportive family, a strong faith, an abundance of free time with lots of friends, coins in his pocket, and contributions to his family's finances.

Jesse Montoya lived like thousands of children across America. He wanted a bicycle. He earned money selling papers and bought one. Needing clothes, he earned the money to buy the articles. He advanced from hawking to being a paperboy on a regular route with all its advantages: spending money, independence, freedom and fun with friends.

Did all children enjoy Jesse's advantages: an older brother to mentor him and who passed along his route, in a vibrant town where he knew the residents and they knew his family? No.

But then Jesse wasn't competing with the nation's large paperboy population in the 1950s. Learning from his brothers, he transitioned smoothly from hawking papers to running a route, where his ordinary job continued to transform him financially and socially.

For legions of youngsters, the competition to acquire a route and the struggles of settling into a daily routine caused major challenges.

Throughout the country, paperboys were impacted by what seems like a simple task: porching papers every day, year round. During interviews of former carriers, the silver-haired seniors readily described how their past experiences affected them. But why raise a stream of questions to hundreds of previous newspaper carriers?

## "Where's that paperboy?"

In the mid-twentieth century, a half million newspaperboys, 500,000 youngsters, ran routes in large and small communities across America. Their numbers increased. By 1980 nearly one million youth delivered papers. This most common first job changed their lives.

Today people refer to the previous century as a simpler time when life was slower and safer. Grandparents, reminiscing over idyllic fleeting decades, envision nostalgic scenes of folks leaving their door unlocked; of walking up town to shop on Main Street, just as Jesse and his mother did. In the evening, long-time neighbors sat at the kitchen table or on the porch swing chatting, rehashing the happenings at high school sports and the church socials.

But a small paperboy scurrying down a dark alley, alone, sending rats scuttling experienced a different affect. Newspaper carriers delivered fast before daylight or at dusk rushing on winter evenings in spite of the snow and ice. Legions of rambunctious children with remarkable fortitude hustled day after day. And a tyke had better "porch" the paper on time because customers clocked his arrival.

Subscribers expected punctual doorstep service as their lives pulsed to daily routines. The school dismissal bell rang at 3:30 p.m., followed by the factory whistle at 4:00. Out by Woods Crossing, the 4:27 Wabash freight train blew a long warning. Before 6:00 mashed potatoes, meat loaf and green beans steamed on the dinner table. Favorite radio shows, *Amos 'n Andy, The Lone Ranger, the Phantom Knows,* broadcast on the minute. Church bells called congregations to be prompt for services. Why couldn't that paperboy obey a rigid schedule?

Well, sometimes he slipped, even without icy snow. A clanging alarm re-routed him to the fire station. A windy March day drew him up hill to fly his homemade kite. A sandlot baseball game, a slide to home base left his papers on the sidelines. Down the street a customer stomped on a porch step fuming, "Where's my paper?"

My older brother, Carl, was one who strayed off schedule. In the middle of the twentieth century, in the middle of Ohio, in the middle of the supper hour, the black dial telephone rang. An irritated voice complained: "The paper's late! Where's that paperboy?"

Our supper was disrupted, again. Carl, and consequently the family, stayed fettered by his paper route.

Trying to straddle the path from childhood to adult status, this "man of the house" struggled against external conditions and internal confusion. Childhood is complicated. More so when penniless, brotherless and fatherless. Our Father was dead. No tears, fears or hopes alter the absolute state. Hope would not bring Daddy home; he remained in Normandy. Carl remained brother-less. He attacked his penniless condition; the only thing he could change.

Without a dime for a comic book, this energetic, determined imp didn't intend to remain broke. Running a paper route, he figured he'd laugh at the comic strips, like the *Katzenjammer Kids* and *Beetle Bailey*, or tremble with *Terry and the Pirates*. And he'd buy *Superman* comic books. Eventually, he'd buy a used bike.

So, not yet eleven, barely ten, a skinny child with short legs and unruly hair became a businessman. The business half came quickly; the man evolved slowly. Small hands smeared with printer's ink, a sturdy, though dirty, canvas bag slung on his slender shoulders, he stumbled along. On his way he acquired more than pocket money and material stuff. He was a mere boy in men's boots living through a slower life, one supposedly simpler and safer.

## Time Passed

Now six decades forward, I tried to tell the grandchildren about my big brother's experiences: delivering papers in the historic 1950 Buckeye blizzard, his stash of Christmas gifts, hiding comic books under the mattress, earning money to purchase his first car when he outgrew the used bike. Most days he enjoyed too many sweets, too many sodas, and some days encountered a few complaints.

Our grandson, Robert, born a century late for being a paperboy, asked questions, because little ones are filled with questions like a marsh filled with mosquitoes. I tried to answer, yet realized I held neither a broad nor detailed view of Carl's efforts, or any paper carriers' experiences. Did I know about paper routes because of novels or the movies, with more myth than reality? Was my limited memory accurate? What lay hidden in the boys' actual activities, long concealed by adult assumptions? The profoundly disturbing element: it was too late to ask Carl.

Catching Robert's contagious curiosity, and knowing this familiar job for youth has nearly vanished, I engaged friends, family, neighbors: "Were you a paperboy?" Everywhere I questioned ordinary "silver-haired youngsters" about their former days as newspaper carriers. Oldsters shared sensitive stories, along with their silly acts committed on the route, which entailed more than casually plopping a paper on the porch. Instead of a slower, safer life, their record demonstrated multiple, disturbing experiences. Fast registered as the standard pace, since speed trumped safety.

Breathing in the seniors' spirit, I determined to give carriers their say. They revealed untold truths about communities, newspaper companies, and carriers' circumstances in the unequal trichotomy of two parts adults and one part child.

Their adventures, whether stumbling in severe weather, facing snarling dogs, nonchalantly peering through windows and seeing through sheer lingerie, cashing in at saloons, emphasized an opposing position to the child labor reformers' arguments that paperboys were "exploited." Young carriers gained significant advantages amidst adventures and misadventures, as they explored opportunities. The children matured.

The goal of registering experiences from a paperboy's perspective, required locating seniors with accurate recall. The alert elderly, who were able to discuss details about delivering newspapers in the 1920s, dwindled to a minute number.

Thus 1920 established a good baseline. Besides the limit with older carriers, research demonstrated that the *Roaring Twenties* ushered in irreversible differences from the dismal, deadly 1910s. The census of 1920 documents a population increase, not surprising from vast numbers of immigrant arrivals. But the major emerging change: for the first time the majority of the population shifted from rural to urban centers (at the time defined as places of 2,500 people or more). Over 59 million lived in locales of fewer than 8,000 residents, a small town with local newsey papers. Just the place for young ones to work paper routes.

The newspaper carrier project also focused on subjects who carried papers through a minimum of four seasons during their most formative years. These curious children, with an innate creative and competitive spirit, committed to a task day after day regardless of external conditions or their gurgling constitution. Immature kids made mistakes, coped with the consequences, acquired confidence seeded in common sense and settled into their first steady job. They grew incredibly resilient.

Neither over-protected or over-praised, and not over-paid, the children managed without being coddled. There was no obesity problem. If they struggled with a weight problem, it was the heavy load on their shoulders, not around their waists. Newspapers and responsibilities weighed them down yet strengthened them physically and psychologically.

For hundreds of thousands of youth, running a route covered a fleeting period in childhood. Still, the year-round job, during development, embedded a significant influence for life. Their formative years were transformed with changes lasting long after the route.

This American icon rests on misconceptions and myths. The advantages to being a paperboy, promoted by newspaper owners, clashed with the vehement claims of the child labor reformers. The opposing adults collided in lengthy controversial arguments, while the carriers enjoyed adventures that outweighed their occasional adversity. Reformers argued that raucous paperboys should be stopped, not simply by state law or municipal regulation but by a constitutional amendment. Proposed in 1924, would such an amendment halt the heathens, whom the proponents considered to be in an embryonic criminal position?

Come. Follow paper routes as carriers swerve through traffic, shiver in subzero temperatures, smell the stale alcohol and smoke in the saloons, spend dimes and save dollars to eventually soar with excitement over their rewards accented with recognition.

# CHAPTER 1
## WANTIN'

Stepping on powdery snow, David sank into the fluffy piles where even with snow shoes, (not that he owned a pair), his skinny frame would sink. The extra weight slung over his shoulder pulled him down through the sparkling surface to a stop so cold his shivers froze. He hoisted himself out of the snow drift, paused at Pearl Street to shift the heavy load of newspapers and readjusted the wide strap in an effort to keep the bottom of the canvas bag from gouging the pristine white blanket. Blowing flakes softly brushed his face, a pleasant touch, better than sand and dust that often circled the streets of Ellensburg.

On the eastern side of the long, rugged Cascade Mountain Range, Ellensburg, Washington, registered cold in the winter, hot in the summer and windy in every season. Strong currents flowed through mountain passes and swirled down the rocky slopes towards the unsheltered town. Dust clouds often flew against folks.

David Bowles didn't object to snow drifts hugging his legs, so happy with his change in circumstances. Besides, the fresh powder was an improvement over the frequent rain he had previously endured in Bellingham and in Seattle, when he hawked on a street corner hollerin' for an hour or more. No, this was better. Dry snow didn't soak the papers. Moving through the clear, still air, puffs of breath formed small clouds around him. His world was lit by the only light over the path: tiny twinkling stars vast light years away. Crossing the railroad tracks, David headed out South Ruby Street to leave a paper at the Munz farm. Beginning a new opportunity, he was determined to prove, "I can do it" the specific words he pledged at the newspaper office.

Mr. Val Comstock, the circulation manager for the *Ellensburg Evening Record*, expressed concern when David asked for route number two.

The change in carriers occurred because Paul was quitting the job and a friend, Mike, said "I'll take it." Then Mike asked David if he'd go halves with him, it being a big route and all. After school Paul guided the two friends along the streets. That was Mike's only trip. One evening plodding through a two-hour delivery in ten inches of snow, he quit.

David figured that was fine. Without a partner, he wouldn't have to split the earnings. He fervently wanted a paper route, wanted it with every blood cell working down his arms, hands, legs, feet, into his freezing toes. Determination sent him to Mr. Comstock to ask for the assignment, only to hear, "Well, you're pretty small. The bag will drag in the snow."

David replied without hesitation, "I'll fix it so it won't."

Mr. Comstock looked down at the young school boy. Cigar smoke fanned out as he said, "Aren't you too small to carry this big route?"

"No, I'm not. I'm strong so small's no problem." He described his chores: feeding the cow and horses, cleaning the barn, milking. "Besides the further I go the lighter the bag gets."

"All right. Try it." Less certainty rang in Mr. Comstock's voice than in David's. But it was agreed: he could at least try.

From his experiences selling newspapers in Seattle, on the soggy west side of the mountains, David felt confident. Once again he'd be happy with coins in his pocket. A route meant steady, weekly money, which was excellent for an after-school job. Pennies would accumulate until he had a dollar, $2 a week, as much as $9 a month. A lot of money in 1924.

High snow drifts, stupefying cold harsh enough to crack teeth like ice cubes, dusk changing to dark, wind blowing the news sheets to smithereens---none of this discouraged him. No defeatism frozen on his face. Besides, Ellensburg was flat. Not like steep hills in Seattle with bullies chasing him off corners. This paper route was easier, though hardly easy.

His early struggles strengthened him, developed his strong shoulders and strong confidence. Before Ellensburg, the Bowles family lived in Bellingham in the northwest corner of Washington. In 1917, starting when he was almost six, David joined his older brother, Carl, selling papers. In street school he learned to make change before he learned to read and write in a traditional school. Handling several publications, eight-year-old Carl taught David to look at the different designs around the headline. Bellingham's 35,000 residents, stayed informed with three daily papers: *The Bellingham Herald*, *Reveille* and the *Journal*. Plus papers were shipped in from Seattle. David learned to distinguish *The Seattle Star*, the *Seattle PI*, and the *Seattle Union Record*. The mill workers were particular about "their newspaper," so the tyke had to identify each publication quickly. Speed was essential.

Each morning, well before school bells, a dozen boys raced to the railroad transfer office to sign up for bundles of papers that arrived from

Seattle. Since the Bowles family lived near the Great Northern Railway Depot, Carl and David appeared first. They always held spot one and two, an important advantage that dismissed the disadvantages of living next to the station. Lines from the Chicago Milwaukee & St. Paul, the Northern Pacific, Northern Canadian Pacific Railways, spread dirty soot, blew loud railroad whistles at all hours, and brought in gruff railroad men along dangerous tracks. Just the same, holding the best street corner, the brothers swiftly sold papers. Their pockets filled with pennies and nickels. They went directly to mama with earned money to help feed the family.

On Sundays with store fronts shuttered and only a few dim street lamps casting light in the early hour, the two boys pulled a rattling wagon along the empty, silent streets. They hustled to deliver large stacks of the *Seattle Sunday Post Intelligencer*, the *PI*. During the week, David used the wagon to earn a dime hauling piles of cans and trash to the dump.

With Sunday papers delivered, before customers raised the blinds for the day, the boys next cleaned a barber shop. They scrubbed the floor, chairs, sink and counter being careful not to spill the shaving soaps and brushes. The barber gave them free haircuts for their efforts.

Learning street lessons, working any small job, starting grade school, there was an order to David's routine. Then the order ceased. Dad, Mom and 11 children moved to Seattle leaving the customers and system David just learned. His new home was a downtown hotel by the waterfront on South First Street. Ships from Alaska and as far off as Asia anchored near the warehouses. Sailors scattered to saloons and houses of satisfying business.

David acquired further lessons on the hills of Seattle amidst ruffians who were entrenched on their corner spot. His persistence increased. He took his newfound determination and street-smarts with him to Ellensburg, to an opportunity for a steady route.

So on his second evening covering the route, he pressed himself to lighten his load. Only 22 papers delivered, another 110 to drop at the right house. Coming across Kittitas Street, down Water, over to Pearl Street, his path was correct. Now, if he could just find the scrawled chalk marks he drew last night on porch columns, when Paul pointed out the customer locations. Blowing snow, grey light closing to dark made it difficult to see chalk, if a mark was even there.

He plunged forward putting his thoughts on home where he'd eat something hot. Eat anything, hot or cold, only first he'd have to feed the farm animals and complete his chores.

# Why?

Why would David, like thousands of young children all over America, who crossed streets day after day, endure the challenging conditions of a paper route?

For the money!

A child was penniless unless he earned his own money. No one said nickelless or dimeless. Just plain penniless. Not even a half-pence with God's blessing. When David wanted pieces of penny candy, a nickel for a birch beer, a movie ticket, he had to earn the money. When Jesse desired a bicycle, he hawked papers to pay for one. As carrier Dale Wirsing said of his childhood, "Receiving an allowance was a foreign concept."

No money struck like an empty swimming pool on a sweltering day. All the space ready to receive an eager boy, but only hard, dry concrete existed rather than cool water. His empty pockets were the same as an empty pool. With an energetic countenance, he shoved aside possible misery and stepped forward to attack his situation.

Decision: obtain a paper route, the most common path for youngsters wanting work, or in truth needing money. The problem? The path was congested, downright crowded with a plethora of kids clamoring for a limited number of routes.

## One in a Thousand

Countless children struggling to win a paper route were turned away, as the circulation managers had droves to choose from. Desperate economic conditions in the 1920s, far worse in the 1930s, required youth to search for opportunities to work. The community, the family, and the child all believed in being productive as they had been for generations. Indeed, small ones were selling paper sheets since the colonial times, and with the advent of the penny paper in 1833 even larger numbers became newspaper handlers.

On September 4, 1833, Benjamin Day sent little urchins onto the crowded, bustling streets of New York City, into coffee houses and taverns shouting and waving his new production, the *Sun* newspaper. For one cent men read the news sold to them on the spot. Mr. Day's successful paper spawned more penny newspaper businesses, until every crowded city teemed with hustling ragamuffins eager to earn a few coins selling sheets of news. Publishers could depend on an abundant supply of little merchants to call out the latest edition. The "newsey" became a common American icon.

And Mr. Day's success increased. In five years the *Sun* had a circulation of 30,000, the largest in the world. As the 1830s ended and additional competitive publishers emerged, the newspaper business raced forward. Selling penny papers continued into the twentieth century. However, the rising costs for print production, additional materials and increased wages led to a 100 percent increase in cost. Now people paid two pennies, and still readily bought the news. Also, with the growing urban population, with electricity lighting city houses, the shift to the home delivery system increased. Residents appreciated their newspaper companion.

## Identified

As Professor George Douglas explained in *The Golden Age of the Newspaper*, "In the 1920s the American newspaper reached the pinnacle of its glory---and influence." This was a decade when public trust in journalists and editors excelled, when radio stations did not yet compete with publications. Douglas's statement expressed more than a narrow assessment of the number of papers sold, because three decades later in the 1950s the population soared to over 151 million Americans and total newspaper sales exploded as well. Actually, 1950 sales statistics state, "increases more than twice as great percentage-wise as increases in the population."     However, in the Roaring Twenties, popularity and profit beamed from large, established newspaper buildings, and the editions exceeded a mere news product promoted on just production numbers. Folks favorite columns had personality. The atmosphere of a community in the 1920s radiated from the desk of a journalist, whom people considered to be similar to a likeable next-door neighbor, regardless if he wrote his columns miles away.

## Not Yet

With the number of subscribers and the number of routes increasing, were adults making it easier for children to obtain a paper route? Sadly, no. An active segment of the adult world intended to prohibit those under 18 from working by establishing a federal regulation. The best monetary opportunities for tens of thousands of youngsters almost disappeared in the 1920s, in the nascent golden years of youth managing routes.

Stop the cheerful paperboy, stop the helpful child meeting family needs, stop a boy from working until he reaches 18? No way!

Eighteen? By the time children entered middle school, they acquired two or three jobs based on their paper route experience. The first year-round job was augmented by seasonal work---picking berries, mowing lawns, harvesting apples, hauling coal, shoveling snow, all sandwiched between daily home chores. It was hard enough to compete for routes, manage extra jobs, and chores without the powerful body of the United States Congress interfering.

This was the governing body that decisively denied U.S. membership in the League of Nations. From international to national, political reformers stopped the flow of alcohol on January 17, 1920 with the Eighteenth Amendment. Prohibition was in its fourth year of blocking bars and saloons from serving alcohol when another strong restriction went into effect. The Immigration Act of 1924, or Johnson-Reed Act, superseded the Immigration Restriction Act of 1921, further limiting immigrants from entering the United States. Into this legislative atmosphere, a constitutional amendment, not just an act, was drafted.

Educators and child labor reformers in cities and states had built a case against small children slaving in deplorable conditions. Earlier, the tireless efforts of dedicated progressives produced strict regulation to prohibit minors from laboring in clothing mills, coal mines, or on machinery in a manufacturing hub. Such dangerous, deadly jobs for little ones stopped. The monstrous toiling by small bodies ended because of reformers' fervent arguments. Children's lives were saved; also, the community and the country benefitted.

These monumental changes kept progressives operating on high power as they fought for additional restrictions: minors should not work. Moving forward, members in the federal government prepared to stop the largest segment of youth, ones under the age of 18, from filling jobs. Keep children off the streets. The reformers threw accusations in more directions than a boy threw his rolled paper missile.

Union leaders, child-labor committees, activists joined forces to intervene while each day newsies hustled. Opportunities to be a paperboy continued to expand in growing urban populations, and newspaper company changes helped increase the number of routes. However, the reformers testified that juvenile detention centers stayed filled with dirty hoodlums, nothing but heathens right off the street. According to testimony prisons remained packed with criminals who began as newspaperboys. The reformers passionately believed children should not work, and absolutely not on dangerous, licentious streets. A young paperboy was on a direct route to becoming a criminal. "Exploited," children must cease selling papers.

In 1924 Congress succumbed to the combined forces of reformers. An amendment to the United States Constitution, the Federal Child Labor Amendment was sent to the forty-eight states for ratification with bipartisan support. The concise amendment read: *The Congress shall have power to limit, regulate, and prohibit the labor of persons under eighteen years of age.*

Newsboys certainly registered under age 18, many not yet 12. Youth, selling and delivering papers, faced a possible job elimination if thirty-six states ratified the amendment. And if minors stopped handling newspapers, would juvenile criminal behavior cease?

With no deadline established for ratification, supporters kept arguing for the state legislators to ratify the amendment. In 1925 four states agreed, and two more by 1931. Calendar pages kept turning and the Depression deepened. Suffering severe unemployment, fourteen states signed on by 1933, and in 1937 eight additional states supported the amendment. With twenty-eight states in support, would eight more agree for the necessary thirty-six state ratification? And while the amendment to be approved or disapproved languished in the states, the newspaper industry became increasingly energized. Was the amendment a balanced approach to a problem?

Bombarded with accusations and unjustified exaggerations, the opposition fought the dour, dismal tones of reformers whose distorted data was unreliable. Well aware of the pressure by activists, the newspaper leaders were not idle nor indifferent. First and foremost, these paperboys were not employees of the newspaper company. Independent and employee collided. Why should the Little Merchants be regulated by child labor laws? Each youngster worked as an independent salesman, salesboy. A youthful labor force functioned for a few hours a day on its own. The independently owned newspaper company would regulate their young delivery force.

The legal struggles roiled in the courts and efforts to accept the child labor amendment were argued in state legislative chambers. Eventually the position to restrict all children was modified to allow exemptions for youth involved in: acting, baby sitting, farm work, a family business, making Christmas wreaths, and the largest number, the newspaperboys.

If the legislative branch, through a constitutional amendment had not yet stopped youth, from working, (in particular for newspaper companies) reformers into the 1930s pressed the executive branch to move forward to stop minors from holding money-earning jobs. Why not, when millions of men were out of work?

The immense total count of paperboys drew the attention of union leaders. The unions' interest flowed in both directions. In some cases, the unions previously solicited paperboys to form their own union, like the Local Seattle Newsboys' Union of the A.F. of L. Yet, in other areas, they argued to have children removed from the job. In the 1930s, with unemployment figures reaching 25, then 30 percent, the unions actively joined reformers to pressure President Roosevelt to stop newspaper sales and delivery by minors. The United States executive branch, the Congress, powerful unions, and the secretary of labor stood against the national newspaper organizations, and against the multitude of paperboys who earned and learned.

Circulation managers, committed to the business of youth distributing papers, confronted reformers to save a system that customers wanted and families needed. With the devastating Depression, there were families desperately dependent on the earnings from paper routes. News about the proposed amendment and progress for passage, if reported, was printed on an inside page of the newspapers that David, John, Ed, Dick, and thousands of others, delivered. It did not catch the boys' interest. They focused on their route. Let the reformers help whoever these so-called "exploited" kids were that adults argued over. As for themselves, the carriers worked harder to expand an opportunity.

While state legislators debated the amendment, and 20 states already agreed to it, the newspaper industry independently produced a code. One hundred years after Benjamin Day established the *Sun*, successfully circulated by a force of little knaves, the newspaper leaders developed a code in 1933 defining age limit and hours young boys might work.

In the throes of urgent economic measures and pressured by child labor reformers and union leaders, the President of the United States argued for an older age limit and less hours for children to be involved in newspaper distribution. With negotiated changes agreed to in the stipulations, President Roosevelt signed a regulation on September 14, 1933. Further debated and modified over the months by newspaper leaders, a final code became effective on March 12, 1934. The rule, in general, stated: a paperboy must reach age 12, or older in some locations, before a circulation manager assigned a route number. A restriction that the national newspaper leaders agreed to and the reformers requested, or in some jurisdictions strictly required, meant an abundance of energetic children faced an age challenge. The regulation gave a circulation manager a backup to his, "No, not yet" answer.

The requirement funneled boys into a narrower range extending from 12 until about 16, when they became old enough for another job that provided more hours and income. To a little tyke, it was like being a girl. No girls were to be assigned routes, age 12 or any age.

The best and the worst situation prevailed. Plenty of playmates to form a ball game. The best. However, at the same time, too many unwanted competitors existed against an individual struggling to acquire a newspaper route. Numbers explained a youngster's woes.

## Too Many

When David Bowles began his competitive race to sell papers in 1917, before he was six, he entered a crowded market. Dr. Anna Reed, hired by the Seattle School Board, conducted a study of newsboys in the city school system in 1914. She incurred no difficulty locating 1,008 children who sold papers on the city's streets or who delivered to residents. Seattle offered 10 dailies for sale, similar to the larger American cities in the east. And with established corner locations, young kids readily entered the paper selling business, supplemented with home routes.

The cities in the populated east provided a plethora of jobs. Professor David Nasaw's book, *Children of the City, At Work and At Play,* devoted a chapter to "The Newsies" documenting that selling newspapers was the most common occupation of youngsters. "Hundreds of thousands of boys who grew up in American cities in the first decades of this century sold papers."

Add in the extensive number of daily papers printed in county seats and small towns across the United States and the newspaper routes for youth rose ever higher. As newspaper delivery became more commonplace, recognition of these diminutive servers expanded.

The nation's population in 1920 reached 106,021,537, with 40 percent (more than 42 million) at 18 or younger. Also significant, for residential delivery purposes, the growing population shifted from predominantly rural to urban.

In Iowa, *The Des Moines Register,* and the *Tribune* praised their 3,500 paperboys at their lively 1933 convention, while a national code for age 12 was waiting to be instituted.

In 1940 Henry McDaniel conducted a country-wide study of paperboys and their school progress, for his Ph.D. at Columbia University. He opened his dissertation with: "Every day more than 39,000,000 newspapers, the world's most perishable commodity, are delivered to consumers. An army of 350,000 boys is involved in the high speed distribution."

The newspaper industry pressed forward to expand and promote a national Newspaperboy Day, which in 1948 saluted 500,000 enterprising youngsters. In 1949 for the Newspaperboy Day recognition, Governor Arthur Langlie of Washington applauded the 10,000 carriers in his sparsely populated state.

In 1950 America topped 151,325,798, with cities and suburbs showing a major increase under a baby boom already into its fourth year. The youthful nation was growing. By 1952, the *Des Moines Register* and the *Tribune* now managed 6,500 carrier boys. On the national level, the circulation column in a July, 1952, edition of Editor & Publisher stated, "Nearly a million newspaper boys," are provided practical opportunities and character development. However, the "nearly" stretched upward toward a million, by 300,000 or so.

The *Tacoma News Tribune* circulation office praised 1,050 carriers at banquets for Newspaperboy Day on October 20, 1962, as the national organization of circulation managers applauded America's 600,000 paperboys.

On October 16, 1965, the *Seattle Times* published a salute to "more than 3,500 Times newspaperboys," which they referred to as "the young man who delivers the newspaper to your doorstep, rain or shine." The special full-page tribute estimated that there were, "...more than one million other young newspaperboys in the nation." Again, a million stretches over the top. If past carriers were added to that current list, yes, the number would reach a million, or surpass it.

In the same year *The Indianapolis Star* and the *Indianapolis News*, based in the heartland of the country, applauded the service provided by 8,500 home delivery children.

National and local statistics documented that youth served as the primary newspaper delivery force. Children populated the circulation offices across America until the 1990s. But, these statistics on populations held little interest for the child without a route. From his world, he saw kids at the drop-off station and firmly believed "everybody was a paperboy," except for him. The 50 rowdies within the residential blocks near his home discouraged him. The forlorn fellow wanted a route and had to do something about his predicament.

For legions of children, the opportunities that a route provided overtook any obstacles. Advantages along with a few adventures tipped the balance against adversities. They favored excitement as they read *Swiss Family Robinson, Treasure Island*, the *Call of the Wild*. Even funnies contained escapades. The *Katzenjammer Kids* came alive to boys.

A child recognized adversity because physical, social and economic struggles abounded. Rather than stall him, the troubles spurred him to action. Coins in the pocket, recognition in the community, and the enjoyment of a few adventures, all these wishes capsized the obstacles. Optimistic and opportunistic, a cheerful outlook spurred him forward past life's difficult reality. David Bowles was a prime example of how youngsters managed.

## His Changing World

Between 1917 and 1924, grade-schooler David Bowles moved through historic changes, permanent shifts, catastrophes, and personal struggles. His business efforts began before he entered first grade, before his tiny baby teeth dropped out making his smile quite charming. Except missing teeth affected his happy whistle, so he sang tunes. Then his singing was curtailed with tonsillitis, and abruptly halted when he was hospitalized during the deadly influenza epidemic of 1918. Besides, singing was prohibited in school classes.

Recovered from the flu, David hawked the special newspaper editions on Monday, November 11, 1918, broadcasting President Wilson's announcement that the war to end all wars was over. Alongside his brother, Carl, the two boys raced to sell their bundles. Peace was the major message, but the *Seattle Times* also allotted front page coverage for the notice, "Ban Lifted Tomorrow." On Tuesday, November 12, the theatres, dance halls, churches, and all places of public assembly re-opened after being closed since October 5, because of the influenza epidemic. However, people must wear gauze masks in public.

As another precaution, the Seattle School Board stated: schools to remain closed. Oh well, wearing masks interfered with recitation. Enjoying no school-days, David was busy selling an incredible supply of papers on the street, though the gauze slipped as he shouted.

Adjusting and adapting to personal changes and many national developments, David straddled the closing years of the 1910s and grew into the vibrant 1920s. The dismal 1910 years had filled people with despair. The Titanic sank on April 15, 1912; a horrific world war began raging in 1914 in the immigrants' homeland, where mustard gas and machine guns slaughtered young soldiers; the Russian Revolution in 1917 reverberated fears throughout Europe and over the ocean into America igniting a Red scare; deadly diphtheria, scarlet fever, polio epidemics and the deadliest of all, the 1918 Spanish influenza. The virus spread around the world killing an estimated 20 to 50 million people in any socio-economic class. September, 1919, President Wilson rested in silence following a stroke. The world was spinning with seismic changes. For David, in 1919, his narrow economic world changed with a fierce city-wide strike by workers in Seattle, which brought production to a halt. Federal agents closed the *Union Record* newspaper shop, affecting David's profitable sales.

David's life had shifted from Bellingham in 1917 to Seattle in 1918, all the while rushing to sell newspapers, especially when headlines increased the citizens' fears. His family returned to Bellingham in 1919, but back to Seattle in 1920 as the cataclysmic 1910 decade ended. The 1920s opened to saloons drying out. Prohibition was instituted. However, the 1920s brought the jazz age. Skirt hems rose with the spirit. Bloomers bounced and raccoons had better beware lest their fur warmed an ivy-league football fan. While cities literally and figuratively electrified, the urban setting lit the way to brighter times.

By 1920, population figures passed 106 million. Nearly 14 million additional people claimed America to be their home, and the 40 percent comprising the youthful nation were exuberant. Advertising helped fuel their excitement.

## Control the Problem

A steady shift, building faster than sand in the Mississippi Delta, began in 1913, when a group of businessmen in Chicago's vibrant and growing advertising business began to attack a problem, one involving money. They organized their ideas into an active plan to control the troublesome situation as they designed the first uniform standards to determine rates for advertising space in publications. It was determined that when a merchant on Main Street paid for his advertisement in a one or two-cent newspaper, he should know how many potential customers read his ad and thus pay on that basis.

Rather than the customary "buyer beware" approach, these men in advertising instituted a basic requirement. An orderly annual audit was to replace the cut-throat chaos of random numbers spouted in a sale's proposal. Once established, the dependable audit information would be posted. The Audit Bureau of Circulation (ABC), a self-policing organization with a controlling board, was created for the Associated Advertising Clubs. The primary role of ABC: protection of advertisers' monies. The purchaser bought his ad space with confidence because of verified circulation numbers.

While the advertising industry established this for their agencies and association members, in a year almost a thousand publishers accepted the process. The new procedure offered benefits for both sides. And young children also benefitted with circulation departments working for more controlled subscriber routes. Circulation managers knew the audit would occur each year. Hawking, selling single papers on corners, was less than satisfactory for extensive sales data. Paperboys sporadically selling penny papers provided an inconsistent profit for themselves and a circulation department. Newspaper company business changed, communities were changing, and the common urban newsey changed.

A familiar American icon in knickers and a newsy cap shouting headlines on city corners transitioned to a new icon, the neighborhood newspaper delivery boy. It's true, talk over the clotheslines, party phone lines, back yard fence lines wove information throughout communities. But nowhere did the web of information reach more residents than by the plethora of newspapers distributed from the hands of youngsters. A quiet, fast paperboy raced to "porch" his papers for the convenience of his subscribers who read in the comfort of home. Folks just reached outside the door and retrieved the news, exactly when they expected the drop to arrive, or close to exact.

For a kid, everything could turn better with a route. Almost everything. Sort of better.

# CHAPTER 2
## WISHIN'

With a steady paper route, each day a boy shouldered his papers and delivered to his list of subscribers.

If a child wasn't lucky enough, like Jesse, to have an older brother who passed on a route, he had to scramble. A kid could gain valuable experience by hawking special editions, serving as another carrier's substitute, or delivering weekly news sheets until he finally acquired his goal: an assigned route. He needed 'sperience because a small-fry smile was insufficient to nab a route, even if a missing-tooth grin was captivating.

### Snickers

The oldest journalism school in the United States, University of Missouri's School of Journalism, founded in 1908, produced graduates who wrote the news in every locale. Oh, if those future journalists would only create more routes, at least more in the quiet college town of Columbia, Missouri, with its own dependable local paper, the *Columbia Tribune.*

Luke Chase liked his hometown of Columbia just fine, without contemplating how important the long-established School of Journalism was to Columbia and to the nation's informed citizenry. The School's relevance was fine, but Luke focused on acquiring a paper route and his concern centered on one college student.

Luke benefitted from the wisdom of Mr. Francis Pike, the revered circulation manager of the *Tribune,* who insisted that when papers came off the press, the carriers must be ready to deliver or have a trained reliable substitute standing by. So an organized carrier cajoled a kid wanting a route to fill in, when necessary, and fulfill the job.

Luke "became a substitute for an older boy who was attending the University." The student "had a big paper route. I was required to go along with him regularly to keep up with the route. Getting the job was not as easy as it sounds. There were lots of boys in competition for a route, and I'm sure Mr. Pike chose those boys he considered to be reliable and trustworthy, based on his observation of their periodic performance." Luke was steadily proving himself.

With World War II growing more intense, the *Tribune* ran extra editions. "Mr. Pike put out a call for his boys to come in and sell the special edition." So Luke "sold papers right and left" in his neighborhood noting which house wanted the latest news. He kept track of the two cents he made on each sale. And in the meantime, he made sure he was available if his college student requested him. Luke acquired knowledge--- and a bit more---as he substituted. "My guy was generous. He gave me a dime and a Snickers candy bar every time."

## Without any Money

In the 1950s Cadiz, Kentucky was a smaller spot on the map than Columbia, Missouri. However, hoping to be a paperboy was no small issue. The carriers, "those lucky enough to have a route would usually keep it until after the summer of high school graduation, so open routes were few and far between." To eight-year-old Vyron Mitchell, "there was nothing more important than being a paperboy for the local *Cadiz Record*. I was lucky to be a sub for a couple of the fellows, which meant I had to learn each one of their customers, make weekly collections for them and deliver any missed copies."

Vyron was an energetic, reliable substitute, albeit a penniless one. "My pay was the knowledge that if I did this long enough and the paperboy graduated, then I was first in line to take over the route as a full-fledged paper boy." And full-fledged, he'd earn money for a bike. He definitely needed a route, instead of a no-pay sub position, in order to buy wheels.

With set subscriptions to be delivered every day, regardless of any circumstances, a substitute was essential. When Leonard Lair lay in pain after an emergency appendectomy, his newspaper bundles rested at the paper station ready to be delivered. His sister and mother managed while he recovered. A tyke hanging around the drop-off spot couldn't be nabbed and instantly know a correct route. The dependable paperboy reeled in a reliable, trained substitute. Otherwise, the carrier endured blame.

# A Bright Solution

A very conscientious paperboy, Mike Rhodes grew in experience and salesmanship with his route in San Jose, California. As a result he received several incentive trip rewards from the company. But to enjoy a long outing, a substitute was necessary. With over 100 customers, and having tripped through several mistakes learning to be a top carrier, he became a careful teacher for his sub. The student tried to remember each subscriber's house; however, he confused specific homes so Mike solved the identification problem. He painted a bright neon slash at the customer's place. Since it was Mike's fault if a paper wasn't delivered, and he worked for a complaint-free record, the flash of red and orange fluorescent paint solved his potential problem and made it easier for the helper. Sure enough, people complained about the permanent identifying swath. Apparently brightening the neighborhood was unpopular.

# Insufficient

Sporadically hawking a special edition or substituting with little or no tangible gain, although a free candy bar was good, a kid desired a more dependable source of income. If only he could deliver every week, year-round, he'd gain experience and count on money, little as it might be. With weekly earnings, a fellow could plan his spending. And show the manager how reliable he was. Counting on 50 cents a week, he'd buy a baseball glove or start paying for a used bike. A carrier inconsistently required a substitute, but the 50 cents for the bike had to be paid regularly. Once a week, stop at the hardware store and pay.

Yes! Deliver a weekly paper for better experience, and possibly be lucky enough to have some customers who gave tips. He'd still hawk with hellacious, salacious headlines, substitute intermittently on other days, but one day a week he'd have a job.

# Dependable

Every Thursday evening John Satterthwaite delivered 300 issues of the *Seattle Buyers' Guide,* right to the peoples' doorknob. Except for one knob on Bagley Avenue N. When John "started up the walk, the door opened. Out came a police dog." This lady had no intention of allowing a boy near her private barrier. Common sense directed him to continue to other houses.

Across Bagley Avenue, as he completed both sides of the street, he saw "a lady stand behind her curtained glass-paneled door to see if I attempted to throw the paper on the porch. If so, she opened the door and threatened to complain to the office." A registered complaint meant a ten-cent fine, reducing his small profit.

# Does It Matter?

Jim McArthur began his first paper carrier job with the *Beacon Hill News*. Not the Boston Beacon Hill with old line Brahmans. This hill was in southeast Seattle, a working-class neighborhood. The paper rolled off the press on Friday destined for 3,500 homes throughout the compact residential area. At the end of the school week, Jim's bundles were on the front porch. And on top of the stacks lay a quarter and a dime. Pocketing his two coins, he started walking along 15th Avenue South, proceeded for a mile and half and then began his return. His three miles expanded beyond the street because the paper was placed on the porch---not rolled and thrown. As a beginner, "I was very proud to have earned those 35 cents each week." So pleased, he never analyzed that the pennies per time stretched more than 15,840 feet in three miles.

Despite pride, his 35 cents didn't go very far in 1945. However, Jim was reliable and advanced to a job delivering 225 papers, the *Shopping News*, that encouraged people to buy now that rationing had ended. This effort after school netted 75 cents, and he passed the *Beacon Hill* job to a younger brother, John.

Jim placed all the shopping specials at each person's door. Every week, one by one he left printed sales suggestions for people. Walk a block, walk another block through the seasons. Lights came on in kitchens, dark settled down before supper, colorful leaves turned brown and dropped in the terribly wet and windy Northwest weather.

Would people go shopping in lousy weather? Probably not. Did it matter if the *Shopping News* was distributed this week? Probably not. Since Jim slipped the paper inside the screen door, slipped quietly away and never collected for the free shopping guide, who knew the difference? Enough! Jim developed "quite a dump site in the woods."

Young John McArthur skipped a run into the woods with his stack. No sense covering more territory. He pulled up a loose piece of stone pavement "on the walkway at the family home and hid the *Beacon Hill News*," right there like a scavenger hunt sight. Tucked in, the sheets wouldn't blow around. Papers pushed down in the depressed hole, heavy pavement replaced, he thought he had cleverly taken care of that bothersome routine.

Not so. An astute mother, alert to what her sons could do, found the papers. Darn, need to dig deeper, and probably dig in the woods. Furthermore, residents began asking why they no longer received the *Shopping News*. People phoned in complaints and requested the paper. The manager insisted a boy learn that 75 cents received for work, or supposed work, meant the job must be performed. Besides, throw-away wasn't in the ABC audit plan.

# Sting

Beacon Hill was not an exception in producing weekly shoppers' guides. All the various Seattle neighborhoods, with stores ready to sell to customers, spread the word about shopping specials. Another small boy, James Grout, gained a job dispensing the *Northgate Journal*, north of Seattle near Haller Lake, a beautiful natural area with dense woods.

Winter frosted the evergreen trees creating a lovely green and white scene, but the beauty was cold, painfully cold. So frigid even salt in Jim's tears couldn't keep the watery drops from freezing his cheeks. Forget the shoppers. Enough! He took the *Northgate Journal* into the woods and he too dumped his load. Miserable stinging cold eradicated any thought about the consequences; no thought of the sting from a parent's willow switch.

## Another Step

A step up the stairs to experience in delivering, or occasionally hiding, the free shopping guides led to the opportunity to deliver a small weekly paper, or a specialty paper like the *Union Record* that David hawked in Bellingham. In the transition to routes, the farming, the fishing news, the foreign language papers, ones printed less than daily yet not free, offered boys the opportunity to learn how to sell, similar to the hawking step.

Striving to be ready for a daily route, by age 12, grade-schoolers settled for a weekly edition with a regular delivery schedule and the essential collection responsibility. Or a kid tried to peddle a less competitive paper, one that sold sporadically, though not very readily.

## Rain, Rats. Rain, Red-lights. Rain

Mom, Dad, two boys, Burnie and Barry, and a small Boston bulldog named Bruce "arrived in Ketchikan on the *USS Alaska* on a rainy day." The rainy day occurred every week in Ketchikan, since annual rainfall measures 165 inches, give or take 10 inches. This particular rain fell at the end of December in the end of the 1930s.

Traveling from Boise to Seattle, before heading north to Alaska the family celebrated Christmas in a motel room, far different from the Biblical, "*no room in the inn*." Packages unwrapped, the Dunphy family waited to sail north through the Inland Passage for Dad's new Coast Guard assignment. The large *Alaska* steamship left the Seattle dock at night, so to pass Christmas day, dad took his boys to the theater. "Dad, Burnie and I watched five consecutive double-feature cowboy movies (a family record that we never surpassed.)"

After six unsettled days at sea, the family arrived in Ketchikan for the New Year, and the start of the 1940s. No one imagined the changes and the horrific challenges for the world in the new decade, but the Dunphy boys recognized incredible changes to their new home.

In the wet town with steep hills, situated in a temperate rain forest, waterfalls tumbled and chattered down cliffs. The waterfront was regularly swept with extremes of high tides. Sea water rose and fell. Rain just fell. For the days, tides measured 17, 18 feet. The rainfall measured about 14 feet in a year. And Barry's earnings, measured per his feet, like Jim McArthur's, calculated to a less than exciting amount.

Ketchikan was not a typical small town, even with the usual grocery store, Champion Shoe Store, bakery, theater, public school, churches--- Methodist, Episcopal, Lutheran, Presbyterian. First, most of the downtown area was perched on large pilings. To provide sufficient commercial floor space, buildings extended out over the water. Sidewalks were constructed from wood planking. Barry and Burnie "soon learned to just step over soaked and sprawled men who had too much." Though not the main economy of Ketchikan, bars stood on every corner. The most prevalent type of business with "more saloons than all other businesses combined," bars served as banks for workers' earnings. With daily rain, men were soaked outside and then soused inside the saloons.

The other thriving business, near the center of town, was the red light district. Unbothered by the brothels and bars, the brothers were interested in the Butterhorn Bakery and the Revilla Theater. In order to have funds for treats and movies and to learn more about their new home, but mostly to earn money, they located the newspaper office for the *Ketchikan Chronicle*. Burnie was fine. He was 12. As the town's only paper, and with no operating radio station, his sales were good. He quickly accumulated nickels.

Barry, five years younger, was stuck. Stuck with the rain, with no money, stuck being seven. Not letting age stop him, he'd try to sell the *Ketchikan Fishing News* down along the waterfront. This was a challenge since he was "supposed to stay out of bars and saloons, and not many people seemed to want *Fishing News*, not even most fishermen." Plus the bigger drawback, Barry "only made a penny for each one sold." To sell more papers than Burnie and sell a lesser paper in order to have a dime for the movies, he'd better get started.

The *Fishing News* wasn't heavy as he walked toward boats tied behind the breakwater. Wearing his sou'wester rain hat, mackinaw jacket, and his rubber boots, he was dry. He sloshed through rain, about a half mile out to Tongass Basin.

Told to stay out of saloons, yet "that was about all there was along the way" Barry's common sense took over, considering he "still hadn't sold a single paper." He pushed his small shoulder against a door and stumbled into a cavernous room. Dark was settling over Ketchikan in the winter afternoon, but he stood in a darker space on an old plank floor. He shoved his wet cap back and pulled his bundle of papers from under his jacket.

His eyes adjusted quicker than his nose. A smorgasbord of smells slid to his lungs. The odors of permanently impregnated wet wool with fish scales blended into the stale beer, stale cigarette smoke, the stink of a splattered spittoon, all diffused into a redolent soup making his stomach jerk. The rain washing Ketchikan didn't reach the innards of the stench-soaked saloon.

"Want to buy a copy of the *Ketchikan Fishing News*?" Barry spoke to a large man slouched against a table.

"Yeah, I'll buy your papers." He grabbed the copies, nearly spilling his beer and pushed dimes across the table.

The happy paperboy grinned. "Thanks."

"Here, I'll help yah." The man pushed himself up.

Barry wondered if the guy's suspenders could extend to hold one more beer. But his concern turned to the man's hands as he shuffled all the news pages, scrunching a few sheets and shoving the stack back across the table.

Perplexed, Barry figured he was to resell his messed up bundle. The paper's manager told him to sell each copy. Though only seven, he had learned to follow instructions.

The bartender must have sensed the child's dejection. "Kid, you wanna see something?"

Barry nodded yes while keeping an eye on the dimes scattered on the rough table surface.

The huge man stumbled toward the back wall with the bartender beside him. Each grabbed a baseball bat resting against a side door.

Barry shivered. He wanted to sink through the floor, past the pilings supporting the saloon, into the dark churning sea. He locked his knees. His wide eyes watched every move. The sound of scratches seeped under the door. The bartender slid his hand along the frame, flipped a light switch and flung the door open.

Foot-long rodents, bigger than raccoons ran everywhere; big rats with big incisors raced to escape. The men swung the ball bats knocking the critters against the walls, causing stacks of crates to fall. The rodents squealed and sssccreched as their fat grey bodies careened through the air. Tails, entrails, decapitated bodies smeared the men. The executioners shouted, belched with laughter, and swung faster.

Barry thawed his frozen stance. The screaming animals, the splattered sight along with the stench, socked his stomach. Clutching his dimes, but leaving the scrunched newspapers, he hurried into the welcoming fresh rain and gulped the moist air. Whatever film he and his brother attended, it would not be as gory as the price he paid to watch a movie.

He understood why he was told to stay out of saloons. But they were the best place to sell papers. Well, maybe this ratty one, far out on the wharf wasn't as good. Plus, was there any chance the weather would be better and the tide lower than 17 feet so the movie theater could open? Sitting at sea level, the movie house was closed during very high tides, lest the patrons sat with their feet in seaweed and the tide water slapped at their bottoms.

Barry's nausea subsided. Breathing slower, he looked for Burnie to check how his brother's newspaper sales had progressed.

## Assigned. Sign on the Line

Even with experience from being a substitute, with hawking special editions and delivering weekly shopping news, a boy understood he couldn't just pick up bundles of papers and run a route. With order to the system, the Little Merchant held an assigned route number before he secured a social security number or a military service number. No dog tags around his neck, only a canvas strap across his shoulder signifying service to the community.

Some newspaper companies issued more than a simple route number. To be certain the child's understanding of the business system was perfectly clear, his manager's handshake was reinforced with a signed or even a co-signed contract. The legal content spelled out all the terms with no exceptions allowed, like being late because of school detention, a drunk ran over his bike, or the dog chewed the papers. This formal contract precluded excuses.

Could a binding contract exist between a newspaper company and a minor? Yes and no. The carrier's name was printed on the form; his signature was included. However, the legal piece was signed by his father and by a newspaper company's representative. A bondsman also signed.

If only a mother's or a grandmother's signature was available, then a co-signer was necessary, one the company considered to be a reliable party, like the working, next-door neighbor. A home-maker position was insufficient.

In 1940 when Henry McDaniel studied 706 paperboys in 15 communities he recorded, "Approximately 70 percent of all carriers work under written contracts with the newspaper company." And of those defined contracts, 75 percent required the "signature of parents." A decade later, the *Racine Journal-Times* in Wisconsin described their three-year contract that was signed by the carrier and parents, along with paying a bond.

The "Home-Delivery Dealer Agreement" or the "Carrier's Lease" came printed on a formal, legal-size sheet of paper with an outlined structure of a standard contract. A date, the specific route number, the parties identified as the seller, as the dealer and a statement that the route belonged to the newspaper company, but they were willing to lend or lease it, these comprised the front of the form. A child had to agree to give either two or four weeks' notice of termination. The company held the right to terminate at any time. Details were stated as to when and where the carrier paid the company for the wholesale price of his papers. Clear words explained that he received no right for reimbursement of expenses.

With a sealed handshake and a signed contract, an arrangement was established to deliver papers. Never to dump them. Was a contract necessary? Perhaps not. If a problem arose, the paperboy answered to dad. And that required no legal contract.

## Start

On September 1, 1939, Joe Forsee joined other school kids selling "Extras," which headlined the horrendous news of the German invasion of Poland. World War II began. Joe's experiences as a paperboy started on the "street corners and along residential districts selling newspapers" in Columbia, Missouri, in the heartland, safe from the horrors of Europe.

By the next school year, his experience expanded to "selling single Sunday editions of St. Louis newspapers from a cart on the corner of 10th and Broadway in front of a Presbyterian church." The *Columbia Daily Tribune* was Monday through Saturday, so Sunday editions came in from St Louis. The *Post-Dispatch*, *Globe-Democrat*, and the *Star-Times* sold readily to the car drivers, as well as to "church goers who constituted a huge segment of sales."

His successful sales role expanded into a morning route for the other six days. Subscribers selected one of the St. Louis papers for home delivery Monday through Saturday. Joe was at his agency's pickup point by 4:30 a.m. After early delivery, in mid-morning on Saturday, he repeated his route to collect subscription fees at a convenient hour for residents.

"After a goodly time waiting and hoping, I finally got a route for the *Columbia Daily Tribune* . There was fierce competition for such routes." The students at the University of Missouri, in Columbia, found a six-day afternoon delivery convenient for college schedules. Joe didn't evaluate a route by convenience. For more than a year, he continued to rise very early to deliver the St. Louis papers, and then after school handled his local *Tribune* route.

# No Different Next Decade

In March, 1951, "After four years of unsuccessfully trying to get a *Democrat & Chronicle* route," Ron Anderson gladly accepted route A-3, in Charlotte, New York. The route was being vacated by a boy who would graduate in spring. Though the state of New York in the mid-twentieth century constricted the field of applicants by requiring paperboys be age 12 or older, and entirely disallowed girls, "the demand by kids for routes far exceeded the supply." Unconcerned about rising at 5:00 a.m., Ron was ecstatic over his good fortune.

Children expected to make money, to capture fun and adventures as they walked through the neighborhood before school, or with an afternoon edition following the school day. Whistling, a boy was ready to begin the rounds in the same routine every day, like writing the week's spelling list over and over. However, with his paper route he was excited. A route was better than a merry-go-round at the carnival, round and round. Everything would be easier now. This meant money. No more waitin'. What could go wrong?

# CHAPTER 3
## WAITIN'

### Brave

Mesmerized by flickering stars, Don's eyes searched for figures in the multitude of constellations suspended in the sweeping sky. Blackest before dawn, blacker than wet tar, the earth's ceiling looked like a giant had scattered millions of sparklers across the universe.

He rotated his gaze past the North Star to Leo to the Big Dipper⁻ but growing dizzy with staring upward, he returned to Earth. Stepping along the rough ground, he paused half way to the top of a long hill. In arid north central Washington, distant from the few dim lights in Electric City, he saw the vivid patterns of stars in a dark silence as extreme as the immense, cold cosmos that enveloped him at 4 a.m.

A reliable fifth-grader, Don Hubbard rose at 3:30 seven mornings a week, through four distinct seasons. Neither a soft spring nor hazy autumn compared to the drama of winter or the stifling heat of summer in the desert where Grand Coulee Dam altered the ancient path of the Columbia River. None of the seasons delivered the theatrics and violence of the ice age floods that gouged and ripped the ground that Don now covered. Prehistoric waters left boulders bigger than trucks scattered like pebbles over the landscape.

The Grand Coulee Dam was no ordinary place. In 1935 Electric City rose swiftly, the way western gold mining towns rose in a few weeks. But this community never deteriorated into a ghost town. Families lived in the usual way with their shopping, church, and school routines. Living in the government community, created during the dam construction, Don's main activities were the Boy Scouts and his daily paper route. He had fun with school friends and Scout buddies. During tourist season, he sold newspapers and talked with people from all 48 states, even foreign travelers, who came to see the largest concrete structure. For now, walking in the dark morning, he was alone.

An occasional sound kept him company as surface gravel rolled under his feet. Rattlesnakes remained hidden deep under boulders until the afternoon heat would draw them out. A coyote howled on a farm miles across the hills

The fiery stars shed no warmth. He delivered papers to his 135 customers before the earth's closest star rose on the horizon. He stared at some falling stars, but they never reached him. A double canvas bag hanging around his neck helped warm his torso, as he trudged to the top of the steep hill and reached the intersection where the streets from town, the county roads and the main highway crossed.

"Good. The construction lantern's lit." His self-talk fashioned a grin on his face. He knew one of the highways was under construction, again, and a lantern alerted motor traffic.

Everything in the territory was in a state of construction: more housing in the new Electric City, and additional generators added to the immense Grand Coulee Dam, the largest hydropower producer in the United States. Roads were being built around and up to the greatest sand pile anywhere in the Northwest, or even the entire United States. School kids argued that the gigantic dam was higher than Superman could leap. Don checked their claim with his dad, who operated a shovel and crane at the dam site.

For now, he felt the quiet solitude before the brilliant coral streaks of a desert sunrise transformed the cold air to warm, the black to sandy shades. Wind swirling down the slopes of the northern Cascade Mountains and over the crusty desert into central Washington made eerie swooshing sounds. And then the wind ceased. Silence spread down from the cosmos.

Kicking aside some jagged stones, Don stomped his cold feet. Shivers ran through his thin body. In the limited light of a traffic-warning lantern, he saw the drop-off spot for his bundles of papers was empty. Settling on the gravelly dirt, he shared space with rocks and the hidden rattlesnakes. Alone, he watched the lantern flicker more than the distant stars. His yawn echoed like a shout. His arm a pillow and the double canvas bag covering much of his chest and back, he curled into a fetal position with the construction light near his center core. He scooted in closer to the warm kerosene oil lamp, secure in his noiseless, small world.

Since the delivery truck, with stacks of the *Spokesman Review,* was late coming west across the 86 miles from Spokane, Don rested. He knew he'd have to rush through his route, grab breakfast before speed-walking the one and a half miles to Columbia School to beat the tardy bell. With no control as to when the truck arrived, Don cuddled next to the lantern, a light speck in an immense, dark universe. He waited. He soon slept.

## Into the City

When an Alberta clipper blew Arctic air across Iowa, waiting in zero weather for the *Des Moines Register* bundles to arrive, Pat Eng became resourceful. Being resourceful, and with a bit of guidance from his mother, he first acquired a newspaper spot in Iowa City at age seven. Pat began his paperboy career in an easier manner than other second graders entering a first job. Inside the University Medical Center, away from any wild weather, he sold papers. No bicycle, no rolling the papers and throwing the tube to the porch. Just stand and sell. Then mother and sons moved. Pat's new job switched to outside, facing into every weather condition.

Nevertheless, he felt lucky to have a route. For warmth, Pat sensibly used sticks from the nearby woods to build a fire and ease the miserable cold that cut into his bone marrow. He needed to defeat the bitter air before Jack Frost bit his toes, fingers, ears, and nose.

Moving his stiff body around, he searched for more small branches and sheets of discarded wrapping paper from previous bundles to expand his tiny fire fanned by the wind. Sparks burst into flames. The burning debris and twigs snapped and crackled. Swirling shadows in the flickering light added company to his lone spot. Small rivulets of water ran off the ice. His eyes became heavy watching flames. He tried to bolster his nascent bravery.

When the delivery truck appeared, warmth spread from the exhaust fumes but only for a minute. The warm truck disappeared and Pat began his frigid route as the small fire burned down. The steady pace of delivery was better than waiting.

Distance, late drivers, icy streets, press problems, even freight trains caused bundles to arrive late. Most anything could, and often did, disrupt the schedule.

## Late Again!

Bob stared into silent black space as though entering a cave. Leaping off the high platform, he landed in a snow drift and groped in the dark until his toe stumbled against the railroad tie. He brushed aside white powder and knelt over, pressing his head next to the freezing metal. The rail stung his skin but no sound reverberated in his ear.

"Darn! Train's late again." At least moving thwarted his shivers. Hugging his canvas newspaper bag to his chest to squeeze out the cold, he wiggled his numb feet before struggling back up to the depot platform to wait. Bob needed his *San Francisco Examiner* bundles that were shipped in the baggage car each morning. The small town of Klamath Falls, Oregon, was one of a string of stops on the Southern Pacific Railroad line between San Francisco and Portland. Due to arrive at 6:00 a.m., train 12 was behind schedule, again. Consequently, so was the paperboy.

Bob Barr was experienced and knew how to manage a paper route. Starting as a hawker on a street corner, he successfully earned a dime his first day. He felt rich. In 1936 a dime delighted a kid. Of course it was difficult to accumulate money since he bought a double-sided canvas bag, then a bike. But his regular delivery route allowed his savings account to rise, in spite of an irregular train schedule.

And since he rose early to be punctual, another late train disturbed him. He must be to the station when the engine pulled in, because if he missed removing his papers from the freight car, the bundles were tossed out in Portland, 240 miles to the north.

On a dark, cold morning, he stood vigil, waiting to hurry through his route, grab breakfast and possibly 20 minutes of sleep before hurrying on to school, For the moment, Bob felt dejected. With more experience, maybe he'd capture a local afternoon route. The silence was suffocating. The child coped, alone.

He heard the train, like a thunderstorm rolling up the Cascade Mountains to Klamath Falls, before the platform vibrated. The brakes screeched as clouds of coal smoke and steam shoved aside fresh air. He grabbed a handle and with a wide swing jumped into the baggage car. To avoid a bad error, he checked to be certain he grabbed his designated bundles.

The engine pulled away. Bob shifted into high gear with his arms working like the pistons of the train. Smeared grey ink coated his stiff fingers but added no warmth as he folded 75 papers into a tight square, alternately filling the double bag front and back. He glanced at the lead story, *FDR Delivers Second Inaugural Address*. Not wanting to, but needing every minute, he had to skip the comics.

With the canvas flaps slapped over the papers, he slipped along the icy road into the dim light of dawn. A few kitchen windows cast pools of light on side yards and a faint aroma of brewed coffee drifted past him. He walked as fast as possible, through deep drifts on his seven mile route. Klamath Falls, almost 4,300 feet above the Pacific Ocean, received heavy snow, often making his bike useless. The wet snow packed inside the fenders, halted the wheels, tossing him to the ground. Thick snow was great for snowballs, but terrible for a rushing paperboy. At least the Sunday edition, which had the most subscribers, wasn't delivered on a school day. He knew he'd be challenged, again, when he entered his class late. He was beyond tardy. A seven-mile route required time. Tomorrow would be better---if the train was on time.

# Shut Out

According to standard pediatric tables, Leroy Modine was small. At seven and a half, the half did not sufficiently elevate his size and strength to the table figures listing an age seven height as 46 to 49 inches and the weight as 43 to 53 pounds. Leroy was on the slight edge of that table. The opposite of physical stature, his determination was huge and drove him. That is, until he was stopped by a gigantic door.

He wouldn't let Dad down, not after Dad helped him learn to make change, because a paperboy had to be accurate when collecting. Mom also helped. She hooked up the canvas strap on his big newspaper bag so it hung above his feet. His parents were certain he could manage a route. Mr. McDonald, the district circulation manager, thought he could and gave him a Nutty Buddy bar when Leroy signed on. Right now he felt real uncertain.

He stretched, strained, and shoved. The defiant door refused him. As he leaped up his shoe laces flapped. With fingers still developing dexterity, he hadn't mastered twisting shoe laces into a bow. At the moment, his tiny fingers were wrapped around the large, thick skeleton key. If only he could reach the high keyhole to the freight room. The newspapers arrived around 1:30 a.m. When the train was thirty minutes late, or came at 2:45 a.m. it didn't matter to Leroy happily slumbering in bed. Now, at 5:30 a.m., time was important. Even more crucial, how was he to grab his papers on the other side of the monolithic structure?

The railroad man, who used a skeleton key to unlock the door and fling the bundles into the freight room, was a long way down the tracks. Leroy strained upward to insert the big key into the hole. He shoved the solid door with his small frame. Folks were waitin' for their morning paper. Leroy's first job, which would open doors of opportunity, was in jeopardy. The instructions and regulations he received, when granted a route, stopped short of specifying how to shove open an immense structure.

# Behave

While there were managers who sensibly recognized that bundles needed to be dropped at the carrier's home when a single paperboy managed a morning route, the greater majority of boys ran or bicycled to their pick-up point when the school bell released them. The desolate silence in a lone child's wait vividly contrasted with a large group of after-school carriers, their exploding energy expressed in noise. They created a racket similar to a Boeing 747 jet lift off.

For decades, afternoon editions dominated morning papers by three to one, and the difference only increased as time wore on. In 1952, of the

1,773 daily papers, 1,454 were afternoon dailies competing with only 319 morning papers. Into 1960, 312 morning publications competed against the 1,763 afternoon editions. After school, this drew numbers of children to the newspaper loading dock. The kids' active, competitive spirit challenged the liveliness of a circus. They rushed to congregate in an assigned place with a purpose.

And one of those places happened to be in a pleasant town with southern attributes, though not a slow center since it was a college town. Living in Columbia, Missouri, provided local youngsters an excellent opportunity to be a paper carrier for the *Columbia Daily Tribune.* The key reason for their exceptional opportunity rested with the circulation manager, Mr. Francis Pike. He screened fellows, like Luke Chase and Joe Forsee, who first hawked and substituted for the *Tribune.* Mr. Pike signed on boys who had at least reached middle school, and ones he knew to be trustworthy. Once assigned, this dedicated manager retained his carriers.

Mr. Pike cared about the paperboys, and they could trust him to be fair as well as considerate. One of his charges, Cary Thorp, progressed forward in life with service in the navy and a formal education through the Ph.D. level. Each stage reinforced his assessment: Mr. Pike was "a marvelous role model." Over four decades, Francis Pike was a revered leader of children who matured under his guidance. He instructed them in proper paperboy protocol, lessons that fit for life. Afternoons when the carriers lined up on the north side of the *Tribune* building, Mr. Pike was there to greet them. Order prevailed.

Not all newspaper office pick-up locations ran so smoothly.

## Enough

An experienced newspaperboy, Cliff Benson, by age 16, had run around the Everett city blocks quite a few times delivering more than one route, so the antics of scuffling, jabbering carriers seemed usual to him. Their arms, legs, lips, and tongues flew in perpetual motion, especially after sitting seven hours in a restrictive school room. The noise in the *Everett Daily Herald* office on Wall Street rose to a train locomotive decibel level. Any school teacher, scout master, Sunday school superintendent knows children's excitement and wild ideas grow exponentially with an additional youngster. Sort of similar to a March windstorm whipping to hurricane force. With 125 puerile carriers for Cliff to manage, their venial actions and noise competed with the loud printing press.

From age 12 or a bit younger and progressing to age 17 or 18, the boys showed a large disparity in size and maturity. Little ones wanted to prove themselves, to rise quicker in the hierarchy. Older fellows expected recognition, to be the big boy on the block, and they picked on the upstarts who defied the plan. Both sides, the large bullies and small victims, worked on ways to level the other guy, the way it could ring out in boxing matches.

Boxing was a favorite sport, further enhanced with Golden Gloves tournaments established in the 1920s. Sponsored by newspapers, radio stations, Boys and Girls Clubs, tournaments piqued the kids' interest, their pugilist heroes leaving them with dreams of becoming amateur boxers. The heavyweight champion, Joe Lewis, won a Golden Gloves championship in 1934. Children absorbed this important information.

While not a champion in Golden Gloves, one of Cliff's paperboys was nevertheless good for his size and ready to prove his prowess. Finding "bug off" to be an insufficient warning, the boy quickly found the perfect opportunity to demonstrate his prowess.

In five quick, strong jabs his opponent's nose spewed blood. Both eyes would be black tomorrow. The victor was the champ without a regulation Golden Gloves title. For the next few days, the loser's black eyes fit with his swollen sore nose. His ego battered, not looking around for a little squirt to shove aside, the big bully never entered the newspaper boxing ring again.

Most carriers stayed focused to avoid losing their route. Frank Gennarelli knew plenty of boys in Binghamton, New York, who, like everywhere, wanted a paper route. As the oldest of four Gennarelli boys, at age 13, he "couldn't mess up" after a long wait for one.

Such circumstances helped restrain boys from trying antics that became too troublesome. Yet, youngsters misbehaved when waiting for their block of papers. Immature and told to "act your age," kids at seven or eight did that, acted silly, noisy, even devilish. Ordered to "grow up," ruffians tried, but only time and experience moved them "up."

## The Holding Pen

In charge of more than 100 boys, Cliff Benson issued warnings, constant warnings. At only 16, his patience stayed exceptionally high. Placed in charge of the bundles to be quickly distributed, Cliff made certain no one left the newspaper company short on their count. The boys also checked their pigeon cubby hole for pink slips, a notice that stated a change in their number of customers. Or possibly a complaint.

Invariably on a windy, rainy Northwest day, a common weather pattern on Puget Sound, when the schools' outdoor recesses had been cancelled, when the carriers wanted their papers in order to hurry through the lousy weather, that's the day the press malfunctioned. The boys crowded inside trying to keep the canvas bag and themselves dry as long as possible. Some loitered outside for a smoke and more space to say unacceptable words, but most stood inside.

The papers must be delivered, so Cliff refrained from removing the little menace right as the bundles rolled out. Dozens of carriers watched, annoyed with listening to the blabbering pip-squeak as he pushed and punched others.

ENOUGH!

Cliff finally decided the kid's wild antics required containment. In he goes. His arms and legs won't bother, annoy, or aggravate anyone. Laughed at by the observing carriers, the kid quit. Confined inside a large bag, secured around his neck, he was set in the corner. The thick canvas mail bag rocked, but he was like a hyena under a tranquilizer dart, going nowhere. Instead of holding rolled newspapers ready to drop at the post office, the long bag served as a straight jacket, a one-person jail cell. Furthermore, the imp recognized his mouth had better button up or he'd be further down in his holding pen.

One under control, only 124 more to dispatch. Cliff's method subdued the nuisance and created a settling affect on the others.

Everett, Washington, Columbia, Missouri, Mount Vernon, Ohio, towns with a local paper where the circulation manager knew which boy belonged to which family; each community of carriers behaved under a watchful eye. Or were taught how to behave.

For cities with more than ten dozen paperboys, locations that exceeded a thousand young carriers, the bundles went to drop-off spots throughout the metropolitan region. The stations, with sparse supervision, provided wild, free-range places for boys, at least by reformers' assessments. The lone paperboy in the early morning hour was brave. The supervised newspaper office guided children to behave. These contrasted with the city newspaper substations that supported an enclave.

# CHAPTER 4
## ENCLAVE

Around the supervised newspaper building, boys fingered their cigarette lighters, snapped it at other boys' noses, but held back lighting a cigarette under the eye of an adult. The semi-control at the newspaper office with disciplining a menace, the cussin' held in check, and certainly no cussin' with a revered manager like Mr. Pike, youngsters behaved. The company pick-up areas were sedate in comparison to the corner substation, a chaotic hornets' nest.

The competitive drive to acquire a route did not dissolve with an assignment. Instead, it often energized competition causing an aggressive stance that rocked neighborhood substations, a haven of intermittent fires and fights. Yet, for the majority a "paper shack" was consistently a center of steadfast friendships.

With no private bedroom in their crowded homes and having outgrown rickety tree houses, the fellows thrived at the newspaper shack, a place they claimed as a clubhouse. Carriers felt a connection with pals who also worked a route every day, enjoying the camaraderie, capturing fun and freedom with friends.

City paperboys, unfettered and unconcerned with consequences, headed to their "shack" after school, to a station free of adult supervision. They arrived early and when papers arrived late, a terrific time and space surrounded the gang. One guy's antics lit a chain of activity, and like a wind-driven fire in dry grass, kids ignited restless energy. Their engines raced on full throttle as though fed on high octane. Free from hours of sitting still at a school desk, keeping hands to oneself, mouth shut, all unnatural positions for a robust, devilish child, their released energy awkwardly radiated from the arms, legs, and vocal cords as they wrestled and uttered irreverent words. New carriers were curious about what big guys knew. The inquisitive instinct ran strong. The competitive instinct even stronger.

Each late-minute arrival of the day's newspaper bundles, and then multiplied by 15, 19, or more boisterous kids, they often used the time to break-out in fights. Wild sounds reverberated over a block away. The carriers' view of their clubhouse, against a neighbor's opinion of a horror house run by controversial heathens, grew further apart than just a generation. The center often became a contentious place and adults demanded closure of the structures. The newspaper company obeyed the adults' demands.

The best part in hanging out at the paper shack: absence of parent or teacher restrictions and criticisms. School regulations---no bubble gum, no swearing, no spit balls---were enforced at home by hovering adults. Unsupervised space in the shack gave roustabouts freedom for unbridled fun. The neighbors considered the loose gang as hoodlums, demons. If social reformers knew even half the trouble.

The substations showed basic similarities whether in Seattle, Milwaukee, Columbus, Lewiston, or elsewhere. As long as the structure bore a sufficient roof to protect thin paper sheets, the place met a primary purpose: a dry drop-off spot. An abandoned garage with a dirt floor, a deteriorating empty real estate office, a dull green wooden frame with a plank floor that the newspaper company provided---any of these filled the need. Or at Jack Moore's heated station in Oklahoma City, the gang enjoyed a sturdy structure with steel benches.

Besides the essential roof, other basics made the clubhouse better. A bench for piling newspaper bundles, preferably two benches and maybe an additional one outside under the roof overhang, plus a table for figuring records of distribution, these made the structure more functional. Serving as a waste receptacle, a dented rusty barrel might be included. A touch of décor was occasionally nailed on an inside wall for the boys' private viewing: movie star pinup or a guy's calendar. A potbelly stove for those freezing winter days was appreciated. When a shack included an icebox, where an occasional block of ice cooled the stolen bottles of beer, the clubhouse became the Ritz.

To pitch marbles, a thick twine ring or a gouge in the dirt sufficed, as did a broken yo-yo string. A crumbled queen of spades tossed in the corner, the result of a gambling loss on meager earnings, lay next to a scrunched-up spelling list. Kids who perfected an accurate aim with spitballs, snowballs, basketballs, and the daily rolled paper to the porch, usually missed the trash barrel with bundle wrapping paper, old advertising inserts, and other trash. Chewing gum wads, dried wads of chewing tobacco, Snickers and Hershey candy wrappers, pop and beer caps, flattened cigarette butts, a broken ball bat, all these lay scattered around. Dried cola streaks smeared sides of the shed where rowdies competed to see how high fizz in a pop bottle shot. Stray dogs marked the corner of the shed and scrounged for any scrap of food. Only a sniff left.

In Seattle, a contest to clean out the shacks improved a few structures, for awhile. At one shed, the carriers painted a crescent moon on the door, like grandpa's outhouse, which delighted the guys and disturbed neighbors. The mess and the moon were there 24 hours. Twenty-two hours a day, empty silence surrounded the building and trampled grounds. Wild noise enveloped it the other two hours, depending on how late the papers arrived.

Kids shared candy, colas, and comic books as well as coughs, colds and cigarettes. Fellows slugged, spit, swore, shouted, smoked---such activities forbidden in school. The stink of sulfur from a freshly struck match, stale cigarette smoke, wet wool, sweat of older boys, rotting apple cores, horse manure along the street curb, a dog pile on a clump of weeds, a wad of chewing tobacco, all infused the air---not a parlor potpourri.

A centrifugal force drove their venial actions faster and wider, with energetic carriers vying to out shout the ones yelling. The shack was no place for a wimp. Better toughen him 'cause he was headed into tough experiences, handling the weight of 115 papers, the rough weather, the riled adults. Initiation was baptism by full immersion with no saintly language.

Reflecting the brawn of big cities, some paper shacks were hotbeds with hot-headed rogues. Others were small versions of college campus hazing. Regardless of the situation, the new kid, like Henry Petroski entering his paper carrier position for the New York *Long Island Press*, incurred a rough initiation. He was stripped of his trousers. In the cauldron of excitement, a kid was unsure of how much further his capture would progress.

At an Oklahoma City station, for devilment, a boy aimed into a small hole in the side of the hot potbelly stove. The inside steamed. A single yellow stream wouldn't smother the fire but the pee stunk. Silly acts by kids. Heck, use the bushes in the alley. Inside the smell increased the usual odors and irked others walking in the door.

Rogues at a station in Kenmore, on the north shore of Lake Washington, near Seattle, built a fire, stoked it, fed the flames until a worried adult called the fire department to report, "There's a roaring bonfire." The boys scattered when the siren approached.

# Fights

In a family with 12 children, John was used to squabbles, jostling for position. He had hustled for a route, with a "nudge" from his father. Earlier he delivered the *Queen Anne Buyers Guide* and weekly grocery store flyers, but 8-year-old John Kearns still had plenty to learn, at school and on the street. Assigned a route, he learned fast, through experiences.

His family resided at 4th W and W. Galer Street on the top of Queen Anne Hill in a friendly neighborhood with a magnificent vista of Puget Sound, Bainbridge Island, Lake Union and of course the Seattle Smith Tower, the tallest building west of the Mississippi, which gleamed like a steeple. A vast world spread before him. He knew his way all around the adjoining streets and alleys. However, to pick up his 100 newspapers, the small boy had to scamper off the steep hill to the flat Denny re-grade section. Twenty-five years later, the area would host the exciting, *Century 21*, the 1962 World's Fair.

Back in 1937, into the seventh year of the destructive Depression, folks ached for a fun time. People drew together but some turned mean with discouragement. John "witnessed serious fights, vicious fights" by the "tough older boys at our station house." These were unrestrained melees eschewing any Golden Glove techniques in favor of fierce pounding, face battering, nose breaking, cheek and eye gouging and repeated groin kicking. The violence echoed the way the tough Depression years beat folks down.

Too scared to even eke out a little squeal, John sucked in awful scenes, afraid that his next breath might be knocked out of him. Just seeing such violent, vehement acts, an explosive vomit might erupt from his stomach. He wanted to grab his bundles of papers and be gone. Youngsters liked excitement but less vivid than bloody, painful fights.

## Stopped by Fights and Coughs

Walking along wooden planks, passing stores on the hills of Ketchikan, seventh-grader Burnie Dunphy was busy selling his newspapers, alone, since his younger brother, Barry, wasn't selling the *Fishing News* that evening. Burnie was carrying a stack of the *Ketchikan Chronicle* when he noticed a crowd. Inquisitive, he crossed the street and edged into the dozens gathered in front of a saloon. He saw why. "An Indian and a Chinaman were fighting," though not with their fingers, fists and feet. They slashed and sliced with knives. Unlike the exciting cowboy and Indian movies Burnie passively watched, this horrified him. He stared at the dripping red scene. It ended. He headed home. Forget selling. As his brother, Barry, relayed, it was "pretty gruesome to watch Burnie. He came home all white and went into the bathroom to throw up." That was one of only two nights he skipped selling papers.

The two men who caused Burnie to lose a night's pay didn't appear on the front page. The brothers checked the *Ketchikan Chronicle* each day. "A few weeks later the Chinaman was fined 'for disturbing the peace,' about $30."

The first time Burnie stopped his sales was because he inhaled a mosquito when yelling the headlines. For hours the small bug caused endless coughing. Alaskan mosquitoes are referred to as the state bird, and more prevalent than birds in the territory. Choked on the big buzzer, Burnie "insisted he could feel it crawling around in his chest." The incessant coughing continued. Burnie shared a bedroom with Barry and that night Barry" wondered if the thing was ever going to die." A boy choking on a mosquito or choked by vomit has difficulty shouting to earn dimes.

## Fires

Along with fights, fires brought out the ruffians' pecking order. In wintry weather, boys at a substation used a glowing potbelly stove to keep their hands flexible instead of numb. Occasionally a few chunks of coal increased the warmth. In the midst of summer, they enjoyed the fun of lighting firecrackers that raised the noise level and irritated neighbors. But sometimes hellions in pure devilment started a fire in the "hotbeds" of paper shacks. The opposite of cozy occurred when a fire gutted the shack space. Along with fights, fire pushed power stances, because flames fascinated boys and badly influenced trouble makers.

## Why Make it Worse?

Mr. Janecke spoke little English. Emigrating from Poland, his labor as a longshoreman on the Seattle water front required hard work, not talk, and he labored whenever a job was available in the Depression years. He shared the language of family and of freedom. When his oldest son, David, acquired a paper route and then another route and assisted the younger brother, George, obtain a *Seattle Star* route, Dad helped them with buying a sturdy used bike.

The route manager taught George how to fold the *Star* in a tight roll so he could bicycle and throw at the same time. George's dexterity improved. "Younger than any other carrier in the group, it made me feel much older than I was." He stood taller in the family unit, placing most of his earnings in the family coffer.

He hustled and demonstrated reliability. The manager soon changed George from south Seattle "to the area east of 15th Avenue South, by Maple School, continuing over to Cleveland High School." Congregating each afternoon with 12 to 15 carriers who met at the "shack" he gained new friends, older boys who also delivered the *Seattle Star*.

One of the big boys, Tom, had been delivering papers for several years and was able to buy the "classiest bike built, a World bike." Another boy, Ralph, was six years older than George, and a rough kid, but Tom liked Ralph, so the three of them, Tom and Ralph, with George tagging close behind, hung together at the shack.

One afternoon, George left his simple used bike resting on the kick stand next to the newspaper substation. He went inside, grabbed his bundles and began the routine of stuffing papers in his canvas bag. Focused, unconcerned with any other activity or his bike, he intended to soon pedal the route. Guys were giggling, some griping, what teachers called goofing off. With his bag filled, stepping outside, George quickly fastened the heavy canvas bag over the back fender rack and grasped the handlebar grips to push off.

"Owwhhaawwhhh! OOOWWWHHHEEA!"

George's scream caught everyone's attention.

"I immediately tried to jerk my hands away from the handle grips, but the thick melted rubber just stuck to the palms and fingers, burning, blistering and blackening the tissue." He failed to peel rubber from his skin as the fiery material fused to his thin tissue.

Unlike smelling cigarette or cigar smoke, or the acrid smoke of burning leaves, the unusual odor of burned flesh was repulsive. Ralph's laugh, not at all contrite, was disgusting. A smoker, Ralph used his cigarette lighter to heat George's bicycle grips to "boiling hot."

Right there in the afternoon, in the daylight, George's hands turned from smeared grey to seared black. Swelling, seeping, the burned flesh stunk. He still tried to handle his folded papers. Delivery would be extra slow. Hands were important to an efficient carrier, as important as they were to a baseball player or boxer. Here was a cruel boy who deliberately hurt another's essential fingers and palms. This wasn't a fight like in Golden Gloves rules. Joe Lewis, up front, face to face with an opponent, won with strength in his fists. The Depression was tough but this fire burned because of an angry, festering meanness. Why make it tougher?

To say the Depression years contained the exclusive cause of fights and fires is simplifying it. If the newspaper office dropped the bundles on schedule, the busy boys couldn't fill the time with bad acts---at least not much of the time. For a few boys, creating trouble was their incessant preference no matter when.

## Fun with Friends

Carriers had waited long enough for a route. They were ready to count and roll papers starting from the loose end, or when papers were thicker fold the pages, stuff the blocked sheets into the canvas bag and be off. Rolling papers was time consuming, but with friendly chatter and laughter the task went faster. Choosing a tight roll, a triangle, or a square, each shape a different aerodynamically designed missile, captured a boy's interest. A carrier competed with himself, first to see how quickly he'd prepare papers and next, reduce the weight in his bag as he covered the distance quicker than yesterday. He loved creating his contest. And just as much, he loved competing with other carriers. Competitive acts drove paperboys' behavior.

At the substation, chaos settled into calm, or the boys' version of controlled calm. Now it was like a thunderstorm instead of a tornado. They moved through a regular monotonous flow. Though they raced to fire and fights, far more often their energy ran directly to friendships. The boys valued their gathered corps.

# Friendships

The district manager, the station manager, experienced carriers, and older brothers advised the younger ones, the fledglings, but with only a sprinkle of advice. The veteran carriers knew that actual accidents, challenges, true experiences were the best teacher.

"Throw underhand. Gotta do it underhand and it'll porch just fine."

"Dodge cars, dogs, curmudgeons and geese."

"Stay out of ice ruts on hills. Better yet, stay off the bike on ice."

Rules and restrictions rose to subjugate the children. Why a feller could be tied up in requirements and bound with too many restrictions, roped into awful confinements. No, he needed to be free and the paper shack was a fine place for free expression and occasional expletives among friends. Like the cowboy singers, he chose not to be fenced in.

For all the shoving, slugging, and swearing, hanging out at the newspaper station helped the boys develop social skills. Kids recognized what was fair and reasonable based on their definition of unreasonable. Work it out or remove the unreasonable rogue.

To Loren Day, from a family of 12 siblings that included a few older brothers, his friend and station manager, Ron Cameron, was the best big brother imaginable. Ron and Loren developed a lasting friendship at their paper shack. Fires stopped, fights ceased, friendships lasted. For many carriers, "the best part of having a route: meeting at the paper shack." The station manager "could count on the fellows," in spite of the devilment, rough initiation of new boys, and frequent teasing. Friends understood a paperboy's struggles. Stand together and build teams for ballgames, which circulation managers promoted for carriers.

Excellent competitive teams developed at substations. Knowing that a group of 14, 17 energetic guys, with developed arms and a natural spirit to compete were congregating, often kids arrived early. When papers arrived late, a game ensued. The station manager and the district manager supported their enthusiasm, specifically for retention and prevention. Boys on a basketball court, rather than in court of law, helped prevent bad acts. At the same time, the carriers would continue as a paperboy for the team rather than for just the carrying and collecting. The best part of Jim Ruck's *Tacoma News Tribune* route in 1942: "playing on the paperboy softball team." Nearby in Seattle Jack Gahan, "especially enjoyed all the *Seattle Times* sponsored sport programs: basketball, softball, bowling leagues, and more. I know for a fact, lots of us continued delivery to participate in the sports events." And teams won trophies, though single trophies weren't distributed to each kid for simply showing up at the paper shack.

For others, congregating and performing as a carrier group supported their interest. With 1,000 carriers, the New Bedford *Standard-Times* managed a broad range of sports activities but then just as important, they had "hobby classes and a newspaperboy band," and the band was recognized at community events and services. In New Jersey, the *Elizabeth Daily Journal* formed an orchestra of paperboys, which regularly played for military groups and the veterans' hospitals. Group activities with a purpose developed social benefits, beyond just the carrier route that provided financial benefits.

## Prohibit

Coping with waiting to be 12, waiting for an assigned route and for papers to arrive, all the youngsters' frustrations and struggles had nearly come to naught, with a constitutional amendment effort to stop minors from working. In place of the amendment, a code stipulated they should not begin before 6:00 in the morning, and for evening, finish before 7:00 p.m.

The involved subjects focused on delivering with no complaints, rather than reading legal decisions, particularly ones that conflicted with finishing morning delivery by the expected 6:00 a.m. However, in 1924, the route to retaining youth for delivering papers almost ended.

## 1924

Children competed, aware only peripherally of any national or state efforts to stop them. They enjoyed their own rough physical tug-of-war and avoided harsh verbal, adult wars as reformers fought for the child labor amendment. Activists believed in the regulation and waited for approval from the states. Passionate adults fighting against the newspaper industry persisted.

The tumultuous 1920s closed with the stock market crash, October 24, 1929. "Black Thursday" struck. On Black Tuesday, October 29, the terrible slide sent the market into a further downward spiral. The vibrant times of the 1920s were vitiated in the 1930s.

Circulation managers knew a paper route placed youngsters in a routine, more routine than the schedule at a standard school, which was just nine months, and only five days a week. This was tested discipline. It established helpful habits and provided necessary financial aid. To a boy, most importantly, it developed the maturity for which he was striving. As Washington D.C. adults, in 1924, began arguing for eliminating youth under the age of 18 from working, in Washington State an ambitious boy completed his daily trudge.

## "Guess I'm a man now."

David Bowles continued to make his daily rounds in 1924 delivering the *Ellensburg Evening Record*, unaware of amendment efforts. In addition, every Saturday the 13-year-old saddled his horse, Ted, and rode through the route to collect. He sat as fine as any cowboy in his spurs, chaps, a checkered neckerchief and a big hat, too big. A folded newspaper on the inside band helped keep the hat above his eyes.

Returning one Saturday, David tied his horse to a post and went into the Warwick Pool Hall, which until 1920 had been a saloon, when Prohibition closed that portion. The long bar and large mirror behind it remained in place. A man served non-alcoholic drinks. David walked into the hall, pushed his hat up, and stepped around a splattered brass spittoon.

As he reached the bar, a client said, "Hey hat, where ya' goin' with that kid?" Making no reply, David asked for his usual: "the best and coldest Birch beer in town, dark, sweet and creamy." It was similar to a root beer only better in the boy's opinion.

Reaching up he placed his arm on top of the counter, one foot on the brass rail, and peeking over the top of the bar, he answered the bartender who asked for his order.

"A cold Birch beer."

"One comin' up. How ya' doin feller?"

"Just fine. This is the best drink in town. I want a sugar maple bar for my horse, too."

David paid the dime, took his purchases and started back to Ted.

The bartender bid him good-bye, "You come back again feller. Nice talkin' to ya."

David nodded as he left. "Not once did he call me kid or sonny. I guess I'm a man now."

Seven years of hawking papers, sometimes in Bellingham, other times in Seattle, David's transition to managing a route in Ellensburg provided an orderly structure for earning money. A young salesboy became a confident salesman. David no longer struggled against Goliath in the communities or with newspaper companies. The gigantic newspaper industry was transformed by the Audit Bureau of Circulation system. And millions of paperboys, through the decades of the twentieth century, were transformed by the responsibility of a paper route. An opportunity for youth to mature and to earn money was saved by leaders in the publishing business.

Distractions and disruptions sent paperboys off course and just as suddenly they slid back to the route to responsibly finish delivering. With a list of customers and addresses that served as a map, the carrier began his journey, a short smooth trip. The world awaited the paper but did not want to wait on the paperboy.

Carriers raced out of their clubhouse or the newspaper office, scattered fast into the community as if playing hide and seek. Except the customer was often "it" and had to seek the paper. Boys circled round on routes every day, rotating through a fun time. Nothin' to routines.

Until the routines ruptured.

# PART II
## STRIVE

Another daily ritual squeezed into a slot alongside a child's monotonous school schedule, chores, scouts, sports, and church: delivering newspapers. A paperboy in stride, one full canvas bag at a time, one season at a time was striving, in a slower, simpler time.

So when his additional mundane routine ruptured, the disruptive event was welcome---well, almost always welcome. From distractions to sudden disturbances to down-right dangerous interruptions, a paper route snapped instantly from dull into a disaster.

### Absurd

With two previous days of warm, dry weather, another mild autumn day directed folks to continue clearing the last rows in the garden, wash the storm windows, store the lawn chairs. By afternoon, ocean air flowing into Puget Sound blew in a chill. Tomorrow's forecast: cold rain.

A squirrel, his cheeks bulging, darted up the tall, reddish madrone tree as Robin kicked a pile of leaves. *I'll try for a raking job before rain spoils an opportunity.* A strong acrid smell told him others had burned leaves. He'd speed up, finish his route a bit sooner.

One after another his tight rolls sailed to the porch, right to the door as easily as throwing spit balls. Appreciating the modest homes set close together, 10-year-old Robin Paterson tossed his *Seattle Times* papers, easing weight off his shoulder. His customers set their watch, almost precisely, by the newspaper arrival regardless of changes in weather, his health, school activities.

Rules at school included be on time, no chewing gum, no spit balls, no shouting. These accumulated with similar rules of the route: be punctual, be polite, be accurate throwing the folded paper to avoid breaking milk bottles, screen doors, flowering plants.

Oops! Step back. Remember: use the walk. Another specific rule: stay off the lawn, unlike stray dogs that ran over the yard. Robin only wanted to cross the grass, not leave a smelly fly-attracting deposit. Ahh well, dogs weren't leashed with rules.

*Hey, flowers are still blooming.* As he turned the corner to cover the last four blocks of his route, he saw the trim colorful garden. Vivid red zinnias, yellow dahlias, lavender asters, burgundy chrysanthemums, the colors bright in the filtered sunshine. As soon as he completed his last drop he'd swing back and "pick a small handful for mom, make up for negatives." Of course he'd pick ones where no dogs had paused.

Robin never meant, at least not consciously, for his mom to be disturbed with negatives. Things happen, the way the *Seattle Times* occasionally landed on a porch roof. He didn't intend for it to rest there, and Mr. Balch did not intend to retrieve his paper. Robin caused the error. He must correct his aim, plus manage the high retrieval. Accomplished.

Misbehavior and misdeeds came naturally from time to time. Why this past summer, a day hotter than usual for the Northwest, he was sweating on steep hills, toting his heavy canvas bag. Walking, he prepared the papers. "Folded into a square, the tight small piece sailed like a Frisbee." Almost every house he passed, even when a structure was not at street level, the thrust in his shots contained enough power to zoom up the extra 15 feet and right through the door.

Through the door?

Yes.

Since it was hot, the windows and doors stood open in hopes of bringing in some breeze from Puget Sound. However, this breeze was blocked by the occupied doorway. A solid delivery swooshed at chest height. Awful sounds shot out of someone's lungs. There wasn't time to investigate since he had to stay on schedule. And hearing such a guttural noise from a person with innards hurting, the guy might not feel like talking. Robin sucked in his stomach and hastened to other houses.

With the sunny sky losing its brightness, he'd better skip recalling past mess-ups. The aroma of onions and meat frying for a supper meal reminded him of the dinner hour, so he hurried up the walk, his bag growing lighter, his throwing arm stronger. The route was fun. His fingers flattened the crease of a paper, folded over the sheets with the loose end inside, and formed his tight square. Pitching the paper underhand, 30 feet, 40 feet his aim was as swift and straight as a pro-ball player's.

He crossed the street and scurried along the top ridge of a steep hill. Swish, another paper missile arched in a smooth line toward the door. He turned his head to watch as it landed on the porch, not the roof. Wow! Perfect shot. Right on the door.

Right *on* the door? "Oh my gosh!" Robin's mouth opened. A large wad of chewing gum rolled off his tongue. The newspaper arrived with a hard hit, nearly to the planned destination, but not at the bottom of the door sill. It was right smack against the lower section of the door. Why? In a flash, he grasped the answer.

News pages stuck to the wood slightly above the expected location. Black ink began to bleed. The front page and some additional sheets would rip when pulled off.

His customer's instant reaction expressed nothing about the nice weather or pleasant afternoon, nor appreciation for the improving war news. No comment on the exact arrival of his paper. None. Mr. Stone choked on an exhaled shout, which collided with his inhaled gasp in an angry expletive, "Gawdallmighty!"

Amazing! Incredibly astounding! Robin delivered the paper every afternoon, same time. His customers could count on punctual service. Therefore, when Mr. Stone finished his chore, why not set a chair in front of the door? Place a sign: FRESH VARNISH. Or better, walk out to meet Robin for the paper. Instead, he encountered an adult's absurd absence of common sense.

## Routines Regulate the Routine

For residents, their paper just appeared with little thought or even a sighting of the carrier, especially on early morning routes. The news came, dropped at the door as part of people's daily ritual.

Like Robin, a carrier was stunned when splatters of paint flew in every direction, uncoordinated with the day's newspaper delivery. Papers absorb puppy pee, canary droppings, and the juicy pulp of melons. The thin sheets absorb paint, varnish, shellac, and the wash water used to scrub the porch floor. Splotches, streaks, smears on the pages, as well as messy footprints from trying to retrieve the wet, stuck paper, broadcast a message to adults: be sensible.

Folks expected their paper drop inside the storm door, or just to the right of the frame, maybe on the side porch. Customers' lives pulsed with set routines, which included receiving the newspaper at a specific time in a specific place, as rigid as the pendulum of a clock. Paced by the seasons, by daily schedules, folks stuck to a pattern.

The image of a quiet street with stately oak trees along parallel sidewalks in front of two-story homes graced with wide, pleasant porch-sets of welcoming wicker furniture was completed by a boy on a paper route: the tranquil scene for a Norman Rockwell or Edward Hopper painting. Some routes were picturesque, reflecting the staid life of the community.

Despite innumerable advances in the twentieth century, more than in previous centuries combined, the majority of Americans held to steady routines. For working citizens, the Roaring Twenties rippled over their lives. The console radio, the Model T Ford, the silent movies arrived in a slow march through towns across the U.S.A. Changes came, but the clock, the seasonal cycles, the calendar stabilized life.

In truth, existence was uncertain regardless of the regiment of a factory whistle, reliance on train whistles, tolling of church and school bells for assurance that all is certain. The honk of a Greyhound bus, rolling on schedule down Main Street, provided reassurance.

Peas are planted February 22, George Washington's birthday. Set tomato plants after May 15, because Jack Frost snitches them earlier. Corn best be knee high by the Fourth of July. Indian summer ripens pumpkins in time for Halloween. Before long children savor ice cream snow with fresh boiled maple syrup drizzled on the white scoops.

Celebrate Easter, Thanksgiving, Christmas; respect Memorial, Independence and Armistice Day with flags fluttering. The calendar dictated customary observance. Predictable schedules made life easier against the uncontrollable, like tornadoes, diseases, sudden death.

Every week was a pre-planned pattern: wash day Monday with wooden poles propping up sagging clotheslines, Tuesday Masonic Lodge meeting, Wednesday bridge club and church guild, Thursday choir rehearsal, Friday evening ball games at the school. Saturday meant shopping on Main Street before stores closed at 6:00 p.m. and remained closed until Monday. Everyone knew that. Sunday sit in the same church pew, wear the same Sunday suit and hat. Fall asleep. Nap over, home to a chicken dinner of mashed potatoes, gravy, biscuits and well cooked peas. Relax and finish reading the paper that plopped on the porch before 6:00 a.m.

Grinding through the work week, folks relished their chance to sit in an overstuffed chair or relax on the porch swing with a cup of coffee, the steam mingling with smoke drifting from a Camel cigarette, content with a newspaper companion. A reader was loyal to his paper, like a Brooklyn Dodgers' fan loyal to his baseball team.

And in the heart of the neighborhood, a plodding paperboy darted through his route, whether or not it rained Monday, wind whipped on Tuesday, he sneezed on Wednesday, ...a cold by Friday. Nothing interfered with the routine of newspapers delivered from a variety of lads. Adorable children who charmed old ladies, down to the arrogant sneaks that infuriated adults, the angels and the assholes with all the average ones in between, kept the community conveniently informed with doorstep service 52 weeks a year.

The wide web of routes in the cities and towns provided quick news over the community, more accurate than telephone party lines or backyard clothesline conversations. Paper routes extended into apartment complexes, hotels, hospitals, nursing homes, funeral homes, residential homes, trailer homes, houseboats, court houses, an outhouse, houses of ill repute, bakeries, barber shops, police stations, military posts, pool halls, saloons, and provocative places like Seacat's or Maud's haunt, all on a set routine.

## His Fault

Jerry hurried to escape from the windy, snowy conditions lashing northern Ohio. A small youngster for his ten years, Jerry Peter endeavored to complete his *Chronicle Telegram* route with no more mishaps. He'd already learned a lesson on balance. The bicycle kick stand must rest on a solid surface, particularly when the dual rear-wheel baskets were unevenly filled with heavy papers. Pulled off center, bike spills occurred on saturated ground. His customers didn't want soiled papers. "Hell hath no fury like the customer whose paper ends up in the mud, wet." Starting as a substitute, Jerry now delivered the usual after-school, modestly-sized route to familiar people in his family's Elyria, Ohio, neighborhood. A simple task? For a grade school boy in his first job: challenging.

Customers knew him, where he lived, and knew their paper was always to be on time and in pristine condition. Jerry finished school about 3:30 p.m., and proceeded to a corner where stacks of papers wired in a bundle lay ready for customers. He left his standard school for a *Main Street School* of common sense. His route covered "a blue-collar neighborhood with factory workers who arrived home at 4:00 p.m. They wanted to read immediately. They didn't have multiple offerings of the evening news." The *Chronicle Telegram* provided a national connection, and more importantly, informed their world of local happenings with the society page, the school sports' records, hospital admits, police reports.

Jerry's schedule lengthened as he hopped off the bike to place the paper behind the screen door. At the next house in the milk chute. He balanced his time. "I had to get off my bike. It was a pain and it slowed down the delivery. But meeting the people's expectations brought the best tips." Then the bike tipped. Forget the bike. Now the snow was too deep. Tough walking "and slippery, the weight of the canvas bag changed my center of gravity. It was a chore." He tried to hurry and stay balanced because a reader fumed by 4:15, "Where's that paperboy?"

Jerry understood, "If the paper was late, regardless of the reason, lateness was the paperboy's fault." No excuses. Furthermore, the customer defined late whether the carrier delivered before school or after school or both. The paperboy must strive to serve his customers according to their requests.

Customers anywhere, whether in Ohio or across the country, held the same attitude: be dependable and on time. Mike Rhodes in San Jose, California, learned that even on "those occasional times when mechanical breakdowns of the press caused late delivery, the blame from the customer was directed towards the carrier." Adults didn't bother to understand what caused a delay. That was when Mike "first received a lesson in tact and diplomacy."

Mere boys made mistakes, yet the boys only expected to make money. By striving, their paper routes provided money, and more, in misadventures with minor and major accidents, mean animals, wild weather, and wilder adults.

In a close community with set schedules, what could possibly disturb conditions and the customers? How did a consistent delivery cascade into inconceivable delays with results that rupture a routine? Was this the stuff that created the comic strips?

# CHAPTER 5
## THE ROUTINE IS ROUTINE

until...

Quickly inaugurated into routines, legions of children held to the ritual of an afternoon paper route, which further tightened their schedule. Boys didn't hang around after school to wipe the chalk boards and pound dusty erasers. Well, maybe Theodore Randall Trauton III stayed to please Miss Harden and giggle with the girls, but for the others, energy exploded, doors blew open as if the dismissal bell detonated a stick of dynamite. Running, racing, and leading the rush were paperboys. They headed for their route, which entailed less time than the seven hours in class, but was every bit as strict as the school schedule. Actually more so, because the newspaper route ran 12 months, weekends included.

Across America tens of thousands of children followed an afternoon pattern of delivering newspapers, since that edition was the most common time slot. They moved through a portion of childhood delivering papers, ready to enjoy any difference in the day's rotation when the mindless repetitive order might be obliterated---temporarily at best. An unpredictable and stimulating accident, an exciting adventure broke the routine. Break the rhythm and momentum was mangled. Even a little disturbance, falling off the bike or tumbling down steps, toppled a paperboy like a bowling pin. Of course, stumbles seldom happened on a sunny day but struck when it was wet and windy. Disruptions or disasters forced a paperboy to reset his time clock.

## Choked

Leonard Lair carried over 100 copies of the *Seattle Times* in 1952. He knew how to handle the weight, just as he handled 28 kids at the newspaper "clubhouse." Mature, capable at fourteen, and a half, he

71

became a station manager teaching new boys, "Never throw overhand. Always throw underhand. Otherwise the sheets catch the wind."

And throw was what Leonard proved he could do, though his early attempts broke lots of milk bottles. This was useful at a carnival, with three throws that knocked down bottles and produced a prize. He never won a prize for his breaks that splashed milk across the porch and down the steps causing a busted-glass mess. He faced his mistakes and improved. As station manager he enjoyed the other carriers. The oldest of seven children, his experience with younger siblings and his affable disposition helped produce a terrific team at the paper station. The only thing that riled him was calling the drop-off center a "shack."

Continuing to improve his throw, he became an incredible ball player, advancing to organizer for the "best men's fastpitch softball played anywhere." His accomplishments and success in a world tournament occurred later. For now, he needed to pitch his papers fast, which he did. But accidents happen swiftly, for sure on steep, damp hills in Seattle.

Leonard tripped and tumbled down a flight of concrete steps, down the hill. Head banging, shoulders smacking, weight shifting, canvas bag tugging its broad strap against his throat. In a second he was spread at the foot of the steep incline, feet pressed up, bruised head pushed down into dirt. He came to rest on his back on top of the thin sheets now soaking up the wet Seattle soil. A turtle flipped on its shell. Worse, with the canvas bag beneath him and the wide canvas strap strangling his throat, he couldn't breathe. Stunned, gasping in a comical posture, he wasn't as funny as the daily comics.

Another point to teach his team of carriers: take one step at a time on a solid surface. Accidents strike in a micro-instant, immediately destroying balance. Control careens away when caught on a clothesline, a low tree limb, or drenched by the lawn sprinkler. Worse, stepping into a window well. The jerked knee instantly jerked the mind.

## One Giant Step

Cliff raced through his routes. He delivered four different routes between 1951 and 1955 for the *Everett Daily Herald*. At first he handled only 100 papers, then he went to 120, and his current route was above 130 papers. When he expanded to more customers, he bought a double-sided canvas bag balancing the weight over his torso. He learned by experience not to load all the papers into the back hold because it pulled against the throat, even pulled a guy over.

However, weight was not a problem on Saturday because the edition was light. Plus, the afternoon became quieter as shoppers in downtown Everett finished buying before the stores closed for the remainder of the weekend. Cliff hurried to deliver to the residences and a few stores. Last, he reached the Snohomish County Court House.

Of course, the court house was closed on Saturday afternoon, but he still delivered to various offices. Sometimes people worked in solitude and would break for a little news, plus the subscription included their weekend paper.

An out-of-the-way door was left unlocked. Cliff stepped inside as usual, walked past a window and turned into an unlit hall. He knew the way even in the dim, progressively darker interior. With limited light, his ears responded to his familiar sound, the echo of shoes clicking on the tile floor like a cane. He punched the elevator button as though using Braille. Without citizens coming and going, the clinking cables of the elevator indicated a quick approach. He was daydreaming of Saturday evening fun.

The elevator door clanked open. He stepped in. And down, way down. His heart thumped, his head bumped, legs flailed as the papers finished plopping all around the caged space. The elevator was out of sync. Cliff's long stride was not sufficient for reaching the elevator floor. Stuck on a quiet Saturday afternoon in the closed court house, alone in a dark space between floors, his daydreaming disappeared. Another point to teach young carriers: look first or you'll leap farther than legs reach. Maybe down into a dark elevator.

## Disappeared

At least Leonard, Cliff and others who tumbled in space struck the ground, which was better than sinking into salt water. The ocean water flowing into the Puget Sound ran deep and cold. The waterway depth ranges from 180 feet to 840 feet and the fjord-like estuaries are nothing like the warm water around Hawaii. Dark evergreens rise straight out of the steep hills, backed by a white 14,410 foot Mt. Rainier displaying sparkling snowy glaciers. This magnificent scenery was washed frequently by rain. The rain also coated a paperboy.

Dale Wirsing was a small third grader when he started a route in the working seaport of Tacoma. "A little shrimp" he was scared of the bullies and dogs roaming the neighborhoods, but adults here and there always looked out for him. "Kids' behavior was everybody's business," so he behaved knowing he was watched in his limited world, as were the bad seeds around him.

When Dale picked up his *Tacoma Times* papers, he tried his best to keep the sheets dry from the "terrible rain." His customers wanted to read all the news, unsmudged, about the horrific, costly war victories. With newspapers protected in his canvas bag, pedaling fast through his route, he coasted to the elevated wooden planks lining the commercial water front. Leaving the gravelly street the bike rolled over the boards covered with mist layered on winter algae. Hurrying, he didn't concern himself with the usual wet ground, wet streets, wet boards. He sped onto the pier gliding faster on the smooth surface. Then his front tire slid.

Eight-year-old Dale shot off the sturdy thick planks of the long pier, flew through the moist air with arms flung out, hands grabbing salt spray, legs flailing for a hold, and lungs expelling yells. His four-foot-frame dropped straight down eight feet to the surface of Puget Sound, and then disappeared into salty scummy water. His mouth snapped shut. Dale's jacket, trousers, underclothes, socks, and shoes absorbed seawater. Even faster, the murky water saturated flying news sheets. His papers sank in the watery environment, and like the dumped loads of shopping guides that entered the forest floor, these too became instant rubbish. Soaked, a boy, a bike and a bag sank.

Fortunately, the boy and bike escaped once they were fished out by boat builders, those watchful adult eyes responding to his urgent screams and sudden splash. They pulled him up. He left the starfish, octopus, and clams down in the watery world. Crabs could look at the comics.

Streams of water ran off his hair, his nose, off green strands of seaweed hanging like dangling earrings. Icy water ran down his fingers. The runoff carried away some of the scum and the salty gulps coming up from his stomach. His shoulder felt jammed but the cold wet clothes eased the pain. Hurrying in his sloshing shoes, he rushed back to the company for dry papers. Customers do not expect to fish for news in soaked printed sheets. Dale's dump in the Sound was a disaster to his timely routine. But with the rapid response of adults, he still delivered and lived to deliver seven days a week, 52 weeks a year, for a decade.

Adults helped paperboys. Adults also hindered.

## Discouraged

Like controlling tires on a slick wet surface, controlling a bike on ice and snow is hazardous. Starting at age 10 with the *University District Herald,* Ron Ballough improved with each new experience until by age 12 he managed a bag of 125 *Seattle Times* papers. Now, wrangling a thick bag in heavy snow, Ron found the going quite rough. Yet, delivering in the heart of Seattle to apartments around the University of Washington, he darted along dry hallways while his bike lay in snow, the drifts growing deeper. And then, darn it, the afternoon deteriorated. When he returned, his bike was a mangled flattened wreck. He was discouraged. "A drunken driver ran over my bicycle." Handlebars, seat, the pedals scrunched onto one flat plane. The hindrance of an adult became downright annoying.

Kids sometimes rode bikes in an uncontrolled manner causing drivers to swerve. Though trouble, the paperboy never caused the awful problems created by a driver under the influence of alcohol. Boys didn't pedal drunk.

# Disgusting

Beginning at age nine, Sam Smyth sold weekly magazines: *Ladies Home Journal, Country Gentlemen, Women's Home Companion* and other publications for five cents a copy. Along with his sales experience, Sam also subbed for his older brother. Before long he had inherited his brother's paper route.

Under the summer afternoon heat, Sam joined friends to swim in the deep, cold waters of Lake Washington. But then, "Leaving the other boys happily playing on the log booms I would trudge a mile to home." Grabbing his canvas bag, he scurried to the designated drop-spot envious of friends still splashing in the cool lake.

In 1932 his *Seattle Star* bundles were dropped from a street car south of Seattle in the town of Renton. The tracks passed a three-way intersection formed with the joining of Third, Main and Houser Way. A regular stop, the papers were tossed off and the street car rolled on. Besides a newspaper pick-up, the triangle was the location of a "comfort station," a very questionable claim. It was not a comfort to the eyes or nose. A fellow must have a very dire necessity to enter the horrific stench and stomach-wrenching, filthy enclosure.

Sam grabbed his bundles from the pavement and moved to fresh clean air. Recognized as a paperboy, he headed purposefully down the street, his stride a bit longer now that he was 12 and handling a paper route instead of magazines. His shyness was diminishing. He enjoyed a sense of belonging in his community.

On a pleasant, warm day, one where folks stopped to debate any indications of when the Depression would end, Sam didn't pay attention to the conversation of two men on the corner. He had his own thoughts and concerns, like wondering if the "dreaded south Renton boys" slouched nearby. Those meanies easily battered a small kid. For now, he stepped toward the two adults, moving in his own safe world and staying alert to possible attacks.

Abruptly one of the men turned. His "spat of a generous stream of tobacco juice" slid down Sam's nose, dripping off his chin, staining and stinking his shirt. Blended with ropes of saliva, an arc of brown tobacco juice made its mark. He saw the juice attach. He smelled the sour splat. Though eyes wide open, nose engaged, there was a silver lining: his mouth stayed shut. He gagged smelling the foul dribbles; he didn't taste them. "It took quite some time to clean up my face and body." The rhythm of his job was disrupted.

Still, Sam appreciated his opportunity for learning about folks. The perpetrator was considerate as he apologized, "Sorry sonny. Didn't see you there." Pushing his wad to the other cheek, he resumed talking. Sam, handled the issue like a man, removed what slobber he could, glad he received only a soft splatter rather than a solid strike by a street bully.

"Being only a boy, I had no recourse. It was up to me to dodge." He guessed the chewing man didn't advance as far in school as to learn the No Spitting rule. Sudden accidents and annoying adults who drank and spit were upsetting. Then animals also joined in the fray.

## The End

Progressing in his business acumen, Max was past delivering the shopping news. Next, he tossed the *Everett Daily Herald*, and now he managed a *Seattle Star* route in his Edmonds neighborhood, a delightful small mill town situated on Puget Sound. He knew his customers and other newspaper carriers, and knew how to race down a steep hill on a bike while throwing the paper. His practice resulted in a few "minor accidents when hit by cars."

The major problem---as if being hit by cars wasn't significant---came from being chased and bit. Max Fisk moved quickly. He was athletic and alert, yet the repeated "pinch on the leg hurt." It was not easy to stop cars, but he intended to stop being bit on his legs or his backside and being laughed at by school mates.

His nice subscribers were unconcerned when their two honking, flapping geese hissed, chased and caught Max. A tough beak clamped into the flesh "hurt worse than a dog bite." Day after day the geese were irritating, actually infuriating Max and causing sores in unmentionable spots. Enough of their confounded interruption.

"I dispatched a goose with a willow stick to the neck." That's one goose that didn't end up on the holiday dinner platter.

## Stewed Rooster

Gerald Horna started with just 32 customers, gained his stride and before long his route grew to 400, covering 10 miles and continuing for six years. He delivered the weekly *Chester Times,* the regular *Philadelphia Bulletin,* the Sunday *Philadelphia Inquirer,* and a half dozen *New York Times.* The families lived in several stretches of housing developments, and new home owners became customers under the eyes of an alert paper carrier.

Though alert, attacks could strike him at anytime from anywhere because of a disturbed critter. Settled into a routine, knowing his area, it was easy for Gerald to mindlessly roll down the street. Be aware. Farm territory transformed into residential lots was not limited to lawns, white picket fences, and well-pruned roses. One large rooster defended his space. A paperboy crossed the rooster's limit.

When Gerald pedaled past each evening, the hissing furious bird came right at him. No bicycle hot-dogging around this guy. It meant to be mean. Move fast regardless of a load of papers. The attacker had Gerald in his sights and a couple of bike wheels rolling on the pavement were insufficient to block the big wings and menacing beak. The tough, old bird should have been a stewed rooster. Gerald would have provided the cooking pot.

# Be Accommodating

Mr. Gamel decided his 10-year-old son, Bill, should work, since he wanted to buy sports equipment for hunting and fishing, to enjoy a bike, a sled. Earning was the route to buying. Not a problem. He didn't face a line of competitors for a paperboy position with the *Anchorage Daily Times* in 1949. The company needed sturdy carriers, so during four years Bill crossed streets in Anchorage. Arriving for his afternoon bundles at 4:00 p.m., he reached all 95 customers by 6:00 p.m. under bright skies. The summer sunshine in the Alaska territory was long and pleasant.

However, as his four-mile route increased to 115 subscribers, as dusk appeared earlier, his dinner came later. The family supper hour held without shifting to accommodate his schedule. Still, he progressed with school, his scout troop, and now the paper route.

He was making money. A large route, supplemented with successfully selling on Saturday in the mile of downtown bars on Anchorage's Fourth Avenue, the coins clinked in his pocket. Unlike the saloon Barry Dunphy encountered on the wharf in Ketchikan, the Anchorage bars along Bill's mile of amber liquid had far more customers than rats.

A mile? Well, not exactly 5,280 feet, but a paperboy mile when hoofing in and out of the dark environs. Just as fish grow in fishermen's tales, the paper routes grow in the telling of each boy's travails. So, maybe it was 4,820 feet, or thereabouts. His sales and tips continued for about six months, until his father learned of his extended position. Dad ceased his son's hawking job because as Saturday afternoon wore on, the bar patrons became boisterous and belligerent. Bill's father didn't feel this was a safe spot for a child. Better his son manage newspapers in the open residential areas, away from trouble.

Bill progressed through the seasons from the midnight sun, to autumn sunsets, to early dusk and then dark winter. He enjoyed himself and was happily buying outdoor equipment, which helped him as he advanced to Explorer Scout. Besides, customers were considerate. When he delivered at minus 30 degrees, -30° F., people invited him in to warm his mukluks by the oil stove. Mukluks, made from chewed leather, which softens and molds the hide, smell when heated, but that was okay. Thawed feet overcame odor any day. However, he couldn't sit and chat. People down the line wanted their paper.

As winter descended over Alaska, Bill's route became quieter. Each exhaled breath was his only company. Children played inside. No one gardened in frozen ground. Keep walking quickly. Movement and carrying a load of papers generated body heat. The frozen snow crunched out soft squeaks as he plodded forward, his warm ear covers protecting him from the bitter cold and allowing only muffled sounds. He crossed the solid ground, head down to avoid painful wind whipping into his face. On a shorter path than in summer, when the area was too marshy to cross, the still silence, the frigid air almost encased him in a stupor. No, mustn't slack.

Bill stepped in the center of a bush and willow tree-lined path before he heard the branches break. STOP!

He instantly knew not to confront a thousand pounds that could out-run him in seconds. Ten times heavier, taller, and faster, this was an uneven match for a school boy using a soft canvas bag against solid four to six foot wide antlers. One accommodates a large moose, granting it the right-of-way. Halted, he wondered how long the huge blocker would stall his service to the remaining customers a mile down the way. Watching small, brown, placid eyes staring at him, Bill was uncertain if he'd continue standing still in the twilight in sub-zero snow. The moose replied with a snort. Alone, in the open residential area, was it safer than a saloon?

## Guilty Until Proven Innocent

Self-inflicted accidents, large, unpredictable approaching animals, or worse, attacking ones, left boys quaking. And then big, unpredictable people powered over the cheerful, helpful underweight messenger. Learning their ABC's in school, carriers soon learned the ABC's of the adult world when involved with a route. Carrying papers taught children essential lessons in handling people-encounters with customers' attitudes and actions.

## A is for Accused

With an uneven gait, Cliff Benson hurried across Hoyt Street in downtown Everett. Delivering 130 newspapers, stuffed in a new double-sided bag, he swayed off stride when he grabbed an *Everett Daily Herald* paper and threw it to the porch. Though heavy, he was glad he bought a double bag and figured the cost would be paid in a month. He cut through a vacant lot and ran to Rucker Street progressing into a residential section of maintained homes, shade trees, and trimmed yards.

Cliff increased his pace knowing the faster he delivered the sooner the weight would ease off his back and shoulders. Also, on the open street, there was no chance of falling into an elevator shaft, again. At the corner of Rucker and 23rd, he shortened his path by stepping over a flowerbed.

A voice shouted. "I saw you stomp in the peony bed. Stop destroying our lawns! Look at the path you've made." Mrs. Frecklend stood on her porch with a broom poised by her side like a marine sergeant, only much sterner.

Cliff stared from her long finger to a worn line running parallel with the length of the wide porch. He stepped closer to glance down the side yard. She raised her voice with a continuing flow of complaints.

"Sorry ma'am." He returned to the sidewalk, peered at the other side of the yard as he continued his route.

Mrs. Frecklend yelled after him. "I'm reporting this." Her shouts were punctuated by sharp barks from the terrier shut behind the screen door.

The next afternoon Cliff read the pink complaint slip placed in his cubby hole at the newspaper office, with explicit instructions: *No riding on lawns, flowerbeds, no...*

He spoke to the manager. "I don't use a bike."

"Well, stay on the sidewalk. That's why they put 'em in."

"Sir, the path goes around her house."

"Don't use the path. This ain't complicated." The manager clipped his words.

Cliff pressed, "I walk past the front, not around four sides of the foundation. That mutt of Mrs. Frick 'n Fat runs her house and all around it."

"Oh, makes sense. She complains regularly. And it's Flecklin."

"Right, Mrs. Frecklend. I won't forget."

Dogs often disrupted the rhythm of delivery. They knocked over trash cans in the alley, fought as viciously as bullies, barked at every cat, squirrel, and pedestrian that approached their turf. Man's best friend was the worst trouble for children who delivered the very item used to help train the puppy's natural way. The mutt outgrew peeing on the porch mat, but grew in his hatred of the paper and anyone connected to a newspaper, other than the owner who fed him.

## B is for Blame

Once George Janecke acquired a route, he pursued perfect service even when that other mean paperboy burned his hands. He learned excellent methods because his older brother, David, was a top carrier. Their dad, a longshoreman at the Seattle docks, was a model of hard work. However, the continuing Depression cut his work, some months into a lot fewer hours.

The boys valued their route money. With steady consistent weeks of delivery, they gave regular earnings to the family. Just a dollar profit in a week bought bread, lard, and beans. Depended on by parents and steady customers, a strong sense of responsibility grew in David and George. After his severely burned hands healed, George became so good at rolling papers, really tight, that the tubes were "hard as rocks and I could throw one a mile."

A mile? All 5,280 feet?

Well, again, a paperboy mile. He had the arm, the aim and the attitude that made him an outstanding paperboy. The kind of kid that neighbors wanted next door.

With daily pumping on his used bike, he gained strength in his legs until he kept up with older guys on the streets of Seattle's Georgetown area, a working-class section, if work was available. Alert, George dodged rough potholes as well as barking beasts, because he knew when to expect a growling flash of fur that burst through broken fence slats, or off porches. One German shepherd was growing more persistent as it lost its puppy playfulness. George wasn't concerned. The dog started a loud continuous bark the moment it heard the swish of bike wheels, giving him an advantage in his paperboy "mile" of 60 or so feet. He revved into maximum speed.

The dog was fast. The paperboy faster. The ferocious animal grew close. George leaned closer to the handlebars. Neck and neck the two raced. Horrific barking blasted George's ears.

HHHHhhoooaawuulll!

George echoed the wild cry, "AAaahhwoohh." when suddenly his front tire struck the curb, bending the wheel in half and bringing the bike down on a crumbled child. The left pedal stopped turning as it shoved against his mouth. Barely conscious, he heard the faint whine from the disappearing dog. Too dazed to rise up, and with fiery, painful stabs starting to advance in every direction on every appendage, he took a deep breath, which ratcheted the pain to excruciating. His misery informed him he was alive, if barely.

A blurry form appeared above him. His ears told him he certainly was conscious.

"You injured my dog. You deliberately hurt him. He's in pain. His tail's broken..." The incessant shouting, directed right down on George, made him dizzier. The dry metallic taste in his throat stirred his stomach. If he vomited blood, it would shoot onto the woman. *It would serve her right,* he thought. Her angry attack, shouting that he was a "dirty little kid" was worse than her dog's bark. George didn't snap at her. Children were not allowed to talk back to adults.

When she stomped up her porch steps, he crawled to his knees. Blood seeped from several places as he moved about gathering newspapers from bushes, the rough ground, the gutter, the street. A car swerved around him. He leaned against a post waiting for the dizziness to subside and the nausea to recede.

He counted his papers. "Ahh good. All here and useable. Not perfect." Propping his broken bike against a fence, he limped down the walk. He knew he'd be late for his last deliveries. He tried to rush.

## C is for Caught, for Chastised, for Criticized, for...

Dale Irvine was progressing. As a small tyke, his efforts to perform satisfactorily challenged him. With over 100 *Seattle Times* customers, more on Sunday, his Dad built a cart that Dale pushed up steep hills. Fortunate to have apartment customers, he could work fast.

The *Seattle Times* offered another of their many incentive trips to reward carriers. The prize captured his interest: a ski trip. Struggling against facing "scary" adults, but wanting to ski, he figured out a system. In his route area, a large apartment complex, large for housing centers in 1948, was the answer. He quietly scurried to the sixth floor of the building.

Dale determined he'd solicit at every door. Difficult for a shy boy, he clenched his hands, breathed faster and raised his fist. He pounded on the door. Begun. Half way to a win.

The door opened. A tall man stared down at the little fellow staring up at him. Dale stammered out his request just the way his sales manager instructed the boys. Only his supervisor left out one critical detail. Dale was facing the "apartment manager who was furious that some kid was in his apartment building, soliciting for the *Seattle Times*."

Why did the first apartment he approached turn out to be the manager's? And why did the guy have to be a devoted subscriber to the *Seattle PI*, and who vehemently disliked the competitive *Seattle Times*? Caught in the act, Dale was out of the guy's reach, fast, like a fireman sliding down a fire pole.

### "Almost my last"

In California, Mike Rhodes took over a *San Jose Mercury News* route in 1955, a boom time for the Golden State. The afternoon routine in his modest neighborhood pleased the grade-schooler. Yes, he was supposed to be 12 but 11 was close enough, particularly for a reliable, courteous youngster.

At his pick-up spot, a fellow carrier taught him to box his papers. Sliding his fingers over the news sheets, he creased all 100 papers in a hard press, and with loose ends tucked in, made a tight square ready to be thrown along route 1233. Fun with other carriers, riding along familiar streets, his first six delivery days progressed uneventfully. In control, his bike functioned fine and his throws reached the porches. He was home before supper. Delivering in an expeditious manner, his additional new routine after school was going well. And then Sunday arrived.

"The route became an intimidating experience in light of the large Sunday edition that challenged and tested my physical endurance. My first Sunday almost ended up being my last."

In the early morning hour, Mike tried to secure his double canvas bag on the rack over the rear tire of his English racing bike. "The weight of the papers caved in the sides of the rack."

Plus, with increased weight on the back, the front wheel raised off the ground. "It was like trying to ride a wild horse." And Mike was neither a rodeo star nor a rodeo clown. House by house he continued and weight slowly decreased. Then the rear tire blew.

"The last straw came in the form of drenching rain." Mike was finished. Enough! He hid the remaining 40 thick papers in a field. Wet grass, about four feet high "would nicely conceal the papers." Task finished and exhausted, he walked his unrideable bike home. Pulling on dry clothes, sitting down to breakfast and hearing Dad's assurance that he'd help with the bicycle, everything was okay now.

Only it wasn't. Forty customers, inside, quite comfortable on a rainy Sunday, expected the comics, the Saturday sports results, the editorial,... "Confound it! Where's that paperboy?"

The district manager, under a hail of complaints and the downpour of rain, carried the delayed, though dry, Sunday papers to the irate people. Then knowing where "that paperboy" lived, gave Mike, "a very stern warning that basically translated into one more foul-up and my paper route was history."

The message penetrated. Neither rain nor sleet, nor a flat tire, nor an angry manager deterred this carrier. No more lectures. A chastised Mike delivered. The weeks passed. He noticed tall grass in an area of the field "was withering and turning brown" exposing a pile of yellowed, blurred newsprint conveniently dumped months earlier. Darn. Thin sheets stuck in a dense stack were not disintegrating. "Under the cloak of darkness one night I returned to the field, procured the papers, and transported them to a nearby Dumpster." Considerate and conscientious, he went about his routine without confessing his foul-up. Confession may be good for the soul, but not for saving a first steady job despite an unsteady bike.

Little Merchants

# More is Better

For some customers, a paperboy was never reliable or responsible. One adult lived for the purpose of complaining and his constant cascade of complaints finally passed the annoying stage. It reached fiery irritation. Glen Carter devised a response. One of the man's frequent complaints centered on a tight rubber band around his *Seattle Times* paper. Was one band worth complaining, criticizing, and castigating a carrier? Not really. The captious guy's attitude was like a burr in Glen's underwear. Better to give the curmudgeon a more substantial reason to react.

Though he paid for each box of rubber bands, Glen felt his effort was worth the small cost. His hands slid down the rolled newspaper, installing each band until the entire paper was encased in 50 slender, stretchy rubber pieces. Nothing in his paper carrier contract stated only one rubber band per paper.

Struggling against animals, avoiding accidents, answering to adults, the paperboys stayed on track, most of the time. At least the newspaper industry hailed the entry-level job as near perfect with many ideal benefits.

# Goofy

In mid-century in the center of Ohio, a skinny sixth grader headed to the Mount Vernon newspaper office. Lingering with friends after school to play ball, Gary, an agile, typical eleven-year-old, left the play field, regardless of a tied score, to pick up papers.

Managing a full canvas bag, he would stride across the town square, past the tall Civil War statue, and continue another block to the steps of the colonial-style, red brick post office. No matter the weather, his health wilted with a stomach or tooth ache, a school-closed holiday, Gary Kost remained reliable. And always sitting on the bottom step at the busy post office, as dozens of shoes clicked past, waited a devoted beagle, Goofy.

The pair set off together encountering and speaking to neighborly folks. Well, Goofy only sniffed. Like figures on a decorative Glockenspiel clock, the two made the rounds criss-crossing familiar streets with the dog mastering the pattern as perfectly as Gary, who "seldom learned the house numbers of customers, but knew them all by name," the same way subscribers knew him. Riveted to the routine, he knew the people, their choice of churches, and the names of their children and pets.

Mount Vernon served as the county seat, average among the 88 county seats in Ohio. A modest town, it was picturesque in spring when a profusion of dogwood trees flowered in the woods. Bright red cardinals sang to their mates. On the knolls, acres of apple orchards displayed soft petals. Apple trees had been blooming in the Ohio Valley since John Chapman cultivated them in the widening frontier. Mr. Chapman, called

Johnny Appleseed in legends, even held the deed on a couple of lots by the Kokosing River that graced Mount Vernon.

In the closing Indian summer days, hardwood trees splashed colored leaves over the sidewalks. On farm fences bittersweet vines added bright orange-red berries amidst a resting spot for red-wing blackbirds. Crisp red apples generated tangy cider and the Knox County Fair awarded blue ribbons to outstanding 4-H boys wearing vivid blue FFA jackets. Globes of golden pumpkins lit brown cornfields. Colors brightened people's lives.

Through the seasons, Goofy and Gary held to their schedule, timed by factory whistles and an intermittent train whistle. In the next decade, when he was teaching in Mount Vernon High School, the town received in April, 1966, an All-American City award, except it was not a congested city. This was an active, attractive locale, a composite of small-town America. The national recognition reflected what optimistic and opportunistic citizens had created. And like Gary, they continued a steady, productive existence founded on a respect for history, an energetic focus on the present, and a dedicated effort to invigorate the future.

As Gary said, "That's the way it was," the way people lived, worked, and believed. The town was a model of thriving America with high farm yields, functioning factories, and a unity of family and faith. Church bells tolled on Sunday drawing members of every denomination to fill the pews. Nothing auspicious or suspicious about the vibrant residents. Their conservative Yankee mettle was moderated by Southern genteel courtesy.

The statue in the central square, facing south, was a replica of a Union soldier honoring valiant service to the nation's cause. However, northern Mount Vernon, named for Washington's Virginia plantation, claimed a contribution to the sentiment of the South. The town's son, Daniel Decatur Emmett, wrote *Dixie Land*. Throughout the South, spirited voices soon sang *Dixie*.

So, balanced with Southern attributes and Yankee sturdiness a cross-section of America persevered. Finished materials rolled forth from the massive factories to the moderate foundries. Production radiated from the Cooper-Bessemer factory, Timken Roller Bearing, the Mount Vernon Bridge Company, Pittsburgh Plate Glass, Continental Can Company, and the Lamb Glass Company that produced milk bottles faster than broken bottles needed replaced. The services and stores provided necessities for the town's 12,000 citizens. They bought at the Farmers Exchange and the Round Hill Dairy, a place selling eggs, milk, cream, butter, and ice cream. Coming to town on Saturdays, Main Street shoppers frequented a Rexall Drug Store, Woolworths, a Singer Sewing Store, J.C. Penney and the usual family-owned businesses for jewelry, groceries, insurance, shoes, and more.

Relaxing, people listened to the radio and cheered for the Cleveland Indians or the Cincinnati Reds. Neither team often competed in the World Series. However, that Cleveland Indians 1948 pennant victory over the Boston Braves caused discussion for six, eight years, until another possible win from Ohio. When summer baseball concluded, fans grew excited for The Ohio State University football team, rooting for a Rose Bowl game. Competitive enthusiasm rang out, regardless of any wins.

For an important game, folks headed to the Mount Vernon football stadium on Friday night. The high school band, the acclaimed *Marching 100*, with Gary stepping high with trumpet players, led the excitement down the center of Mulberry Street to west High Street, across the railroad tracks with a police cruiser's flashing lights leading the parade. This wasn't River City, Iowa, with 76 trombones, but the school's music stirred the fans' spirit with snappy marches.

And all the football calls were covered in the Saturday edition of local news. Gary's junior and senior year in high school, the football team went unbeaten and untied, holding the title: Central Buckeye League Champions. Those headlines caused discussion for decades.

Listening to neighbors, looking out for one another, laughing together, the friendly residents formed a community of proud citizens. Patriotic people flew the flag from the porch or it fluttered from a pole. They practiced the faith of their parents and stayed interconnected to all the happenings in the community through their newspaper, the *Mount Vernon News*.

Gary earned $7 to $10 a week, above $30 a month, more than $350 a year by collecting 25 cents each week from customers. After placing money in his savings account, he stopped by The Donut Hole, ate Coney Island hot dogs at Beck's Drive-In, and bought tickets to Saturday movies. Through four years he held his route. And the best part, he became acquainted with a cute member in the Banning family, a customer of his. Pleased with the slightest change in his routine, he was delighted when his school friend, Beth Banning, watched for him to bring the paper to the door. Happy in a budding romance, he considered his moderate after-school route, with no Sunday edition and nothing scary in his familiar hometown, the ideal beginning job.

In the core of the American Century, in an All-American town, he models a nostalgic, reminiscent view of youth managing a paper route. Is Gary's ideal the way paper routes always ran? No. Is it wrong? No. Just incomplete, like showing a still life picture rather than addressing the subject's difficult reality. The perfect setting and people's proper behavior misconstrue the realism affecting many paperboys. Their experiences, from poignant to repugnant, challenge the myths and misconceptions that exist. What was it actually like, alone on the route?

# Down With The Sun

Immature kids made mistakes, tripped on their missteps. Older ones caused mischief. And a few miscreants, impossible to control, kept managers busy. But most paperboys didn't try to be trouble, or didn't try very hard. Trouble just appeared, like sudden rain showers. Scolded, chastised, and blamed, a boy felt discouraged. Then he noticed the daylight growing shorter, shadows longer and evening air colder. His enthusiasm waned in the sunset.

Robin Paterson only saw wilted autumn flowers; no fresh ones to pick for his mother. He shivered as he walked in the twilight under a few skimpy leaves clinging to limbs. He felt low, hearing less birds chirping, seeing less children skipping rope or roller skating. An occasional porch light shone on the door. Soon he'd finish his route on dark streets. Still, the growing dusk after school wasn't as black as his 5:00 Sunday delivery, so early.

Add to it, that paper was the heaviest edition and included the most subscribers. During long winter months, it required delivery before dawn or before the folks appeared. No one else, not the postman, milkman, garbage man, grocer, none of them crossed a paperboy's path on his Sunday hour. His *day of rest* began with neither rest nor the light of day.

Geez, afternoon carriers had it easy. Why a lot of local papers didn't produce a Sunday edition. Even if a guy delivered on Sunday, that was just one morning a week, and not a school day. Yet, a single a.m. delivery challenged carriers more than six afternoon deliveries combined.

Well, try rolling out of bed every morning, on school days, snowy days, sleepy days. Try seven, dark, silent rises before 4:00 a.m. repeated for weeks, months, into years. Along with the challenging hour, significant differences existed between a morning route and the common, simple after-school routine.

# CHAPTER 6
## MORNING HAS OPENED

### after the paper arrived.

A sharp ring stabbed his eardrums. With the alarm clock pressed against his head, where the teddy bear use to nestle, the shrill clang blasted away a dream of flying above clouds. He slapped the top of the clock. Silence re-entered the dark room but sleep was dismissed. Familiar scenes had disappeared, concealed in the blanket of night. He blinked a few times and glanced around for a touch of comfort.

Another jolt: bare feet on the frigid floor. Once the warm feather comforter slid off, Jim was doused with the cold reality of his unheated bedroom. Every cell of his skin vibrated into goose bumps. After a full night's sleep, a person woke energized; however, a morning paperboy's sleep ended incomplete, with three hours sliced off by the 4 a.m. alarm.

Experienced from handling the shoppers' guide one day a week, but wanting his own business, when offered a morning route, the boy leaped at the opportunity. The last time he leaped for the delivery. Awakened every day, not just Sunday or Thursday, but seven days repeated again and again meant his system must tilt, whether his biological clock shifted or not.

Maybe Hobson's choice for a morning route could be a stepping stone---though lots of steps---to a convenient afternoon time. Yes, it was difficult to leave a ball game, or as Sam Smyth said, "leave the swimming hole;" nevertheless, afternoon carriers arrived at the paper substation awake, active and driven to compete with other kids. But darn, too many others asked for that easier time.

Morning publishers usually recruited carriers, since tumbling from bed in the dark was an unpopular choice. People quipped about the early bird gets the worm. Who wants a worm? And anyway, migrating birds are smart to fly to warm weather during winter, rather than chirp about winning worms. In the summer they stay in the nest until dawn---after papers were delivered.

To rise while the family slept raised a boy's discipline to a higher level. He made a commitment. He kept his agreement, contract or not. His subscribers signed on expecting to receive the news before 6:00 a.m. Forget the newspaper code concerning time limits. Children started their rounds with a deadline pushing against a drowsy head. Operating on a time table, they delivered by daybreak and appeared at school on time.

In the rugged, barren desert surrounding Grand Coulee Dam, Don Hubbard respected his early morning responsibility. "I always completed my route. Sometimes I was so tired and sleepy that a fleeting thought of dumping the papers over the bank crossed my mind. The consequences weren't worth it." So when bundles came late, he caught a nap, curled up on the road warmed by a lantern, until the delivery truck arrived from Spokane. Then he hustled.

## Wake-Up Call

Sleepy, stomach growling because eight or nine hours had passed since supper time, a boy tried to wake himself and hurry outside while his family nestled in the quiet house. John Knight's place was silent. His father wasn't stirring for work. He had died. John was a responsible conscientious fellow, once he was awake. With 100 customers expecting the *Patriot News,* which must be delivered regardless of rain, hail, or a blizzard covering Harrisburg, Pennsylvania, he needed to roll out of bed.

Even though he should be underway John slept on, slept and slept through the ringing. Fortunately his sister, Emmalou, heard it. In her pleasant soft voice she answered the persistent phone. "Yes, John'll be right there." After his sister roused him for the route, he "came home soaked to the skin, shivering, dog tired, but never missed a delivery day. I'm proud of that."

Fortunately, for the young district manager, the brother continued to over sleep. His sister answered wake-up calls speaking nicely to the manager, who ultimately won her hand in marriage. The wedding was not held in the wee early hours so John attended, wide awake.

## Up, Right-side Up

Across the country, another John delivered a large route in Tracy, California. John Wilson recalled that the "worst part of the route was the winter months, the very cold and wet months. Once you finished delivering the papers on a rainy day, you never felt warm and dry until you got home to change clothes."

Whatever the California weather, nasty or nice, he worked to be on time and to increase the size of his route. Beginning with 135 papers, he advanced his subscriptions to 150, a load. Consistent, he rushed to start at 4:30 a.m., to finish by the 6 a.m. deadline.

"One early morning I woke and looked at my watch. It was 6:30 a.m. I panicked. I was late." Dressing fast, John raced his bike to the *Tracy Press* office. "There was a crew working in the press room. They should have been home hours ago. A second look at my watch and I discovered I put it on upside down. It was 12:30, not 6:30 A.M. I glanced around to make sure no one saw me." He scooted home for a real bonus: four more hours of sleep.

## Together

As opposed to depending on an alarm clock, phone, or wristwatch, a paperboy with parental help for the wake-up call, and maybe older brothers hurrying to dress, could almost tolerate the morning routine.

Pre-dawn hours felt best when shared with a father, a brother, or a friendly pet. As the Roaring Twenties closed, unable to foresee what the Terrible Thirties would bring, two young brothers "rose at 4:30 each morning in Spickard, Missouri." Just a speck on the map, south of the border between Iowa and Missouri, Spickard was a village of friends.

Led by their father's example, brothers Robert and Winton walked a few blocks with Mr. Wyatt to Grandmother Wyatt's home. Dad hurried on to work at the grocery store, which opened early because those folks without an ice box needed their perishable foods for the day. Across a back yard, a rooster crowed.

The grade-school boys entered Grandmother's small cozy kitchen. The room was lit by a coal oil lamp and warmed by the wood stove ready to cook breakfast before dawn broke. Hats off, the youngsters sat down at the extended wooden table covered with a faded oilcloth. They poured homemade syrup from a tin cup over stacks of pancakes. "Grandmother welcomed our visits and continued making our hearty breakfast each morning." For their part, the boys continued carrying the *Kansas City Journal Post* in their small town of 600 neighbors. They "delivered in all sorts of inclement weather, with special care to place the papers in a proper place and at the same time each day." Windy stormy days often thrashed across the plains, particularly from September to May. Regardless, the reliable paperboys "delivered early enough to get to school on time."

First parting with dad, then leaving Grandmother's comfy kitchen, Robert took his half of the small town and Winton the other half, though not alone. Winton owned a bicycle with "a wooden box on the back carrier and Lucky jumped in the box." His black tail curled over his feet, pointed ears straight up, away they rolled with the wind ruffling his dark fur.

Robert was joined by Brownie. No clock needed, the customer knew exactly when "to let Brownie out each morning at the same time and he ran down the street" to join Robert. Brownie's small ears, short tail and short hair were long on energy as the two scooted along together before the egg and milk man arrived.

Rather than racing through his routine, in the 1920s, Robert walked the neighborhoods. Not rushing to leave Grandmother's comfy, slower style, but recognizing rapid endless change, he transitioned into the increasingly faster-paced American century. An American model for the time, the Wyatt brothers and their furry companions could have posed for an Edward Hopper painting or an Andrew Wyeth picture.

## Another Father Model

Tom Rockne thought ahead from his dark winter hours to the coming daylight in pleasant summer months. Think ahead. His dad emphasized planning and stressed the future. Mr. Rockne's oldest son (though age 10 wasn't old) should aim for college. So, assisted by dad's 5:00 a.m. wake-up, father and son talked about Tom's future over a quick breakfast.

For the present, he opened the door and stepped forth into an adventure, alone, his first daily job, which before dawn was actually a nightly job. He set out seven days a week on foot or intermittently pedaling a bike. The bicycle was okay in clear weather, but the paper must be inside the storm door when blizzards swept across the yards, building high drifts in Jamestown, North Dakota. In deep snow, his bike was useless. With the big Sunday edition of the *Minneapolis Tribune,* Tom used a wagon when possible or in the long, ferocious winter months, he depended on his sled to manage the load.

The damp chilly air, often downright freezing, gripped him with new sensations. Braced against the wind, he stumbled into the dark. Naked streets disturbed him. There were no children jumping rope, playing hopscotch, or any clacking mowers crossing lawns. His senses groped for familiar voices, a friendly wave from the porch, an open kitchen window releasing aromas.

Stripped of the usual attractions, Tom moved past the vacant lawns, empty porches, and shuttered store windows. It was even too early for Mrs. O'Donnell to hang a load of diapers on the clothesline. She waited until the sun cleared the roof tops. Mr. Cutter snored on the sleeping porch, his loud snorts rumbling down to the street in the night air.

When the weather was beautiful (the qualifier "when" ruled out lots of weeks), the dim morning hours stimulated the eyes. Once dawn appeared, shrinking the large shadows, a perfect picture developed for a

Christmas card scene. The still life provided an appreciation for the privilege in witnessing the undisturbed community.

## But Until It's Light

With no light, a carrier responded with increased awareness to any lone sound. The morgue-like stillness made him suspicious on spooky streets. Later, checking the scenes in daylight, a boy assured himself a looming, ghastly form was just an old bent forsythia bush. At 4:00 a.m. the sleeping community rested differently from the noisy, busy afternoon with kids at the play field, auto horns beeping, folks talking at the post office. Now, the town smelled empty. No cigar smoke, no exhaust fumes from a delivery truck, fresh cut grass, or a redolent kitchen with fish frying. No one burning the last pile of wet leaves. The dark didn't invite a skipping, whistling time. A carrier's sensitivity to raw sounds, long shadows, and stale smells held his reaction system on alert. Some black moments were downright scary.

## Definite Difference

Harvey Knizek stayed small for his age, though he'd finally reached 13. He'd been hawking the afternoon *Seattle Star* for two years. Then he switched to a full-time *Seattle P I* route, a routine unlike selling on busy streets with crowds of businessmen heading home. Bright mornings in the Ballard section of Seattle, with its popular, tantalizing Scandinavian bakery, brought folks around for sweet pastries. But before sunrise, Harvey, starting at 5:00 a.m. utterly alone, the black mornings shook his confidence. He suffered "pure hell at first."

## Nothing to fear, but...

Delivering on Sunday once a week was awful. But every morning meant seven times as much fear. A novice paper carrier was scared of the dark, any and every day, until he adapted. Cutting through an alley, his body snapped to attention when the sound of metal cracked the silent air. The sound magnified as though a giant steel door slammed. A trash can lid struck a rock when knocked off by a feral cat. Staying alert he hurried on. Icy tree limbs creaked like a person groaning. Breaking an icicle off the corner of a porch, he sucked on the ice to refresh his dry mouth. Pings resounded. *Did someone throw gravel? Whew, just sleet.* With his sixth sense honed to a high wave warning system, he imagined more than actually occurred. Was he safe?

Mothers called kids inside when street lights came on. The shadows broadcast: be safe in the house. Aunt Edna said children should not stay out in the dead of night. *Why is night dead?*

And on Sunday the stern minister reading the *Old Testament* threatened the congregation that sins led to a dark hell. He pounded a message of fear: fear the Devil, fear burning fires in hell. *Huh? A fire gives off comforting warm light. Why fear illuminating fire?*

Toward evening, the family settled in the home listening to radio programs like *The Shadow Knows,* which heightened a young one's fears. His imagination soared even more, up to a terrified level, if he passed a funeral home. It took no effort to locate a haunted house at Halloween. All the houses appeared haunted at 4:00 a.m.

Even the film industry expanded young imaginations with scary movies. A cackling sound brought the wicked witch from the *Wizard of Oz* into his neighborhood. Dang, why did he spend a dime to see the *Frankenstein* movie? Just as bad, he listened to older kids who recreated awful scenes. In the movie theater with other boys, he was unconcerned as candy wrappers crinkled, pop corn crunched, feet shuffled. In the theater's dark  he closed his eyes during a terrifying horror scene, with just a few peeks. Jack London's *Call of the Wild* ran from Alaska right to Maple Street. The English teacher made it worse by reading Dickens' *Great Expectations.* Pip was scared speechless, gripped with fear when that creepy criminal rose from behind a tombstone and grabbed him. *What if some crook grabbed him right now?*

He asked for a route. The circulation manager questioned his size and strength, yet never checked his scale of scared. Probably because there was "nothing to fear..."

Nothing?

His footsteps and his breathing made a rhythm. Each sound distinct because so few existed in the stillness. Smells faded into a mush of stale scents. Familiarity breeds confidence but this wasn't familiar. Sitting in school before Halloween, reading Washington Irving's tales of *Sleepy Hollow,* was exciting. Now the hollow, the woods, and the roads became kind of scary.

Those halyards on the flag pole at the library slapped like horse's hooves. Ohhh, the headless horseman's coming. A looming shadow swayed. Ohhh, not the headless horseman. His blood dribbling. Fast, hide with Ichabod Crane.

Whew, relief. It was only a drunk relieving himself at the corner of the brick building. Actually, this was darn scary. Yes, a concealed spot for relieving himself was a good idea.

At this hour, alone, he suddenly pivoted from sleepy to scared. With a hidden noise, his imagination exploded like a water main bursting. Fear was huge, black, and as powerful as a train engine running loose. Those terrible crime stories in the newspaper came from somewhere.

Why, that sinister Captain Hook could stomp toward him with Long John Silver, or that awful Injun Joe. Even Tom Sawyer was scared of the Injun.

The carrier's sensitivity to swaying shadows held him rapt on high alert. Weird shadows stretched into weird body shapes. His own elongated shadow gave him a height that even a wild imagination couldn't match. Was a giant around the corner? Lonely smelled like dusty gunny sacks, leaving his mouth as dry as baled hay. The vast silence screamed, opening its jaws to swallow a child. A slight breeze stirred the pine trees scattering needles. He never heard that in the daylight. He tried talking to himself, whistling or singing.

Nothing to fear but dark corners, a stalking dog, the Devil. A crescent moon faded as a streak of sunlight bordered the horizon. His self-assurance rose quickly with the sun.

## "I leaped that morning."

Stillness showered over Richard. He shivered. His eyes adjusted to the shades of black spaces. He climbed a steep hill, huffed, and tracked on, stumbling over a branch concealed with leaves and snow. Only his footprints marred the snow. No smell of wood or coal smoke drifted to him. Folks would fire up stoves in about an hour. Richard Ruth's route covered the small community of Geistown, just beyond Johnstown, Pennsylvania. For now, Geistown was still. There was no one on the porch of the general store when he picked up his papers. The family dog, Bo, had chosen not to run with him today.

Hurrying, without time to yawn, he headed for a quick path. *Oh good, a depression.* He stepped into a hollow, like a footprint, and then another making his strides easier. With limited light from glistening snow, his ears took on twice their usual sensitivity, maybe more.

Alone in the dead of night, hearing his heart beat like an Indian drum, his senses sparked his imagination. Covering the mountainous terrain, Richard delivered before 6:00 a.m., before a long walk to school. He knew his routine, the scenes, the usual distant sounds, and any smell of smoke and farm life along the way.

He rushed to cover his three-mile route. Time was crucial. Cows had to be milked, then leave for school. He shouldn't arrive late, again. At least the snow and ice were less thick today. Having suffered one bike accident down a steep hill on the harsh ice, now he was more careful about riding his bike. Gee, when his older brother, Robert, on this same route, tripped over a body frozen in the deep snow, it was awful. The drunk was as stiff as a grave stone. Robert, startled and scared, needed to report it and yet hustle to school on time. The younger brothers remembered that, and listened to talk of the many souls awash by the horrific, tragic 1889 Johnstown flood. Just a generation ago, relatives recalled the grief.

Richard chose a short cut rather than walk another long, secluded street with no street lights. The snow provided a faint reflection as daylight barely seeped through. In the graveyard, drifts buried half the tombstones. It wouldn't be easy to play their usual hide and seek game there today. He was part way through the cemetery when he heard a noise, he distinctly heard something unfamiliar. Sort of a whistle, a whirr. A tremor of fear reached to his feet. Slower steps. There it was. Using good sense to clear out of the desolate grounds, he headed straight to the edge of the cemetery, racing away from a strange, eerie sound.

Richard "jumped a four foot fence" with his full canvas bag of newspapers. His weight, the bag, his boots pressed him into the snow, on the safe side of the fence. He leaped up and rushed toward the safety of home out of that cemetery.

The school hours ticked away, but his scare stayed right in the front of his thoughts. He needed to test his prowess. "Later that day I returned to the fence to see if I still could jump over it." Calmly eyeing the rails, feet flying, "I couldn't even come close." He missed his mark, missed it without the weight of papers. Ability receded with no adrenalin pumping. An Olympian track star clearing a four foot fence might win the hurdle division. Richard, just 12 in 1936, wasn't competing in the track events at the Berlin Olympics that year.

## Halt!

Though less severe than in Europe and Asia, the opening of the 1940s grew darker in America, particularly on the West Coast. As if early morning---or closing night hours---were not dark enough, the World War II blackouts for vulnerable war-time factories, ship yards, and military posts near the coast made paper routes during night hours more challenging.

The nation turned scared. Fears of survival had subsided as the Depression eased, until Sunday, December 7, 1941, when Japan attacked a harbor far out in the Pacific. School boy, Art Armstrong, looked over his parent's shoulder at a map to locate an island, identified as Hawaii. Fear rose, worry worsened. In the winter of 1942, authorities established blackout regulations to make the night as dark as a deep coal mine. Ensure total darkness, at least if the moon was not full. Street lights, dim though they were, offered a little light. No, all public lighting off. At night if folks left the bed, out of necessity or for a trip to the refrigerator, blackout curtains had to conceal even the small appliance bulb that might shine through the kitchen window. In some war production places, with mills belching sparks and flames, wet coal, tar and oil were burned to create thick smoke for camouflage at 10:00 a.m. The dense air hid the beacons, however small, from enemy planes, unless the wind interfered. The smoky blackness stunk.

Art's parents told him he should be glad lights came on even under limited hours. The newspaper headlines and stories made it clear the lights went out all over Europe, Great Britain and China. For those suffering people, the United States and Canada raised the only beacon of hope. He accepted the concern.

Enveloped in fog, his head down to protect his nose from pointing into wet winter air around Everett, Art's route turned blacker than his usual night rounds, darker than his bedroom when he was jolted awake at 3:30 a.m. Much darker than the movie theater.

Darn, he'd rather be watching a movie, sitting next to others in a theater not totally darkened. Maybe the newspaper company would give carriers another free ticket, but better not see horror movies. His back to Puget Sound, he walked up Hewitt Avenue blinded by blackness. He might as well be wearing a blindfold. No street lights, no porch lights, blackout curtains across windows. Unlike refreshing mist, Everett lay choked by fog. He needed a bat's sensory system. No bats were even flying around in such dense moisture.

The fog stuffed Art's nose. Creeping mist coated his hair, his hands and clothes leaving a clammy chill that seeped inside his cold skin. Thick fog muffled sounds, not that any usual daytime town movements existed.

"HALT!"

Art stopped. Speechless, his internal alarm system wasn't stopped. Shivers raced along his spine keeping up with the pounding heart, churning stomach, racing urinary tract. He needed to flee this scary scene.

Dutifully patrolling the streets of Everett's sleeping seaport, the stern blackout warden checked Art's purpose. After questioning him, he and his canvas bag were released. The powerful adult authority penetrated the fog. Fear was a big brute.

## Adults Were Scared

More so than children, many adults were scared, sometimes frightened even in the daylight. Following the horrific bombing of Pearl Harbor, fear swept over folks up and down the West Coast. It increased after mixed news reported a bomb at Ft. Stevens, Oregon. Located by the mouth of the Columbia River, there it was: a shell crater. In the long daylight of June, who knew where the Japanese intended to strike next?

Gene Reiber began his *Tacoma Times* route in 1942 as people's fears escalated. He was conscientious with his new job and completed the year without a single complaint. Delivering in his own residential area, he was acquainted with most of the customers. But one home-owner startled him, at least for a short time.

Though first he startled her. Downright scared her. Growing in expertise but still perfecting his aim, on a calm autumn afternoon Gene threw a rolled *Times* paper through the window in the front door. Stunned by the shattered, clinking glass, he parked his bike and walked toward the porch trying to prepare what he'd say.

However, his subscriber reacted faster. An "elderly lady, oh, in her 60s, came out the door quite agitated." Distraught, eyes blinking, hands clasped tight, voice shaking she repeated an urgent request for sand. She wanted sand thrown on the incendiary bomb. "Help. Dump a bucket of sand on the bomb. Hurry!"

Although Gene's rolled papers flew like a missile and, if improperly rolled might burst open, the *Times* news was not going to explode in her hallway. His presence and an apology became reassuring; his spoken lines so comforting that she didn't file a complaint. Of course, giving her "two months of a free newspaper" also softened her state of fear. Her "replacement of that window cost much more" than his weekly 15 cents for six dailies and 10 cents for Sunday. He appreciated her kind consideration.

## Nearly Shattered

Accidents happen suddenly. They capture attention. An occurrence with afternoon routes—broken milk bottles, a broken screen, storm door, broken Christmas lights---changed to monumental problems in a motionless, predawn hour.

The Depression was finished. World War II ended. Everything was good in Utah, until the 1948 winter. That brutal winter registered the worst in Utah's record with farmers' livestock freezing to death; hundreds died. The horrific storm costs rose. Still, Ron Petersen delivered the *Salt Lake Tribune* without pause. It's challenging to finish a paper route before 6:00 a.m. It was worse completing a route through the harsh winter months, when the bicycle bogged down in deep snow, when drifts stopped the wagon, and his sled was difficult to pull. However, very extreme "icy weather was not an obstacle" that stopped Ron.

Porch a *Tribune*. Keep hurrying. Porch another paper. Just be finished and sit at the breakfast table by the time the neighborhood stirred. Swish, another delivery.

SHATTER!

Glass exploded in every direction. The window shouted, breaking the silence like a disturbing police siren. The tight flying missile broke the sound barrier between a sleeping customer and a scurrying carrier.

Ron didn't need a "Halt!" He was stopped, riveted with fear. He stood dead still before the myriad of pieces that a second earlier fit into a large plate glass window. The picture window burst in microseconds. The splintered glass instantly sliced away the quiet air. Every broken particle sent sound waves across, around, and through the night. Elongated seconds held as shards scattered on the wooden porch and broke into more bits of glass.

He listened but didn't look through the space that opened into the house. Instead he stared down two holes, two round dark circles with an edge of glint. He was shaking. The holes held steady, aimed close at his face.

Fortunately, the customer glanced first, before he could send a shattering blast through the boy's head. "Oh, thought you were a burglar." Good thing the guy recognized a kid with a canvas bag stuffed with newspapers, one who sent a paper to the wrong place. Releasing the cock on the lowered gun, the shivering guy in his flimsy shorts hurried back into his warm house. Ron continued his delivery on trembling legs.

Rather than intimidated, Ron was downright scared. Ahh well, only a window shattered instead of his head. He'd fix a little broken glass. In truth, plenty of glass, which broke his bottom line of profit for weeks, even months.

Add adults to a scary scenario and a boy's stability was tested. Disturbances magnified in the dread of dark. Alone, unknown sounds produced fear which seeped from the marrow of his bones. Familiarity conquered fear, once the familiar finally appeared at dawn.

## A Juvenile Criminal?

Bob Spahr substituted for his friend for two months before his classmate's dad offered Bob the route. The father worked as a distributor of the Seattle *Post Intelligencer*, the *PI*, for the outlying towns through Washington State's southwest sector. With the local *Chehalis Courier* available in the afternoon, Bob only had 78 customers for the city morning paper.

Off to the east, sunlight didn't glisten yet on Mt. St. Helen's glaciers, and would not for another hour. Still, this day was brighter than yesterday, when he rushed out to begin his deliveries and discovered the back tire on his bike as flat as any sidewalk. Thick, crawling fog from the Pacific Ocean made the hour and his situation darker. He ran into the house for help. No one offered help. "Got a problem, take care of it." He handled his trouble by walking the five mile route. Not planning for the long jaunt, the starting school hour deepened his trouble.

This day was lots better. He woke before 5:00 a.m. A strong breeze erased all the fog. He rushed through his route. With the bike tire repaired, he delivered 40, 50, 70 papers, down to five left in the bag. He loved to compete with himself. Maybe he'd break his time record.

Wait a second! There's eight houses left. He slacked off pedaling. Tapping across fingers on his right hand he named, Erickson, Hanson, Johnson, Carlton, Postal. Oh Dang! His mind flashed over the route. All in order. He stopped pumping. "No way I left extra papers anywhere."

Rushing home he dialed the district manager. A drowsy voice answered.

Bob burst out, "I'm short three papers."

He listened. Quickly replied, "No, I didn't misdeliver. I got 75 papers. I'm sure, 75."

The man's voice was awake and explicit.

"Okay." Relieved, Bob thanked him and answered, "I know where that is."

He swung his bike around the corner and into the shopping streets, well on the way to handling his problem. The grocery, like bakeries, opened before the rest of the stores in the quiet town of Chehalis. Dropping his bike and canvas bag against the wall of the market, he dashed into the alley's delivery entrance. His district manager said he'd left a bundle of papers near the door, by the candy racks. "Pick up three, 'cause on Tuesday Mac doesn't sell all the papers."

Yep, a full stack. Bob tugged three papers out with just a crinkle to the top sheet. He ran down the aisle and out the stock room nearly falling when he slid on wet celery leaves. He paused to fold the papers into a square. As he creased the third one, a vice grip jerked his shoulder. Spun around, Bob faced a Goliath.

Shouting down at the paperboy, the gruff grocer said, "You steal from me and I'll have you put away. You'll have readin' time in that juvenile detention hold." Yelling louder, "You belong in jail, in the rogues' gallery." The giant shoved Bob back inside, pushing him along like a crate of lettuce, though less concerned if he bruised a kid. The Paul Bunyan figure had no trouble tumbling a boy over to the phone, all the while ranting about Bob starting his life of crime, a definite career criminal. Why he'd be in the penitentiary before he drove a car.

When the grocer paused long enough to locate the police listing, Bob hastily said, "My manager told me to pick up three papers. He's the *PI* manager." He raised his shaky voice a bit, "I'll give you his number."

Bob was scared. He knew about the juvenile jail. A really tough kid at school was sent there. Going to the principal's office for another late slip would be easy compared to this. Just, "Please call my manager. He'll explain. I won't use your three papers."

Many kids acted rough around the newspaper shack, became smart alecks at the bicycle shop and the gasoline station. However, youngsters shook when captious, controlling adults threatened them. Power rested with the elders, including parents. Tempered with experiences, the imaginary fears were conquered by a child's resilience. However, fear of adult action could reduce self-assurance, even permanently scar it. Adults failed to recognize how severely they frightened children. Other times, a scare produced unexpected results.

## Bad to Better

On a bright morning, without erratic Denver weather that Jim Rudy and his buddy endured throughout the year delivering the *Rocky Mountain News*, they were relaxing in the Dutch Boy Donut shop, a favorite hang-out. Brushing glazed sugar off their fingers, the two enticed by the sunshine and energized from eating sweet donuts, formed an idea.

Finished with the daily delivery and having a few papers left, which they didn't feel pressed to sell, the boys created a simple contest. Wherever two shall convene, competition will ensue. Heck, the *Rocky Mountain News* competed for subscribers. Competition occurred in sports, in politics, for a girlfriend, anytime, anywhere. It was fun.

With routes completed, the guys couldn't try speed to roll papers or distribute them the fastest. Besides, that's a common paper carrier test. No, the boys wanted more. Instead of fastest, why not farthest? Yeah! Jim Rudy accurately porched papers to the customer's door from as far as 60 feet. Each was confident he'd throw farther. Where Colfax Street and Niagara meet, they would torpedo papers over a four lane boulevard divided by a center median, into a large space.

The competitors stood at the bakery, looked across the wide street to the Niagara House Motel, to a long pool where guests enjoyed a fresh dip or swim. An inviting place to stay, both well maintained and well managed.

The boys successfully threw their tightly rolled papers the distance over the busy lanes of traffic, landing them right in the pool. Out of extra papers, satisfied with the missile shots, the teenagers lost interest and started forth to find other activities.

## Not so fast.

The manager flew out the motel door, shouting, thrusting his fists in a rage. Very angry, he accused the kids of vandalism. Newspapers floating in a pool were apparently worse than candy wrappers and cigarette butts. After the kids removed the soggy blobs, which had not unfolded nor conked anyone on the head, he ordered them into his office.

Rather than bolting and running off, or throwing the manager in the pool, the boys obeyed him. The two sat in his office, fidgeting, wondering why a fun stunt caused such fury. Gee, the pool wasn't grey with ink mingling into the aqua color. What's the big deal? The manager reached for the phone. Oh no. Not the police. Their competition stunt deteriorated.

Mr. Fracton asked Billy for his phone number. Billy spewed off some numbers. No one answered. Madder because of the mendacity of the kid, Mr. Fracton asked Jim for his. "Naive, I'm scared, dumb me, I gave him our phone number."

Still enraged, Mr. Fracton dialed Jim's dad and related quite an episode. Oh brother, Jim would have preferred that the mad motel owner phone the police.

When Jim arrived home, he received a double dose of furious. He tried to explain how it came about, ending with, "No harm, no foul." Wow! Wrong response. A parent was harmed by a fellow citizen thinking his kid was some hoodlum. Furthermore, Jim was misguiding his younger brothers. Mr. Rudy, a member of the old school, sent his oldest son directly back to Mr. Fracton to work off the damage. For sure, the police call would have been better.

Jim strained all day, hour after hour working in the parking lot, around the manicured grounds, along the room corridors, working off the damage. Whatever that was? Billy, his pal in crime never came around. "He ended up in juvenile detention, a real jerk." Obviously, Billy committed more acts that escalated to actual trouble.

Jim's long day of discipline ended with a new opportunity. Telling the truth with his phone number, having a stern father who held him accountable, a strong effort for an entire day, the manager proclaimed that the culprit was "the hardest worker he ever had." Mr. Fracton gave Jim a job on weekends for 85 cents an hour. Continuing to prove himself, he became a manager when Mr. Fracton took a vacation, something he had not allowed himself for a long time.

Jim valued what he learned. He did not like his boss, an incredibly strict man, but Jim appreciated the opportunities he provided. A bad situation turned better under dad's sentence and a business man's opinion. Fear disappeared once Jim worked through his incident.

## Serene Solitude

Physical exertion in delivering papers, enduring the sleepy and hungry state, nevertheless, quiet, empty space gave the morning paperboy time to think. Alone, though not a loner, an independent carrier crossed tranquil streets before sunrise, his scared state absorbed once he confronted his fears. Frightened disappeared the way winter passed into spring. And then summer would bring an easy time, or at least easier. He'd still rise in the dark, but in air that was cool and refreshing rather than freezing cold.

Ron Richardson's *Seattle PI* papers had been dropped at the shack on time and without the usual rain, he was able to finish his route earlier. His Madison Park neighborhood, to the east of central Seattle, was framed in the beauty of glistening snowy peaks, deep reflecting water, tall spreading evergreen trees and flowering shrubs. He paused to survey the smooth water in Lake Washington that shimmered as the sun crested on the Cascade Mountains and lit the towering Mt. Rainier with a coral glow. He breathed deeply. Satisfying air filled Ron since his asthma was no longer a problem. Peace showered over him and he relaxed at the lake's grassy edge, clothed in the pleasant freshness. For a short time he thought of himself, enjoying the moment while he stood in his world on his small island, not isolated but a part of the community, surrounded by the rare gift of silence. Sunrise belonged to him. He savored the solitude.

Experience assured him the community would soon yawn and stretch. Until then, the interlude of silence was dissolving like a sunlit icicle, drop by drop as daylight winked and softened shadows. The day began from a stillness so quiet one could hear a morning glory open.

In a few minutes he saw the University of Washington crew team, their shell gliding over the lake past ducks slowly gliding by. Life sang out. Robins chirped a cheerful greeting. Morning appeared slowly, then with haste to a cacophony of human motion that shattered the solitude. Vehicle motors idled, an awning was rolled up, shop owners called out greetings. A plethora of sounds fused with the streaks of dawn, and activity came bounding forth.

Smoke began rising from furnaces and stoves. The milkman and the baker were working. He saw the bakery front lights come on and his stomach growled, ready to enjoy a warm treat. In family kitchens the coffee percolated, bacon sizzled, the dog ran out the front door, and a hand retrieved the dropped newspaper.

Starting early day after day, week after week, season into season, it was monotonous, but so much required stuff was routine. The route, heck, it was alive. Ron had the whole day ahead. His day would be noisy at times, but rising at 3:45 a.m., sunrise now allowed him brief joy. His paper route guided him on a start to the day; his first job guided him to a practical start in life.

# CHAPTER 7
## MAIN STREET SCHOOL

Managing the sleep schedule, controlling fear---real or an ethereal scene---a morning carrier faced an additional challenge nine months of the year: the school bell. Children by age 6, 9, 12 or older who ran an early route required rigid discipline. Awake earlier than school mates, the paper carriers with morning routes needed another hefty layer of order. No excuses accepted. A paperboy was expected to deliver and be in school on time despite any distractions, disruptions, or dangerous encounters. It was clear: settle at his desk, scared and sleepy or not.

From drowsy to adrenalin-filled, a morning paper carrier left his unstructured *Main Street School* and entered a standard school to sit quietly in a row like a stiff corn stalk. Commit to prompt attendance no matter how challenging. Oh, and be in an active learning state, as well.

In the heated room, his trousers thawed, shoes semi-dried, fingers began to lose their tingling numbness. By the start of reading circle, his yawns increased, his stomach rumbled. Lunch period was three hours away. By lunch a full eight hours in his day had passed from having risen at 4:00 a.m. It seemed like the dinner bell should ring. A stick of Wrigley gum would ease the immediate hunger pain, but that brought the pain of whacked knuckles. "Don't chew gum in school!" He swallowed a lick of white paste from the sticky jar and chewed on the pencil eraser. Sitting at a desk his curiosity and competitive enthusiasm disappeared, as he conjugated regular and irregular Latin verbs. Slowly writing each spelling word five times, a tired body fell asleep.

## The Enclosed Classroom

For kids, a new year started after Labor Day and wound down by Memorial Day, May 30th. Three months into the nine-month school year, students enjoyed a long weekend for the Thanksgiving Holiday. In December school closed for a two week Christmas break. George

Washington's birthday and Good Friday clipped off two days. Added to weekends, the holidays compressed the learning year to about 180 days of school---less than half of the standard 365-day year. A "school year" redefined a Gregorian calendar.

Even better, a shoulder-deep snow, a spring flood tearing out bridges, or a tornado-induced power outage delighted children with an exhilarating extra day of play.

The opening bell rang at 8:00 a.m. A child was tardy by 8:10 a.m. The classroom provided a warm, dry place with drinking fountains, a lunch room, and restrooms, only who wanted to "rest" on a toilet? Children were confined to the school grounds until 3:30 p.m. dismissal, which still left time to play in the daylight, unless detention interfered.

## Year-round

Located in the midst of the community was a school system with shorter hours though a more intense schedule. The newspaper carriers' street school rotated in a Monday through Friday plus Saturday and Sunday routine. Unlike a standard school with holidays and vacation days, *Main Street School* operated on a 365-day calendar.

A postman was off on Sundays, New Year's Day, Memorial Day, the Fourth of July, Labor Day, Armistice Day, Thanksgiving, Christmas, and other possible days. But like the farmer milking cows, the carrier attended to delivery every day. His extra school remained open in snow storms, in wind and ice that snapped power lines bringing deadly wires to the pavement, or in road-closing floods. The worse the weather, the more folks, driven inside their home to the fireplace, expected the paper.

No matter if a toothache or tummy-ache, the paperboy appeared at *Main Street School*. In epidemics of chicken pox, measles, mumps, even in the heightened polio season with community swimming pools and theaters ordered closed, boys delivered papers. When Seattle schools closed in 1918 because of the influenza epidemic, David Bowles had time to sell newspapers. The carriers' street school was in session: Monday, Tuesday, Wednesday, Thursday, Friday, Saturday, Sunday, back to Monday, and around for weeks into months.

His starting bell clanged by 4:00 a.m. and after 6:00 a.m. the child was late. No excused absences, no sick leave, though when critically ill he provided a substitute. Perfect attendance went unrecorded on a report card. If he missed deliveries, he could be dismissed. Children enrolled as young as six, and often by 14 or 15 changed to longer jobs. Paperboys participating in *Main Street School* learned the same basic lessons: be fair, be honest, be considerate of others, wash your hands before eating, especially when grey from printer's ink.

This school of hard knocks, a euphemism for many youngsters' lessons in daily reality, taught practical, common sense. The material learned on Monday was put to use on Tuesday, and repeated with frequent pop quizzes, none of which resembled the easy multiple choice tests in his other school. Nor did his route list receive a gold star.

Unlike the prim plaid uniforms or white shirts (definitely not white) and long ties with school blazers seen in regular schools, the carrier's uniform allowed a cap or hat during school. His shoe soles, worn thinner than writing paper, were re-enforced with thick cardboard when large holes damaged his socks and the stones punctured his feet. The sturdy canvas bag, with the "school letters" advertised across the side, hung heavier than a book bag. Hand-me-down patched trousers lacked the style illustrated in the *Dick and Jane Reader* series. Maybe that's why he enjoyed the cartoon-like appearance of characters in comic books: he related.

Not lock-stepped into lines, a paperboy ran through his session. Recess came once the route and daily chores were completed. Or it was supposed to be after duties were fulfilled. His street school ranged from loud and raucous to eerily silent. The superintendent, in the form of the newspaper owner's position of power, reigned supreme. Since talking in *Main Street School* was acceptable, a paperboy became a conversationalist with his subscribers, developing his social skills. However, he lost any debate with ones who balked at paying.

The regular school subjects, readin', 'ritin, and 'rithmetic remained important. But the *Main Street School* immediately taught physics with lessons applied to overloaded bikes and canvas bags around the neck. Laws on bodies in continuous motion and the aerodynamics of a rolled paper against a window taught a specific lesson. The open classroom was a laboratory with daily experiences that proved the truths in life.

Unlike sitting in a row of wooden desks, with a hard seat undercoated with wads of chewing gum, the carrier passed through orderly rows of workers' company cottages or along dimly lit hallways of apartment buildings. Criticized for being late and fined for repeat offenses, there was no sitting in a classroom writing 100 times, "I will not be tardy again." His street school was more intense, physically and psychologically.

With the help of circulation managers, carrier buddies in *Main Street School* formed year-round softball, basketball, and bowling leagues. A group of boys who understood speed and had a strong throw made the fellows a natural for teams. The carriers loved belonging, keeping the route longer just to play for their clubhouse *school* team. The paper shack was a dual sports center. And best of all: the boys competed against other newspaper carrier groups.

The *Columbus Dispatch* (Ohio) carrier stations organized slow pitch softball competitions. More than an impromptu back-lot game, played if enough kids showed, the paperboys became intensely competitive. In September 1949, station 52 won their second straight championship, defeating stations 34 and 17 in a rousing play-off that made the sports pages of the *Dispatch* newspaper. Their customers, neighbors, other carriers, any sports followers saw the group photo of happy *Main Street School* winners acclaimed in the week's newspaper, some delivered by a team champ himself.

## A Team of Two

Rather than leave the pet dog outside on the lawn, the way a standard school required, many paper carriers chose to make their pets, (like Goofy or Brownie) their consistent companions traversing the open classroom of *Main Street School*. His personal Achates mattered even more when the two covered sidewalks in the stillness before sunrise.

In 1974, Tom Rudy followed his brothers, Jim, Dale and Greg, as a paperboy for the *Rocky Mountain News*. Bicycling the streets of Denver, porching papers 70, 90 feet, his customers knew him "very well." Receiving the morning edition from a Rudy boy since 1959, people counted on the paper regardless of weather and Tom's "interrupted sleep."

In no way a loner, he nevertheless felt the quiet, dark residential streets as he pedaled all by himself, in a sleepy trance. Until a friend appeared. Tom found a dog at his school. He coaxed the small, ordinary black dog to his house. Cared for, given a home and named Hannibal, the dog attached himself to Tom. So he ran along every day on the two-mile route.

And then Hannibal figured out the constant path. "He was wise." Running on his short legs next to the rolling bike wheels, after seven or eight city blocks, the smart dog paused. He located a fire hydrant, sniffed bushes, watched birds stirring and sat down by the curb. He waited. In a little while, just as he expected, here comes Tom back around finishing the last blocks of his route. The friendly, devoted companion diverted Tom's feelings of being alone on a monotonous route. Hannibal was a "Wonderful dog."

## Mentor, Model, Mr. Manager

The carriers answered to so many people who acted as teachers: the customers, the businessmen, circulation managers. And the district manager wore another hat: counselor. Not expecting infallible behavior, he helped mold the actions and attitudes of his young charges. As Henry

McDaniel found in his study of 706 boys, "in many cases newspaperboys are more influenced by their district managers than by their teachers."

In 1938, by 2:30 a.m. John Reed traversed the streets of Sacramento seven days a week delivering the *San Francisco Examiner* to 140 customers. For six years, he reliably dropped the papers at residences without any problems. Naturally difficulties arose, but Mr. Keane, John's manager, "took care of the fellows' problems." Though John was scared at times and struggled with minor mistakes, he could count on Mr. Keane because he was "fair, a wonderful man."

Ross Webb felt the same about his district manager. Learning the discipline in his steady daily job in Portland, Oregon, Ross gained confidence managing his route and talking with customers guided by, "a great Boss, Don Concannon. He treated us fairly and encouraged us to do a good job. For a first time job, he was very influential" offering his humor, directives and patience with boys' errors.

Paul Meyer began carrying the *Tacoma News Tribune* in 1948. Expanding from 100 to 200 customers before 1952, "felt very special" under Mr. Barnwell's supervision. His manager "often showed up at the paper pick-up point and talked to all the paperboys. He kept close tabs on what we did, establishing a relationship." Experienced with all ranks of people, having been "a professional boxer, he set a good example of conduct, decorum and dress. He always wore a double-breasted suit and a huge fedora." Not flashing any air of superiority, "he loved to shadow box with his boys and kidded around." But the carriers were accountable because "each month Mr. Barnwell paid a call at my home and collected the newspaper's share of the proceeds."

## Problem Solved

After waiting four years to be assigned a *Democrat and Chronicle* route, Ron Anderson's customers could count on their morning paper from him. So, when one subscriber missed an edition on Monday, and then the next Monday, they reported the error. Operating a mom and pop store from the front of their residence, they knew about service.

Ron was certain he had walked behind the building and "placed their paper in an open wooden box attached to the back door jamb," the same as always. He talked to his district manager, Bill Goettel. Listening, Mr. Goettel instructed Ron to be "doubly sure to place the paper there next Monday." Manager and carrier needed to rely on each other's action.

Ron knew Mr. Goettel was "a full-time probation officer in his main job. He carried a gun." The teenager had seen it. What he didn't see was a complaint slip on Tuesday.

That morning the manager appeared on the route to explain the solved problem. He'd been present when Ron, as instructed, delivered the

Monday paper, though Mr. Goettel hid from view in the bushes. The paperboy continued on; the probation officer waited. "Very soon a rubbish collector came around the house and stole the newspaper from the box when he picked up the trash. Bill caught the thief." Ron was sure that an officer with a gun and ID, "scared the thief big time. Bill Goettel was certainly my hero."

The common denominators of respected managers were regular presence, focused listening, and constructive criticism. They helped rather than hinder the children's development. However, the paperboys' educational benefits in managing a route and interacting with a special supervisor nearly stopped with the attempted 1924 Child Labor Amendment. Before those legal lines were even written, in 1915 an astute educator named Anna Reed wrote results of her research on the coordination of paperboys' street learning and classroom learning.

## Permanent Value

The concerned, pro-active teacher argued for an expanded education of newsboys. Not conforming to the warnings by child-labor reformers, Mrs. Reed proposed changes for the Seattle City School's curriculum. Her report reflected her sensible knowledge.

Anna Reed was a married woman and a mother who worked in the 1910s. More incredible, she was formally Dr. Reed, having earned a Ph.D. from the University of Wisconsin, in a period when an 8th grade education certificate was considered an acceptable achievement for any student. The daughter of a New York judge and the niece of President Grover Cleveland, Mrs. Reed was current with the growing opportunities being made available to schools through the Smith-Hughes Act. The legislation provided millions of federal dollars in financial assistance to states and local communities for vocational training in the classroom.

Dr. Reed recognized the practical connection between newsboys and vocational training. To justify and institute a change to the Seattle Schools' curriculum, she conducted an extensive study with 1,118 working children and their families. The majority of her subjects worked in the city in newspaper sales.

These youngsters did not see *Main Street School* as their only education system. They knew the value of formal school. Why heck, without the standard classroom, how could a guy learn to read the comics, the sports page, the notes on complaint slips, or even the headlines? How could he calculate the total amount owed in a delinquent three-month account? The standard school and *Main Street School* enhanced each other. Both made him more capable as he learned practical lessons day by day.

Strongly supportive of vocational education and defining all the ways the newsboys benefitted from their learning, Dr. Reed's published book concluded: "No academic assignment is entitled to the interest, or even the attention, of pupils unless it offers something of permanent value---unless it makes a definite contribution to future usefulness and success."

Her report stressed the impact from the newsboys' daily activities. "Many minor influences impel newsboy service. Practical motives dominate all others." These children understood earning money and the benefits from earning. But Dr. Reed stressed points beyond the financial gain. She knew childhood was the time to establish good habits as well as independence. She wanted to improve the education of a young newsboy to, "show him how to think right and how to act right, and do both instinctively, courageously, and independently."

The Seattle School Board dismissed Dr. Reed, and her report.

## A Better Route

In the prosperous 1950s, while education, social, and child labor reformers continued to target newspaperboys, circulation managers grasped the struggles carriers faced. Most managers had themselves been paperboys in the more challenging 1920s and '30s.

Circulation managers established a system. They met with parents, principals and teachers to design weekly training sessions with the carriers. This was cooperation, a constructive system rather than constant criticism. The newspaper business argued their case fervently, citing examples of outstanding businessmen, governors, judges, and mayors who began as paperboys.

Managers shared methods and positive results in professional publications and at their circulation association meetings. They drew on the expertise of a renowned professional, Dr. George W. Crane, who stated in his nationally syndicated column that America's newspaper circulation managers are the "best professors of practical economics." He encouraged parents to allow their sons to deliver papers.

As graduation approached, newspaper managers collected reports from schools on attendance, scholarship, and the community efforts of paper carriers. From Cleveland to Los Angeles, Salt Lake City, Dallas, Indianapolis, and Atlanta, they presented paperboys with scholarships of $500, $1,000, $3,000 and even more toward a college education.

The proposed constitutional amendment of 1924 would not have enhanced vocational education as Dr. Reed recommended, nor even allowed for the existence of the *Main Street School*. The amendment would have deprived tens of thousands from the educational opportunities of being a paperboy. Rather than eliminating these benefits, or as happened, placing industrious children in the middle of an adults' tug of war, why not allow youngsters to gain a structured education complemented with a sensible, practical one?

## Time Enjoyed

As America entered World War II, into the nation's dark hours, Howard Wagner, age 10, began managing a compact route of 200 customers. Yes, he was to be 12, but morning route managers needed paperboys so 10 was accepted. His Montgomery Ward bicycle, with heavy balloon tires and a sturdy basket in front, helped as he quickly porched papers.

Howard delivered the *Columbus Citizen Journal* from 3:30 a.m. to 5:00 a.m., in his neighborhood in the south sector of Columbus, Ohio. Once they were up, folks read the horrific news about Pearl Harbor while drinking their first cup of coffee. They read details of the Battle of Midway; learned that North Africa was secured as coffee became a little bitter because of sugar rationing. The months continued with headlines: "Patton Takes Sicily." In another year: "Successful D-Day" and finally on September 2, 1945, "Japan Surrenders." He had delivered detailed war news on the safe streets in America. The troops came home, prosperity broke forth, the essential Berlin airlift began, American soldiers arrived in Korea, and the century crossed the half way mark. Howard would soon complete a decade of finishing his delivery by 5:00 a.m.

He passed from fifth grade to sixth, seventh, eighth, ninth with no indication of dropping the route. At times he expanded his delivery routine. In the summer, softly singing to himself, he increased his outdoor morning time to deliver three and four extra routes for other paperboys who enjoyed family vacation time. From his work, he shared half of the earnings with his family.

Finishing the morning rotation, he prepared his breakfast. Then like other morning carriers, he closed his eyes for a short snooze before school beckoned. His nap was brief because his school included choir practice. After an audition, Howard was selected for the Columbus Boychoir School, a nascent program that soon produced singing comparable to the famous Vienna Choir Boys.

Founded in 1937 in the Broad Street Presbyterian Church and assisted with funding by the Columbus Kiwanis Club, the music program accepted 52 students committed to a full school program, rigorous music study, and a performance schedule. Howard added in paper route time. The choir grew. He grew. By age 14 he exited the boys' choir and returned to regular school studies, staying on the steady morning route, except for that one week in 1950.

The long Thanksgiving weekend was unsteady. Ohio and surrounding states were paralyzed for several days with deep snow, sub-freezing temperatures, ferocious wind. Nevertheless, he trudged with his papers during the Buckeye blizzard, as hearty as the college football teams who played that Saturday. The University of Michigan beat their rival, The Ohio State University, 9-3 in a game dubbed as the "Snow Bowl." The two college teams were about the only ones moving during the blizzard. Oh, plus Howard and a very few other paperboys.

A rigid schedule, but not a rough system because Howard "enjoyed the solitude from 3:30 to 5:00 a.m." From a childhood of consistent early mornings (or midway in the night at 3:30 a.m.) he appreciated the "friendliness of the people." His subscribers, many of them German and Hungarian immigrants or first-generation Americans, admired their dependable paperboy and expressed it in tips, which he appreciated.

Completing eleven years of delivering before dawn, Howard considered the army's reveille bugle call a mid-morning summons. His time in the military and at college was an extension of his paper route discipline. He earned a bachelor's degree and then a master's degree from The Ohio State University, resting on the training he adhered to in a set route schedule, that began in grade school and continued through high school.

## Switch To Easy

For others, when an opportunity to acquire an afternoon position arose, they grabbed the chance. In Klamath Falls, Bob Barr decided waiting on a late train for his *San Francisco Examiner* bundles had occurred too often. He snagged an afternoon *Klamath Herald & News* route with 100 customers. This increased his earnings to $30 a month in 1938. The paper was "quite a bit smaller than the San Francisco paper so I was able to fold it and throw to most of my customers. I could even throw a curve." Best of all, no more early mornings, none. The local edition did not produce a Sunday paper.

But if it had, heck, anybody can do one morning a week, just Sunday, with no school pressure. For children staying on the morning routes, such a busy schedule: paper route, altar boy, school, endless chores, scouts, boys' choir, how did anyone shove additional tasks into the day? Who could commit to more than seven mornings a week? For sure, no paperboy.

Wanna bet?

Some delivered as constant as the sunrise and sunset, witnessing both with a morning and an evening route. Plus each week rotated through the ring of subscribers to collect at a convenient hour.

# "Wrong"

"Look. Look here!"

"You sound like a *Dick and Jane Reader*." Len laughed at Chet.

Chet ignored Len's comment as he pointed to the cover of a weekly magazine showing a boy on scales. "This article's talking about obese kids. Me and my brothers weren't obese." He shook his head in disbelief. Three senior-citizen buddies, each a former paperboy, Chet, Len and Joe, sat in a coffee shop recalling childhood.

"I delivered papers morning and afternoon," said Len. "After the early run, I served as altar boy for St. Paul's at 6:00 a.m. mass, raced home, grabbed a hunk of bread lathered with lard and walked a mile to school, sandwiched in chores, mowed lawns, shoveled snow, always outdoors and healthy." He punctuated his words, "My stamina and strength rose to stellar."

Chet cut in, "Yeah, walking, pulling a wagon or sled full of heavy papers, my brothers and I stayed slim. Throwing tight tubes of newspapers, gosh, my legs and arms grew as muscular as that ancient, ahh, Greek statue. You know, David. "

"Huh?" Joe looked puzzled. "Oh, Michelangelo's *David*. Wrong century."

"Yeah. Well, there's something wrong with this century if kids are fat. How can they be overweight?" Chet slapped the article on the table.

Joe said, "I had a weight problem."

The guys glanced at Joe's thin wrist holding up a cup of coffee, his watch band sliding loosely on his arm. "No way! You were never heavy," Len said.

Joe smiled, "Wrong. The newspaper bag over my shoulder was heavy."

# CHAPTER 8
## THANK GOD, ONLY 24 HOURS

A single daily paper route, whether walked or biked, trimmed youngsters. For kids with a morning and an evening job, including a hefty Sunday edition, their torso and time registered lean. Furthermore, a route extending seven, ten, twelve miles involved enough distance for two runs. In some situations, boys handled two and three separate routes each day, Sundays too.

### Above Bartlesville

On dusty roads near Bartlesville, Russ pedaled his bicycle 10 miles delivering the morning *Tulsa World,* then repeated the process for evening customers who subscribed to the *Tulsa Tribune.* Folks also requested the local *Examiner-Enterprise.* At times he rode his horse, which trotted along the route just fine. It was the simple bicycle on the unpaved Oklahoma roads in 1936 that required greater effort from 11-year-old Russ Tobey.

Bartlesville is located south of Kansas---tornado country---as immortalized by Dorothy in the *Wizard of Oz.* Frequent winds buffeted the region, swirling dust into his tired eyes. He also faced an additional challenge because of ruts on his daily round of 20 miles, half in the cool dawn and 10 more miles before dusk. The bumpy dirt surface stymied his speed, but he stayed with the task through six years of sweltering, triple-digit summer temperatures and winter freezes falling to minus double digits.

Why?

His lengthy paper routes provided the funds for lessons in flying a single engine airplane. Soaring high, a young paperboy surveyed all the dry terrain that he crisscrossed every morning and every evening, recognizing that as he flew he enjoyed the flight more than the rough bicycle pedaling. Though he "could only afford 10 or 15 minutes of instruction" at any one

113

time, he persisted, just like with his delivery job, so he would accumulate flight time to pilot an airplane.

# FUN

Like Russ, others repeated their rounds each morning and each afternoon. Dick Irvin, by age nine, joined his older brother, Bede, to deliver the *Des Moines Register* at 5:00 a.m. and the *Des Moines Tribune* in the evening. For the Sunday load they used a wagon or sled. With no bike, no horse, and no possibility of saving for a personal goal such as flying lessons, Dick walked his route for nine years from 1923 to 1932. Not coerced, not complaining but feeling "fortunate to have a route," he tromped through every kind of Iowa weather. Why? "To help. Only money coming into the house."

The major economic panics of 1920 and 1921 left millions unemployed as businesses failed, and extreme deflation took hold. Farmers on limited family-farms endured depressed prices through the 1920s, which affected all agriculture businesses and associated services. Across acres of heartland, past miles of fertile soil, the Great Depression spread early through America's bread basket. Like a suffocating sludge, it progressed to devastating severity.

For the Irvin family, the 1920s did not roar or feel jazzy. For nine years, through 468 weeks, Dick committed himself to morning and evening rounds to sustain the family finances. He delivered reliably and with a remarkable attitude of gratitude.

In a similar manner, Ed Norlin rose by 4:15 a.m. to drop papers for ones who subscribed to *The Daily Oklahoman*, and in the afternoon completed a route for *The Oklahoma City Times*. On the day of rest, while subscribers rested, he delivered *The Sunday Oklahoman* before dawn.

The canvas bag Ed bought in 1926 was stuffed as he began walking to 150 subscribers, all of whom he knew by name. Rather than being a chore, his route allowed him to do "less household chores," shifting indoor drudgery to outdoor activity. And like Dick Irvin, all of Ed's money, that he earned from the two-cent papers, was dutifully deposited with mother rather than put aside for a bicycle.

Asking Russ, Dick, Ed and others, "Did you have fun delivering papers?"

Without hesitation or reservation each replied with a resounding: "Yes."

# Not the Easy Way

Joe's accumulated newspaper selling experience landed him a coveted paperboy position for the *Columbia Daily Tribune*. Now, he could settle for an after-school route, only one round, just six days with no heavy Sunday edition. But operating under competition for the preferred job, Joe Forsee pushed ahead, continuing to rise at 4:30 a.m. all seven days to deliver three St. Louis morning papers. Then in the afternoon on school days, holidays, Saturdays, and summer days, he was punctual to start his delivery of the *Tribune* to 240 customers. Earning more income to help his mother, he shouldered a heavy load of newspapers and personal responsibilities.

## Got it Covered

By his sixth birthday, Dominic Soriano joined his older brothers to sell papers on the streets of Everett. The siblings, Pat, Mike, Joe and little Dominic---age six is small, he was smaller---hawked on corners and also delivered to homes in 1934. In the morning, customers received the *Seattle Post-Intelligencer,* and in the afternoon the *Seattle Times* or *Seattle Star*, along with the *Everett Daily Herald.* Dominic was available before breakfast, after school, Sunday, summer, autumn, winter, spring for eight years, during the desperate Depression. When he was old enough, he added serving as an altar boy to his schedule. In 1940 he turned 12, meeting the newspaper code age requirement instituted in 1934.

Just like David Bowles, Dominic figured coin values for his two-cent papers computing subtraction and addition before he learned to read. Still, with regular school attendance, he soon successfully read the headlines and the front-page local stories to sharpen his sales to folks crossing the busy intersection of Hewitt and Rockefeller streets. The Soriano brothers controlled three of the corners, the way other sets of brothers dominated their locations in the central business district of the working mill town.

At the Soriano home, scrumptious Italian dishes were passed to each member at the family's dinner table. The boys' one sturdy World bicycle was shared among the brothers. Mended clothes for the six boys and three girls were handed along. And when an older brother left his newspaper customers, a younger Soriano boy stepped up. In 1941, Mike was leaving for the United States Navy and this brought young John to the sales team, the fifth brother to join.

By age 8, John was hawking, running into business buildings, delivering a route. How could he walk to the *Everett Herald* office on Colby and Wall Street, deliver papers to homes grab bundles off the bus from Seattle, and stand on a downtown corner all at the same time?

Trust and honor. When bundles arrived, he left his cigar box on top of the stacks of newspapers. Folks left their money in the small sturdy box as they completed a self-serve purchase, a transaction similar to one customers used when they "left a dime on the porch for a Sunday paper." During week days, John returned to his corner an hour later, his cash register box setting just as he left it, though filled with more coins. Occasionally, when not working on the Great Northern Railroad line, his father stood by the box, or the older sister, Mary, assisted. Deliveries completed, John checked the papers he still needed to sell to enjoy a profitable day.

As street traffic subsided, if he had extra papers, he headed to the "for-sure sales spots: taverns." Relaxed patrons, who recognized the regular paperboy, "handed him money but didn't want the newspaper." Holding his supply, he "sold the papers over and over." Moving along Hewitt Avenue, he conducted a few transactions at a cigar store, and then in a quick, stealthy manner "snuck upstairs to a pool hall." Invariably, he was kicked out quite soon, but with pockets a bit heavier. Unconcerned, he returned to his "good sales spots over and over." Sales results, not rules or restrictions, guided his work.

So he ignored the rule that he was to be 12, or ignored it the best he could in his haste to sell. Then Mrs. Batten appeared. Dowdy in her stark gray suit, no make-up, she looked straight down at John with an accusatory stare. She strutted her important child-patrol position. Child labor legislation, city ordinances, the newspaper industry code, any and all of these were to be enforced, or so the agents insisted who were dedicated to restricting street children. She marched him into the police station.

The sergeant, familiar with the rumpled street seller and the stern authoritative adult, contacted John's father. No argument ensued between Mrs. Batten and Mr. Soriano. She cited reasons and rigid age regulations until their ears stung. Mr. Soriano nodded politely.

He had arrived from Italy at age 13, worked hard, and raised responsible American citizens with sons serving in World War II. Mr. Soriano attempted to interpret her arguments against a boy earning money. He said his few words of English, stood still, looked at his scuffed shoes. Proud of his children, he left with no intention of unnecessarily punishing John. Mr. Soriano cooperatively returned any time a request came from the police office.

As war production expanded, John raced to a shack near Everett's thriving water front. Keeping the large shifts of departing and arriving shipyard workers reading the latest news, he sold the *Seattle Times* and *Everett Daily Herald* at an even faster rate than in the taverns. And on the very fastest sales day, the street warden cast no interference. John's older brother, Mike, had been assigned to a navy ship serving in the Pacific that was blown up by the Japanese. Mike survived. John sold the local *Herald* to people who cared about their former paperboy and his little brother. Customers felt compassion for all of their hometown boys dutifully serving.

# Jeep is Free

Like Dominic and John who wanted to be outside making money, Jack Moore chose to be involved with a newspaper job. He hung with his neighbor, Ronny, who delivered to Jack's home, and Ron was glad to have an assistant serving as his "jeep."

In Oklahoma City a young boy who helped a guy with his assigned route, was labeled a "jeep." Thus Jack served for two years as a free assistant. Jeep and free linked together.

But out of bed by 4:00 a.m., to scurry to the paper station ready to provide service before 5:00 a.m., caused a problem. How does a young tyke rise in the dark? He wasn't about to lose an opportunity to be a free helper.

Slumbering under a warm cover on the quiet second floor sleeping porch, Jack received a wake-up pull. With a rope tied around his foot and the loose end hanging out the open window, a fellow paperboy came past, tugged the rope. Cooperation worked.

Two years as a jeep, quite experienced at the rowdy paper shack and speaking the jargon, Jack was assigned a large route. With no difficulty he "was chunking my wipes." Translation: delivering the Oklahoma paper wipes in the morning, evening and on Sundays, to customers whom, in short order, he knew. Mr. Gaylord, owner of all three of the city's papers, was potentially unaware that his company's essential delivery service meant "chunking his wipes."

# Some Changes

Twenty-seven years after his father walked the streets twice a day in Oklahoma City, Ed Norlin followed in his dad's steps. Sort of. In 1953 Ed covered his route using a bicycle to deliver 130 papers in the morning, then repeated the task in the afternoon for 95 customers during the week, and a whopping 200 on Sunday.

Ed, unlike his dad, didn't personally know every single customer since Oklahoma City had grown considerably in 20 years. Plus, prices rose from two cents a copy to five cents. In contrast to the father, the son "always had money in my pocket." Though not too much since he bought his school clothes, school lunches, and placed money in his savings account. When the younger Ed began the routes, his Grandmother Norlin opened a savings account for him with a $10 deposit. Thinking back to her son, who gave her all his earnings to help support the struggling family, she started a savings plan for her grandson. For father and son, some aspects of doing two routes didn't change: Oklahoma weather and a routine every 10 to 12 hours.

# Expanding Further

Having substituted throughout the summer in 1959 for another paperboy, Bill Ruth, Jr. acquired his own route by autumn. As his father had, nine-year-old Bill, Jr. rushed out every morning in every season. Nature's conditions were similar in Columbus, Ohio, to what his dad endured in Johnstown, Pennsylvania, in the 1930s. But young Bill was unconcerned with weather, because "you can adapt to any kind of weather and still be functional. It's not an obstacle to good service." Just like his dad, he moved through the early hours with energy and spirit, while also serving as an altar boy and attending school on time with fine results. However, being a product of the 1960s, in the ever expanding Ohio capital, Bill Jr. got to avoid chores like his dad's, such as hand-milking cows before school. Still, the youngster was no slacker.

Along with the morning *Columbus Citizen Journal*, he delivered the afternoon *Columbus Dispatch*. He sandwiched school, additional lawn jobs, and chores between his routes with 6:00 p.m. as the deadline. He served morning readers before 6:00 a.m. and evening customers before 6:00 p.m. For six years, his discipline held every day.

Performing as a paperboy was similar for father and son. Naturally, prices for papers increased with the increased size of the paper. The bicycle costs and optional features for bikes increased. However, the measurement of a mile remained the same. Whether the 1920s or into the 1970s, carriers who delivered twice a day and Sunday tallied miles of exercise.

# All the Way to L.A.

Paper routes of eight, ten or more miles existed either as a daily run or a combination of the morning and evening routines, and the miles rose to a significant total. Examining a common distance, a four-mile path, which is not exceptional, provides an example of a carrier completing both an a.m. and p.m. schedule. Even on a simple one-mile route, a 5,280 foot mile, unlike a "paperboy mile" it was accomplished by exercising feet and legs.

Covering four miles each morning and repeating the route in the evening (excluding Sunday evening) the distance comes to 52 miles for the week. Also, collecting was not welcome before sunrise and making change slowed the delivery so he added a trip to collect. This return is based on every subscriber paying with the first collection attempt---quite unlikely. But including only one collection effort, the 52 miles climbs to a minimum of 56 miles a week.

Week in and week out the 56 miles accumulates through 12 months to over 2,900 miles a year. Specifically, 2,912 miles for a basic four-mile route.

4 miles x's 7 days =28 miles for the mornings

P.M. adds 24 miles (no Sunday afternoon): 28 + 24= 52 miles a week

Collecting at a reasonable hour, adds 4 miles: 52 + 4=56 miles

Total for a year: 52 weeks x's 56 miles =2,912 miles, as a base.

The four-mile, year-long example would take a paperboy from Boston to the outskirts of Los Angeles. And there were days he felt like he crossed the country coast to coast, walked the monotonous plains, climbed the Rocky Mountains, struggled over deserts, and raced to a city. Boys wore out shoe leather, bicycle tires, canvas bags and yet the worn-out carriers kept moving.

These miles continued for three, four, six or more years on thin soles. Remember Russ Tobey circling 10 miles at dawn and 10 again at dusk near Bartlesville for six years?

10 miles x's 7 days = 70 miles for the morning runs.

P.M. adds 60 miles (no p.m. on Sunday). 70 + 60=130 miles a week.

Collecting at a reasonable hour, 10 more miles: 130 + 10 = 140 miles

Total for the year: 52 weeks x's 140 miles =7,280 miles.

The 7,280 miles x's 6 years = 43,680 miles, for a base.

Russ's distance equaled one and three quarters times around the equator. Riding his bike, he could have prepared for the Tour de France. No wonder Russ signed on for flight lessons.

Why state a base? The calculated route length excludes walking or biking up and down long driveways, climbing porch steps to place the paper inside the storm door, or running flights of stairs in an apartment building.

## Race to the Top

At age eleven, Raymond Bloomer rose every day, including Sunday, before 5:00 a.m. He had to reach his first customer who demanded that his *Cincinnati Enquirer* arrive by 5:00 a.m. The guy lived at the bottom of one of the steepest hills in Cincinnati. From there, Ray delivered papers for his other 199 customers, proceeding on foot up, down, up the high hills above the Ohio River. And his long route contained another challenge.

A student at Xavier College, in the heart of Cincinnati, wanted his newspaper dropped at the door, a common expectation. Ray entered the apartment building and sped up to the sixth floor, the stuffed canvas bag slapping his thigh. He could choose the stair run at the end with no load of papers, or race into the building complex in the order of the route and cover less distance by not back-tracking. Either way, he stayed slim, the same as other boys who daily climbed flights of stairs in apartments, office buildings, and hospitals.

The length of a route, augmented with side tributaries, captured part of the challenge. Merely strolling along a tree-shaded street splattered with sunshine, pausing to pick lilacs for mom, omits the remarkable rugged distances many paperboys covered. They make the energy bunny of advertisement fame seem like a slacker.

## More Miles

Of course school-age carriers, like other children, walked to school, often a mile. Back and forth adds two miles a day, in five days a ten-mile hike for each school week. During the 180 days of school, this accumulated to 360 miles along with playground time and sports. Some children walked more than a mile to school, with or without deep snow drifts like the kind in dad's lecture, "When I was your age... "

After the delivery truck driver awakened Don Hubbard from his nap next to a construction lantern, he delivered 150 newspapers to neighbors near Grand Coulee Dam before continuing one and a half miles to school. With three more miles added to his day, he needed an occasional nap whenever he had the chance.

Helpful carriers who completed an additional route because a friend or a brother suffered a broken leg, faced restriction with disease confinement, or left with their family on outings, accumulated a string of miles. Gary Rhinehart knew four routes and, while also covering his own, assisted the paperboys for their routes when needed. In the summer with three or four carriers enjoying vacations, Howard Wagner made his rounds to 200 customers by 5:00 a.m. and then filled his morning with these carriers' routes. Bill Miller could have enjoyed an idle summer, except for a couple of hours each afternoon serving 150 customers. But instead of free play, he added a morning route, Sunday too.

The carriers' exertion placed them on par with athletes training for the Olympics, though their attire didn't include shorts and sleeveless shirts. The youth on a school track team competed without a lopsided load over their shoulders, diminishing aerodynamic efficiency. And track teams ran on an oval track that was flat as news sheets, safely out of the way of cars, and pesky, barking dogs. Paperboys trained every day as long distance runners and discus throwers, even if the discus was a paper tube. Also the broad jump, with carriers clearing hedges like equestrian jumpers. Why he could be Superman. Actually Superboy, leaping over tall buildings, or at least a four-foot graveyard fence as Richard Ruth had accomplished in his heightened state of fear.

# Distance <u>with</u> Resistance

A carrier circling his route sometimes enjoyed nice balmy days. These delightful breaks were bracketed by the stiff resistance of gale-force winds, slap of stinging sleet, or misery of stifling heat. And rain added weight as his protective apparel absorbed water.

Bicycling on unpaved roads in Shoreline, a growing suburb north of Seattle, Harry Peifer pedaled along dirt streets in 1942, bumping into mud ruts from frequent Northwest rains. Then winter increased the hindrance. He parked his bike to plod through drifts pulling a sled loaded with *Seattle Times* papers. His wrists and back felt the drag from the snow. However, exertion kept him warm as his wet hat, wet jacket, wet trousers and shoes became heavy. Unconcerned for his comfort, he worried over how to keep news sheets dry and prevent customer complaints. Plus 144 soggy newspapers added weight and fatigue to his twelve-mile route. Twelve miles, seven days a week, 84 miles times 52 weeks, and...

# Weight

Good days occurred when mild dry weather coincided with Monday's lighter papers. But then Wednesday and Thursday brought increased thickness from full-page shopping ads for market specials on baked beans, pork chops, Del Monte peaches. Mother Nature should schedule snow or heavy rain only on Monday and Tuesday when papers weighed less.

The most taxing edition: Sunday. And of course the thickest paper drew the most subscribers, who enjoyed their day of rest with time to read all the sections. The cities' newspaper business specialized in the Sunday edition, shipping bundles to outlying towns. Carriers like Joe Forsee, who delivered the local *Columbia Tribune* that published only six days a week, acquired a Sunday route delivering the big city papers.

Filling their double canvas bag, the front bike basket, the rear bicycle rack, carriers balanced the thick papers and additional subscriptions until they were loaded like pack donkeys on the ancient streets of Morocco. Mike Rhodes learned the hard way that Sunday required a sturdier bike, when his rear wheel buckled. As editions grew and the weekend inserts increased, using a cart or the common Radio Flyer wagon became necessary. In deep, clumping snow, carriers attached a crate to a sled. Pulling it demanded greater exertion, tiring their arms and legs.

By the 1960s, distributing large stacks of Sunday papers often became a family affair, when sons exchanged a little red wagon for dad's station wagon. Hopping in and out of the car, handling the weight of only a couple of papers at a time, children appreciated the help and, more so, enjoyed their focused time with dad in the early morning once a week.

## The Ruler of Weight

Moving forward to another generation, in the current century parents drive grade school children to the school door. Youngsters tote a backpack, though the book bag does not remotely approach the weight of 70, 80 or 100 newspapers. Today's colorful school packs come with a booklet featuring health instructions that lists the benefit of balanced double padded straps. Also, warning: *Pack NOT to exceed 15 pounds for a child's weight of 100 pounds.* This rule is to manage less weight bearing down on a child's frame.

For a paperboy in the golden era of delivering, his full 30-pound bag slung across one shoulder pulled his back down. It altered more than the gait. Whew, the *Lord's day of rest* offered the greatest challenge as Sunday bundles reached 45 pounds or more.

On his twelfth birthday, Russell Baker's present, acquired by his mother's efforts, was a city paper route. On the streets of Baltimore, in the depths of the Depression, he was to finish the Sunday delivery before dawn. Striding forth in the dark, Russell balanced "forty pounds of the [*Sunday American*] newspapers on my hip..." With forty pounds on his hip, he walked "easily." The "easily" is a question.

By the mid 1950s the weight of thicker newspapers was beyond the weight that Russell had "easily" managed. Henry Petroski handled two bundles each with 50 papers bound tightly in wire. Rather than walk, his "bike helped immensely." It helped, except when the bike fell over, spilling the newspapers out of the large front basket. Just the same, the basket was a major asset, "since a day's papers could weigh as much as 50 pounds."

The newspaper loads "weighed a ton." Okay, a paperboy ton, but that double bag over the head pulled on the front and back, if he remembered to balance the bags over his torso. Kids requested the distribution driver drop bundles of papers along the route. Others dropped their several bundles every few blocks before starting the full distance to deliver. Fortunately, weight steadily decreased as the route unfolded street after street, mile after mile.

Considering distance, resistance, repeated routes, and bundle weight, another impacting factor was the age of the child. Though age is an ineffective indicator for physical capability, since boys' growth spurts vary. Some do not reach full development until their eighteenth birthday, when paperboys usually advanced to other endeavors beyond routes.

By age 10, boys became a reliable substitute, or better, a full-time carrier regardless of the age-12 code regulation. Reviewing a pediatric book, *The Child in Health and Disease,* published in 1948 (in the midst of the paperboys' era) and featuring clinical tables listing normal measurements, the height for a 10-year-old boy ranged between 5l and 55 inches. He would be 15 before he reached five feet or 60 inches. In weight, a 10-year-old ranged between 57 and 71 pounds. The 6-year-olds, like David, John, Dominic, who joined older brothers to hawk and manage a route, extended just past three and a half feet and weighed a mere 39 to 48 pounds.

Boys wanted their height and weight to expand, particularly by middle school when girls stretched taller. And especially if others taunted the little guy. But to grow, young bodies must have sustenance and sleep.

## Not snow, nor sleet, nor sleep...

If a paperboy went to bed by 7:00 p.m., not too difficult in the wintry school months, and rose at 4:00 a.m., he captured nine hours of uninterrupted sleep. However, the ten hours recommended by pediatricians for children in their formative years, dictated a challenging bedtime of 6:00 p.m. Unlikely.

Finishing his morning route no later than 6:00 a.m., the time required by the newspaper company and the time expected by the customers, a paperboy could potentially catch 30 or 40 minutes of sleep during school weeks. He managed a bit more in the other 185 days of the year, if the household was quiet.

As newspaper carriers moved through monotonous routes, they daydreamed along the way. Or because of dark mornings, more like a night dream. It was even possible to sleep walk, though not if one wanted to successfully porch a paper. Sleep bicycling was impossible.

By 5:00 a.m. Walter Johnson was well underway with his six-mile bike route in the foothills of the Cascade Mountains. Learning to be reliable as a berry-picker, he expanded from his seasonal first job into a year-round position, with solid people rather than squishy fruit. Walter "knew every one of his customers" in the small Northwest town of Mount Vernon, and knew which paper or papers they requested. The *Seattle P.I., Seattle Times*, and *Seattle Star* were shipped north into Skagit County. And the county seat published the local *Mount Vernon Argus.*

Besides knowing his customers, and remembering which paper they requested, he knew the streets. That certainly helped when mandatory blackouts began. "Just a small slit of light was permitted from flash lights and headlights. Nothing from homes. No street lights of any kind." Such darkness further impacted a sleepy state. Then daylight savings time was inaugurated. His alarm clock, set for the savings time, rang at 4:30 a.m., which was the standard 3:30 a.m. More sleep lost until the body's time clock adjusted. Finagling enough sleep was a struggle for Walter. No surprise, "I fell asleep more than once in my school class room. I noticed other morning carriers did the same."

## 24 hours. Enough

Rising at 3:00 a.m. to have the paper shack open on time, Paul McManus, as the station manager, made sure the counts for the *Seattle P.I.* were correct and all his friends were underway. Then he bicycled his own route. Finished, he settled into school on time. With school completed, he delivered his *Seattle Times* route in the late afternoon. His district managers were oblivious to the fact that he carried for competing papers. They just knew he was reliable.

If a morning delivery, and school, followed by an afternoon route didn't interrupt or eliminate free fun-time, dogs disturbed his routine. Paul was under time constraints, and "some dogs were kind of a pain." To avoid being attacked by Max, a large German shepherd that frequently threatened him, Paul sharply stated, "Max, NO." The trained shepherd obeyed his explicit command. Less successful were his repeated orders to a small cocker spaniel. The yipping, snapping dog eventually bit Paul's leg. In pain, he kept delivering.

"It was a seven-days-a-week job, a long day at times." Very long for a young boy.

Paul, Walter, and other youngsters, who delivered every morning and evening, never wished for more than 24 hours a day. Their daily childhood schedule was long enough.

## Additional Exertion

Living near the South Dakota border in Pipestone, Minnesota, a small town of about 5,200, Paul Fellows helped connect his neighbors to the world through the *Minneapolis Tribune* in the morning or the *Minneapolis Star* in the afternoon. Living in the north country, "No matter the weather, I was out on my route." And he obeyed his agent's orders: "Never toss the paper in the yard!" Paul made the rule a strict habit because for weeks lawns were buried in snow. Regardless of conditions, rather than porching the paper, he placed it inside the storm door. A captious customer often waited by the door watching for him, and if the man felt his paperboy was "late, he complained." The man was the authority on late.

Paul tried his best to avoid justified or unjustified complaints. But learning control required a few lessons, ones he instituted quickly. For example, the paper bundles were bound in wire. One day, running behind schedule, he snapped the wire. Immediately the North Wind caught him, and "caught the papers before I could put them in my bag and just peeled away page after page. I lost quite a few papers." No additional lesson needed: "put the bundle in my bag before removing the wire," or trouble with tardiness extended into later.

With streets covered by hard-packed, icy snow, and some days encumbered by a larger edition, the route often mandated the use of a sled. Pulling the sled meant he walked in the street, because the sidewalks in most places were cleared and sled runners didn't work on bare walks. Paul tried his bicycle, but a bike on icy spots, well, invariably accidents resulted. He fell "more than once when the bike skidded on ice," causing the pain of a complaint for a late delivery. Studying his situation, he "tried wrapping thin rope around the bike tires and through the rims, like snow chains on cars, but the ride was bumpy." Bumps or blame? He went with bumps, but lessened them by "going through loose snow."

Other carriers, like Paul, who struggled in snow drifts that shackled their boots and legs and slowed them down, found the extra exertion made them hungrier. Pedaling over a gravel road or through snow on a bike loaded with papers, the sustained effort built muscle in legs, built stamina, and built an appetite. Furthermore, newspaper delivery was not the singular energy expender. Boys mowed lawns, shoveled snow and coal, participated in sports, outran bullies, all creating maximum expenditure in the formative years. Perpetual motion meant perpetual hunger.

## Sustenance

Mothers know growing boys frequently ask for food. Add the physical effort of carrying papers and paperboys were famished. When the customers' strawberries ripened, cut through the patch. When apples ripened, pick a few. Cherry trees, pear, peach, heck, boys enjoyed all of them. A hunk of bread slathered with thick, white lard was insufficient, particularly for dual routes. Delivering in the early morning before breakfast, he was always hungry. Delivering after school before supper, his hunger was further stimulated by spreading kitchen aromas: onions, fish, and potatoes frying, spicy Italian sausage bubbling in pasta sauce, goulash simmering, baked pies cooling. The names on his collection ring: Schneider, Polanski, Zuretskei, Lugiano, Mickelonovich, Schwartz, Murphy brought the foreign names to life through the savory smells.

Along with redolent kitchens, he passed aromatic cafes with coins burning in his pocket. At a bakery on Main Street, a carrier indulged in warm sweetened dough. Why be a stern Puritan and deny himself an array of delights? Every day he filled the coal bucket, the milk cans, the dog's dish. To diminish his gurgling growls, a paperboy filled his stomach.

Dr. Anna Reed writing her conclusions on Newsboy Service in Seattle in 1915, quoted a newsey, "Whether we have anything to eat or not depends on what I sell." When grade-schoolers, David and Carl

Bowles, sold papers in Bellingham in 1917, they "took the money home to Mama to help her buy groceries." But early Sunday morning, while the town slumbered, the daylight not yet cresting on the Cascade Mountains, David and Carl finished on Holly Street, where Mr. W. H. Giles served them "breakfast at Giles Cafe. I ate my first waffles there." Food was a priority. The funds from selling newspapers bought satisfaction and sustenance.

The same held true in the 1920s. Dick Irvin explained his morning and afternoon Des Moines routes provided "the only money coming into the house" to buy essential food. Such situations prevailed in the long, economically depressed 1930s.

In Hazleton, Pennsylvania, John James contributed his earnings to his mother, almost every penny earned through the 4/5's of a cent on a two-cent newspaper. However, John and his furry companion, Bepo, sometimes "stopped at the Berlitz's Bakery for a goody." In the early dawn, the wafting sweet aroma coating the air along Third Street, drew him in the door, especially when he was able to hawk extra copies there. His bowl of oatmeal that mama served at 4:30 a.m. pumped energy into his blood for the three-mile walk into the newspaper company. Now he replenished his stomach and Bepo's tummy too.

In 1932 Sam Smyth contributed half his earnings to his family, and then he invigorated his enthusiasm for the route with a treat. "Occasionally when I had an extra paper, I was able to sell it for three cents to the watchman at Pacific Car and Foundry. Though it might have affected my appetite for supper, I quickly exchanged the money for caramels at Mrs. Peterson's lunch counter." Chewing gooey caramels, which stimulated saliva and blended into sweet buttery juices, young Sam could spit a stream as colorful as the slurpy tobacco shot that had struck him. But why spit out anything so tasty? Common sense prevailed. He ate them.

Ray Bloomer captured an opportunity to reward himself in the long Depression years. Delivering 200 morning papers up and down steep hills in Cincinnati, he needed energy, which he replenished with items from the Heineken Bakery. At his favorite spot, he bought three rolls for a nickel. Ohhh, so good.

Boys enjoyed choices on a regular basis. Dodging the stiff Mrs. Batten, avoiding the police station in Everett, John Soriano frequented his preferable spot: the Elgin Cafe on Hewitt Avenue. His brother Dominic, after finishing deliveries, entered the Top Hat Cafe on Colby Avenue and bought a hamburger for a nickel. The sons savored the morsels, but not more than mama's authentic Italian cooking.

The pleasant environs of Missouri turned hot and humid in the summer months. Delivering 175 *Columbia Tribune* papers, James Ausmus felt the steamy afternoon heat. Crossing the intersection of Broadway and West Boulevard, he rode his bike to Sunset Market, a mom and pop grocery store. "Practically every day I would make a pit stop there to get a Grapette or Royal Crown cola," a nice habit, even when temperatures weren't soaring.

Why, a guy liked a cold drink right on the porch step. With milk delivered to the customer's door, a quick advantage appeared: alluring chocolate milk. Unless, the empty glass bottle sat among full milk bottles, and if the customer wondered why the chocolate milk wasn't included, and if the delightful drink was enjoyed again, and again, and, oh shucks.

## A Chocolate a Day Keeps...

Ron Haringa was devilish, or a bit more, yet he was "hesitant to be too bad." He was raised by parents enforcing their strict Dutch heritage, who quickly put a stop to anything naughty. Besides, Ron's time for mischievous behavior was curtailed by the demands of delivering 115 *Seattle Times* papers, and then a second route with 150 customers pressed on him by the district manager. Delivering 265 papers, he grew hungry. So, with money in his pocket, he scooted into the candy store "every night and bought chocolate." Not wanting to upset his mother, he ate the sweet delight before going home for supper.

The chocolate refilled his energy gage, enabling Ron to make a regular bicycle trip up Holman Road with his filled canvas bag. Holman was a long hill used for soap box derby races. Healthy, strong, though still growing, he competed with himself to race up the hill.

## So Convenient

Doug Larson always arrived for his papers no matter the weather in Lincoln, Nebraska. At the pick-up spot, he folded the 90 *Lincoln Journal* papers, a monotonous time, like the hours of school he just finished. His route had to be completed before supper. Since bundles were dropped at a gasoline station and because his mother, like Ron's, scolded him for consuming sweets, he used his profits "buying a bottle of pop at the gas station every day," and drank all the cola without perturbing mother.

## So Conscientious

Purchasing more than treats, if the bread winner died or was out of work with a union strike, the son's paper route fed the family. For 10 months, Gerald Horna provided necessities while his dad struggled through a long Westinghouse union strike. "My father worked in the Steam Turbine Division in Lester, Pennsylvania, and in 1955 the union struck for 299 days. My newspaper route was the sole support of the family during the strike." Building his route, over five years, from 32 to nearly 400 subscribers in an expanding suburb, he managed the duty for the growing family, which included four younger, hungry brothers eating full meals.

## First Treat of the Day

Tasty sources tempted a morning carrier, craving food in the quiet hour of predawn. A youngster sniffed a bakery a mile away (a paperboy mile) in the clear air. In a community, full of ethnic bakeries, and with his stomach growling, when shops opened they offered opportunities to buy day old and broken pieces of pastry, or even better, treats straight from the oven.

As sure as the sun would rise to the east of Lewiston, Idaho, the baker could count on three paperboys appearing at his counter before dawn for their daily purchase of his warm Butterhorns. Lee Desilet and his best pals, Mike and Ted, were on the street year-round by 4:00 a.m. to deliver their *Lewiston Morning Tribune*. Only first they fished a nickel from their pockets and fed their stomachs, with the soft sweet dough warming their hearts. Eating the Butterhorns provided a respite from the growing war worries and fears as the nation faced the 1940s.

## Lines of Customers

For decades the Denver donut shops were an extra special place for *Rocky Mountain News* boys. They ate more donuts than darting swallows devour mosquitoes. In the 1930s Dugg Holmes, finishing his long rural route, made the donut shop at 10th and Ogden Street his last stop. In the '50s David Stonington and his buddy frequented their tempting spot, even enjoyed occasional free donuts from the baker. For sixteen years, 1959 to 1975, the four Rudy brothers stopped at Dutch Boy Donuts located at Niagara and Colfax Street. "This was a unique donut shop, one of a kind. People came from all over east Denver, " purchasing quantities of the fresh treats. "You could always find a policeman there."

The oldest brother, Jim, enjoyed his on weekends, particularly on pleasant summer days. "Donuts were eight cents, and 50 cents a dozen." But Jim said he "couldn't frequent it too often on a paperboy's wages."

Other paperboys in various locales ate cinnamon rolls or hot cross buns warm from the oven. But none became a model for the pudgy Pillsbury doughboy. Boys added revenue at Mom & Pop stores buying penny licorice sticks, nickel Hershey bars, packs of Wrigley chewing gum. And, packs of cigarettes off racks displaying a selection of tobacco products.

The attributes of daily outdoor exercise and sunshine produced an increase in vitamin D. These and many nutritional benefits became modified, and severely reduced, by a paperboy's daily doses of cigarettes. Seeing adults, movie heroes, ministers, teachers, coaches, the United States president, dad, granddad, and other paperboys smoking the cool status symbols, carriers often began the habit by age 13. For the braggart who wanted to puff out his chest, he puffed smoke in the face of kids and dared them to join him. With coins in his pocket, he bought cigarette packets as easily as chocolates and colas.

The nauseous act made a child's eyes smart, curbed his appetite, and caused a cough unlike the usual cold. But a stuffy cold didn't stain the teeth, tongue and fingers, coat the lungs in nicotine, nor make the clothes, hair, and canvas bag smell smoky. Regardless of committing to the habit, he'd smell like a burning cigarette since there was incessant smoking in restaurants, taverns, stores, elevators, dentists' and doctors' offices.

Furthermore, his appetizer sweets seemed moderate alongside home cooking, which offered bread spread with lard, pie crusts flaky from lard, meals lathered in butter. Breakfast brought a calorie bonanza as he poured whole cream off the top of the milk bottle onto cereal and accompanied it with fried bacon. From the bacon fat, a child enjoyed fried potatoes, fried bread, fried eggs. He burned the calories and cholesterol hurrying along the pavement.

Overall, his hunger pains inflicted less discomfort than bodily aches and pains, which periodically annoyed or turned worse for a paperboy. Then no amount of chocolate, donuts, or colas offered any satisfying relief. Cigarettes certainly failed to help.

# CHAPTER 9
## ACHES, AILMENTS

Though active and agile, young paperboys were plagued with a variety of pains. Headaches in the severe summer heat, stomach aches from too many plums plucked from a customer's tree that caused diarrhea aggravation and inconvenience, earaches in the winter, even aches in the spring: heartaches brought on by puppy love. Too many chocolates and caramels guaranteed toothaches. Blisters and bites turned to irritated, sore infections. As paperboys entered adolescence, acne appeared. Sadly, children endured the stigma of pimples, even scars.

Paperboys delivered because a route was a responsibility with a capital R. Just as the other carriers, Paul Meyer delivered even when he didn't feel like it. "There were some pretty tough days when I was sick yet managed to finish my route," for 200 customers.

No star-gazing to wish away an ailment. No whimper or whine if it didn't go away. When symptoms became serious and expanded to severe, a boy's pain required slowing down or finding a substitute, but until then, he struggled down the street.

### From Aches to Bites

On a warm, sunny, June day, with roses blooming, what could be nicer than a stiff breeze? A swift wind to drive away mosquitoes, especially the huge ones like the Alaskan variety that Barry Dunphy's brother swallowed. Though wind caused havoc with loose newssheets, at times a paperboy actually wanted the wind to start blowing so he could quit swatting mosquitoes, or stop squashing them on his forehead as his bike flew into a swarm.

Why couldn't all bugs be like lady bugs and lightning bugs---fun and tickly? Yet, it wasn't only buzzing in the ear that caused a pain. There was a bite that lasted, returning winter after winter, one that couldn't be smashed or blown off. It silently bit ears, noses, cheeks, fingers, toes, and was actually quite dangerous.

## Avoid Frostbite

As Jim Stingl worked through three and four feet of snow blanketing Milwaukee, handling 115 papers with steady plodding helped warm him. Snow insulates bushes and house foundations; however, it is poor insulation for fingers and feet. "Outside in sub-zero weather" and temperature further "lowered with dangerous wind chill," Jim tried to move fast on snow and ice while layers of clothes protected him from the chill, though the added girth hindered swift delivery. He managed through the severest season, and "never got frostbite."

Tom Rockne faced horrific conditions in Bismarck, North Dakota. The bike was no help. A sled worked okay, at times, but what did not work well: numb fingers, especially when collecting. "My fingers would get cold and my mind foggy" to the point he figured he "gave back the wrong change." Uncertain about the money and potentially suffering from "frost bite on my fingers and toes," Tom kept moving, using good Boy Scout techniques to protect himself.

The same with Bill Gamel in Anchorage. His Boy Scout wisdom and the knowledge gained from hunting in the wilds of Alaska taught him to be sensible and measure his progress over a four-mile route. The exertion from walking and carrying loaded bags for 100 customers usually warmed him, until the extreme struck. Freezing is 32° F. When the temperature dropped to minus, - 30° F., a loss of over sixty degrees, his paper delivery slowed. Customers, who were settled inside waiting for the paper, coaxed him inside to warm himself and his mukluks by an oil stove. The boots smelled but that didn't matter as warmed toes and numb fingers revived.

Fairbanks surpassed Anchorage with low temperatures. In the long, dark, Alaska winter, Kent Sturgis bundled into a parka with the hood extending beyond his face, its long sides holding his warm breathes in closer. The banner on the *Fairbanks Daily News-Miner* explained his cold route: "America's Farthest North Daily Newspaper." The town was far enough north it registered -50° F., which is terribly dangerous for exposed skin. His speed through apartment complexes made the route tolerable. However, back outside his occasional falls on ice, when he smacked a surface as hard as concrete, were painful. Yet, he rushed because functioning without thick, clumsy gloves meant he needed to finish fast.

Paper carriers in the north were conditioned to tolerate harsh winters and owned clothes necessary for protection. For ones who lived in milder climates---mild compared to Fairbanks---an onslaught of extreme wintry weather often caught them by surprise.

Richard Reed began his five mile *Spokane Review* route at 4:00 a.m. When the thermometer hovered at minus, -15° F., he tugged on two pairs of long underwear and then two pairs of blue jeans, the extra layers keeping him moderately warm. He walked as fast as possible, but with his outer blue jeans frozen, the icy, stiff pant legs reduced swift speed and led to another challenge: finishing before the school bell.

Alaska, Idaho, Wisconsin, all the northern states are recognized for cold winters. But Kentucky is viewed as a southern state, and certainly the southern hospitality shines through. However, when a severe winter struck, the outdoors was not hospitable to Grant Wise, who delivered both a morning and an evening edition. With the temperature hovering "around 20° below zero and snow on the ground, my bicycle wheels actually froze where they wouldn't roll. I had to scoot it along." The bike held the papers while Grant slowly moved through his route on the hills in Hodgenville. Hours in cold air, under a fifty-two degree drop below the freezing index of 32° F. (32°F. down to -20°F.) "By the time I was finished I had frostbite to my feet, hands and ears. My eyebrows were frozen and when I wiped my hand across them they actually broke off." Nevertheless, Grant delivered his papers starting from the post office at 3:15 a.m. He returned in the afternoon for his next load.

## Daily Dose of Diseases

No question, delivering papers was a physical job which engaged the whole body: shoulders, arms, hands, legs, feet. Well, maybe the eyes didn't always engage. Uncoordinated eyes and hands trying for a fast throw landed the paper in the bushes, on the porch roof, or through a window. The boy committed to the task must be physically fit to go the mile, and then another mile and another. Along with the distance and physical rigors of delivery in mud, snow, up flights of steps, and hauling the heavy bag, a young ~~Superman~~, no a Superboy, completed the route every day for months and months during times rampant with severe health issues.

In the core of the American Century, in the golden age of youth dominating the newspaper delivery system, their time of managing routes paralleled the period when serious illnesses prevailed in youngsters. Childhood. Diseases. The words go together like boy and bike. Boys' infectious smiles and laughter occurred alongside a myriad of infectious diseases.

People thought of these maladies as the "usual run of things." When asking former paperboys if they were ever ill, they replied with, "all the normal childhood diseases" or "you know, the usual childhood diseases." The common cold and epidemics of chicken pox, measles, and mumps spread through neighborhoods and school as though someone was sharing candy-coated germs.

The "usual" lice did not cause a calamity; ringworm wasn't a catastrophe; a cold wasn't considered a crisis. Grandmas, aunts and cousins helped mom administer folk remedies. On a sting, she applied a dose of apple cider vinegar, a baking soda paste, a blob of toothpaste. A raw fresh onion rubbed on a bite reduced scratching that occurred from dirty fingernails. Chicken soup, hot ginger tea, grape juice, any of these certainly eased a cold. His stomach growing upset from a long spell of hiccups, and so many folks with so many remedies, the child became motivated to escape from treatments.

In a home with seven, nine, ten children, or only four or five young ones, they regularly shared a bed, shared a bath, a bowl, even a toothbrush. Mom swept, mopped, scrubbed, and scoured, while Mother Earth continued to disburse dirt, grime, germs on, and over everything, always with the assistance of little hands and mouths.

For mother, when the first case of measles or chicken pox broke out, she accepted that three or four of her brood would soon be speckled. She did not scoff at the fevers but placed her youngsters in bed and added nursing to her long list of daily chores.

Furthermore, the natural way of sharing reached outside the residence. September ushered children back to school packing more germs per inch in compact, warm classrooms. Coughing, sneezing, and swiping the nose along shirt sleeves occurred as regularly as chattering. Grade-schoolers exchanged a partially eaten sandwich, a cookie with a bite removed, whatever part of lunch was worth bargaining away. The school nurse, if the school employed a nurse, tried to identify classmates with scabies, impetigo, pink eye, or measles. But the visible symptoms of red-peppered skin or scratchy eruptions meant the contagion period had already begun inoculating additional roustabouts. Diseases spread from home, to school, to the paper station.

The germs advanced in the small paper shack through boys' sniffles, sneezes, and coughs. To pass time as they waited for their bundles, boys spit on their glass marble shooter. They spit for luck; spit for emphasis. They also shared a half-eaten candy bar, part of a cola, or the last partially smoked cigarette.

On a daily basis, dirt attached to small bodies like burrs. Pulling a wagon of trash cans to the dump, followed by exploring thrown away treasures, a boy found more than germs. And items from the dump interested him more than his chores of carrying the cinders out, scooping the chicken coop, spreading old manure, weeding the garden after it rained, digging soil for potatoes, carrots, turnips, slopping pigs wallowing in mud. When he wasn't restricted with chores, a boy wrestled a bully on the ground, rode through puddles, the bigger the filthy puddles the better. His scruffy, worn, canvas bag showed dark, scattered splotches.

Saturday meant a bath in shared water. Working on the farm, helping with the chicken coop and delivering papers in the 1930s, the Ruth brothers bathed regularly on Saturday. Mother heated water on the kitchen coal stove and then three boys washed in a tub.

Kids ingested dirt with dirty hands, like when children picked berries off dusty vines and popped the fruit in their mouth. All dirt forms are not dangerous, anymore than all bugs are bad, although it was bad--- especially for the bug---when a boy sailing down a long hill inhaled one.

A youngster existed in an unsterile world, spending hours outdoors growing healthier. Continually exposed to dirt and germs, children's immune systems strengthened. A child in a scrappy world, built his defense system as he fought off germs, dogs, and bullies.

Paperboys were unaffected by mysophobia. How could a boy be afraid of dirt and yet seek out mud puddles? His hands were vital for earning funds. And with his enjoyment of playing ball, throwing dirt paddies, and collecting empty bottles, he suffered no fear of filthy hands. Boys stopped in the woods without a sink, soap or hand sanitizer next to the mossy urinal, and then hurried on to throw the customers' newspapers. The grey-smeared printer's ink created no worry or any rush to scrub with lye soap.

Dirt was. Sharing was. And, yep, lice, a cold, or ringworm was. Maybe colds were common because carriers considered them common, or as Dale Wirsing said, "a condition of life." By accepting sickness and infection as inevitable, prevention was seldom a priority. As Ed Hahn, the oldest of seven children, stated "Oh yeah, I had all the normal childhood diseases, usual run of things. Better to have mumps as a boy. Get it over with."

But normal and disease are not synonymous. Normal OR disease. Illnesses of a week, or maybe less but still bearing the possibility of complications, deserved attention.

However, a child saw the cigarette dangling on adult lips, heard dentures clicking, smelled the smoky cigar, felt the spittle of chewing tobacco. Alongside the unhealthy adult habits, youngsters scratched their poison ivy, rubbed impetigo, openly sneezed and coughed readily spreading germs. The same with the highly contagious conjunctivitis or pink eye.

Doug Coleburn's conjunctivitis certainly itched as he trotted along Virginia dirt roads in the summer heat, swiping sweat off his face. In Washington, Paul West's cough became more than irritating. The incessant hacking added fatigue to his early morning run. But if he was ten minutes late, a customer reported him. He did not deserve the complaint fine. However, rushing in cold morning air made his whooping cough grow worse.

There were many illnesses and hurts that impacted active paperboys.

A. Aches, acne, ailments, allergies, asthma, appendicitis, accidents to start the A's

B. Blisters, bruises, breaks, burns, bug bites, bat bites, bites of spiders, scorpions, dogs

C. Canker sores, carbuncles, cuts, chicken pox

The list ran on to measles, mumps, meningitis, pneumonia, polio, on through to rheumatic fever, small pox, strep throat, scarlet fever, typhoid fever, typhus, tetanus, whooping cough. How did a child ever rise from bed, survive and grow?

Ailments and accidents pulled a carrier off track but rarely stopped him. Deliver when hungry, deliver when sleepy. Mike Hall reliably delivered the *Spokane Daily Chronicle*. On one occasion, he was "so sick" his Mother drove him through the route as he made the effort to climb steps to the customer's door. "Never missed doing the route. That would be irresponsible." Carriers delivered whether they felt like it or not, unless...

## Stopped

Deadly diseases stopped young carriers. Prohibited by parents, doctors, the public health authorities, a paperboy had no choice but to remain in his home. The only time John James missed selling his morning papers was because his brother, Vallent, lay still with scarlet fever. Vallent's throat burned as though a fire ignited his tonsils making it too painful to talk or argue with his older brothers, William, Robert and John. Public health authorities quarantined the boys in their house for 15 days. And that was the only time John missed any school days.

Doug Wilkerson declared the best part of his paper route: "parents couldn't ground me anymore." But he was grounded, the same as Vallent, by microscopic bacteria that made him too sick to care. As Doug's strep throat advanced, his feverish face looked like he was badly sunburned. The strep throat led to the rough rash of scarlet fever, caused by streptococcus bacteria. This caused him to give up his *Seattle Times* route for six months. The restriction was also important for other paperboys, since strep infections spread with open coughs and sneezes. After months, and finally strong again, Doug returned to the fun of the newspaper shack, the rain, the dog bites, and the steep hills to reach his 115 customers.

Dale Wirsing, glad to do his daily chore delivering the *Tacoma Times* because it meant doing less chores at home, was suddenly forced to spend time in the house. He developed more than his usual cold. Dale's pneumonia sent his mother and sister out to cover the route until he recovered and was sturdy enough to function in the Northwest weather.

By the last half of the 1940s, newspaper carriers were blessed, if being seriously ill ever has any blessings. In the close of World War II, antibiotics for treating injured or ill soldiers from the battlefield had produced miraculous results, creating a rush for very high production of penicillin. This now gave family doctors a reliable treatment for children's ear infections, strep throat, pneumonia, and infected injuries.

Despite the promise of penicillin, a plethora of health issues could take several paperboys down on any given day or week. Substitutes were essential. And then an influenza virus, undeterred by penicillin, invaded and gripped an entire community. That's when the supply of substitutes rapidly decreased, especially if they were also sick. In New York, in the mid-1950s, an Asian flu invasion struck the *Long Island Press*, leaving over 100 paperboys too weak to pedal a bike and too dizzy to venture away from home. The company printed requests for customers to be patient.

After eleven years as a paperboy followed by graduation from Seattle University and service in the army, Jack Gahan had advanced to managing the district managers for the *Seattle Times*. Though consistently reliable and accountable, one week he was sidelined after a trip from a newspaper carrier outing.

In 1961 hundreds of paperboys and their chaperones returned from Victoria, British Columbia, on the S.S. Princess Marguerite, a Canadian Pacific ship that carried passengers across the Strait of Juan de Fuca. During the four hour boat crossing, a full course turkey dinner was served. Hungry boys received large portions with all the traditional accompaniments. A fantastic trip, until: "more than 250 carriers and supervisors became severely ill." The circumstances and cases turned so serious, "the state health department intervened. They required stool samples from the patients." The food poisoning specimens had to be studied. Jack was "sick for three days." He sympathized with the boys' misery. They had no thought of delivering papers. The drop-off centers lacked necessary facilities when kids suffered with food poisoning. At least they were not contagious.

## Wrong Diagnosis. Right Response.

Any family developed concern when a robust child became too sick to talk. Nathan Everett arrived home after an incredible newspaper incentive trip to the Caribbean, which he won by effort. But he was not talking about the cruise. He felt too miserable.

Earlier, when his stomach cramps had increased, he went to the cruise ship's doctor. No, he was not seasick at the beginning of the travels. Yes, he ate the ship's rich food but not more so at the completion of the trip than during the earlier days. Talking to Nathan, the doctor figured that his patient's indulgence in the plentiful cruise food had resulted in another one of those prevalent -itises. People have bronchitis, laryngitis, tonsillitis. Not a major concern. "The ship's doctor diagnosed gastritis and gave me an antacid." The trip ended and the doctor was hastily finished with treating patients.

Back home, knowing their son was not a complainer, the parents recognized that his condition was urgent. The stomach "pain turned really intense." The hospital surgeon removed his appendix before morning. Fortunately, the cruise had not lasted longer. But until he recovered, he still needed his substitute.

## Gripped with Fear

Parents did respond to a child's severe affliction. They tried care when diphtheria, tuberculosis, or rheumatic fever was diagnosed in the neighborhood, and even for any illness when effective preventative measures hardly existed. People made an effort to be healthy. Their greatest concern came in the steamy, stagnant dog days of summer. Worry grew to serious fear, increasing from one decade into the next, when good ol' summer days held ghastly days.

At midpoint in the twentieth century, Americans' spirit soared. The optimism of more than 152,000,000 citizens prevailed after the intense struggles of the 1930s and 1940s. An explosion of consumer goods became available for weekly shopping on Main Street. The baby boom was giving birth to bedroom communities as cities pushed into the suburbs, but the long strip malls had not yet disrupted chats in the family-owned bakery, meat store, or vegetable stand. People whistled and sang the music of *Guys and Dolls*, cuddled at the drive-in theater, listened to radio's Sunday afternoon baseball games broadcast from as far west as St. Louis. And a large new electric box began entering homes. By 1955, 40 million televisions were altering porch time. Life became good for Americans.

Except for the seasons when parents were gripped with fear, because no immunization existed for the disastrous disease: polio. No one ever scoffed at infantile paralysis or relegated it to a common status. Influenza, scarlet fever, whooping cough didn't leave the visible scars the way polio marred a body. Penicillin helped against many ailments, the smallpox immunization protected, but nothing defeated the polio virus. Unlike the world's deadly influenza pandemic of 1918, in which the strain did not repeat in the next decades, polio epidemics occurred in cycles. And each time, parents grew terrified as outbreaks increased. Through the first 60 years of the twentieth century, "nearly half a million people in the United States contracted polio." The 1916 summer polio outbreak flowed into states, but New York City suffered "the greatest number of cases."

As the newspaper capital of the nation, the horrific news spread to dailies in every location. The 27,000 cases instilled a lasting fear.

A 1921 polio survivor, with legs permanently paralyzed, Franklin Delano Roosevelt provided a proactive voice for fearful mothers when he led the founding of the March of Dimes in 1938. The Foundation provided education instructing parents on what to avoid during outbreaks. As important, families with polio victims received financial aid to ensure access to whatever care was available.

## Clean Coins

In his closing years of grade school, during the height of World War II, Jack Gahan had a residential *Tacoma News Tribune* route, along with delivering newspapers to the Pierce County Hospital. In surviving polio patients, the fever and muscle aches subsided, yet the disease's damage remained. Jack witnessed the twisted crippling effects to legs and spines, and the chest paralysis in hospitalized victims. In 1944, 19,000 cases across the U.S. frightened mothers and paralyzed children. Jack saw young ones struggling in heavy leg braces. He heard the steady hiss of iron lungs. Longer than a casket, the cold steel airtight chambers pushed and pulled the diaphragm of victims. The breathing body tanks lined polio wards, which he visited each day.

Those isolated in enormous iron lungs, with only their small heads outside the coffin-like cases, appreciated Jack's visits connecting them with the vibrant, outside world. He talked with confined patients unable to breath by themselves, surviving because a giant cage exerted the pressure necessary to move their chests. His maturity grew faster than his thin, lanky body. Before he walked out, he was required to wash the coins he carried from the polio ward.

## The Best in the Worst of Times

Rising early in order to have his bundles of *Seattle PI* papers delivered by 7:00 a.m., Roger Leed enjoyed the benefits of his special route, "a plum job, indoors. I went all through the hospital every day." And patients, eating breakfast in bed while they waited for a newspaper next to their food tray, looked forward to his visits. The 10-year-old didn't observe visiting hours at Seattle's large Harborview Hospital in 1949, or any of the usual restrictions placed on children's visits. He obeyed one restriction: "not to enter the surgery area." Other than that, Roger covered the nine floors, none with private rooms, walked into the maternity ward, and occasionally passed badly injured patients in the hallway. "Someone unconscious, hooked up to lots of tubes, was in a corridor because the wards were full." An overflow of the injured occupied every space.

The sterile world around his route lacked dogs, a neighborhood bakery, or space to race a bike down the street. Rather than pass by dark houses with shades closed, this morning carrier visited with his customers and the hospital personnel. Spending no previous time in a hospital, Roger, an only child, nevertheless responded well to the white-starch uniformed nurses and the orderlies. He learned patients' names. Without television, not even radios in the room, the people were happy to have a paper and paid "on the spot." If asleep or away from their bed, "they left a dime on the bedside table" not wanting to be skipped.

Holding the position from 1949 to 1953, the fifth grader began his route during the deadly 1949 polio epidemic; the worst yet, it bore 42,000 cases across the nation. He reliably continued his morning routine, walking into the polio ward, "filled with iron lungs. I had several steady customers there." With the close of the 1940s and the beginning of a new decade, it was hoped that severe polio outbreaks would recede into history the way influenza, diphtheria, and smallpox outbreaks diminished.

Reaching teenage status in 1952, as fear roiled through the nation in the greatest polio outbreak in American history, the 13-year-old still made his early, seven-day rounds in Harborview Hospital. That year hospitals received 57,000 cases that struck anywhere and anyone regardless of socioeconomic status. The number of cases did not reach the pandemic level of other disease epidemics, but the quick deaths or permanent specter of crippled legs and spines spread a profound fear. Roger's regular customers in the polio ward were "glad to see him."

## Continuing, Regardless

During that year's horrific epidemic, the National Foundation for Infantile Paralysis produced another effective poster. Titled, *1952 Polio Precautions,* it issued steps for people to follow. In a block of four separate scenes of children, the large design instructed people,
"When polio is around,
Don't mix with new groups; Don't get chilled; Don't get overtired;
But Do keep clean."
The concise poster was well presented. However, it wasn't possible for paperboys to obey the instructions. They became chilled, exhausted, and dirty. Boys didn't want to shun new kids. No polio poster hung in the paper shacks. The young carriers weren't special, exempt, nor immune, just busy completing rounds every day that for some included crowded polio wards.

As an epidemic spread, communities cancelled Fourth of July celebrations and church socials to eliminate crowds. Swimming pools, theaters and libraries were ordered closed by public health authorities in desperate attempts to stem the rising number of polio attacks. Doctors avoided performing the common tonsillectomies during summer polio scares. News of the advancing disease and the closure orders were distributed by more than 500,000 paper carriers, who continued as usual on their routes through the summer of 1952.

Seeing instructive polio posters at school, walking past the closed movie houses, regardless of where, paperboys kept delivering. In Cleveland, Ed Schroth dependably covered his multiple routes. Howard Wagner finished his eleventh year of dropping the Columbus *Citizen Journal* before 5:00 a.m. Gerald Horna, building a ten-mile route toward 400 customers, bicycled his rounds, and Ron Haringa biked two routes for 265 customers. Dale Wirsing, with or without another nasty cold, pedaled through Tacoma in the eighth year of his paper route. Paul West could be glad he agonized with only miserable, severe whooping cough and not polio.

## Hazardous Job

And in the small farming town of Marysville, Washington, customers in the 1950s received an evening paper from a new paperboy as he tossed the *Everett Daily Herald* to their porch. Nils Ladderud had periodically substituted for his paperboy-neighbor since the boys were "together a lot." So when the boy became ill, his mother asked Nils to take the country route, which he did, bicycling the 10 miles delivering 120 newspapers. He repeated it for several days and then the route became his in spite of his mother's fears. She was extremely worried because Nils "was using the paper bag, bicycle and even a rain coat" of the sick neighbor who had been, "diagnosed with polio." The boy's death and that of his older brother, who also died of polio, profoundly disturbed Nils' mother. Just the same, he went to the drop site to roll papers alongside other carriers, all of whom missed their young friend. Without his pal, Nils certainly felt an emptiness, but he continued delivering the route, even to homes with more cases.

Though polio severely invaded the community, "we didn't have any closure at school, sporting events, or the theater." Nils stuck to his routine. Required to finish by 5:00 p.m. he rushed along, except for one afternoon. A driver turned in front of his bicycle and he crashed into the side of the car, throwing him to the hard ground. From time to time, careless drivers and ferocious dogs made the job hazardous.

## Contribute

Like Nils helping his neighbor, hundreds of carriers in locations across the country wanted to help against horrific polio outbreaks. When the March of Dimes conducted their annual porch light drive, the paperboys pitched in to contribute to the fund. Giving was as American as apple pie and baseball. In addition, the contact with customers and the consistent collecting, along with organized sports teams formed in city stations and their love of competition, made the boys a natural for benefit ballgames to further support donations.

A 1947 polio benefit drive in Rockford, Illinois, had carrier teams playing a softball game with all the proceeds donated to the National Foundation for Infantile Paralysis. A successful start, the event became an annual fund raiser. In 1950, "3,000 spectators attended." The *Rockford Morning Star* boys and the *Register-Republic* carriers played a team from Madison, Wisconsin. They met their "goal with $2,269" donated to the charity. By 1952 the paperboys for the two newspapers reached more people than usually watched a local ball game, as the polio virus reached ever more victims. With both enthusiasm and a competitive spirit, they also distributed charity cards to their subscribers. Customers inserted dimes in the card slots raising a "total of more than $9,000. Since 1949, Rockford carriers raised nearly $50,000 for the local county polio committee."

In Peoria, Illinois, a benefit drive crossed state lines when, in 1950, the "fifth annual polio baseball series" was played between all-star carrier teams from Peoria against teams from Columbus, Ohio, who in 1949 demonstrated champion play. Donating the entire proceeds, they intended to equal the "approximately $6,000" raised in 1949.

And in Nebraska, in 1952, paperboys for the *Hastings Tribune* "collected, on their own initiative, more than $4,400" toward the purchase of an iron lung. The money increased a community fund drive underway for the Mary Lanning Memorial Hospital, which that year received more polio cases. The simple caring by carriers and customers demonstrated deep concern for the fight against the cruelest disease. Since it was 3 cents to mail a greeting card, 5 cents for a newspaper or an ice cream cone, the 10 cents mattered to folks. But the people tucked their dimes in slotted cards until a card was full. The filled March of Dimes cards provided the highest benefit contribution amounts of any health charity.

In April, 1955, bold headlines throughout the nation created the greatest euphoria and a very welcome reversal for Americans. Children lined up to receive a moment of injection pain for a summer of carefree play. The potent Salk vaccine to prevent the scourge of polio was readily administered. The looming fear of polio outbreaks disappeared, changing to happy relaxed times and a return of summer social events. By 1961, the number of cases decreased to 1,312, contrasted with nine years before when 57,000 were attacked by polio.

# CHAPTER 10
## ACHATES TO ATTACKER

Dogs ran the gamut from special, furry friends to the vicious fiends, creating a range from the faithful, delightful pals to the worst dangerous enemies, with numerous canine play and problems between the extremes of best and worst.

Paperboys liked dogs running beside them as constant companions, especially alone in the dark or under tough conditions, similar to some of Ron Haringa's challenges. When a high school bully, who was a wrestler, decided to beat up Ron and his brother, Bob, they were scared. Bob took off running, as Ron's pain was rising. Fortunately, Bob returned quickly with their dad who rushed into the unfair encounter and stopped the bully's pounding. Ron was out of trouble. However, he was soon in a worse predicament.

He wanted to drive. He bought his first car at 13. It didn't run. His mother allowed him to drive the family car, or attempt to drive. He "blew the low gear out of dad's 1939 Dodge." Though mother defended him, dad, again, stopped trouble.

Ron's daily dose of purchased chocolate eased his woes, yet no matter the troubles, his dog, Duffy, raised his spirits every day. Duffy also ran into a few scrapes, but his master was there to bail him out. Simple solution: hide the dog in the canvas newspaper bag. The two moved down the street, and soon the "feisty" mischief was free of the bag. He was running fast, ears flat, barking wildly. Duffy's greatest thrill: chasing cats. Squirrels would suffice, but cat chasing was the best. Dad didn't stop him. Ron certainly didn't. And Duffy served as Ron's delight, because with nasty conditions or curmudgeons affecting them, Duffy, who allowed no felines to cross his turf, amused Ron and kept the route less mundane.

## Speed up

Don Hubbard's family left the Grand Coulee Dam region because dad transferred his construction work to the McNary Dam site, connected

143

to Umatilla, Oregon. Don took his bicycle, that he had purchased, to his new home and shortly acquired an evening paper route delivering the *Oregonian*, which arrived from Portland. Saving money with this route, before long he bought a Cushman motor scooter. The motorized wheels provided a great advantage on flat and downhill streets. The speed was countered by the uphill slowness, since Don couldn't push the scooter very fast up a steep hill. However, it provided the best advantage: Shorty's seat.

Shorty, a small, loveable mix of Cocker Spaniel and Spitz, rode behind Don. Perched in his kingly canine seat, his fur swept back, head erect, Shorty "thought he was big stuff," surveying his world from on high. When they passed another dog, Shorty barked sharply at the lowly critter. His bark emphasized two messages: *I'm above any dog on the dirt*, and nudging his driver, *speed up the scooter*, just in case the four-legged trouble came near.

## Protective

Harry Peifer began a *Seattle Times* route with 70 customers, in the midst of World War II. Dad bought him a used bike for $5, a major asset as he traversed more than 10 miles across dirt roads north of Seattle. Conscientious, he worked and increased his base to 144 subscribers in a two-hour routine, though longer when he pulled a sled in deep snow. He saved his earnings to buy a Columbian Flyer bicycle for $35, complete with a reflector and chain guard.

As focused as Harry was on reliably delivering papers, Dusty was just as focused on the paperboy's arrival. The dog watched and waited for him. He raced to Harry, tail wagging, nuzzling him with an excited greeting. Then Dusty whimpered, his head down as his friend hurried away. The owners decided to allow their dog to run along with the paperboy. After two months of Dusty living for Harry to arrive and enjoying his freedom, the folks changed their pet's master to Harry. Part-collie and part-German Shepherd, smart and obedient to Harry's voice, Dusty kept any marauding dogs away, allowing the paperboy to flow unthreatened through his long route. Better a companion than a combatant.

Carriers enjoyed the devotion of their Achates, even on those few cat detours or occasional orders to speed up the scooter. The pet entertained with its carefree approach, and encouraged the master to explore, while staying free of unleashed, threatening critters.

Customers could control their mean menace. Town officials could institute and enforce leash laws. Rarely did either happen. Instead, paperboys coped with man's, *supposed*, friend. The neighborhood carriers knew the quiet dog that liked its ears scratched, which pups yipped incessantly until tossed treats, and when to be cautious nearing an attacker that was a danger for the milkman, the postman, and certainly the paperboy. For all the friendly pets, carriers encountered just as many nasty, nuisance-to-dangerous mutts.

## A Mad Dog

Whether it was Goofy in Ohio, Hannibal in Colorado, Duffy, Shorty or Dusty, the companionship between a dog and a child mattered more than school, snacks, comics---well, within reason. His Achates was loved by him and by the family, neighbors, and customers. This furry, four-legged buddy was not the fiend that many paper carriers had to out maneuver, or painfully succumb to. And the collecting often collided with crazed canines, sometimes worse than on a fast delivery. Actually, the delivery set the scene for a confrontation. What made these youngsters more vulnerable than the postman or milkman?

Dogs stop at bushes and fire hydrants. They turn over trash cans and chase cars. However, the owner forbids his pet to pee on the carpet. A puppy's discipline began by being stationed on a newspaper, and it learned from the start that when it missed its mark: swat. Struck with a tightly rolled newspaper, a puppy was conditioned to react, ferociously, when a hand goes up and a newspaper rod comes down. A paperboy was the primary source of the stinging slap.

Without leash laws, once the critter knew when his food dish appeared, he roamed where ever his nose led him. A marauding, mad dog---mad at anyone who smacked news sheets near him---was on alert for confounded papers that plopped on the porch. For the paperboy, a chance to see an annoying dog responsible for trouble, delighted him. However, he stayed continually careful as he hurried past the dog's space.

## Blame the Dog

Nine-year-old Paul Stevens enjoyed walking his after-school route on the friendly streets of Fort Dodge, Iowa. He faced nothing scary in his ideal Midwest town filled with considerate folks. Well, except Paul was scared 'cause of certain dogs. No one needs to instruct a grade-schooler that canines attack.

Paul caught moments of enjoyment as he threw the paper on the porch, and "watched a dog tear it apart. Served the owner right." If an adult didn't have the common sense to spend time training his dog, he could spend time piecing paper shreds together. Or come outside his yard and pick up the paper from the edge of the sidewalk.

Jim Stingl, delivering his *Milwaukee Journal* route, used his trusty bike to quickly reach 115 customers. Nevertheless, "dogs were a challenge" and affected his swift rhythm. At one house "I had to sneak up to the door, whip open the screen and toss in the paper as two beagles raced toward me through the living room." To the microsecond, it was a test of speed and silence in closing the screen door. Guess adults were half right: children should not be heard, before the get-away. Fast eliminated the need to slam a shoe into a snarly snout in foot to mouth combat.

At another house, the customer owned an ugly dog, an unruly pug. As speedy as Jim was, one day he slipped in his race against the ornery guard. The canine teeth "tore the paper out of my hand and started eating it."

A paper carrier seeing a nasty dog rip the paper apart, realized it could rip his pants apart. A kid's satisfaction toward the customer's loss lasted until time to collect. The school-boy line "the dog ate my paper" was more costly when an owner subtracted the paper meal from his weekly subscription fee. Other times, a dog's tail would wag knowing the carrier was caught.

Remember in grade school when the class pest repeatedly annoyed classmates by elbowing and shoving? Just when an umpteenth irritating push occurred, a reasonable classmate gave the rascal his due. But that counter-attack came at the same moment the teacher looked around. Unfair punishment descended on a good boy. The irksome pest's finger-pointing and laughing made his decent classmate steam. An annoying dog could also make a paperboy steam.

## Timing is the Trouble.

Opportunities for youth to earn money in the 1960s were scarce in Johnstown, Pennsylvania. However, Larry Hudson was ambitious and figured out ways, particularly in the summertime. Year-round he delivered the *Tribune-Democrat* on a morning route, and after school handled another route. His manager insisted, in addition to the standard rules of "be on time for the customers and pay the company on time," that carriers "be polite and respectful." Larry personally added: be resourceful, and for that, he rushed.

Running his two routes, he added a job in a bar-restaurant when school was out. Sandwiched between his newspaper deliveries, he washed dishes and scrubbed floors at 4:00 p.m. and again at 4:00 a.m. He also shined shoes in a barber shop.

Week after week he stayed on schedule. Dismissing summer vacation's tempting days, he scurried on his rounds, with more struggles on Wednesday, when the mid-week's big shopping edition filled two canvas bags. Once, Larry fastened both bags over his bicycle handlebars, pushed off and the "forces of nature took over." In other words, the laws of physics propelled the bike. "I shot out of the alley alongside the newspaper building and went careening wildly across a main thoroughfare through evening rush hour traffic." The drivers in their big, fast 1960 cars managed to miss Larry as he sailed through. "Never tried that again." Thankful the drivers gave way, he controlled his foot speed rushing to places that included flights of stairs.

"Many of my afternoon customers lived in old apartment houses, some with six or seven floors." On steamy August days, folks tried to cool off leaving the door open, hoping to move stifling air through the hot rooms. That was exactly one lady's method who lived on the top level.

Her dog, needing a cooler spot and conditioned to knowing the paper boy was coming, waited for Larry at the top of the steps. Hearing feet pound every board, floor after floor, the dog started growling as the enemy approached.

Racing up steps in hot apartment buildings, speeding to be on time, plus finish the route to switch to his next job, Larry needed a break. "I made a game out of trying to hit her dog with the paper." But just like the timing with that pest in grade school, one day as Larry let the paper fly, "the woman stepped into the doorway. Unfortunately the rolled stiff paper hit her right in the head." The dog's growl subsided, his tail wagged, his temperament mollified while Larry received a long, stern lecture. She had not missed his reckless move. On Friday, he would try to pleasantly collect with a convincing "respectful" smile while avoiding a look at her forehead for evidence of an egg-size bruise.

# Surprise!

In quiet Columbia, Missouri, David Berbert biked through his afternoon routine in a mindless manner making sure his "timely delivery" brought the latest World War II news.

One of his pleasant customers stood at the kitchen sink with the same steady activities of any housewife. Her time looking out the small window, like a porthole, accumulated into an aeon as she viewed her world.

Smash!

David's rolled paper, off aim, struck glass, sending the "paper through the kitchen window startling the lady." Startled? For sure, and David was just as surprised. Shattered glass fell in the sink, on the drain board, over peeled potatoes. Slivers landed against her apron and pieces scattered across the clean linoleum. Fortunately, no significant harm resulted. She said nothing about a burglar, or needing a bucket of sand for bomb prevention. A sudden change occurred in her routine and in his. After a diversion, they returned to their usual tasks.

And her dog returned to his "aggressive" barking. Typical of a critter who wanted to be more aggressive than size dictated, the pet sensed a paperboy who shatters glass and causes excitement. Unlike many residents who allowed their dog to interfere with other people's property, these neighbors chained theirs. Each day as David approached, it ran toward him barking, lunging, warning him to stay beyond the length of chain, which yanked the little fellow's neck and furry throat.

Just like the window, one day the chain broke. The clanging snap startled the dog and boy. "I'm not sure which one of us was most surprised." And then the biggest surprise from a small, angry beast. "He stopped at my feet. I reached down, patted him." He liked David offering gentle attention. The sudden release changed the animal's temperament.

Consistent with correcting a problem, the customer, who immediately inserted a new window, "repaired the chain by the next day." David delivered the paper, the lady stood at the kitchen sink watching her world, and "the dog resumed barking." A nice dog angrily strained against confinement.

Paperboys, windows and rogue dogs roiled like the Bermuda Triangle. But paperboys didn't disappear nor was trouble a supernatural occurrence. Unlike violent water, there was no need to embellish dangerous adventures. Disaster loomed in the form of savage teeth.

## Disappeared

Rather than a chain restraining a bulldog, he was in the confines of a house, and "always sat in front of a large living room picture window, the master of his domain. Any sign of trespassing invoked his ire." The transparent view of Mike Rhodes daily appearance with the newspaper repeatedly caused the old bulldog to "bark ferociously and charge the window in an all-out attack mode." For weeks, months, the same burst of fury continued, undiminished.

"One day as if he could take it no more, he assaulted the picture window and crashed right through." The huge glass sheet exploded and a snarling, barking mayhem ensued. Quite loud, Mike realized the fiend was close. A one-beast rebel army was about to secure a strike.

The bulldog raced in hot pursuit of Mike, pedaling his bike with adrenalin-pumping speed for the sake of his back, his legs, his life. This was not the Saturday movie cartoons with a theater full of kids laughing. Real danger existed between a boy and an enraged attacker. Before it reached the sidewalk, Mike quickly assessed he would not be the winner at the finish line. Desperate, abandoning his bicycle and newspapers, he hastily took "refuge inside the house of a very kind and protective customer." Neighbors were well aware of this danger on their street.

The bulldog lost his chance to viciously "maul his victim." The owner retrieved the furious dog. It's easy to surmise the exchange during the supper hour in that household. More than the meal was hot. Mike "never saw the bulldog again." Apparently one immense, shattered picture window was sufficient. And this one didn't cost the paperboy a large sum subtracted from his collection money.

A chain, a window, a door, any of these barriers existed in separating a serious threat from the paperboy's safety. And adults assumed their device was sufficient.

However, a carrier had to be alert for dogs that attacked as they pleased. So he stayed ahead of the threat. If speed was insufficient, he prepared by using anti-dog methods: a squirt bottle filled with ammonia, bleach, or even cheap perfume. With his swift, steady aim, the boy sprayed the dog's snarling snout.

When obnoxious liquids were inadequate, carriers turned to other weapons. Instead of borrowing mom's perfume, Jerry Walsh used one of his mother's very long hat pins to jab a dog, before the dog's teeth could jab his bottom. Or sometimes a boy carried a weapon larger than a bendable metal piece.

## A Neighbor's Answer

Grant Wise stuck to his schedule. He had fun as he delivered every morning and evening in the quiet, southern community of Hodgenville, Kentucky. Then a badgering dog turned vicious. This wasn't just a disturbance. No, this dog threatened with more than an incessant, harsh bark that irritated others. The Boxer's bite from strong, thick teeth would prove worse than his bark. With assistance, Grant's situation was settled.

The beastly creature's next-door neighbor saw that Grant endured a dangerous situation. Darn. Here was a paperboy who did a good job. Direct action was required against the owner's loud, aggravating dog. The annoyed man crafted a tool about two and a half feet long with a leather strap at the top of the piece of walnut. He polished the weapon. Let the troublesome dog sink its teeth into wood rather than into a helpful kid's soft flesh.

Very shortly Grant discovered he was carrying a billy club embedded with ivory from the dog's teeth. One neighbor was satisfied. The paperboy sped along, safe and pleased to have help with avoiding a painful accident.

## A Winning Strike

The billy club worked, but such weapons were less common for protection than other wooden objects, like Bill Gamel's club. He dealt with the challenges of Anchorage weather, dealt with a moose in his path---well, Bill granted the right of way to the moose---and then in early autumn, which in several days became an Alaska winter, he faced a serious problem.

He had purchased his own sled, fishing and hunting gear, and various sports pieces including baseball items because he loved the sport. During the baseball season he talked with his customers, betting them who would win the pennant. The World Series was under way by October as winter descended from the Arctic. With over 100 newspapers to manage, tramping along his four-mile route, he carried his canvas bag along with a baseball bat, scared that Jack London's *Call of the Wild* would become more than a frightening page turner.

By now, seasonal employees left the fishing boats, crab haulers, and their construction sites where they had worked in the mild summer weather. The crews shipped south into easier conditions in a manageable winter-climate, leaving loyal summer pets to fend for themselves.

Bill found himself, "being chased by packs of dogs." Scraggly starving canines ran "wild in packs of five to ten. I looked like a good meal." As temperatures moved well below a mere 32° F., the pathetic, deserted mongrels became severely cold and desperately hungry. Seeing Bill, they started circling. Their "meal" wasn't snarling back, nor kicking or biting like a wolf, moose, bear. The canines grew more persistent. Their ears back, tails down, an outline of ribs with no visible muscle, they even snapped at each other. A frantic, starved dog lunged for food.

Trying to watch the movements of all the beasts, but hurrying rather than standing frozen as the dogs spiraled inward, Bill swung the bat. His purposeful strike hit the lunging dog's skull. A solid blow. The attacker went down, unconscious. The others retreated from the weapon.

The strong paperboy was safe for another evening. Sweaty with nervous fear, Bill clasped his bat and hurried on to his customers' homes. A severe winter in Alaska provided frequent batting practice, until several nights when the temperature dropped below -30°F. coupled with long spells of hunger and it meant the disappearance of the dogs.

Bill avoided an injury, like awful bites other carriers suffered. In time, tissue healed though scars remained and vivid thoughts of dogs continued to inflict fear. Even escaping attacks that left a boy free from being mauled, his walk or ride remained mauled in fear.

## Insufficient

Joel Mast concentrated on his weekly collection for the *Springfield News*. It was winter in Ohio; he stepped inside a customer's home while the man counted out coins. Fortunately, "heavy padding of my snow suit prevented any puncturing wound." Bitten by an English sheep dog, not a loveable, little lap dog, the creature "latched onto my forearm." Its master quickly intervened.

Joel enjoyed riding his unicycle to "break up the routine. It was a great challenge to develop your balance." But on down the street, a

Doberman seriously threatened him. He had to pause on his unicycle knowing he could not safely pass the Doberman. The seconds seemed to be long minutes until the owner commanded the dog to retreat. The paperboy, the owner and the steely-eyed dog practiced its retreat command more than once for Joel's safe passage. Riding his unicycle was less of a safety test.

A closer and worse encounter involved two dogs, a male and a female husky. Joel knew this pair of dogs had killed another dog. Their vicious reputation was established. Focused on his routine, approaching the dogs' residence, in a second he "spotted them charging around the corner of the house and straight at me snarling." Their wild speed, teeth gnashing, Joel's ears and eyes riveted on the dogs' stance. Unlike the incident when he was bitten, Joel was outside with more space for both to charge at him. Their master was not standing by. It was the heat of summer with casual thin clothes that provided no thick protection. Even a strong canvas bag was insufficient, especially against large huskies.

As Joel heard the dangerous attackers, the owner heard them, too. His order came. They heeded his voice in time. Joel was a "bit shaken by that encounter." The fright resurfaced in his clear memory.

Jim McArthur still recalls "being terrified when a dog had me backed against a wall." Though Jim, and also Joel, had fun with a paper route, the interludes with terrifying dog threats challenged them. Over and over former paper carriers expressed their childhood terror of dogs, to the extent of enduring dark nightmares that entailed battling canines.

## Return to Peaceful Sleep

Tony Lee delivered in a quiet neighborhood in North Dallas, Texas. The third grader managed his modest route size, cheerfully pedaling along tossing papers onto porches. Except at one home, where a dog incessantly barked at him "from behind a screened door on the family's front porch." Because it caused such a furor, Tony liked to throw the paper as hard as possible, "so that it would bang off the door and make the beagle go nuts."

The eight-year-old's effort to annoy worked. Until. "One day the beagle got even. The paper must have knocked the door loose because before I knew it, the beagle was tearing across the front yard toward me with teeth bared. I tried to pedal faster to get away but the dog was mad and fast." Catching Tony, its teeth grabbed his ankle and bit with an accumulated fury. "Fortunately, I was able to kick him away and ride off faster than he could run. When I got home blood was all over my shoe, sock, leg and ripped pants. It was Mother's turn to go nuts." Mom doctored the wound and then she drove them to the house of trouble. Tony sat in the car, his ankle throbbing, while Mom went to the door, unafraid because the dog was nowhere in sight. When the conversation ended, she returned and said the dog had its rabies shots. The owner also said to add the price of a pair of trousers onto his newspaper subscription fee.

Tony limped through his route, listening for possible barks, particularly on the slower collection day. But clothing costs and paper delivery costs were not what mattered. In a few weeks he, "quit the route. Thoughts of wild dogs chasing me down the street invaded my dreams. I realized it was time for a career change." Hampered by nightmares, the grade-schooler circumvented his problem of disturbed sleep.

## Faster on the Draw

Times were good in 1948 and Paul Meyer's paper route was really good. Entering junior high school, he purchased a new Schwinn heavy-duty bicycle with a large front basket. He started with 100 customers, which later rose to 200 when he was assigned a different route, as the manager recognized his reliable delivery of *The Tacoma News Tribune*. Mature, the 12-year-old, knew all his customers, knew who had dogs and particularly problem dogs. Paul prepared.

And like critters everywhere, the pests ran loose in the suburb of Lakewood, south of Tacoma. Sensibly, Paul "carried a water pistol filled with bleach." Just aim it in the right direction and be sure it didn't leak in his pocket. Unfortunately, he slipped with the worst pair.

A single dog was awful; two German Shepherds were horrifically awful. "Before I could get the loaded pistol out, one grabbed my leg." Catching Paul in a piercing clench, the dog punctured the skin and ripped muscle fibers. Its thick canine teeth penetrated his leg releasing a pool of blood. It was like being struck with a railroad spike. He was bitten by teeth that tear apart garbage, shred squirrels, and lap muddy water from puddles.

The large dog "left a deep bite wound, a serious injury, which took weeks to heal." Paul continued through weeks of slowly mending as he moved on his painful leg delivering on time.

## Indifferent

Loren Day knew his *Seattle Times* customers and worked to provide good service to all 150 subscribers. Selected as a station manager, the extra $20 a month helped. He also added money with his work at the nearby Zesto Drive-In. Loren, when just seven years old, became fatherless. Though the 1950s were prosperous times, uncertainty hung over his family. Only a second grader, Loren's uncertainty rose on dark delivery days made worse by bullies who wanted to steal from him and beat him up. A worry for a fatherless tyke.

Being banged on by a bully hurts. Being bit on the bottom hurts. Loren was trying his best and doing exceptionally well, and then a dog increased his troubles with a big bite to his backside. His mother, quite concerned, sent Loren to their neighbor, "a doctor. He drove me to his office and gave me a shot. The shot was free."

No charge from the doctor. From the culprit's owner, no sympathy, no apology.

Since the dog was the problem, why didn't he take a painful shot? No, the people said their dog was safe. "Oh, he's had his shot for rabies." Well, he's still rabid in his attacks.

# CHAPTER 11
## ACCIDENTS

The avoided-accidents to actual severe injuries.

When George Janecke suffered burned hands from his bike's melted rubber grips, his pain widened as he accepted the reality that he'd still deliver papers, though slower. It was an agonizing situation much like when the dog's tail jammed in the spokes of his bicycle severely hurting George. Despite the pain, he did not sit in the kitchen expecting his mother to dish out soothing scoops of ice cream and words of sympathy to make him feel better.

Even in a caring family, doting compassion was as uncommon as generous money allowances. Boys faced their abrasions, bruises, even scars. Why, how could a guy be an authentic buccaneer, a soldier hero, Superman, oops, Superboy, without a stoic mindset?

But any swift accident, unexpected and painful, halted a routine and inevitably caused further ramifications for young paper carriers with their scattered newspapers, crumbled, even soggy sheets on a rain-soaked ground that added insult to injury. And then the most challenging part of an accident: deliver the route without any customer complaints.

## A Slice in Time

Once Harvey Knizek adjusted to the "pure hell" of the dark morning hour, and had settled into his routine, he faced another difficult challenge: an unwelcome incident that amplified the trials of his route.

The blade of a scythe cut deep across his hand, the slash causing sharp pain. Blood flowed and woozy nausea followed. First, control critical bleeding, then he'd deal with long-term: how to manage his route. It was difficult to handle papers with a palm swaddled in a thick bandage, protecting news sheets from blood splotches. Worst of all, he simply couldn't roll 110 papers. The scythe sliced his hand and his time as he slowly plopped flat papers on the porch.

Even a smaller cut went from annoying to aggravating when an accident debilitated a wrist, an arm, a leg, any part critical to delivery. Depending on the severity, it could cause a major disruption. And kids were accident prone, whether at the ball park, on the playground, at the swimming hole, sled riding. In summer, additional jobs picking produce and mowing lawns without a shirt resulted in misery a few hours later, as the canvas strap scraped blistered, sunburned backs. A carrier suffered the consequences of carelessness, like many adult injuries that occurred all around him and were reported in a stream of newspaper articles. Accidents happened to railroad workers, factory and mine workers, farmers. What farm child working around stacks of hay held by baling wire avoided cuts? It was similar in the paperboy's world.

## A Cheap Change

To start a route, boys grabbed their packed bundles that arrived at drop-offs secured in wire so tight it cut into the edge of the papers. Like elsewhere, the *Seattle Times* instructed carriers to keep one hand on the top of the wire and with the other hand snap a side of the binding. Hurrying to unfasten this stiff stricture, a kid leaned over holding a flat disc about the size of a silver dollar and inserted the disc's notched edge against the binding. He twisted it. If he wasn't careful, when the lethal wire snapped loose, the sharp ends lashed free to slash a dirty hand, arm, or face leaving a razor blade slice through skin and muscle. Blood shot out.

Less serious than causing injuries, though related to trouble, wires created more problems. The bundle wrapping over papers provided fuel for a warming fire; the wire offered no such benefit. But creative minds put a piece of thin metal to use---whether or not the action was beneficial. The metal strands also became part of devilish behavior to break a day's rigid routine.

As 14 boys boasted and bullied each other at their pick-up shack in Wood River, Illinois, one guy used the wasted metal strands to force another hold. Twisting a long piece around a bicycle wheel spoke and the opposite end to a fender brace, the boy snared his victim. Bruce Dodson leaped on his bike with his load of papers, pushed the pedals, and only moved a few feet. He crashed. His 80 newspapers crumbled.

Mike Hall was a quiet son, a light-weight "string bean." Then he began delivering the *Spokane Daily Chronicle*. His father had delivered the *Spokane Press*, using the street car to reach out-lying areas, along with selling some papers to riders. Mr. Hall knew a paper route was beneficial for his child. Mr. and Mrs. Hall had resided in Spokane for years and so Mike, identified as the Hall boy, actually "knew his customers very well." He faced them when collecting and that "brought him out."

Being prompt, Mike waited at the corner with another paperboy for their afternoon drop. Restless from sitting in school, the two boys decided to amuse themselves and change the monotony a bit, once their wired bundles arrived. They'd create a little enjoyment, maybe a touch of merriment, but no outright devilment. With a developed throwing arm, Mike was able to sling wrappers wound in wire debris into a large leafy tree. Like most children's games, now that the mess sat on a limb, it sparked enthusiasm, which led to more throws.

Under the watchful eye of a woman peering out the window, Mike's entertaining tosses of bundle wraps bound in wire were dutifully noted. And reported. She stopped that demon from desecrating an orderly neighborhood. His entertainment ceased, since his parents were not about to have their son labeled a hoodlum. He cleaned up all the mess.

Trash, trouble, and the most serious, terrible cuts, for heaven sake, stop using wire. A Gordian solution wasn't necessary to eliminate the accidents. Simply replace the troublesome wire with flexible rope. Finally, in the 1960s newspaper company owners made the change. Once it was recognized that twine was cheaper than wire, and resulted in fewer problems to the machines, they switched. The boys benefitted because the rope eliminated frequent stinging cuts and curbed trouble, though they could find other ways to be devilish.

## Ignoring Possible Accidents

Carriers did intentionally cause accidents, from malicious sabotage, like burning a guy's hands with melted rubber grips, to relatively harmless pranks, like spilling him off the bike. However, most accidents happened without conscious assistance from demons or devils. The plethora of circumstances and conditions that the job entailed created a higher probability of accidents, than for children who sat lethargically in the confines of the house.

In 1942, Jim Ruck wasn't just sitting around. With two routes, he crossed busy streets every day of the week delivering 188 copies of the *Tacoma News Tribune*. He was fortunate to stay dry in the large apartment hotels comprising his first route. When he finished walking downtown Tacoma, he hopped on his bike ready to hurry three miles to a second run. From the center of town, he pedaled across a city block at the top of an extremely steep grade, where he "delighted in swinging to the middle of the street and pumping as hard as possible down the hill. Never did think I might get in a wreck." He simply sped on and ignored the likely probability of an accident to his unprotected head, elbows and knees. He raced ahead of injury.

Think of an accident, contemplate the results? When kids were reckless but suffered no accident, it reinforced shoving aside safety. Max

Fisk bicycling fast, wanting to avoid a goose bite, recognized other disruptions but regarded his accidents as, "minor. Hit by cars."

Minor? In 1937 the weight of a car averaged over 2,400 pounds. That force against the weight of a child under 100 pounds is hardly a "minor" impediment. By age eight, Ed McArthur had joined his older brothers, James and John, delivering on Beacon Hill in Seattle. Hurrying seven days a week through four years until he was 12, his accidents amounted to "nothing major, usual bike crashes."

As sharing germs resulted in illnesses, bicycles often led to accidents, particularly when boys sped and swerved around cars, while running a paper route. This also included sharing a ride on the bike's back fender that further altered the balance. Or Jesse Montoya's perch on the handlebars of his older brother's bike so the little tyke didn't have to walk.

## Ice Cream's a Problem

But as Jim Root learned, walking rather than biking did not guarantee safety. Focused on the certainty of making money, Jim hustled to earn pennies. Starting with the *West Seattle Herald and Shopping News,* and then expanding to the morning *Seattle PI* and evening *Seattle Times,* he ran a busy routine. This meant heavy bundles particularly on Sunday. A bike shop provided relief, renting him a small two-wheeled cart with a long steel handle to pull his load.

For a change of pace in his early Sunday morning ritual he, "decided to push the cart instead of pulling it. Not looking forward where I was going, I turned my head just as a wheel on the cart hit a picket fence and stopped." Jim quickly learned a law of physics. Sure enough, a body in motion stayed in motion. "The steel handle hit me, breaking off pieces of my two front teeth." When the dentist looked at the large permanent and prominent front teeth, he enlarged the young boy's acute discomfort with his professional appraisal, "Nothing to do but pull them."

In contrast, Jim made his own personal assessment: "No way." The lesson, pull the cart or pull the front teeth, struck him as extreme. First graders are cute with missing front teeth. A sixth grader is a spectacle. Jim smiled through his school years, displaying the wide gap from his accident. But he managed and "learned how to spit through the opening. No other kid could do that! Still, eating ice cream was hell.!!"

## Speed, Before Safety

Agility and physical fitness developed a confidence that lulled carriers into careless accidents. Hurrying through an alley, he ran into a garbage can. Cutting across a lawn, he fell into a window well, or hung his neck on the clothesline. One more leap over a hedge, but fatigue left him straddled and jabbed by branches. Ouch! Spurts of growth altered his center of gravity, further aggravating the imbalance of his large swaying load. This awkward, accident-prone stage was exacerbated by rushing and "hot dogging." A robust kid, whether or not a paperboy, was just a potential accident, waiting. He performed like a circus clown, the vaudeville clumsy cop, a novice acrobat on a high wire act.

## Stand on the Fender; Sit on the Seat

At the start of the Depression, Dugg Holmes sold magazines door to door at the age of 9, the same as many youngsters in the 1930s. He also helped his brother, Richard, with his *Rocky Mountain News* route. Awakened by an alarm clock, the brothers rushed out before dawn and headed for a long rural route to reach 60 customers spaced along a bumpy country road. Richard pedaled and Dugg tossed the newspaper. Because Dugg was small, less than 50 pounds, and needed height to make his throw carry, he stood. He actually stood on the back fender of the bike, clutched Richard's shoulder with his left hand and threw a paper with his right hand. They worked as a team. Dugg trusted his brother to avoid ruts and potholes, though it was difficult in the predawn darkness. Against the probability, they managed to miss any severe accidents.

Dugg balanced on the bike and balanced his earnings, until by middle school he was self-sufficient, earning more as he managed the route alone. At 13 he was taller, could finally reach the bike pedals and throw a paper while sitting on the seat. Most of all, he was grateful for the route and extremely grateful to his brother who gave him the bicycle.

However, carriers were always in a hurry. They seldom took the extra seconds to roll up the bottom half of their trousers. But when a pant leg caught in the bike chain, it caused a serious delivery delay as a boy lay on the pavement. More than one young rider learned how quickly accidents happen. Some bought bands to clamp the loose trouser material, yet other bike-related injuries still occurred.

## Move On

Len Terrell needed to hurry. Promptly delivering the *Greensboro Daily*, he pushed the bike pedals faster to meet his school schedule. Having earned money to buy a used bike, the speed helped with everything except staying awake in school. That problem persisted.

But the route was going fine. His legs had grown longer and stronger so the bike accelerated. Until...

The bicycle's front fork snapped. Len stopped instantly; bike and boy crashed in a jumbled heap. By the time he untangled himself from the twisted bike, his abraded elbows and knees were bleeding profusely. Yet his burning knees kept going as he pushed the broken bike one and a half miles to home. His simple used bike was not constructed for daily stress.

Now his stress rose because an accident was no excuse for not delivering. Bleed on. Move on. The school bell would soon ring.

Even when a boy was able to control his bike and avoid careless acts, he had to be on alert for street and sidewalk conditions that might throw him from his mechanical steed. Danger with dogs lurked around any corner; speed magnified the danger of problems coming from any direction. Look right, left, glance behind. And watch out below.

Large tree roots, loose gravel, toys on the walk, many obstacles caused dangerous interruptions. Then the seasons brought additional problems. For certain, snow and ice in winter damaged many a bike, the bags of papers, and the tender bodies. But boys expected trouble with winter, so they were surprised when autumn also snagged them. Sam Smyth learned that a trail of wet leaves made an effective ski slope, but rough ground was not as soft a landing as in snow.

Combine Mother Nature with man-made conditions and a boy had to be readily aware. Flint Whitlock delivered half of the *Hammond Times* in Hammond, Indiana, and finished the other half in Calumet City, Illinois. Rushing through his interstate route, he realized the paved roads held a hazard. One day Flint "hit a pothole." Without a helmet for protection, thrown over the handlebars as if he were a rolled newspaper, the scraped dermis, deep bruises, abrasion pains concerned him more than shredded or ripped papers. He survived as did the painful memory.

Sometimes a boy spiraled to the pavement despite warning signs of the dangers around him. Sam Smyth gained speed on the streets of Renton, enjoying the wind through his hair. Pedaling fast was exhilarating, as was his bumpy, lightning-fast passage across the railroad tracks. That is, as long as he hit the metal rails at the right angle. Otherwise, the tracks scored a nasty accident when the wheel jammed down along the rail, and the soft, unprotected body slammed against the solid railroad ties.

Flowing fast, riding with no hands, hot-dogging across *Accident Avenue's* dimly lit streets, directed a number of carriers to the *Highway of No Teeth*. Furthermore, a rider's bike speed collided with the speed of dogs and large heavy cars.

## Jammed

Once the newspaper company bought the route for Robert Hansen, that he could not afford in 1932, he raced forward with his job. "Always healthy. Did not miss a day." With the steady route, his work paid off, and he met his goal: a bicycle. He ordered it through the Montgomery Ward catalog. The bike made the job much better, actually quite terrific.

Usually careful to prevent his pant leg from catching in the chain, one day Robert was "traveling down the center of the road folding papers without holding on to the handlebars." He moved at rapid speed, trying to outrun a "darn dog," who regularly chased him, when "the front wheel of my bike stopped dead." He "flew over the handlebars and skidded on my face and hands." Speed across the rough sand and gravel sandblasted off several layers of skin. Bleeding ensued. Robert was a painful, bloody mess. Breathless, through tear-filled eyes, he saw a man appear; however, the dog had run off, avoiding repercussions for his key role in the accident.

Seeing movement, the guy figured the crying boy "was going to live" so he checked the bike. The complication was the canvas bag. It had been swinging freely over the back fender wire support, and swinging worse with speed, until it jammed between the wheel and the fender, forming a swift, effective brake system.

Robert bled while the man tugged, struggled, and finally released the bag. At which, the paperboy "got on my bike and went home. The guy was glad to see me go. It was his darn dog." With less dermis, less blood and less speed, he learned a tough lesson.

## Watch Out, Watch Around

Cary Thorp felt fortunate. He acquired an evening route in the pleasant, safe community of Columbia, Missouri, under the "marvelous circulation manager: Mr. Pike." Using a bike he delivered 130 papers in an hour. Yes, in winter the dark icy streets put him on alert, particularly as electric lines collapsed under the weight of ice. But Cary considered himself safe.

Was he? When dogs chase cars, the driver has the advantage of being enclosed in a strong metal shield, on four steady wheels, with an accelerator to speed past a barking beast. For Cary, exposed on a bicycle, hearing a ferocious creature, and despite pedaling to nearly the speed of a bullet, he felt severe pain. A rogue dog bit through his shirt, tearing into his back. The agony was worse than being jammed with a large hypodermic needle. Suffering from the horrific injury, and glancing around to see if more jagged bites were coming, he ran into a tree, a hard immoveable stanchion. A bite in the back, a busted bike, a bloody face and a bag empty of papers, the ones he was to deliver on time.

Wrecking a bike is enough of an accident. Being bitten is enough of an accident. Together: maddening. Noisy dogs were a menace, and their attacks made matters much worse. A tree is not considerate of a bicycle or a body, anymore than dogs are considerate of soft tissue when they go in for the kill.

## Bigger than Beasts

Four legs interrupted the route. Four thick wheels disrupted the routine. A bottle of spray, a pin, a club usually worked against snarling dogs but offered no defense against a solid car.

On a quiet Sunday morning, without winter's icy effect, John Kearns felt pretty good riding with no hands, looking at his collection book as he gained speed rolling down the steep Queen Anne Hill in Seattle. If his cap had an anemometer fastened on top to measure the speed of wind as he sailed down the street, the meter would be off the scale.

Then immediately the wind and rider stopped. Striking a parked car, the wind knocked out of him, his bike wheel bent in half, a scraped, bruised youngster sat alone on hard pavement with a lesson learned: watch out for cars, even the stationary ones.

Riding on black ice, in snowy ruts, speeding downhill, striking a parked car, inevitably bicycle accidents happened. And worse ones occurred with a rolling car crossing the path of a fast rider on an out-of-control bicycle. In a sudden encounter, a rider could swerve fast, unless it was the broad side of an automobile, which was too much to avoid.

## What's Okay?

Sufficiently warmed in his classroom after a cold morning delivery in Hodgenville, Grant Wise now hurried through his second route of the day, as the darkening afternoon hour converted thawed snow to icy patches. Racing on his bike to finish so he could be home for a hot supper, he steered around a corner and turned down a hill, but quickly stopped pedaling. Heading onto a slick street, he switched to "letting my feet drag along to keep things going slow. It didn't take long though and I had picked up quite a bit of speed." A steep hill, ice, faster speed, his shoe soles would zoom through the intersection at the foot of the city block.

No, the bicycle and Grant stopped as he struck a vehicle, though not just any 1960s muscular automobile. A patrol car "pulled out in front of me at the bottom of the hill and I hit it," striking the side of the cruiser with a heavy thud.

The policeman hit the brakes, jumped out of his car, "Damn it boy, you hit me!"

Paper's late, blame the carrier. Paper's chewed, blame the carrier. Car hit, blame the carrier. With blame established, the officer immediately continued, "Are you okay?"

What defines okay? The bent bicycle, banged side of a car, crinkled papers, not exactly okay. Standing up, staring at the policeman, Grant stammered, "Sorry." One okay had to suffice.

However, Grant's run-in with the law, literally, brought an immediate recognition. The patrolman was familiar with him. The police station and this policeman knew the town's paperboy. He was identified without a police lineup.

Months earlier, scurrying to deliver one of his routes and focused on finishing faster because of his empty stomach, Grant heard a high pitched sound. It distracted his thoughts about food. A few feet further, the noise disturbed him. He was "hearing a woman screaming for help." As a Boy Scout he was taught to act responsibly. The screech rose again. Since the building was nearby, he pedaled "to the police station and told an officer about hearing a woman screaming." The conscientious boy-reporter and the policeman stepped outside to listen. Another scream. "The officer started laughing." Looking at the puzzled paper carrier, the amused man said, "Damn it boy, have you never heard a peacock?"

Grant's obvious answer, "No, is that what that is?" Like a goose, a rooster, a moose, the peacock was a disruptive pest. But worse than a physical attack, Grant's status was diminished, at least for a brief time.

Sure enough, he faced "the same officer I struck with my bicycle," when the policeman drove in front of the bike rider and they collided. And later the patrolman recognized Grant among a group of boys, who one night decided it would be fun to use a school bus for a joy ride. He learned one lesson at a time.

## Good Ball Player, Good Paperboy

John McArthur enjoyed plenty of downhill runs, any season, in his Beacon Hill neighborhood east of Seattle. In 1950, on an August afternoon when weather was no problem, John hurried to finish delivering the *Seattle Times*. With nice summer weather, the group of paper carriers at his paper drop would be practicing. They were a winning team. John was especially proud of their win against a group from British Columbia. He felt terrific. Papers delivered, he'd be at the ball field. But in a mere second, his chance to play ball ceased.

Accelerating down a steep hill, his bike chain came off. John careened into a rolling car. Two fast moving objects collided. In a flash John heard nothing. He saw nothing more, not his widely scattered newspapers, his crunched bicycle, the ambulance attendants who whisked him to the hospital, red lights flashing. He was limp and unconscious.

When friends, neighbors, and subscribers learned of his serious injury they wanted to help. He was a good youngster and deserved support. The circulation department received a phone call stating John was the "best newspaper carrier we've ever had! He's just spoiled us by his good service." One of his customers, a 65 year-old gentleman, called the *Times* to say he'd deliver the papers, and three older boys in the neighborhood said they would cover for him. John healed while others ran his route. And for weeks, his carrier team missed their good player

# Regardless of Ailments, Attacks, Accidents

No matter the long days, erratic weather conditions, lugging weight, sharing infections, and skirting or enduring accidents, 400,000 youngsters, rising to 500,000, on to 600,000, delivered their papers routinely and amazingly uninterrupted through the decades. Yes, short routes existed, small ones of 70 subscribers without a Sunday paper, yet thousands of children committed to seven days for two hours or longer with 100 or more customers.

Irrespective of route size and distance, carriers developed discipline in the formative years by delivering day after day. Not assessing if they felt like doing the task, not over-protected, hurrying fast, they completed the route no matter their energy level.

Still facing possible childhood diseases and hurting from occasional bike spills, Jesse Montoya, starting at age six, worked consistently. Ron Richardson walked each morning whether he sneezed with colds or felt drowsy in the drippy Seattle weather. Harry Ansted picked himself up from hitting a car and finished delivering. If a carrier didn't show in the morning, as the station manager, Harry did his run and any absent carrier's route. The time pressure became very difficult when he raced through three routes before the school bell. Paul McManus faced the same situation. Furthermore, completing morning rounds, Paul also worked an afternoon route. He even finished it after being bitten by a dog. The papers had to be delivered and if a carrier did not arrange for a substitute, then the young station manager moved the bundles.

In 1939, Ed Hahn, the oldest of seven children, set the example for the other siblings with his route of 100 customers, throughout the seasons in Rochester, New York. He determined "weather is not a problem. Outdoors all the time, healthy, except for the usual childhood diseases." Don Hubbard, in 1948, started delivery at 4 a.m. to 100 customers. Maybe short naps on the desert floor next to a construction lantern kept him well. He "never got sick."

Jim Leo, in 1950, served 165 customers, often walking through dense fog spreading in from Puget Sound. The thick moisture, mixed with vehicle and industrial fumes in a working mill town, produced a stench of unhealthy air that irritated his asthma. Three years delivering the *Everett Daily Herald,* he "never missed a day."

There was no extended sick-leave provision. Accepting that papers were delivered fed the thinking that colds, a disturbed constitution, bruises and abrasions were common and not an excuse to be idle. A healthy attitude won, over any sickly or sore thought.

# Immune

Daily breathing of outdoor air, children inhaled the oxygen that fueled their bodies, assisted by a chocolate and cola boost. However, the oxygenated air was also laden with coal smoke from train engines, coal furnaces, factory smoke, pulp mills and enough cigarette, cigar, and pipe smoke to eradicate every mosquito. Air was not always pure, any more than the end of a handy garden hose guaranteed a flow of pure water.

The paperboys lived in an era when serious childhood diseases prevailed. As developing youth, they were in an awkward stage that is accident-prone. These threats existed alongside a time of dismal protection from severe injuries. Nevertheless, the newspaper carriers were remarkably healthy, active and industrious. Though periodically disrupted with aches, injuries, and illnesses, each time carriers sprang back stronger and healthier. Mentally immunized against excuses, inertia, irresponsibility, indoor-itis, they developed physically and socially.

With a cheerful, competitive energy from small bodies, carriers produced a big spirit. Struggling and striving, paperboys exercised and strengthened their shoulders, legs, arms, and torso for a strong body, supported by a stronger attitude. These mere boys in men's boots worked against more than their physical size. They also worked against the size of the route, the full canvas bag, big dogs and bigger cars, and the size of responsibility on their shoulders.

All this and without today's tremendous improvements in immunizations, antibiotics, fluoride, vitamins, protective weatherized clothing, bike helmets and bicycle paths, less smog, brighter and more street lights, making life safer for currently growing children.

Carriers who delivered in the morning and evening, seven days a week, 52 weeks a year, or who completed two and three routes each day also sandwiched in school, served as altar boy, milked cows, shoveled coal, snow, sawdust, chopped wood, mowed lawns, gathered crops, cleaned the chicken coop, scooped the dog kennel....

Well, maybe not a dog kennel. And one boy did not perform all this list of chores. However, carriers salvaged little time for trouble, in spite of reformers who insisted paperboys found time. Yes, a policeman saw Grant and his buddies borrow the school bus for a joy ride. Jim Rudy fished papers out of the motel pool. Mike Hall removed all the bundle wraps and wire from a tree. Occasionally, some kids stepped outside the confines of acceptable to commit acts not balanced with common sense. Boys felt the consequences and made adjustments, usually.

Certainly they were nothing like the weaker sex, that other gender who grew taller than the males in middle school. How could soft girls challenge sturdy paperboys? Or was the opinion, "weaker," a valid assessment?

Seven-year-old hawker, without a badge. Library of Congress, National Child Labor Committee Collection, Photographer Lewis Hine. 1910 era.

## MEET YOUR NEW CARRIER SALESMAN

We are pleased to introduce the young man who this week took over the Oklahoman and Times route in your neighborhood. He will do his best to deliver your newspapers, regularly, promptly and safely, especially on wet or windy days.

He makes his collections each week, on Wednesday, Thursday, and Friday, following a fixed schedule. His earnings—and the money to pay his paper bill each Saturday—come entirely from his collections. He hopes you will understand how important it is for his subscribers to pay him promptly when he calls.

Your aid and encouragement will help him to make good in this his first business venture. For this and for your continued interest in our newspapers, we sincerely thank you.

Please telephone the circulation department, 2-1211, if service is not to your satisfaction.

OKLAHOMAN and TIMES

JACK MOORE
Route No. L-13; Phone 9-3806

A 1946 postcard introducing Jack Moore, carrier for the Oklahoman and the Oklahoma City Times. He delivered morning and afternoon in Oklahoma City.

Paperboys waiting at the *Everett Daily Herald* for afternoon papers in Everett, Washington. Photo-journalist Jim Leo, 1955.

YOUNG MERCHANT                                    December, 1951

NEW OFFICE: Times carriers in the Beacon district are conducting business in a new location at 2103 14th Av. S. The building front is adorned with the lettering "Seattle Times Beacon Station." Carriers in front of the station were from left Allen Jetton, Clarence Higgins, Tom McArthur, Rio Ciotta, Ed McArthur, John McArthur, Don Daniels and Mike Yurina, all 1200 district carriers.

Paperboys congregated at the Beacon Hill station for *Seattle Times* bundles. Photo published for the carriers' publication, *Young Merchant*. Three of the four McArthur brothers, Tom, Ed, John, are present. James stopped delivering by 1951.

Doug Wilkerson

Doug Wilkerson, a typical paperboy with his canvas bag, bicycle, and ball cap, delivered the *Seattle Times*, 1950 to 1955, in Lake Forest Park, north of Seattle.

Ron Haringa needed a double bag to deliver two afternoon routes in Seattle. He bicycled with a full bag up Holman Hill, site of soap-box derby race trials.

Howard Wagner delivered the *Citizen Journal* (Ohio)for a decade. Age 10, in 1941, he started his route by 3:30 a.m. A member of the famous Columbus Boychoir, he managed his route, school, and met the choir's performance schedule.

Carrier friends, Gene Ausmus (right) and Roscoe Kinkead, biked to the Wabash Railroad Depot in Centralia, Missouri for *Columbia Missourian* bundles. 1944.

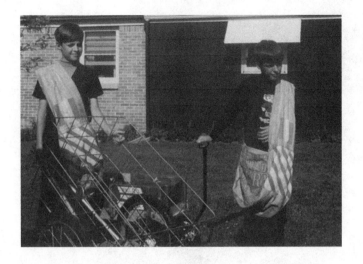

Brothers, Jim Stingl (on the right) and Phil Stingl, handled their large *Milwaukee Journal Sentinel* load on Sunday with the metal cart they purchased. 1968.

Reading the *Seattle Times* Sunday comics, Robert and Jacob enjoy a favorite pastime of adults and children, especially paper carriers. People religiously followed the funnies.

James Ausmus and his dog, Scout, Columbia, Missouri, 1950. Jim delivered the *Columbia Daily Tribune*, 1949 to 1951. Many paperboys shared monotonous route time with their pet dog.

Dwayne Lane on Starlight, delivering the *Everett Daily Herald*, Everett, Washington, 1947. His horse helped him deliver, especially when snow sidelined his bicycle.

A Grab family portrait, 1955. Martin Grab holding Suzie. Mother, Martha Grab. Back row, left to right: Mary Ann, Phyllis, Teresa, Patricia, Frances. Front row, left to right: Josie, the parents, Kathy, Barbara. The nine sisters delivered the *Tacoma News Tribune* from 1950-1964.

Ron Cameron's delivery of the *Seattle Times* slowed, but did not stop, as the bike, in the "frickin' snow." His dog, Mutt (left corner) plodded with him on his hilly eight-mile route, 1953-1958.

A moose, like one Bill Gamel faced on his *Anchorage Daily Times* path. Not stopped by snow, ice, conditions below -30° F., he halted when blocked by a moose of more than 1,000 pounds.

Paul Fellows, in 1956, purchased an English three-speed bicycle, a Hercules with a 50-year warranty. After heavy use on his Minnesota route, the steel frame remains quite useable. Photo by Ana Gaston.

Ed Boblitt porched his papers, while he balanced on a unicycle. 1952 photo by photographer Joe Munroe in the Munroe collection at the Ohio Historical Society's archives in Columbus.

A typical, comfortable sitting porch on twentieth century homes. Paperboy Gary Kost passed such porches delivering in Mount Vernon, Ohio, 1951-1955.

Jim Root standing by his first car, a 1932 Ford coupe, purchased in 1951 with earnings from his *Seattle Times* route, which he worked from 1945 through 1951.

The Kopczynski children (left to right) Allan, Larry (smallest) Joan, Don and Connie. The four older ones delivered the *Lewiston Morning Tribune* in the 1960s.

The Montoya boys, Lee, Fred, Joe and Jesse in 1954 gave $3,500 of job earnings to their father. for a down payment on this two-story house, the Montoya family's first home.

Jack Rodda, age 16, placing a wreath at the Tomb of the Unknown Soldier in Arlington National Cemetery, December 24,1930. He represented hundreds of carriers on the Patriotic Pilgrimage of the Newspaper Boys of America. Jack delivered for the *Butte Daily Post*, Butte, Montana.

A paperboy statue announces Alaska is the 49th. Robert Atwood, publisher of the *Anchorage Daily Times* and Chairman of the Alaska Statehood Committee, commissioned the statue, stating the paper's headline, "WE'RE IN."

Glen Carter received recognition with a Service Award certificate, and the next year, age 14, was selected station manager. He delivered from 1963-1966.

Kathy Grab's program for the 1962 Newspaperboys' Banquet. Only her initial K. was posted and Grab misspelled. Kathy delivered from 1955 to 1964.

During World War II, a poster shows the newspaper industry's encouragement for Americans to buy defense bonds. By 1945, newspaper carriers sold almost two billion stamps, at 10 cents a stamp, to citizens for the purchase of bonds.

The commemorative 3 cent postage stamp salutes newspaperboys in appreciation for service to the country in selling stamps for war bonds. Unveiled in Philadelphia, October 4, 1952. Contributed by Paul Haygood, paperboy for the *Atlanta Journal*.

# CHAPTER 12
## I CAN DO BETTER. YES I CAN

In northeastern Montana, with an emphasis on north, Robert Gilluly slogged through snow drifts selling the local paper. His town of Glasgow allotted no sympathy for a sniffling sissy. Bob was no sissy, just short. His legs would stretch when he advanced to first grade, but for now he ran as fast as any five-year-old while enjoying fun on the snowy streets. With papers tucked under his arm, he raced along carrying the *Glasgow Courier.*

Montana is not considered a sunshine state, because starting in autumn into the long winter until the latter part of spring, rough weather comes with the territory. Bob held the same view as his family, friends, fellow citizens and "just accepted it." When conditions become tough, the resilient residents become tougher. Public school, and of course the carriers' *Main Street School,* remained open.

So venturing forth, since he wanted to buy candy after selling papers, Robert headed for a tavern, for the best bar in town. "Bar patrons were always generous, paying a dime or a quarter even if they were in no shape to read the news." And like Jesse, David, or Barry, grabbing papers just released from the press, Bob rushed, "to be the first to run to local bars and sell copies to customers." Though people didn't have a dime to spare in 1938, they mustered a nickel or more for the five-cent *Glasgow Courier.* Since he received a two-cent profit on each sale, he'd earn enough pennies for candy, if he was fast.

Problem: he wasn't the only one with a tavern plan. Heart pounding, legs racing, pigtails flying, a girl ran past him. She reached the best selling spot before Robert dashed inside the smoky haven. He had to settle for a "lesser bar." At least there were several to choose from. Selecting bars as a prime location and with 10 bars nearby, it wasn't necessary to run to the edge of town, out by the railroad tracks and the red-light district, though it might have been profitable.

At times, in a competitive speed test, a small boy shrugged and admitted girls were better. Other times, they were considered equal especially in the rugged western states where equal was gaining momentum.

Two decades before Robert's birth, Montana citizens acknowledged females' capabilities---well ahead of the United States Congress. The federal government finally allowed all women the right to vote by passing the Nineteenth Amendment in the political, and August, heat of 1920. Prior to the Amendment, Montana joined other western states and granted women the opportunity to vote. Furthermore, citizens of Montana believed women should be part of the legislative scene, and in 1916 they elected Jeannette Rankin as the first woman to serve in the United States House of Representatives.

In Glasgow, Robert focused on his world, oblivious to politics. His success the day he rushed to secondary bars netted him 15 cents, enough for three candy bars, or a movie. He expanded his selling experience, and passed competitors. Survival is not to the slow, nor are newspaper sales, and by age 8 Bob proved his success with an assigned route. He joined the pandemonium of a dozen noisy paperboys leaving the *Courier* office, where Sam Gilluly, his father, presided as the editor. Sam's son persisted in the dark at -20° F., in order to sit in the dark movie theater for three nickels. Wintry conditions never stopped Bob nor other hearty carriers from gaining the benefits in a paper route.

## "Really Scared"

No question, Montana was ahead on issues of equality. Sensibility, along with frontier spirit, extended out to the Pacific and up the Inland Passage to the Alaska territory, where endurance like Bob's was matched by the female contingent.

The privilege of living in the magnificent territory surrounded by wild, stunning beauty, expansive summer daylight, and surplus space for quiet existence is counter-balanced by the pressure to cope with lengthy winter conditions.

Alaska incorporates the largest land possession of the United States with over 570,374 square miles. Two states the size of Texas can't fill the space that contains thousands of radiant glaciers including the highest glacial peak in North America: Mt. McKinley. The Mountain rises to 20,320 feet, dominating the Alaska Range's other 23 icy peaks above 10,000 feet. Against these geographic superlatives, population registers much less.

In 1939, with only 72,524 people, half of whom were native Alaskans, and spreading over more than 570,000 square miles, Alaska placed a dozen people per square 100 miles. With only 12 people populating 100 square miles, it makes a next-door neighbor extremely remote. Along the miles of coastline, mountain streams, rivers and lakes, hearty folks established a home in majestic locales, like Cordova, in the eastern sector of beautiful Prince William Sound.

Averaging 92 inches of precipitation a year, the "city" of Cordova receives less than Ketchikan's 160 plus inches, though between December and March, Cordova is covered with about 20 frosty inches of snow each month. Reaching 118 inches of snow a year, such circumstances would challenge any paperboy. Cordova does not have the temperature extremes of Fairbanks, but at freezing, with over 100 inches of snow, it is cold. Period.

In 1939 during the winter months---quite a few long months---an afternoon newspaper route folded into a cold, early night enveloped in wind from the sea. Frequent rain, sleet and snow settled over the region for a stern winter. The grandeur required granite strength when nature's force grabbed a delicate person of insignificant size.

The affect of such elements diminished around pleasant townspeople. Norm Brown, editor of the *Cordova Times*, provided people a close community connection through up-to-date local news. His paper included articles from neighboring towns such as Petersburg about 570 miles to the south, Wrangell 590 miles away, Anchorage 160 miles north and the territorial capital at Juneau, 450 miles south. Inaccessible through highway traffic or Greyhound bus service, friends, however, from other towns seldom dropped in for a visit.

Within the city of Cordova "everyone knew each other," and folks reached out, not to interfere or restrict, just to extend a friendly helping hand. In the immensity of the territory, Cordova, with under 1,500 people, yet much larger than most Alaska communities, rested like a shiny emerald on snowy-white satin. The emerald color because for three decades green money and green copper filled their port on Orca Inlet.

The same as Glasgow under the long Depression, the citizens of Cordova held together as the depressed conditions lingered, grinding against citizens the way a glacier grinds against soil. Only an economic depression grinds against the soul. The great Kennecott copper mine, the reason Cordova grew to prominence, closed in 1938. No longer the Copper Capital of the World, the town continued on as the Razor Clam Capital of the World. It was a productive capital rather than a political one. And quite magnificent, where stanchions of mountains protected and the ocean reflected the beauty of Ruth Fulton's small world. She valued Alaska's uniqueness.

Life in Ruth's sphere was an adventure, though day-to-day Cordova functioned the same as other coastal towns with the Customs House, a school for 12 grades, post office, and newspaper ads for grocery specials.

The residents attended churches in the denomination of their choice: Baptist, Lutheran, Presbyterian, Episcopal, Catholic, Mormon, Nazarene, or the active St. Michael's Russian Orthodox Church. However, there were differences, such as the Eyak native houses and a significant lack of highway traffic. No highways. But the Empress Theater allowed Hollywood to come to this remote town.

Like elsewhere, children spent their earned money enjoying the movies. So Ruth asked for a paper route, and with no competition, she began her new job as she stepped forth to deliver the eight-page *Cordova Times*. Passing the business district on First Street, past the Masonic Temple, she walked away from town over the snow-covered dirt street to the water front in the fading afternoon light. She was headed to the dock, her first delivery location.

The north wind pummeled Ruth. A strong gale slashed the long dock jutting into Orca Bay. Concentrating on the guardrail, she inched her way along what people called the Ocean Dock. Slippery from sea water and frequent rain, the algae-coated planks of the walkway required that she "grab the guard rail or be blown away." The distance she covered was less of a challenge than the intensity of conditions—a lone figure battling forces. Standing required strong legs and then stronger arms to securely hold the rail.

The piercing scream from a seagull was no help. Seagulls never assist, even with their own as they steal shreds of razor clam from other gulls. The flapping screechers had better stay above on wind currents, because Ruth needed to focus without an interruption by annoying birds.

Facing the fury of icy weather became more daunting in the dark. If blown into Orca Bay, into the deep Alaskan water, where seconds in the freezing waves brings quick death, she'd be unable to float in wet, heavy clothing and a full canvas bag. She gripped the guardrail with cold hands and step by step broke through the lashing wind to walk inside.

Shaking, she entered the dim parlor and became scared, "really scared." Taut facial muscles blocked any smile. Her pupils enlarged. Her olfactory nerve was stuffed with odors as the smell of salty sea air laced with clam shell odors was replaced with aromatic burning cedar, stale smoke, and stale alcohol. The crowd of smells was shoved aside by strange sounds. Wild animal noises, a chain saw, a native Eyak tongue? No! Unusual conversations: in Greek.

Ruth eased into the parlor. She blinked under the bare light bulb. Unlike a sedate Victorian parlor, a chatty beauty parlor, or a silent funeral parlor, this was a Greek Parlor. When she first entered it "was real dark, smoky and really scary until I got used to delivering to the men," who drew together playing cards, smoking, drinking in their clubhouse.

The men came to Alaska from sunny Greece to work in the immense Kennecott copper mines, now closed. The miners endured a tough adjustment, adapting by using their card room. And they appreciated the 10 cent paper with news from the outside world.

## Annoying

Days turned into weeks, on into months, as Ruth moved through the route, her fear long since disintegrated as she delivered to delightful folks: the Cordova citizens, Eyak natives, Greek gentlemen, the pleasant prostitutes. After a long winter and a short spring, warm summer days appeared, which is not 100 percent better. On a windless June day as sun heated Lake Eyak, residents hoped wind would arrive to blow away obnoxious mosquitoes.

The biting annoyances are small---the only thing small in Alaska. On such a day, Ruth was comforted as she stepped into the Greek Parlor, the door shutting out buzzers or the smoky air driving them away. Fortunately, only a few days out of 365 produced windless conditions that benefitted millions of mosquitoes.

Ruth left the thick tobacco smoke to enjoy fresh air and sunshine. Walking along the dock, comfortable and warm, Ruth removed her jacket. Her pretty hair shimmered in the sunlight and fluttered in the slow, gentle air as she strolled along.

A moment later strands ceased to flutter. Her thick hair stopped the rivulets before they slid into her eye lashes. She raised her hand as the seagull flew away, leaving behind its goopy glob on her crown of shiny hair. She swatted mosquitoes, but did not swat the seagull's yellowish-white slime. She couldn't shake the mess out of her tress as easily as a boy manages with short hair. She hurried to finish delivering and go home to wash poop right out of her hair.

Ruth had persisted through punishing winds, and stepped into an unknown card parlor alone. Scared stimulates the senses. Poop infuriates the senses. But only briefly, as Ruth's cheerful disposition wiped away the irritation. From ferocious weather to friendly folks, the friends won, not the fear. The gull won too, but just once.

Clearly, paper carriers faced challenges with inexperience, the conditions, and a few difficult customers. Though struggle was, Ruth's fears faded and her route passed from afternoons of early darkness in the winter to amazing sunny views of brilliant scenery shared with people of strength. Many times the difference between being discouraged or overwhelmed by a situation, and managing to cope with circumstances, was...

# Attitude.

In the northeastern United States, mornings were dark during Beverly Brunner's winter deliveries. Still, like Ruth, Beverly appreciated her surroundings, even if Syracuse wasn't exactly the central feature in a travel agent's brochure for winter escapes. The same as Bob in Montana or Ruth in Alaska, Beverly developed a key element: a cheerful attitude.

She liked the distinctive changes in the seasons. And Syracuse, with weather effects from Lake Ontario and Lake Erie, received extremes throughout the evolving seasons. Brilliant autumn colors splashed over the maple trees, adorned in red, orange, and burgundy. Slowly colors disappeared into the smell of burnt leaves lingering in morning mist. Then suddenly a change to the glistening white of winter with the neighborhood still and silent in the setting moonlight. She continued the route as spring's new green shoots, spectacular yellow daffodils and forsythia were enhanced with the earthy smells of plowed gardens. Smelling fragrant lilacs, hearing robins chirp, Bev "watched the world wake up," with her upbeat sunny attitudes.

Her mood reflected that of Americans throughout the nation. The Depression finally disappeared after 1941, and by 1945 had receded into history as victory prevailed, jubilant troops came home, and the record-breaking wartime production turned to rapid production of consumer goods. Energetic times and prosperity in the closing half of the 1940s were good.

Seven days a week, Bev rose in the dark and scurried to deliver the *Syracuse Post Standard* before 6:00 a.m. When snow and ice didn't accumulate dangerously thick, her bike expedited the process. Completing the last part of her route, she smelled breakfasts brewing, baking, and frying. With such tantalizing aromas, she hurried faster to enjoy eating "breakfast with dad, reading the comics" and still arrive at school ahead of the tardy bell.

Unlike most morning carriers, Bev had no chance to catch a quick nap after the delivery. She left for school, arriving well before classes, to "practice with the high school chorus. Those were fun times." The same way she evaluated a paper route: "fun."

Pushing herself with a route and the choir rehearsal, her discipline had begun at a young age. She responsibly handled baby-sitting jobs that paid 15 cents an hour. Sporadic baby-sitting felt more comfortable than her first job: picking green beans under the searing sun in Rome. Not romantic Rome with beautiful fountains, but the farming fields of Rome, New York. When her brother moved to his next job, he confidently gave the route to his sister, along with his canvas bag. Now, into her year-round job, the morning delivery offered the clear essence of sounds and smells stirring the start of her day, before a flood of distractions began. Everything was good.

Everything? Well, except for "a mean Doberman." Scared, Beverly cautiously moved past him, without a weapon or defense strategy, just her careful, alert approach.

## Quarters and Experiences, for the Movies

The calendar records the seasons evenly with spring and summer covering half of the months. The reality for many locations is an uneven division due to erratic weather changes. In Oregon, Illinois, about 4,000 residents tolerated periodic extremes.

In 1952, Zita Stanley had not quite reached 12 when a newspaper manager came to her grade school in Oregon requesting possible carriers. She signed on for a route, and the expectation of earning quarters for movie money. With a bounty of wonderful movies released in the 1950s, she watched comedies, thrillers, westerns, and the glamorous stars on the screen. She danced down the street reeling music through her mind from *Singin' in the Rain* or *The Band Wagon*. The excitement in *High Noon* was worth seeing more than once. And she earned quarters faster than movies rotated. Though a healthy, average size, she waited for that growth spurt girls enjoy in middle school. But there was no waiting to deliver the papers.

The manager sensibly arranged for bundles to be dropped at Zita's door, rather than have her wait alone, a distance from her house at 5:00 a.m. Her mother helped roll the newspapers at the kitchen table while her baby brother slept. Pedaling her bike, she hurried past the homes of sleeping neighbors, who expected their paper before 6:00 a.m. Her bag half empty, she crossed the street and glanced in the window at a customer's clock to assure herself she stayed on schedule, allotting "enough time to change clothes for school, eat breakfast and read the comic strips." Her bike ride finished, she rushed to dress in a skirt and blouse and then read her beloved funnies. With quarters to spare, the money felt good; the sense of accomplishment felt better. She "enjoyed being recognized" when customers identified her as their "paperboy."

But there were nasty days, when strong gales whipped across the Great Plains into Illinois, flattening corn stalks and indifferently blowing a bike and Zita to the wet ground. Beaten by the wind-bully, her pages of the *Rockford Morning Star* spilled, scattering fast like loose balloons. The wind laughed. Sheets ripped apart. Ignore freezing fingers, skinned knees and hands. She spit back at the wind. She'd rise like Scarlett O'Hare, her favorite star in her favorite movie, *Gone With the Wind*.

No, Zita's strong self-reliance receded. The movie image receded. She needed help. Her mother drove the car for the rest of the delivery, the onetime mom helped on the route. And through the terrible 1952 polio epidemic, Zita delivered papers, though she was not invited to participate in the paperboys' *Rockford Morning Star* polio benefit softball games.

Several years later when her brother wanted a route, their parents said no. Apparently one paper carrier in the family was sufficient. Bob Gilluly in Montana would have understood the little guy's frustration over a girl disrupting his opportunity to make money and be independent.

## An Arrangement

Another brother fared better with delivering papers, not that he actively requested a route. Cathi Vannice scurried each morning, including Sundays. By 1956 advertising inserts were significantly increasing the Sunday size. She wanted a helper, so she drafted her younger brother. Hurrying through the government housing, built as duplexes near Grand Coulee Dam, they delivered throughout their community. The *Spokesman Review* arrived by truck from Spokane for the 150 customers. With a "free run of the town" she and her sidekick covered streets, fast.

Only before dawn, could Cathi manage time for a paper route so the task didn't block her extensive school and church activities: the band, pep club, a few hours of school classes, piano lessons, Rainbow Girls, Girl Scouts. Being active in clubs, academically strong with excellent school attendance, she was selected to attend Washington Girls State. The summer program for outstanding high school students focused on leadership development, and instruction in the principles and processes of American government.

Also, her early hour avoided the terrible afternoon heat radiating off the desert in central Washington. One can pile on clothes for miserable cold; however, a carrier can't peel off the heat. Usually ignoring the weather, she delivered with an orderly, controlled certainty.

But in the autumn of 1957, when the dry summer continued into September and October, the vibrant certainty in America was greatly reduced. Across the vast expanse of sky, which for millenniums had provided direction from ancient constellations, the great highway overhead was split apart. As the sun rose on Cathi's delivery, the dawn of the space age appeared. The Soviet Union's Sputnik launch, October 4, 1957, set the United States on a race against the U.S.S.R. A small satellite invaded confidence in American leaders. On the cold throes of January 31, 1958, the U.S. launched Explorer I. In the dark winter sky, carriers looked for more than the big dipper.

## Alone

While Cathi's brother helped her, adding two brothers and a sister on newspaper rounds provided more service with another girl, a third grader. In Cottonwood, Idaho, Joan Kopszynski, with three of her siblings, monopolized delivery to a community of 800 citizens.

In 1964, President Lyndon Johnson's fight to enact legislation attacking the roots of America's poverty produced the Economic Opportunity Act. It missed Cottonwood. The root problem for the Kopszynski family was money, or a lack of surplus funds, so the four children worked on that problem.

Their newspaper bundles came from Lewiston, through the central panhandle of rugged Idaho country, a challenging hour-long drive from Cottonwood. With bad weather, which occurred during the same months as school sessions, papers periodically arrived late.

From age 8 through her first teen years, Joan's recommended 10 hours of sleep was cut short. "I had a difficult time getting up in the morning. Dad told my sister and me to rise. Then he turned the light on in our bedroom and the brightness blinded me."

For several months, the sun rose later than Joan. The town slept awhile longer. With 10 children in the Kopszynski home, and mom and dad starting the work day, the house bubbled with life as Joan stumbled about dressing.

The young carriers had to be on time, regardless if the papers arrived late. So, scooting along on foot, Joan lugged the newspapers in her full canvas bag, which clearly displayed in red letters *The Lewiston Morning Tribune*. She advertised the paper through the middle of town and up Lewiston Hill, a steep climb for short legs.

The 75 papers were a sufficient load for a child who reached about four feet, and when bundled against the weather weighed slightly more than 50 pounds. Leaving her busy house, facing the Idaho elements, she ventured into her quarter of the route alone. With streets utterly deserted, hearing her footsteps tap the pavement, she "felt eerie walking around in such quiet. The houses were steeped in darkness." Pulling a paper from her bag and folding it in thirds, the crinkly sheets sounded like a pretzel bag opened in church during silent prayer.

Sometimes she saw movement: an unleashed dog. Joan knew her older brother, Allan, was bitten by a Husky so she didn't take chances. She used a method as old as Biblical times: a rock. Finding the dogs pesky on good days, but worse on days they were irritated, she needed to threaten the canines more than they threatened her. She "picked up a rock and pretended to throw it. They never bothered me." Fortunately, for her, this handled the annoyance.

As if disrupted sleep and crossing dark streets shared with dogs wasn't enough, the finale to her route greatly disturbed her ritual. The last customer required her, "to open the door and place the paper in the viewing room of the Uhlorn Funeral Home." The acrid smell of embalming fluid, the sight of a rigid body encapsulated in soundless death, these attacked her senses. With a "fueled imagination" Joan was on high alert. Any second the icy fingers of the lone reaper might touch her. She hated the chills, the starkness. She was sure a stiff body on satin lining could "suddenly rise from the coffin." Halloween ghouls circled around.

Walking alone, surprised by dogs, scared of placing a paper near a dead being, these distractions dissolved in the presence of, "What I really dreaded..."

## Aware

Down the sidewalk from St. Joseph's Catholic Elementary School children marched two-by-two in lines, obediently headed to church for early morning Mass. Their disciplined march led them past Joan. The Benedictine nun's long habit sh-sh-shooing softly ahead of the line did not hush school mates' whispers or block their gaze at Joan's appearance.

Folks in the hamlet of Cottonwood called their neighbors by first name, memorized who married cousin Will over in the next county, discussed competing rivals for the best apple pie at the church social. Cottonwood citizens knew each other. Classmates knew Joan.

Still, she was insulated in her familiar town. Comfortably protected by family, neighbors and customers, she nestled in a cocoon. But like young children anywhere, Joan recognized reality. "We lived below the poverty level and I was embarrassed that I had to work while my buddies spent their free time leisurely getting ready for school."

Joan dressed sensibly in her carrier uniform. For warmth she wore a red hood trimmed with white fuzz, like soft bunny fur, circling her face. "I looked like a Santa elf," rather than a *Tribune* helper. From older sisters, she received hand-me-downs. A worn, blue snowsuit covered her against the cold Idaho wind, along with protection from dirty newsprint smearing clothes. "I looked pretty scruffy." The scruffy, unlike the pretty, drew notice. "I didn't want to be seen by my peers who were wearing their good school clothes." Her snowsuit didn't insulate her feelings.

The *Dick and Jane Reader,* a favorite in reading circles at schools, pictured the little sister, Sally, in a dress, a bow in her blond curls, her bright blue eyes shining as she skipped in the sunshine. Folks continued to idolize Shirley Temple's dimpled smile, wearing a cute, short dress with matching ruffled anklets. The Hollywood darling influenced girls' fashion long after the child-star retired from the screen. No exception in Cottonwood.

A robust boy wearing Huck Finn attire with patches and dirt, grinning beneath tousled hair, was accepted just fine. However, society issued a specific gender delineation when it came to a girl's appearance. That was clearly understood by Joan and classmates.

She moved quickly to the next porch, her hazel eyes downcast before the chorus of stares. Their looks stained beneath the surface deeper than a smear of grey ink. Joan's cocoon unraveled. She metamorphosed. A butterfly emerged and she transformed from childhood into a mature student ahead of her grade level.

On an unpleasant path, the third grader, not yet enunciating and defining "embarrassed" on her spelling list, learned the root meaning of embarrassed in *Main Street School*. Embedded beneath the superficiality of appearance, her strong character rose. Common sense took over.

Joan resolved to reduce the chance of more stares from her peers. " It made me hurry so I'd pass by the school area before the line went down to church." No dallying. Safely crossing the streets with no traffic to interfere, she scampered along, once the bag became lighter. And she counterbalanced her fear and dread with fun and delights.

"Great customers made my route a pleasure. My brothers and sister accused me of having the best territory because I collected the most candy and tips. I smiled so much my face hurt. I possessed the politeness of a southerner." Attitude had corralled the "scruffy" appearance. Joan liked the friendly folks with their cheery greetings. As she continued her rounds and with the peoples' sleep completed, their lights came on. They "came out of the house to greet me."

Now fully awake, Joan placed papers in the door or under the mat. Her daydreaming happily handling the monotony. "I never hardly missed a day of delivering newspapers." Well, once in awhile, "Mom would get a call from an irate customer." The missed delivery meant the little girl raced down the street with a copy. "It didn't happen very often."

Re-walking the route cut into the steady list of chores that absorbed hours. A family of 12 required all hands pitch in. Joan "helped cook dinner, set the table, followed by wash or dry the dishes, pin laundry on the clothesline, fold clothes, mend clothes, make the beds, clean the kitchen, bedrooms, the bathroom, the chicken coop, the woodshed and barn, hoe and weed a half acre garden, tend the flower beds surrounding all sides of the home, pick raspberries and strawberries, help can fruit and vegetables to include making sauerkraut" and then to supplement the family garden, "harvest potatoes, peas, carrots, corn and other vegetables from area farms." If needs at home were met, she helped to clean neighbors' homes and babysat for families in town. Amidst all of this, she managed to do "homework and pray the rosary each night."

The Sunday editions in the mid-1960s were heavy papers, yet the Kopszynski children tried to maintain their usual efficient speed, even in snow. Dad stepped up. Shoving aside the sled and placing stacks of papers on the front seat of his blue pickup, he rolled through the route with windows down. One child balanced on the running board of the driver's side and one on the passenger side, "holding on by the open window." The children scooted off the ledge, raced to deliver, and jumped back on as he drove the snowy streets, headlights beaming. No dogs bothered them. The best part: out with dad. Yahoo! It wasn't eerie, but energetic and exciting. Oh to those classmates: if they could see her now. Wow!

## A Choice

In a family of eleven children, Shirley Hamm was number five on the ladder. Smack in the middle. And as a girl amidst a large family, just like Joan, she found herself confined with household chores, which reappeared faster than it was possible to complete a list.

Coping with her circumstances, Shirley chose to deliver newspapers, an emphasis on the plural. She distributed for more than one newspaper company. Living in East Millinocket, Maine, 10-year-old Shirley began delivering the morning *Bangor Daily News*, and also handled the weekly *Penobscot Times* on one afternoon and on another day, the weekly *Katadin Times*. On Sundays she carried the *Portland Press Herald*. She covered every day of the week with a daily, two weekly papers and a large Sunday edition with all the region's news. A challenge for any grade-schooler.

However, she had already strengthened her discipline by carrying lunches to workers at the paper mill at noon and meals again at 4:30 p.m. The food service routine, along with her school schedule and the never-ending family chores developed her reliable traits. On Saturday, when most children enjoyed idle time, she helped women in town clean their homes. If there was ever any spare time, she babysat a couple of nights a week, an expected role for girls.

In 1946, Shirley thought the advantage of being a newspaper carrier outweighed any disadvantages. "Delivering the newspaper got us out." Not out of routines, nor out of work, but outside a busy house run by Mom's restrictions and assigned duties. Shirley resolved to deliver papers in the northern New England weather seven days a week. She'd capture adventures, rather than be stuck setting and clearing the table, washing, drying and putting away the dishes, scrubbing the kitchen floor, sorting and folding laundry, sweeping, vacuuming---as a start to a list of chores. Her plan was unfazed by the age-12 limit.

On breezy days that snatch news sheets, yachts sailed beyond the picturesque, rocky coast of Maine. With clear sunny days, blueberries ripened. Warm windless days meant mosquitoes, congregated by the millions. And on bitter cold stay-in-the-house nor'easter days, she walked along familiar streets. And familiar residents acknowledged her, or at least identified her as the paper girl. Folks in East Millinocket, "knew everyone by the first name." Almost everyone. Like other paper carriers, she enjoyed being recognized, though it wasn't as Shirley. The people knew Mr. Robert Hamm so she was "recognized as Bobby Hamm's girl." Even the "dogs got to know us so they didn't bother us." Identity was welcome.

Season after season, year after year for five years, from age 10 to 15, she began before 5:00 a.m. with a jaunt to the fire station. She didn't pause to evaluate the worst or the best days, or whether it was a slower or simpler time. For two school kids, it was a scheduled time. Shirley and brother Chester, rolled the papers, stood the tight rolls in the canvas bag until it was packed and then filled the second bag. Shirley carried one slung to the front and right, and the other slung to the left and back. With the route split in half with her brother, who was three years older, the pair covered the sleeping town.

At 13 her brother averaged 85 pounds, which was 15 pounds heavier than his partner. Neither one weighed 100 pounds (meeting the current required child-weight of 100 pounds for hefting 15 pounds.) A bike would have helped, in speed and in relief with the weight of papers transferred from her shoulders and back to the bike, but only during weeks without deep snow.

In four foot drifts even strong legs can't pump a bike. With an average of 93 days of snowfall, a bicycle was left idle on most winter mornings. Shirley was unaffected. Oh, the deep drifts affected her. A 10-year-old female averages 53 inches, which allows a four to six inch clearance in 48 inch drifts.

What didn't apply was an idle bike. She didn't own one. All of her earnings went to her mother. If on occasion she received a nickel tip, she spent the five cents, because it didn't stretch far toward buying a bicycle. Chester, three years older and with longer legs on a five foot frame, bought a new bike.

## Donut Alert

"One particular winter morning after a storm, when the snow was about four feet, I headed for a house where the walk had not been shoveled. It was 5:30 a.m. As I struggled through the snow one boot came off ." Trying to wade through snow with an unprotected foot, the canvas bags slapping side to side, Shirley was caught in a bad situation. No one was out on a dark wintry morning. The cold penetrated more than her foot.

Covering his route, when Chester reached Mr. Hale's house he immediately recognized a problem. Shirley "wasn't there to share the donut." Mr. Hale and his wife, pleasant customers, often bought donuts for the children. Chester knew something was wrong for his sister to skip a sweet, delicious treat. Backtracking, seeing a helpless form, he "helped dig my boot out of the deep snow." More than one reason to love donuts.

# Available

Afternoon newspapers were the most readily available edition. So, John Walsh bought a p.m. *New Bedford Standard Times* route from William, his friend. An enterprising youngster, John held "jobs as early as I can remember, cutting grass, shoveling snow. We were expected to have jobs," Now, he worked the route including Sunday morning, "never late, never missed a day." Through sunny, breezy summer days, when folks headed to Cape Cod, John delivered papers, including to Tobey Hospital where he sold lots of copies. He continued throughout the colorful autumn, with New England leaves aglow, on into the northeastern winters. When he advanced to another opportunity, he kept the purchased position in the family. That way his two small brothers, Tim and James, would have a route.

In the interim, John passed the route to his 8-year-old sister. He was certain she'd handle it, having already demonstrated responsibility. At age 7, Joanne worked in the hot sun picking blueberries for four cents a box. Ready to move from stretching over bushes in a short, seasonal job, she covered the streets of Wareham, Massachusetts, in every season.

Boys struggled to appear taller, struck a swagger to appear older, and kept their lips over toothless spaces until large permanent teeth filled in. All that effort and there were girls who held routes before age 12. It was worse than a classmate cutting ahead in line. Only eight, some girls really cut in front of others.

By the time Joanne was 12, the newspaper code regulation-age, she had passed the route to her two younger brothers. No need for any fussing. Well, maybe she fussed a bit.

If she could have selected a morning route, like Cathi Vannice, Joanne would have avoided nasty heat and humidity. When the fresh, brisk, winter air shifted to blistering heat, the peak summer temperatures were an irritant. She enjoyed her community of Wareham but not the steamy summer days causing "the worst part of the job." Under the blazing sun with her light-weight, sleeveless top, she felt "so hot and the print of the paper stuck to my skin."

# No Girl Need Apply.

In 1950, 8-year-old Joanne had continued John's route. No concerns. Managing one newspaper was not a complicated job for a third-grade girl, even when ink stained her arms. Furthermore, the ties between brothers and sisters ran more than skin deep, which assisted the circulation manager who respected a reliable family.

However, nationally the newspaper industry stated: No girls. Laws in a number of states and large municipalities prohibited "papergirls." So how did female carriers obtain routes? The most common occurrence: the important family unit, bound tightly like bundles of papers.

## Be It Resolved...

The trichotomy of the newspaper company, the community, and the carriers faced a re-stated rule in June, 1950, from the same statement in the 1930s. The rule reinforced the **un-**equilateral triangle as ever more unequal. Parents restricted their daughters, society limited girls, and publishers conformed to the child labor reformers' stance.

A special committee appointed by the International Circulation Managers' Association (ICMA) requested their concise statement be accepted by independent newspaper companies. *Be it further resolved: That no girl will be permitted to engage in newspaper work.*

Reformers pressed for state regulation, preferably national legislation, prohibiting all children under age 18 from working. Advocates for age-restrictive legislation also insisted: *No female minor be permitted to sell or to deliver newspapers.*

Newspaper publishers knew girls managed routes, though they were not a major contingency in the carrier population. In Todd Postol's research on paperboys selling in the 1930s, he determined, "Girls represented an insignificant proportion of route carriers." They were present, but for statistical data they were insignificant. An extensive 1934 survey by the newspaper industry "included 2,530 girl carriers." As the ICMA Newspaperboy Committee in 1950 urged local papers to abide by the recommended standards, they noted a study of the 1949 Newspaperboy Day, which "revealed that 56 newspapers in 27 states were using girl carriers." The publishers' national position was not a criticism of local circulation managers. Leaders urged the standards in order to deflect unsubstantiated complaints against the newspaper business.

The centuries-old gender separation was reflected in higher education. Not until the close of the 1960s did famous colleges admit young ladies. Sex discrimination existed. The national soap box derby races in Akron, Ohio, excluded girls in the competition until 1971.

Thus in 1949, the leaders in publishing urged independent newspaper companies to conform to society's common gender restrictions. However, in a close family, in a compact friendly neighborhood, there was no need for a committee decision. One newspaper edition after school, or in the summer sun that baked the sidewalk and ink-smeared skin, Joanne made her rounds supporting her older brother's choice for her to hold the route for their younger brothers.

# Accountable

Carole Bergeron was the recipient of a decision, rather than independently deciding. With her brother's asthma too severe to struggle up steep hills in Tacoma, walk in the salty damp air along Puget Sound, or inhale the stench of numerous pulp mills, Carole's brother relinquished his route. His mother was not about to relinquish the income from the route.

While the Washington state legislature granted women the right to vote in 1910, this little child in 1949 did not register a vote in her family. A responsible, younger sister stepped forward when her mother assigned the brother's route. Carole was a third grader, another girl not yet 12, who delivered every afternoon, except on Sundays, when she awoke in the early morning to distribute the *Tacoma News Tribune.*

Canvas newspaper bags weren't designed with 8-year-olds in mind. The long strap on the bag was cut according to the average height for a middle-schooler. The designers assumed bags cleared the ground at age 12. Carole's mother sewed an inches-long tuck in the canvas strap, enabling her daughter to tote it each day. Maybe the older brother's severe asthma might improve in 12 months, or 18 months, but not this year. So for days after class at Sheridan Grade School, Carole worked the notched metal washer under the tight wire, snapped the band loose, dropped the papers in the bag and settled into a gait, folding papers one by one for an hour. The frequent Northwest fog, marine mist, and the plain old rain soaked her, but she placed smooth, dry papers inside the screen door in a dry spot. Seven days a week, 52 weeks a year, she moved along the route and moved ahead in school. Mother decreased the tuck in the canvas strap an inch, another year another inch and still another year another inch. Then Carole changed to a double bag as she managed a larger route.

South of Tacoma, army troops shipped out from Fort Lewis for the Korean War. The *Tribune* headlines broadcast Eisenhower's presidential election. As the world smiled, a young Queen Elizabeth II was crowned. Polio vaccine was administered to Carole and her classmates. Sputnik crossed the sky, raising serious concerns. A small papergirl moved from grade school to middle school and into Lincoln High School. From age 8 to18, for a decade, she delivered papers covering all the news events and non-events. Her job culminated with her senior prom. In 520 weeks, she received only one criticism. For whatever reason, the comic page was not inserted in a customer's paper, prompting him to submit a complaint.

The steep hills, rising from the water around Tacoma, offered views of Puget Sound, and the Olympic Mountains capped with sparkling glacial snow lit with colorful, beautiful sunsets. In spring she enjoyed delightful flowering rhododendrons, azaleas, and daffodils.

At other times, the noisome air from the pulp mills really stunk. The stinging, nauseous odor mixed with the exposed, seaweed-strewn sand at low tide when dry crabs and barnacles emitted a smell. But mostly the periodic stench of the mills repulsed people anywhere near Tacoma. Pinching their nose, people labeled it the "aroma of Tacoma."

The smell just was, as the daily paper delivery was, as the tide went in and out. Carole knew her customers quite well and they considered her as consistent as the tide. Knowing how reliable and personable she was, customers asked her to babysit. Earning 35 cents an hour for a family of eight children, she was glad the paper route paid a better, steady income. Plus she enjoyed a "kinship with the customers." Despite the time involved in the route, she looked back on those formative years as enjoyable.

## Sharing

When the Benjamin twins decided to change jobs, they wanted to pass their route to someone in the community. The boys delivered to neighbors and friends, the folks in the small village of South Prairie, Washington, who counted on them. Since they were a pair, people never worried about papers being delivered when one boy was ill. As luck had it, the twins found the right person, or to be exact, persons, for the afternoon run.

A neighbor, Tikie, at 13 met the age requirement for the *Tacoma News Tribune* regulation. If for any reason Tikie was unable to deliver papers, a younger sister would step up, though not the two littlest sisters, being only four and two. And yes, it would be possible to complete a paper route along with the household chores and the farm chores, because everyone in the large family shared daily tasks.

So no question, if two boys handled a modest route, the Grab sisters were capable of surpassing the guys. In 1950, regardless of a written restriction against girl carriers, the *Tacoma News Tribune* district manager wanted the opportunity to cover an outlying village for a decade. Delivery over 10 years stretched to 16 years, but in 1950 he had no idea how many sisters might be available. A substitute would always be ready. The sisters shared the task the way they shared their boy's bike, their clothes, chores, and shared a bed. They even shared the one bathroom just off the kitchen. Sharing was natural.

Riding her boy's bike, Mary Ann, nicknamed Tikie, appeared at the general store that housed the post office in the little burg of South Prairie in western Washington. A truck driver heading east of Tacoma arrived at the village store and dropped stacks of the daily *Tacoma News Tribune* on the rough wooden floor, near the huge glass merchandise case.

Tikie, or a sister, placed the bundles in the bike's front wire basket and rode past two taverns and the church to begin her 10-mile route, as it spread through the fertile, bucolic prairie settled close to the Cascade Mountains.

No need to distinguish between a paperboy and a papergirl since either one should deliver the paper in prime condition and on time. No reason boys deserved an extra metal bar on their bikes. With the metal basket fastened to the handlebars, a boy's style of bike was more convenient to set a small sister on the long bar ready to roll into South Prairie.

Any afternoon, Mary Ann, Phyllis, Teresa, Patricia, whoever was delivering that day, flipped through a *Tribune* bundle, paper by paper reciting each subscriber's name. Rather than count from one to 60, the girls always stated the list of customers by the memorized last name, flowing easier than multiplication tables or Bible verses.

Sixty papers, even on Sunday, were manageable. However, the route was long, especially in the rain, which spoiled a pretty hairdo, or in the valley's hot summer months. Ten miles repeated over six afternoons and one early morning, with extra runs up the walk to a door, stole a chunk of time. It wasn't that the girls lacked for things to do. Situated on the large dairy farm, the growing family always required more help. Chores in the house, chores in the barn, milk the cows, complete lessons for school, lessons in earning money, these all taxed their time.

The girls easily earned babysitting money because the neighbors and church members knew a Grab girl was reliable. They earned additional money during the limited berry picking season. However, seasonal work or occasional sitting did not produce a steady income. Not like a year-long route that consistently provided enjoyable treats when the girls chose to indulge: root beer, Twinkies (two for a nickel), local Nalley's potato chips.

And if for any reason Mary Ann was unavailable, Phyllis helped. Or in case Phyllis missed a delivery then Teresa substituted, or Patricia might be ready to learn the route. And Frankie, age 7, was capable. Quickly proving their ability, age 12 was ignored as age 10, 7, down to 6 started the routine with the younger sisters, Josie, Kathy, and Barbara learning the subscribers. The girls continued, until 1964 when the ninth sister, Suzie, completed the job.

For a decade and a half, nine pretty sisters carefully delivered on time. If they missed a customer, a call to phone number 591 let mother know about the mistake, and anyone else who checked the telephone party line. The printer's grey ink soiled hands and clothes. On one occasion, when Josie delivered on a fresh summer day in her stylish white shorts, she returned home very brown. Cutting across the railroad tracks, stepping along a plank, she lost her balance. Sloppy mud covered her shorts, shoes, knees, hands, under the fingernails. Yuk!

Even before starting the afternoon route, a sister's appearance might be affected. Riding the bike to school, blue jeans properly under her dress, ready for an after-school rush, Teresa discovered the task spoiled her features, hours before delivering papers. "I'd get all fixed up, hair styled, make-up smoothed and when I reached school my hair was straightened, my make-up washed out." The frequent morning fog and Northwest rain interfered with a cute look. However, attitude covered over any appearance as Teresa assessed the situations: "What a wonderful life we had with all our struggles and accomplishments."

Open farm country meant lots of dogs, the chasers and casual barkers, both friends and fiends. The mean mongrel, Juno, was trouble and yet he kept coyotes away. In contrast, a wonderful customer, a lady who bred dogs, gave Phyllis a fluffy, playful puppy. Though larger than a bug, she named him Cricket and, like all gentle collies, he was a marvelous pet. Until! Phyllis faced a dreadful loss, was tearful for days, when Cricket was killed by a vehicle.

The sisters knew their customers, relatives and friends, quite well, and knew all the countryside surrounding their farm home and the village of South Prairie. However, Sunday mornings, or in the winter months when night settled early into the valley and the road was covered with thick fog, the dark scared them. They faced fears the same as any carriers.

Passing from the small community to the outlying farm homes meant riding the bike on the "old road." The back country road, not frequented by traffic, dipped down a hollow into a secluded, spooky section lined with thick trees. The still silence suddenly slashed by the howl of a coyote made a young girl pedal faster. Finish quickly and race for home to be secure with sisters. Of the nine, the middle one, Frankie, could speed the fastest, really super fast downhill.

Frankie, at 7, was already active with farm chores. Finished, she rode their boy's bicycle a mile to school, in her dress, properly wearing blue jeans underneath the skirt, ready for the afternoon delivery. She pushed herself to be with her older sisters and quickly became good at managing the route when a big sister was off on a date. Busy with school, with chores, milking cows, Frankie found the paper route a terrific time to let loose and pedal down a hill. She had just the one. Union Hill was long. Union Hill was steep, not some little turtle hump. In winter, it could make a great sled or ski run for a young, vibrant girl.

Curving into the middle of the road, pumping hard, rider and bike quickly formed a speeding straight arrow. Not sluggish like the tractor chugging in a distant field. Not a bird drifting on air. Pedaling fast downhill, wind swept her hair back. Her skin tingled. Her eyes watered. She felt a lift, soaring as though an albatross. Rising free, "trying to fly."

Her front teeth flew out when the handlebars, crashed "through my mouth. I ate through a straw for three weeks." Severely scraped, spitting out blood, bruised and a battered mouth that caused excruciating pain, she gave up "flying." Another sister took over the route while Frankie healed. The limited healing left her with continuing jaw problems well beyond childhood.

But soon she was back on the route, on her bike with a basket full of papers until an airborne move stopped. Actually, an automobile failed to stop before the two moving objects hit head on. Frankie "ended up on the windshield and got lots of bruises." Terrified as she looked in the window at the car driver, her ears ringing from the screech of brakes, trembling as she slid down onto shaky legs that fortunately were "saved by the large basket of newspapers in front of the handlebars." She survived but not without injury, particularly to her feelings.

Anger does not listen, does not ease pain. Parents who lovingly care for their family slip sometimes. "My parents were very angry and said to the man who hit me, only pay for the repair of the bike, $25." The driver made a serious mistake. The parents misunderstood. Frankie was miserable from mother and dad's criticism.

## Different, But Just the Same

To opinionated social conformists, girls covering routes appeared too different, and they looked askance as gals delivered papers. The movie star image, story book pictures, Sunday school papers, and ladies magazines showed proper lassies in pretty dresses. A girl should be mother's little helper in the home. She was. And then more.

Whether subtlety or clearly stated, imposed restrictions were meant to keep girls off the streets rather than defying the biased rules of society, the newspaper industry regulations, and the state legislatures. For decades newspaper publishers adamantly opposed and successfully argued against child labor reformers on all points concerning paperboys. With papergirls, the leading news executives agreed with the reformers: no girls. Eliminate half of the youth for paper routes: the female half. Even have a co-signer for a carrier contract if a mother was head of household.

Papergirls had to endure all the hardships suffered by the boys: earaches, toothaches, tummy aches. And in addition, girls struggled with monthly aches. Headaches, bloating, tender breasts and the uncomfortable menstrual cramps affected them, if they carried into adolescence.

Fewer in number, defying society's restriction, a papergirl's common sense and independence directed her. Girls wore skirts. Boys wore pants.

That's the way it was. Still, a sensible attitude lifted her over the superficial dress issue. She was not dismissing femininity, but balanced a pretty appearance with functional, unsophisticated attire. The silly corsets, miserable girdles, nylons with a dark seam up the leg, stiff crinolines, none of those uncomfortable items appeared on papergirls. She could deliver in a skirt, which, if she had a bicycle, cleared the bike chain. When schoolmates stared at Joan Kopczynski, she sensed disapproval. However, were their looks actually a sullen desire for money for the movies?

Instead of mindlessly jumping rope in one spot, why not skip down the street, wave to folks, earn money for treats, for clothes, a car and college? The papergirl was disinterested in challenging the system, if even vaguely aware of stated rules. She completed her delivery, earned money, same as boys, in a system that provided equal pay regardless of gender.

Like boys, girls became sick, were scared, and were stiffed by customers. Did girls relish making the rounds facing each customer, the cheerful ones, the crusty curmudgeon, the chronic complainer, hearing the same excuses as boys? The over-arching umbrella of a newspaper carrier job included requesting the subscription fee. Delivering was one segment; asking for money owed was the other half. Boys and girls showed remarkable responsibility, which became evident in their ability to manage money. Were adults as responsible as the paper carriers?

# CHAPTER 13
## THE RAISON D'ÊTRE FOR A ROUTE

Bill scurried along the walk, pennies bouncing in his pocket. Strands of unruly hair sprung from beneath his newsey cap, the wool cover keeping his head warm, unlike his exposed hands. Holding small coins to make change was impossible with thickly knitted mittens, so he managed with naked fingers, not losing a single penny.

He dashed up another set of steps and clapped the brass door knocker. Faint radio music from inside was muffled as a Model A chugged across the intersection. Cars had significantly increased in Brooklyn, cutting down on manure piles and flies. Though right now noxious smells and flies were not a problem in such frigid air. The auto passed and Bill's thoughts shifted to baseball. With extra pennies, possibly he could stand in Ebbets Field in the afternoons and watch his Brooklyn Robins win, if they scored this season.

He turned back to the door just as the curtain closed and radio sounds ceased. His cold knuckles pounded the door frame. When he stopped, silence surrounded him. He stomped his feet to counter shivers that rippled his knickers and ran to frozen toes that he couldn't feel. Another resounding knock jiggled his ring of collection cards.

Each paper Bill Nolting delivered in Brooklyn cost his subscribers two cents. Now he expected the two pennies per paper in order to earn his profit. He heard a slight sound. The high carved oak door slowly opened a few inches. Warm air brushed his cold hands. A small girl, with a pink pinafore over her dress and a matching bow tied to curls, looked up at Bill.

"My mother told me to tell you she isn't home."

### Weight Surpassed by Wait

Collecting---the nemesis of newspaper carriers. Earning was the best, but weekly collecting reached only marginally tolerable. Instead of balancing the bike with a top-heavy load, a paperboy switched to balancing time and the bottom line of his business ledger. A child intended to make money, the raison d'être for a route. And so a carrier climbed steps, politely spoke to customers, and persisted with late payers as weight had morphed to wait.

A boy had turned from riding down the sidewalk using a fast aim to porch a paper, to standing still on a door mat, his throwing arm resting. Delivery focused on speed as he competed with himself to be faster. In collecting, his speed ground to slow as he faced customers telling him, "no money today." Bill's common sense told him the girl's mother was ignoring payment, again. When the cutie closed the door, warm air and pennies disappeared.

While a carrier endured a range of conditions---shivering in snow, rushing through sleet, panting in the heat---collecting brought additional challenges as he tried to catch folks at home, catch them before the curtain closed, catch them with money. With a receipt book in hand but no paper, it was obvious why he stood on the porch and addressed the silence: "Collect for the *Times*." or the *"Tribune"* or the *"Telegraph."*

Running his route, the paperboy learned each street, alley, high hedge, short-cut, apple tree, guard dog; he knew the neighborhood like a cop on the beat. Straight up the steps to collect, he learned details about his neighbors, both delightful and disturbing, when he listened to whistling, singing, snoring, shouting, and swearing.

As Mike Rhodes discovered, he held "more demographic information about customers collectively than any census report ever had." An alert youngster, Mike observed "the intimate and personal comings and goings of people" around the geographic sector he served. He could "spot anything out of the ordinary," and his presence was "within earshot of domestic spats."

Aided by honest wisdom, Mike was "entrusted with and the guardian of a great deal of information that was not for public dissemination." He heard, he saw, he absorbed, and held people's trust in him to remain silent. From an adult's point of view, this was only the paperboy, a neighbor kid. No need to be reserved and proper around him.

So carriers watched live sitcoms running and repeating on their routes. They observed married and unmarried couples, saw who tossed brown bottles in the trash, who left Miss Straight's house before sunrise on Sunday, noted which children went to the tavern to guide dad home, followed people's occupations and sudden unemployment, admired a shiny new Lincoln at the mansion, felt sad for a guy suffering over a repossessed car.

Up the long, curved driveway to double doors gracing a mansion, a paperboy stepped inside the splendid home and witnessed the style and wealth of life enjoyed by others. His feet warmed on the thick pile of a red, Persian carpet. The grandfather clock reminded him to keep working. He'd never set foot in such an imposing residence. His personal assessment of his family's crowded rental flat changed, as he compared and contrasted his world with a dream world. Collecting often meant cookies and cocoa, and also, an abundant taste of possibility. Several blocks later he had moved from mansions down to misery; the opulent wealth receded to odorous filth. He aimed higher.

Besides coins, carriers pocketed their experiences, while still too young to extrapolate the full meaning. Collecting revealed a lot, even a whole body's worth as some ladies came forth in less than a boy expected. With focused eyes, ears, and most of all, a curious nose to smell excitement in exotic enclaves, his innocent views burst open like a jack-in-the-box. Approaching different people, including indifferent ones, he made his rounds to scoundrels, a scrooge, on to the welcome smiles and silks.

The child wanted money for snack food, some fun, and for his family, but first he paid the newspaper company, then for his sundry costs. Parents didn't distribute coins for lost baby teeth, good grades, doing endless chores, or for casual spending. With no allowance, absolutely zero, children never suffered being overpaid.

## Little Merchants

The rule of the company: carriers promptly pay the total wholesale bill. For a weekly plan, they paid each Saturday. In 1951 after waiting four years for a route, Ron Anderson learned immediately not to wait to pay his bill. "Every Saturday at 8:00 a.m.," Ron, along with other paperboys, met their district manager by the gas station at the corner of Lake and Stonewood. For a carrier to miss this meeting or be short on his bill was a "mortal sin."

For the monthly payment, carriers paid by the tenth of the month, but newspaper managers pressed boys to pay by the fifth day. No excuses, no arguing, no partial amount the way some adults operated. Paperboy and manager respected the agreement, whether in a written contract or a business hand shake. The company was paid by the youngster---or by his parents---and then he'd really pay!

Though he disliked collecting, a boy had to get motivated, get moving, to get money. His only way to pocket coins was to collect more than he owed wholesale and in expenses.

So, climbing slippery porch steps, standing at the door in a hand-me-down jacket, too big for a nine-year-old yet with sleeves that loosely covered cold fingers, his patience with collecting was incredible. Furthermore, this little businessboy, acquired debts he must cover. Along with paying the company, his accumulated costs pressured and pushed him up to the door knocker.

Costs to having a paper route?

Yes!

## A Collection of Costs

Buy a route: For decades young city hawkers served as manager, sales force, and financial officer of their small, owned corner, and shouted, "Extra! Extra!" When a boy advanced to another job, he sold his lucrative spot. And then these turfs broadened from shouting and selling on a corner, to silently walking residential streets on a neighborhood route.

Though not common, but not unusual, carriers in like manner sold their route, which was not solely owned and for a lesser amount than the city hawker's real estate spot. If a boy faced buying a route, it was one of several hurdles to acquire a newspaper carrier job.

Living in a rural area of the Appalachian Mountains, Robert Ruth in 1928 bought a *Johnstown Democrat* morning route. Purchase price: $10. This was a sizeable investment for a paper that sold for two cents a copy, when people stooped to pick up a dropped penny.

With $10 a family could purchase a wool blanket or a school suit with a vest and knickers and pocket $3 for other necessities. Here was a boy dealing in dollars. To reclaim the $10 investment, collecting was imperative. Robert, followed by brothers William, Richard and Paul, reaped benefits from the route, until World War II controlled their lives.

Donald Watt wanted a bicycle so in 1934 he bought a morning delivery, the *Toledo Times*. Sold on the basis of customer count, the route cost Donald 15 cents a subscriber. The 53 customers equaled $7.95. This was a sizeable sum for a 10-year-old in the deepening Depression. Earning money, he soon owned a used bike to ride into the wind tunnels off Lake Erie in the challenging landscape of northern Ohio.

Jim Birchman purchased a *Detroit News* evening route in 1941, the usual way to obtain one with "many eager youngsters and only so many routes." The supply and demand market gave an advantage to the seller.

With prosperity came an increase in price. In Hodgenville, Kentucky, Grant Wise began the 1960 decade by buying a morning *Courier Journal* and an afternoon *Louisville Times* route for $45. This was a hefty sum for an 11-year-old in a small, economically-challenged town.

Rent a route: At age 10, Bob Brink did not purchase his huge evening route of more than 300 *Elmira Star Gazette* papers. He inherited the route in 1954 from his brother, who like Bob, "paid a rental sum, which I am guessing was about 10 cents per customer every month. A considerable cost for the right to deliver papers, especially with no guarantee I would ever be able to collect from every customer all that they owed." Bob paid the full rent to a soda-jerk at 14th Street in Elmira, New York, who bought *Star Gazette* routes.

Management finally stopped the man's unorthodox practice. "Even so, we kids would never see any of the rent paid over the years." The rental payments were the kids' problem.

Whether buying or renting a route, the amount started the debit column in the Little Merchant's business ledger. These costs were less common than other expenses.

Sold: With 150 customers to serve, Bill Miller determined he needed a consolidated route in the erratic Connecticut weather. Plus his New England efficiency and work ethic in 1943 rested on common sense, so he sold an out-of-the-way customer. Because the purchaser would make money with another customer, Bill felt he should pay for the addition. The 35 cent sale of one subscriber helped Bill offset his 50 cent cost for a canvas bag.

From the start, a paper route's bottom line taught small merchants a practical lesson: time is money. Making little money per hour, a carrier controlled his time to raise the profit column. Spare minutes needed to be spent mowing lawns, shoveling snow, gathering pop bottles, hauling coal, and selling extra garden vegetables.

## Business Expenses

Bought: A strong canvas bag monogrammed with the newspaper company name---giving free advertisement along the route---carried a price. Kids tried for a hand-me-down, but sometimes the bag was too wasted or someone else picked it up. Paying $45 for his route, Grant Wise also added a $2.50 charge for a canvas bag.

As carriers acquired more customers and coped with the larger Sunday load, they needed an extra bag or a double design. Face one more cost in managing a profitable route.

Bike: Before the 1950s, many a boy started a route on foot, earning funds to buy a used bicycle, and then, hopefully, a brand new bike. Not waiting on an answered wish for one to appear, sprinkled with Tinker Bell dust, he worked for a used one.

In the 1920s, the luxury of a bicycle lay far beyond a family's restrictive budget. Money paid for vital necessities. Playing on a bike was but a pipe dream to Dick Irvin or Ed Norlin in the '20s. Yet they still managed to complete routes every morning and afternoon.

Once the *Toledo News* paid for Robert Hansen's route, (since he couldn't afford the price) he worked hard. "Did not miss a day." He was focused on his reason for requesting the job: a bicycle. As he pulled a loaded wagon, "I had a goal to keep me stimulated. Dad could not get a bike for me," not in 1932. Robert took action. He collected regularly, saved and "studied the Montgomery Ward's Catalog." At last, tallying his profits, he ordered a bicycle with a large wire basket. Then he waited. "It came all crated up. Dad and I had a swell time putting it together." Father and son time, with dad feeling pride in his son's financial accomplishment.

Charles "Bill" Cain needed a bicycle. Delivering in Fort Smith, Arizona, seven mornings, to over 200 customers on his 10 mile, rough path, his used bike suffered. Though it was 1936, Bill saved every month, and eventually bought "a new Schwinn for $40, one with a spring fork."

Vyron Mitchell knew he was lucky when he acquired his route in Cadiz, Kentucky in 1950. A third-grader, Vyron was earning $15 a month, sometimes $20 a month. Saving money as a grade school boy made him proud, especially after his brand new Western Flyer bicycle from the Western Auto company arrived. Pleased, he owned a "two-wheel" auto.

As more prosperous years rolled in, children asked for a new bike and it appeared next to the Christmas tree, or a shiny one stood on the porch with a birthday bow. Others could not expect to freely receive.

Up and down the streets in Lake Forest Park, running along the rough ravines north of Seattle, Loren Day watched boys on their bicycles. With prosperity in 1954, he wanted to emulate his school mates and ask for a bike. But Loren couldn't ask dad; he had died, leaving seven of the twelve children still at home. A brother helped, selling his bike to Loren for a one dollar bill. This lifted him to wheels so he didn't have to wear out shoe leather for five years while delivering 150 daily newspapers. Once he owned his working bike, he had to maintain it. Costs for maintenance were not to enter his expense column. Necessity and thrift taught Loren how to fully maintain it, even how to spoke the wheels.

Bike parts: To most kids, a split tire, broken chain, busted basket from crashing into a tree, bent frame from hitting a car---any of these meant a sudden expense. Collecting that week became more vital.

Bands: The newsboy bought boxes of rubber bands from the newspaper company, just as he bought a canvas bag. All the stretch bands cost him, including spare ones he used for shooting paper wads. The 50 rubber bands Glen pulled over a rolled newspaper, to vent his frustration with the chronic complainer, added a cost. It was worth the price.

Sunday Edition: While the number of Sunday customers often exceeded the weekly count, and the one-day increase added to earnings, additional costs occurred because of heavy stacks. A wagon, a back fender rack, a double bag for the load helped, but meant another expenditure.

Bruce Adams bought a whizzer bike cart. He wanted one with a motor but that cost $100, and already the $73.35 he spent for a new bike in 1946 was a challenge, like his 10- mile route on dirt streets. Leonard Lair, facing the Sunday weight, built a cart using bicycle tires, and Jim

Root rented one with a solid steel handle, which snapped off his front teeth. In 1969, the *Seattle Times* suggested carriers buy a super-size cart for $18. The cost could be paid over a two-month period. However, the bicycle attachment for it was an additional $2.87, owed in one month.

Buy a route, buy a bike; rent a route, rent equipment, and try to stay ahead of being in debt. Under way on his job, a paperboy faced challenges and costs from every direction.

## More Money

Broken: Windows, storm doors, Christmas ornaments, milk bottles, plenty of breakable material jumped in the way of solid paper missiles. A bike breaks: fix it. A window breaks: fix it.

As if burned hands from a mean boy and the harsh blame for a dog's broken tail weren't enough to endure, George Janecke shattered a window. Or technically, the tightly rolled paper flew through the glass.

"I got so good at rolling my *Seattle Star* papers, the roll became as hard as rocks." Furthermore, "I could throw one a mile." The "mile" was measured by paperboy standards. Day after day for "miles" he porched rock-hard papers until the evitable happened. "My paper sailed right through the front window. I was stunned."

Once the ringing of broken glass ceased, George walked up the porch steps. He knocked. No answer. With nobody home, "could I somehow get out of this dilemma?" Not really, since the paper rested in the middle of the living room encircled with broken glass and a few slivers embedded in the "rock." No detective necessary. George left a note, finished his route, and then a forlorn figure returned to the mishap.

"I asked how much money they wanted me to give them so they could fix their window." Prepared for a discouraging bill, his self-conscious thoughts swirled. Anxious to be on his way, he wasn't sure he heard the reply. "They didn't want any money. Wow!"

Really? Were his ears still ringing too much from the glass crash to hear clearly?

No, the people were specific. "They wanted me to fix the window." As if paying wasn't enough, an inexperienced school boy must now repair the break, and of course immediately. Did dad "offer to help? No."

He did explain how to repair it. George listened to what little English his father knew and translated his dad's Polish directions: measure, buy sheet of glass, seal. Using father's tools and putty, he proceeded to install a window. He precisely measured the window frame, bought the glass, carried it ever so carefully to the home, cleared the track of broken pieces, inserted the new window, and placed putty around the edge. He cleaned up the bits of mess.

"By golly I fixed the window!" And he fixed his newspaper throw, down from a speeding mile. Maybe other paperboys should hire him to repair their damages.

Jim Birchman scored a double hit in Detroit. He broke the storm window and the window. Buying his route, paying for two windows, darn it was hard to get ahead.

Purchasing a canvas bag from the *Seattle Times*, Dale Irvine believed he'd quickly pay for it with over 100 daily customers, and more on Sunday. Then in his first month, still learning the rhythm to a route, he broke an ordinary window, which both frightened and discouraged the shy youngster. In 1948 his $27 accident, cost more than his anticipated monthly profit.

The Window Association of America should have sponsored a special promotion and discount plan for carriers. It could include a glass lay-away plan and installation instructions.

Accident Insurance:  As property damage happens, physical accidents happen, particularly in an accident-prone age. But when a child is nine, he doesn't connect stumbling accidents with debts. Nevertheless, for his family to be protected from bills for his physical injury, Ron Casto paid 25 cents a week, a dollar per month in 1955, to the *Marietta Times*. Carriers for the *Seattle Times* could buy 24-hour accident insurance, adding just 75 cents a month to their bill. Mike Hall, in the last half of the 1950s, met 35 cents each week for insurance. To children who never think about accidents, Mike's $1.40 every month would have paid for their choice purchases.

Money Order:  To pay the circulation manager the weekly wholesale subscription fee, arriving with a full bag of coins was unacceptable. The *Seattle Times* district managers requested payment with a money order, which the carrier had to buy.

All these accumulated charges were biting into their expected profit. And then something else would arise, such as a fellow who needed boots and a pilot style hat with flaps to cover freezing ears. The list grew, shrinking the profit line, and a bit more when the customers and the newspaper company cut in.

# F _ _ _ _  Words

Functioning in the work-a-day world, sometimes a child simply couldn't cope with the challenges and conditions in a  controlled route. He failed, forced to travel other avenues.

Since paperboys weren't classified as employees, it's difficult to believe they could be fired. An untrustworthy devil, a kid committing malice, the circulation manager discharged the rogue, dishonorably.

Maybe dismissed deviants were already on a route to jail, with or without a detour around a newspaper route.

More common than kids who failed or were fired was the company's answer to customers' complaints: a fine.

Fined: With mistakes or the missed delivery, the company's documented complaint, known in paperboy jargon as "kicks," came with a price. Without a dime to spare and a debt column at the start of a route, fines did kick. And a child's net profit was affected far more than a company's bottom line.

For Mike Hall, a fine was another cost added to a $10 deposit to start his route. If fined the company's 15 cent charge, the 15 cents would be cancelled when the customer signed his apology note. A greater impact than the fine or facing the customer to apologize was the stigma. To a conscientious child, "a complaint was like the end of the world."

There were customers who behaved like mean, sneaky dogs, hiding to catch a paperboy with a late or missed delivery, but managers monitored the complaint system. And a deduction or a fine was minor compared to failure or being fired from a first job. A kid could make up fines selling extras, earning tips, signing on a new subscriber as long as that other F_ _ _ word existed: FAIR.

The manager's interest was not to inflict a fine on paperboys. The men taught young charges to provide customers with the child's phone number and encouraged them to know their customers. Recalling their own experiences, managers empathized with the newsboys.

Mr. Comstock accepted that David Bowles could carry 132 *Ellensburg Evening Record* papers. The manager valued the small boy's reliability. Delivering during the winter, with roads full of snow, David struggled for two and a half hours. He had "two people that complained, usually in the winter. If I got a "kick" (a complaint called in and the company made my delivery), they would dock me 10 cents for each customer that called in." Mr. Comstock, knowing David tried his best, "would stall them and by that time I'd have been there and left their paper." He still earned his 10 cents, which mattered in 1924 when a dime paid for a hamburger and a hot cup of coffee.

Bond: Like many carriers in the 1950s, Ron Casto paid a required 50 cents a week for a bond, to insure that his wholesale bill was always paid, along with his 25 cents per week for injury insurance, and 10 cents for any complaint. The minimum $3 a month reduced the profit column.

Wake Up Call: Starting in 1938 with an early morning route of 100 customers, Harry Ansted quickly rose to station manager at the *Seattle PI* paper shack on Queen Anne Hill. He earned extra for the position, a real benefit. Of course the additional pay meant more responsibility. Completing an absent boy's route, or even two routes, on the steep slopes and arriving at school on time required running faster than a gazelle. With a heavy bag and long hills, he couldn't reach the speed of a cheetah.

After covering three routes before school, Harry addressed his problem as a mature new manager: He phoned the absent party. Better the kids deliver their papers than saddle him with the burden. Very disciplined, he determined other carriers should learn to not oversleep. Set an alarm clock or pay up. He figured the bottom line would get a bottom out of bed, so he charged 25 cents for a wake-up call. In 1941, a quarter bought lunch. Growing out of the Depression, Harry knew the value of coins as he helped his family and saved to purchase his clothes.

Phone Call:   Many times, a pay phone at the corner grocery or on the wall of the general store came in handy. Of course that required dropping in a dime, but the pay phone, like a pay toilet, covered a necessity. However, should a dime be routinely necessary because of a sleeping manager? To rise by 4:30 a.m. to have papers delivered before 6:00 a.m. and then waste 10 cents per call---no way.

John Wilson's common sense eliminated the repeat cost, sparing the loss of dimes. John earned $20 a month so 10 cents was available; however, he wanted pocket change for his fun. With calls as a quick alarm clock, by 10 calls, he'd spent a dollar, a difference. Starting with 135 customers and increasing to 150 subscribers, plus in a few months he added an afternoon route complimenting his morning rounds, John was a businessboy.

The situation with his publisher, who also served as the circulation manager, was that he wore too many hats. Once the papers came off the press, exhausted, he relaxed and slept.

John needed to disrupt the sleep to leave quickly with papers. He walked to the pay phone and deposited a dime. A drowsy answer. Before long the budding entrepreneur learned that the moment his manager responded, if John immediately hung up, "got my dime back." Appreciating reliable performance, the manager soon gave John a key. When the publisher was "late (as always) I would let the rest of the crew enter, about 20 boys." No sleeping then.

Hired Help:   Bill Miller, with a hefty route of 150 customers, added a morning route in the summer and for a while delivered a paper in Polish. Bill was busy. But he didn't like collecting, what with the dog nuisance and some people falling five weeks behind with their bill. To ease the burden, Bill hired a younger boy for the task and paid him 50 cents a week.

Substitute:   Paperboys realized it was a good idea to pay a dime, or purchase a candy bar for the small fry, who as a sub tried to learn the paper route business. If he did a good job, treat him well, since he might be needed for the next week or weeks.

Christmas Calendars:  In December, folks would want a new calendar for January. Christmas cards and catchy poems had long been a traditional effort by newsies to solicit a Christmas reward. Combining this traditional effort with access to the printing press, newspaper companies helped carriers by producing calendars. And being consistent---sell a canvas bag, sell rubber bands---the calendars were sold to the carriers, who recognized an inexpensive way to substantially increase tips. While the boys paid for the calendars, they could choose to sell or give them to their customers.

Small Claims Court:  For customers who considered newspapers as free, a disgusted carrier took action. With the cost of newspapers increasing, and not being reimbursed, a paperboy in 1969 in Seattle could proceed to Small Claims Court. He paid a $1 filing fee. Then he completed a subpoena form, and added $2.80 for the subpoena to be served. The claim brought him $9.

A single carrier never faced all these itemized costs. Nor did the list of charges occur each week over years of delivering. Once he paid off the route selling price, and his payments for a used bicycle, those line items disappeared. Yet new ones occurred: a larger double bag, a bigger bike, better boots, another box of bands, broken windows, deadbeat losses. Costs whittled down his profits: bike repairs, 25 cents for a money order, 50 cents for help to collect.

Face the circulation manager for newspaper charges, face expenses, whew, collecting was clearly imperative for the important part: pay the carrier. So he prepared, focusing on essential keys.

# CHAPTER 14
## BE . . .

### Be prepared. Be seen. Be considerate.
### And above all, be persistent

Counting customers, so easy. Counting change, so confusing. For young paperboys in their first job, a handful of coins tested them. For inexperienced newspaper carriers, who had never felt coins of any denomination in their pocket, they struggled to accurately collect a week's worth of subscription fees.

Pennies are a copper color. Nickels, larger than a penny are a dull gray shade. The dime, also gray, but oops, thinner than the penny or the nickel. How could a smaller coin be worth twice as much as the thicker coin? The nickel, quarter, and fifty-cent piece are the same color and progressively larger. The quarter is worth five times as much as the nickel.

*"But what's five dimes?"* a small voice inquired.

*"Not dimes. Times. Multiply,"* explained his brother, now a big third grader.

The mix-ups were different from school problems. Standing at the blackboard, when the paperboy committed a subtraction mistake, the teacher quickly pointed out the error in front of the entire class. With inaccurate collecting, lost coins mattered more than chalk dust on an eraser.

The carrier needed to correctly recognize the fifty-cent piece and calculate double digits in his head as he subtracted 35 cents and returned a dime and nickel. Or a dime and the quarter?

*Oh no, a customer owes for three weeks.* That means multiplication, but the math tables aren't taught until third grade. A man held out a dollar bill. Since the pencil lead was broken and the eraser chewed off, a grade-schooler self-consciously figured 35 plus 35 plus 35 in his head as his stomach growled.

*But it's off five cents? Do I tip the guy a nickel or one of those little thin coins?*

Managing money records was difficult. Then a boy tried to ignore a stack of coins that tempted him until he paid the manager on Saturday.

Following baseball batting scores, memorizing players on national teams, accurately citing World Series statistics, knowing the day and time of radio programs, keeping all that data in his head was easier than remembering coin values and figuring change. Oh, and remember the spelling list for tomorrow's test. Sometimes the head was too full.

In 1950, Leroy Modine, who was not yet eight, needed to learn the coins and the math problems in order to accurately collect $1.25 each month. Dad gave Leroy a $20 bill and then "helped with making change." They worked on problems with two $1 bills, with a fifty-cent piece; his customers also helped him. He soon calculated change for $1.30, for $1.50, and whether the handful of quarters, nickels, dimes and even pennies handed to him totaled the amount due. His small, chilled fingers lacked the necessary dexterity to easily separate cold coins, while adding the values before pocketing the money. Determined, he succeeded and increased his route from 55 to 85 customers. With more subscribers, he went from collecting $68.75 to $87.50, and on to $106.25 a month. Quite an accomplishment for a grade schooler.

Delivering to customers in East Lansing, Michigan, Ron Nixon found money more challenging than the wintry conditions on his early morning rounds. He repeated his route to collect at a convenient time, since disturbing subscribers at 4:30 a.m. wasn't smart. The sleepy residents might be confused.

With 135 customers, collecting required considerable time, and was considerably more uncomfortable. Ron "couldn't make change. I just couldn't figure it out. Most of my customers were in married student housing while attending Michigan State University. I used to take out a handful of coins and ask them to make their own change." Living on tight budgets, the students knew the value of nickels and dimes. They were honest and helped him.

For many boys, nearing age 12 and no longer struggling to figure correct change, they soon fumbled with coins when a pretty, slim school mate answered the door. Distracted with internal excitement, the cool confident approach was clipped by her smile and curving figure, which caused math figures to disappear.

Whew, the chaos at the newspaper shack was more appealing than keeping receipts in careful order. A kid needed to carry extra change, his receipt book, a pencil with unbroken lead, and remember his manners as he spoke to a dense looking fellow, who knew very well why the paperboy was standing in the doorway. Collecting required pluck and strong motivation to address an adult for money.

When circulation managers held weekly sales-development meetings, the boss emphasized: collect at a set time, be prepared with change, carry your receipt book, and look right at the customer. No slouching, stand up straight and make eye contact.

*Jed raised his hand.*

*"Yes Jed."*

*"Should I carry a stool?"*

If little Jed stood straight, shoulders back as the manager advised, and looked straight ahead, he'd see the guy's belt buckle or bulging beer belly.

Collecting was not easy, particularly for a small, shy child reduced to stuttering under the stare of a tall adult. Many grownups avoid public speaking, but a tyke on the porch platform had to swallow shyness, stop shaking, and speak up without lisping to request payment, while his cold nose dripped. Ask for a paper route: fine. Ask an adult for money? He never approached his parents for any, and now he was to approach customers. Gee whiz.

As Dr. Reed reported in the collecting section of her *Newsboy Study*, "Knowledge of human nature and the way to meet and handle different types of people are recognized as essentials to success." A paperboy met folks in the collection process. He was okay with a neighbor, parents of a school mate, relatives a block away, or nice customers down the street, but a stranger stalled him; yet, he wasn't allowed to stall paying the manager.

Instead of balancing on his bike using no hands at break-neck speed, he switched to standing with a hand extended in order to keep a receipt book balanced. And be respectful, when a grouchy adult did not respect how uncomfortable he was.

## Be Seen, and Not Heard?

*Ask and ye shall receive.* Sunday's sermon emphasized Jesus delivering his sermon on the mount. For the week's Sunday school verse, children memorized Matthew, Ch 7 verse 7, 8: "*Ask, and it shall be given you; seek, and ye shall find; knock and it shall be opened unto you. For every one that asketh receiveth.*"

However, in practice, the newspaper carriers' lessons were fraught with restrictions.

Parents and grandparents, raised in the Victorian era, preached to the younger generation that children should be seen and not heard. That principle left paperboys confused. How can you ask and not be heard, or with open curtains, not be seen? And some people intensified the ordeal. Is it any wonder kids hesitated to converse with adults? The tyke requested the route for money, just a little spending money, because wanting a small allowance was futile.

## Slow and Intense

Simplicity disappeared, replaced with complexity for those who delivered large routes twice a day, or more than one local and regional newspaper. True, the collecting portion was not repeated seven days a week. Still, the financial process was more intense than tossing papers. The slowest part of managing a route was as irritating as a dentist's slow drill without Novocain.

In addition, mistakes and misdemeanors became magnified in the eyes of the customer holding the money. Remember the person in the open door, the one Robin Paterson blasted in the gut? Or the lady Larry Hudson hit in the head with a tightly rolled paper? Santa knows who's been naughty and nice, and so does the customer with 50 rubber bands around his paper. And what about the dog that chewed the paper and now has a chance to chew the pants, or even deeper, as the kid stands at the door? Collecting required strong determination to address a perturbed customer for money owed. Then at times an intimidated child had it worse with a raspy cough and a drippy nose. His splattering sneeze spread on a customer as she hands coins to unclean hands hardly endeared the paperboy to the adult.

Knowing all his customers, enjoying the friendly neighborhoods of working families in the prosperous '50s, managing one afternoon route, Gary and his side partner, Goofy, collected consistently, at a set time, with coins ready for change. They rolled right along.

Unfortunately, thousands of carriers stumbled into different scenarios.

## Labeled Simple When Complicated

With a 4:30 a.m. route, a child needed to collect at a convenient time from people he seldom saw. Or he delivered in neighborhoods other than his, on impersonal city blocks asking strangers for their subscription fee. He counted on considerate customers answering the door.

Charles Cain delivered seven days a week, over a 10-mile route in the pleasantly cool Arizona sunrise. His discomfort appeared as he tried to raise his profit column at a comfortable hour for his customers when the mercury column was rising. The hot sun challenged him, as he maintained pay records on 200 people. Some folks paid regularly, others missed two, three, even five weeks. There were Sunday only customers. Yet, Charles considered his job fun, and enjoyed $25 a month in the midst of the Depression.

For paperboys with a morning, an afternoon, and a Sunday route, more complications occurred. On multiple routes a price difference existed between the daily, the daily and Sunday, and the Sunday only customers. Also, factor in a customer who pays sporadically and collecting turned complicated. Even more so with complex people.

Harve Harrison, from 1932 to 1935, in the nation's desperate economy, appreciated his paperboy position. It was "a privilege to have a newspaper job." Harve balanced his time around school and the handling of morning and afternoon newspapers that came from Seattle, Tacoma, and Portland. His father served in the army, which was why Harve's route was located in Fort Lewis, between Seattle and Portland. He delivered the *Seattle Times, Seattle Star, Seattle PI*, the *Tacoma Tribune, Tacoma Times* and the *Oregonian* to 80 subscribers. He kept track of requests, because the customers had a "distinct preference for their paper." He also kept track for collecting. The price of the papers could be the same; however, the totals tallied different amounts for different companies. His job was not the usual, one-local-paper, each afternoon.

Nevertheless, with six carriers at the drop spot, Harve and the gang had fun competing to see who rolled their papers the fastest and threw the farthest. After a quick respite of fun, he and his terrier dog set off across the large army post. His pet kept him company as he traversed the streets, though police dogs on the military grounds frightened them. He felt little comfort with just a canvas newspaper bag slung between a strong, mean attacker and his best pal's short legs. But rolling through the rounds, he finished in the wards of the General Hospital, and headed to his last stop: the hospital kitchen. Guys on KP gave him a full supply of food for his dog, an extra collecting benefit in a challenging route.

Rather than deliver every afternoon, Shirley Hamm supplemented her daily morning routine with two afternoon routes, one day the weekly *Katadin Times* and the next day the weekly *Penobscot Times*. In order to pay the newspaper companies, she maintained customer payment records for daily, weekly, or Sunday-only subscribers, and paid the *Bangor Daily*, the *Portland Press Herald*, the *Katadin Times* and the *Penobscot Times*. As a 10-year-old, she managed a full record system along with her lengthy list of chores and school studies.

Ed Norlin's route in 1953 was not small. He delivered *The Daily Oklahoman* to 130 customers in the morning, another 95 homes in the afternoon with *The Oklahoma City Times*, and for *The Sunday Oklahoman* he dropped 200 papers. The Sunday delivery often required three hours to finish. Each week he completed thirteen delivery rounds, and then made his rounds to collect, keeping his records accurate on which subscribers were daily, daily and Sunday, or Sunday only. He gained a slight advantage with The Oklahoma Publishing Company owning all three editions.

Connecting with the customers, collecting the correct amount, challenging themselves with stacks of tempting coins, these steps tested the paper carriers, but were not the dangerous threat boys encountered at some homes.

## Drop the Bike

Going about his weekly task, in the difficult 1930s, Robert Hansen's collecting system worked. He checked off dozens of customers as he methodically collected from all 124 people, which led him to his goal: buying a bicycle. Another collection day, one more house, one more customer. Rather than casually drop his newly purchased bike across the front sidewalk, he carefully parked it along the side of the house. Bad mistake.

"I guess too close to where the puppies were." He hadn't seen the German Shepherd who just produced a litter. Like a mama grizzly, she attacked. This was the only time Robert was bitten, because once was a sufficient lesson from a terrible, bloody bite out of his body.

## Faster than The Road Runner

David Mushen built his *Detroit News* delivery from 45 customers to 98 daily papers and over 100 on Sunday. In the 1960s, Sunday papers stacked ever higher with multiple sections, a Sunday magazine, and numerous advertising inserts. Delivering the route for five years, he knew his customers "very well." He also understood his route mattered because he paid his school tuition, all his personal expenses and gave Mom money. His father died when David was nine. But he met his difficulties head on and conscientiously managed his school work, chores, scouts, altar boy duties and the paper route, which he considered "fun."

There was a place along the route that scared him. When he reached a particular door to collect, a "large, aggressive German Shepherd" was guarding the house. David approached the open door, with just a screen separating him from the angry, charging shepherd. He saw the large shoulders, the ears back, the slimy throat. He smelled the saliva and his own reasonable fright. Week after week, into another year, David never relaxed his tense fear of the beast.

The test came: the day his subscribers forgot to latch the screen door.

The frame slammed David's face. Though painfully smacked in the head, with his fastest reflex he shoved against the wood frame a second before the dog could sink its teeth into his nose, ripping off cheeks and lips. Like a competing Olympic athlete, David won by a millisecond. "Fortunately, I was quick enough to push the door closed and hold it until the owners put their dog away."

Unlike a scene from a *Road Runner* cartoon, the thin wire screen held, and the people arrived quickly, though they were not as fast as David. Nothing slow about his racing heart. David's split-second response was critical. His collecting time had switched from very slow.

## Be Considerate

Ron Anderson delivered the *Democrat & Chronicle* before 6:00 a.m. To be considerate he repeated his route on Thursday afternoon to collect from, "nice people, middle class working folks in modest homes in their very neat, clean, well-kept neighborhoods" of Charlotte, New York. "I never had any trouble collecting from them." Ron conscientiously managed his route, to include hiring his brother on Sundays, for $1, to deliver the long Sheppler Street.

Collecting for the entire route remained Ron's responsibility. One home on Sheppler Street only subscribed to the Sunday paper, a cost of 10 cents a week. The people owned "a small but very energetic, very loud dog. I used to think that if he ever got out while I was collecting that he would bite me."

Just a matter of time. Evitable! The dog broke out. "He did bite me."

Ron needed a doctor to attend to the painful injury. "The dog's owners were not very sympathetic with my plight." Could they spare a little sympathy, more than a dime's worth?

## Lost out

The usual 80/20 response held: 80 percent paid on time. They paid the correct amount, no question, no complaints, and no terrible dogs. The best subscribers placed the correct amount under the door mat, in the milk box, or left their exact change on the hallway table for a straight forward transaction. Such people demonstrated a model of efficiency.

The 20 percent who were perpetually out, or held out, or deliberately cut out, created more than four times the annoyance for carriers. Charged for the number of newspapers issued, and working for pennies of profit, why should a mere child reach into his pocket of meager earnings to pay for a daily paper conveniently delivered to his elders?

Learning different coins and grasping basic number problems, carriers just as quickly learned the simple ABC's of adult antics. Kids figured out the pattern, figured out which people would pay, and figured on a profit---the primary reason for a paper route.

Those few complainers and curmudgeons that made collecting a challenge became a major irritation. In addition, paperboys tried to corral people at home, often during their set supper hour. Carriers didn't always succeed. Or some people were simply unresponsive. For the money, a child returned as persistently as a squirrel to a blocked bird feeder, or a bear opening a latched trash can lid.

A paperboy just wanted the 65 cents, or whatever amount, people owed. For this he approached adults who persisted in failing to pay a small bill. Aloof, the folks functioned under their procrastination privilege.

Children who delivered before breakfast and before supper, completed chores, and attended seven hours of school, had to sandwich the required collecting into a limited time slot. If Thursday and Friday weren't sufficient, they tried Saturday, their free day from school now sliced into parts---one part delivery and a repeat to collect at an agreeable hour in the daylight or when the porch light was still on.

## ABC's and D's

**A.** A is for Avoidance or Argue. Also for Aggravation

Avoidance was common among the dedicated non-paying folks. A week after they received and used the newspaper, a very inexpensive commodity, they considered their bill tossed aside. Whether it was Friday evening supper hour or Saturday morning before market, people recognized the familiar paperboy's approach. And he knew the visible, audible signals and smells, which clearly demonstrated folks were home: a car in the driveway, radio playing, fresh cigarette smoke drifting through the screen. His loud knocks rattled the door frame, reverberating around the living room where light peeked through the thin rip in the window shade. Yet, when he knocked, talk ceased, the lamp light disappeared, the radio program faded. A customer actively hid and passively avoided opening the door. The aroma of fried sausage lingered in the silent air.

No fool, a child understood a customer sat silently holding out against his request. With 175, 200, 300 customers, a carrier could develop calluses on his knuckles trying to roust the moles. He needed to knock long enough to be emphatic, but just short of annoying. The youngster might succeed, but more likely did not.

People who lived in Avoidance Haven---that deadbeat residence for elusive critters---definitely disgusted the reliable carrier. Their game was slow, slower than checkers. If a subscriber avoided payment, a child paid his subscription in full. During delivery a customer clocked the newsboy; when it came to paying, the customer closed the curtains. Folks away from home: frustrating. Adults at home who refused to answer: infuriating.

Avoidance came before arguing (though not in spelling lessons). Avoidance was passive, while arguing was an aggressive stance with a heated, "I already paid." Holding out the receipt book, the blank receipt with the stub still attached, the paperboy tried to explain. A logical statement against an adult's arguing-posture was futile and quite aggravating. Adults ruled.

Enduring patience with poor payers was not a virtue to be cultivated if a boy wanted to keep his route, the bike for which he still owed $3.50, and buy a pair of school trousers.

**B**. B is for Blame

Settling into his routine, Jack Gahan developed into a model paper carrier. Starting with a *Tacoma News Tribune* route, he increased it from about 30 customers to over 100, with Sunday numbers being the largest. His system seemed smooth, along with steady sales to hospital patients. Sometimes it was unpleasant when a patient asked him to sort in the bed stand drawer for pennies scattered among strands of hair, dentures, and used hankies. He accommodated their request. He cared about the patients, in spite of a messy reality.

Knowing people were waiting for him, he hurried from room to room in the hospital, passed a nurse in her white starched uniform, stiff white cap, white nylons, and white shoes. In his grey attire, it was clear he wasn't a nurse. But he brought comforting care to folks who were glad for his brief visit, happy to stay connected to the community, and they paid him.

One afternoon, with a few papers left, he turned into the room of a single patient to whom he sold on a daily basis. The man was always pleased when his paper arrived. Oh my, he was so anxious he toddled out of his bed and stepped towards Jack.

Jack looked down and reached in his bag to be quick with a paper for the eager gentleman. He wanted the *Tribune* even faster. As the two met, not face to face since the man was tall and the 10-year-old slim and short, the patient came right against him. The slight child pressed his feet firmly on the smooth, scrubbed linoleum and tried to brace his small frame, supporting the man propped against the newspaper bag.

"Are you okay?" No reply. The man's head drooped down on Jack's shoulder. Help! Should he drop the patient? Should he dash for a nurse? He heard a gurgle of air. Then Jack was alone, only a boy and a body. The breathless, dead weight scared him. The experience with loss stayed in his heart. Though his family moved to Seattle, where he started a new route, he remembered his lost customer who always wanted a newspaper.

Reaching age 13, Jack delivered the *Seattle Times* three-cent papers and collected the subscription each week. Straight forward. The customers were conditioned to his weekly collection and held a mindset that a newspaper only cost three cents. Jack, like hundreds of thousands who held routes in the late 1940s, faced tempers. The newspaper industry, working to control innumerable cost increases, raised a single paper to a nickel.

Why blame the messenger? People certainly did. Carriers received the brunt of anger for a price increase. Subscribers remembered paying only two cents for a newspaper; then they paid three cents for years. Now the company increased the daily paper to five cents! Customers stormed about the outrageous price. A carrier was challenged to be polite while being cursed. The obdurate posture aimed at a child, just because people now paid a nickel for an inexpensive, yet, valuable commodity: so absurd. Caustic people really expressed their two cents worth.

## How Beastly

Bob Spahr, delivered the *Seattle PI* before 5:00 a.m. Like other morning carriers in 1950, he did not connect with his subscribers until the monthly collection. If he repeatedly missed finding a customer at home, the bill extended into two months. By three months of effort, the amount owed rose to over $5.

Bob finally caught up with a guy who was several collections past. *Whew, good for me.* Happy to know he'd have his money, Bob was all smiles.

Wham! Words shooting at him jerked the happy expression off his face. He had tried many times to collect, yet he was being blamed for not being responsible for the monthly task. Bob pocketed the man's owed money, but his cheerful mood was replaced with discouragement, caused by a very angry customer who was the one delinquent in paying his account. The jingling money didn't make Bob merry.

The avoidance by deadbeats, the arguing and blame from dead beasts, these lined up alongside people who blatantly cheated.

**C.** C is for Cheat

There were people who actually cheated over a simple transaction. For little Joan Kopczynski, in the chilling dark, dreading dogs, facing the line of prim classmates, what she, "hated most about the job was collecting." Other school children played after school, but Joan, stuck with her disliked task, "usually collected after school."

Making progress, she knocked at another home. An old lady looked out the window, old to an 8-year-old. The woman opened the door a few inches. A one-sided argument ensued in which the lady insisted she had already paid for February. Joan showed her the blank receipt. The woman still insisted she paid, and accused Joan of forgetting to punch the receipt that confirmed payment. The customer flat out stated that Joan was "trying to cheat."

The woman pushed the door closed. Joan rang the doorbell. No answer. She knocked on the window. The customer pulled down the blind. Joan left. She didn't pocket her money due, but the third grader grasped a nasty realization that an occasional adult cheats.

Cheating without hesitation or reservation left a child realizing in the head, or in the stomach, that some people can't be trusted. The amazing audacity of an adult who would chew out a carrier, who would cheat a kid all for a few cents.

**D**. D. is for Disappear, for De_ _ Oh, my gosh!

An apartment complex provided a dry interior without wind or sleet. It also formed a compact route. However, these daily delivery advantages disintegrated at collection. A paperboy moved along dark hallways to doors, most emitting a smorgasbord of smells, appetizing to repulsive. He knocked, which alerted other customers within the sound range of his approach.

The route advantages were lost as children saw mail and papers accumulate outside a door. Renters moved away, some in the night, unconcerned with paying for their paper. They disappeared and the newspaper payment along with them.

## Stop the Paper.

Jim Root's customer was neither a deadbeat, nor a dead beast but Jim reached a dead end trying to collect from the gentleman, who previously always paid. Frustrated with another unanswered loud knock, he walked to his uncle's home located nearby. The two returned to the customer's house. Finding the home unusually quiet, the uncle forced the door. It opened. They saw newspapers and mail scattered on the floor beneath the mail slot. Odors drifted toward them. Over by his favorite reading chair, the subscriber lay still. Jim would never collect.

## Time to Pay

Unlike the delivery schedule, when papers arrived at a specified time---or nearly a specific time---the hours for the collection task were set by a carrier. The newspaper industry's Little Merchant system held the paperboy accountable for collecting. He must collect, convert the coins to a check or money order for the company, and also convert some bartered goods to his benefit. Compassionate with customers who deserved concern and care, in the meantime he cursed the curmudgeon and the cheat.

If a paperboy couldn't collect at a dark, still house, then he had to find where the money flowed. Saloons were an answer. However, stale beer odors and sweaty men in a dark, smoky tavern were less than enjoyable. True, saloons were better for selling papers, but definitely unpleasant for a child's ears when collecting.

Be . . .

Josie Grab figured the South Prairie Tavern was a sensible place to collect. She knew "that the men had to have money since they were buying beer." Plus, they were with their friends so in front of other guys, "they had to pay me! They did and swore at me. But, I got the money."

Children started with people they could count on, or count on having money. Also, they approached speedy ones first, because the slow collecting slowed further with sociable chatterers.

# CHAPTER 15
## C. FOR CONSIDERATE, COMPASSIONATE. FOR CONVERSIONS, CHRISTMAS

Leaving the school room and running into the real world to deliver papers was not a philanthropic endeavor, in spite of leeches who felt they deserved papers placed on the doorstep for free. Disgusted with deadbeats, dead beasts, and his ears drained from listening to blamers and complainers, the carrier altered his approach and changed his attitude. He switched from people with whom he could not pry open the door, to ones he struggled with to slip out the door.

### Considerate

The paper carrier was not a stranger, a suspicious snooper, nor an itinerate salesman. The majority of people found his stop welcome. Most customers cared about him and didn't appear at all malicious in using time when they asked him about school, his effort in sports, or lessons at Sunday school. And friendly, personable boys chit-chatted with subscribers, the way Bill Miller often paused for a talk.

The paperboys enjoyed a brief chat, a pleasant rest under the shade of the porch ceiling and the offer of a cool drink of water. Invited inside in the winter, as a radio played and the clock ticked like a metronome, he sipped hot chocolate while the cat sank into a faded gingham pillow, quite cozy. The cat napped and, without a nap during school, he nearly dozed.

Coby Lamb began his route at age 10. Wanting a route, he circumvented the manager and asked the publisher directly. "I guess maybe my guts to go to him was why he hired me on the spot." With 120 *Daily Forum* subscribers, Coby sped through Maryville, Missouri, ensuring "prompt delivery." Then he addressed the customers for collection. His speed stopped.

"The elderly ladies loved me and lots of times had hot chocolate for me on cold days," when trying to walk through a foot or two of snow challenged him. The older ladies "wanted to visit and it was sometimes hard to get away." Of course, to a boy of 10, women over 40 appeared elderly. Taught proper manners, how could he respectfully ignore his elders?

## Endless Chatter

Paul Meyer worked his collection schedule. Unable to rush as fast as when he delivered 175 newspapers, he still tried to hurry, and so he switched his pattern to visit the slowest payers last. He followed the school teacher's example: send chatterers to the end of the line.

Miss Meddle peered through her lace curtains. She looked forward to Paul's pleasant monthly visit, a male visitor who politely listened to her. He said please and yes ma'am. She understood he was there to collect, but if she gave him his money right away, he'd leave and end her time to share, time to spare.

Millie Meddle asked about his mother, his father, other customers on the route. Paul answered patiently; he turned his ball cap from hand to hand. The hall clock chimed 4:30 p.m. The stores would close soon. Miss Meddle was a shopper people avoided standing behind at the grocery cash register. Before she finished talking, a cut of meat spoiled.

Finally, she paid the $1.50 for the month. Paul wrote her receipt, said thank you, and stopped at another slow customer. Mr. Reston covered all the sports happenings for the season, compared records to past years, discussed which baseball teams would be in the World Series. Listening to his chatter, Paul would rather be playing ball with his friends.

He adapted to customers who chatted. "They would draw me into conversation which took time away from my collections. I tried not to be rude and break away, but this aspect of collecting was frustrating. I enjoyed the give and take in conversation, but at the same time felt an urgency to get the job done."

## Comfort Comes Before Collection

For 10 years Carole Bergeron stuck to endless collecting. More than 90 percent of her customers paid promptly. She enjoyed "a feeling of kinship with them," particularly those who hastened the process with the correct amount "left under a rock." However, she wasn't fond of the annoying "10 percent who were terrible payers," and ones who took advantage of her time.

Managing her collections, she quickly learned to stop last at Mrs. O'Kelly's. The sincere Irish lady "poured out all her troubles and woes" to the polite, young papergirl. An especially bad day occurred when, earlier, a

Jehovah's Witness follower knocked on Mrs. O'Kelly's door. A one-sided conversation ensued. The devout Catholic was not about to change her religion, not after the Witness told her "she was surely going to hell." For that visit, Carole's agitated customer required even more time. The school girl consoled, comforted and reassured Mrs. O'Kelly she would go to heaven. Carole also made certain to collect.

# The Last Home

Finished with residential homes, Doug Larson completed his slowest challenge last. He chomped on a bite of candy, sighed and pushed the door open. He smelled the familiar astringent, pungent air filled with cleaning chemicals mopped over floors and swiped across counters to maintain cleanliness. It was fumigating the heated rooms. Frigid Nebraska air did not reach the patients settled in their rockers or wheel chairs, buttoned in wool sweaters, blankets over their laps even though the nursing home was quite warm.

Doug politely removed his cap, and for sure, he certainly didn't need anything warmer. He resigned himself to knowing he couldn't dash in and right out. The collecting pace slowed to the speed of a turtle stroll, incredibly slow to an active adolescent. Winter in Nebraska was long, just the way his task lasted among infirm patients whose days were lost in the 1960s. Collecting in the nursing home, "took FOREVER. The folks were lonely and wanted to visit."

No taciturn clients in this sedate home. Doug's interest focused on the weekly 50 cents, or the flat $2 a month for the *Lincoln Journal*. His paper route supported a greater purpose. Staying on target, he'd earn his necessary, "two hundred dollars to go to the Boy Scout National Jamboree in Valley Forge, Pennsylvania" However, first he had to be patient.

"People at the nursing home were so lonely. It was hard not to stay and talk to them. They would show me photographs of their farms and teams of horses." The patients covered every detail of their past life in a lost era. Doug knew the finish to their story, but if he interrupted before the ending his visit took longer as the gentlemen switched to another of their many memories. Unlike a private residence, a nursing home didn't have any treats to offer a boy, only the pills, ointments, and cough syrup.

Finally, he excused himself and moved down the hall to Mr. Steiner's room. The waning glow of January's short daylight spread over the blanket covering Mr. Steiner. Doug tried to rouse the fragile gentleman, tried a couple of times. No luck. Already Mr. Steiner was two months delinquent. In February, Doug persisted once again, wanting the 90 days owed. He never roused Mr. Steiner. To receive his $6, Doug "had to collect from his estate."

# Sit a Spell. Light Up

Jack Moore took advantage of America's expansive spirit in 1946, enjoying the rowdy fun at the "clubhouse" shack, playing on the carriers' softball leagues, even visiting with the pleasant prostitutes over at the Osage and the Columbia Hotel. Still, he stayed on a daily schedule for his seven-day morning route and another run in the afternoon, and then added a collection round on Wednesday and Thursday evening from 6:30 p.m. to 8:30 p.m.. He tried to finish the 100 customers on Friday, for their combined bill of $2.20 a month. Held to a routine, he paused to sit a spell and socialize with a widowed lady.

Seventy years his senior, Mrs. Lacy chatted and laughed with Jack, delighted by his engaging smile. No need to act their age. They even shared a smoke together. And in the heat of Oklahoma, why not wet the whistle with a tasty slug? She and her young caller shared a spirited shot. Jack swallowed the blended whiskey and immediately the fiery liquid caused a blush to form on his cheeks. He appreciated his respite, particularly since Mrs. Lacy paid regularly.

His customers very seldom stiffed him. Most were respectable, honest folks, who when they could not pay said so right up front. Furthermore, taught to respect his elders, he was considerate with chatterers who eventually paid after slicing off a chunk of his time.

# Compassionate

There were mean people who finagled their way out of paying the small subscription fee, but there were others who had no means to pay. A child experienced a long arc from deadbeats who chose to be unaccountable, continuing on to those unable to count out a few coins. They had none. In these cases, the carrier advanced to a compassionate level.

Vernon Franze delivered *The Wenatchee World* to some customers who didn't have 15 cents a week, not three nickels to spare, not even a penny. They were truthfully penniless. Beginning his large route in 1931, Vernon and the rest of his Wenatchee Valley community succumbed to the Depression by the following year. To hold *The World* from failing, the company owner reduced salaries and printed scrip to pay employees. They used the paper scrip at local shops where store owners redeemed it for advertising. Just keep moving ahead.

With 160 customers requesting the *World*, Vernon collected from enough residents to earn between $5 and $6 a week, a very fortunate sum for a boy when many families had nothing. Managing his opportunity, Vernon "could support himself," freeing his parents to better care for his five younger brothers and sisters. He recognized his advantage and felt compassion for the very poor subscribers in strained times.

In the East, coal miners, already physically strained in their dangerous work, became just as severely strained for money during the Depression. Ten-year-old Sam Rarig respectfully acknowledged their harsh circumstances. Suffering through the Depression, from 1935 to 1943, in the small town of Catawessa, Pennsylvania, Sam accommodated his customers. At 2 cents a paper, some "could not afford to pay. Sometimes I paid for them or granted credit for several months," still delivering. Miners needed the *Shamokin News Dispatch* to know which anthracite coal mines were open, since that information was published regularly and it could save them a long, unnecessary ride. Sam managed well enough, carrying his papers and carrying their credit to establish a savings account.

Compassionate with folks unable to pay the low subscription price, many a paperboy politely accepted an individual's pride when a person offered the little he possessed: a friendly nod. The carrier's manner spoke better of youth than the actions of some nasty, evasive adults.

## What's the conversion rate?

Time is money. A slow time turns little money. His lifesaver melted, and still pondering how to convert time spent against his earnings, a boy's tabulations showed him in arrears. Though confounded with the figures, such problems were better than arguing for collection fees.

Following a method older than any currency, penniless people used a barter system. The delivery boy wore one more hat. On top of being a collection agent, a financial officer for a periodic parental IOU, he wore a barterer's hat. Considerate, and as certain times dictated, compassionate, carriers matured as they coped with every aspect of financial management, including a grasp of how values circulate through a society when money is severely limited.

Instead of cold clinking coins, which he counted to keep his records correct, a carrier might request or receive the money due in forms other than what the United States minted.

## Street Car Desired

After walking three miles to the newspaper office and securing his bundles of papers, John James rested just a bit. Having exchanged a paper for a ride, his short legs dangled above the floor of the street car. With limited resources, since he gave his pennies to his mother and wanted her to have as many pennies as possible, he handed a paper to the conductor. He sat for a slight distance until the street car stopped near the mansion of Hazelton's most prominent citizen, who was John's first delivery. He rode each day for a two-cent paper, which helped him be underway quicker with his morning route. That way he made it to school on time. Also, he'd sell extras to other riders for an additional benefit.

## Pressure Versus Pleasure

Despite the awful fights in the paper shack at the Queen Anne station and the steep hills in Seattle, John Kearns, a small tyke, moved along through his route. To assuage such conditions, each day he placed a newspaper over a clean dairy counter in exchange for an ice cream cone, a special treat for an 8-year-old in a family of 12 children affected by the Depression. Finished tossing 100 papers, he walked along licking the creamy treat one delicious swipe after another. He "loved it." John was a terrific advertisement for the ice cream store with sweet drips sliding down his ink-stained hands.

Sometimes an exchange wasn't swift or sweet and yet a thoughtful offer was granted in appreciation for the paper. The 1930s were the worst, and yet, when the Depression faded, when the war ended, not everyone participated in the prosperity explosion of the 1950s. Pockets of poverty remained, but the newspaper company wanted customers retained. The customers wanted the news, even when they could not pay. However, they tried to be fair to the boy who cared enough to always bring them the paper. Such circumstances called for different measures in order for a fair exchange.

The feeling of compassion carried into corners of the community, though not to complainers and cheats. Caring was granted to legitimate folks without money.

## A Grocery Bag, Too

For customers who couldn't afford even the most inexpensive purchase, the local newspaper, often a paperboy continued to provide them with a vital link to their community. In the 1950s, 8-year-old Vyron Mitchell didn't see terrific financial gains flashing across the porch of every person in Cadiz, Kentucky.

Vyron considered himself lucky. He was past the substitute stage and had become a "full fledged paper boy. There was nothing more important than being a paperboy for the local daily newspaper." Boys holding routes usually kept the job until graduation so, "an open route was few and far between."

Feeling fortunate, Vyron helped those without a similar advantage, ones without a dime to spare. These customers did not avoid collection, did not cheat, complain or disappear. And he accepted them rather than feel anger towards their condition.

A subscription cost a dime for the week and Vyron spent each Saturday doing his rounds to collect. When 10 cents was a stretch, his paper route would include a short admonishment: eat your veggies. Over the weeks, into months people met their obligation with garden vegetables, or in the sparse winter months, a chicken. His canvas bag became a grocery bag. That was fine. The paper route was what mattered.

## Like Ancient Times

Similar to Vyron and many others, Max Fisk felt good about his paper route---except for the confounded goose bite. Max considered his "parents the best" and his "wonderful family" of two sisters and a brother part of his good fortune, right along with his route. However, trying to earn in the Depression meant convincing everyone to pay. One customer met his debt, sort of.

The subscriber, with a painting and wall paper interior business, "never had the money to pay for the paper." Just the same, his lack of accountability bothered the gentleman. To pay his due, he provided, not a mere pint, or a flask, nor a quart bottle, but a half gallon of dark, frothy beer. Max "took the beer home to Dad." In 1937 treats weren't plentiful, yet with prohibition removed in 1933, alcohol was again openly available. Anyway, beer had been used for payments since the building of the Great Pyramids in Egypt. A functional system lasts.

## Developing a Profit

Rather than a jug of beer, Doug Coleburn received live specimens as his payment. Delivering the *Richmond News-Leader*, he covered five miles down Virginia dirt roads, across muddy streams, to mostly poor neighborhoods. The cost to his customers for his efforts: 25 cents a week. They received newspapers on time, whether or not their quarter appeared on time.

Leaving a dirt road to tread on a long, unkempt path, weeds scratching his legs, bugs scattering, Doug faithfully took the newspaper to "an old woman who lived with her disabled son." As her past-due bill stretched into six weeks, instead of paying the $1.50 owed, the elderly, tired mother, who resided in her simple house where she protected her son, offered Doug what she could spare. He saw, "behind her wood-burning kitchen cook stove, little chickens roosting and staying warm." She paid him with three bantam chicks.

Though the barter system existed for centuries, at a young age Doug wasn't familiar with it. However, his father raised chickens, a common task like tending large vegetable gardens. With chickens, their family's Sunday dinner was close by---or they might sell a Sunday dinner to neighbors. And mom collected egg money. Now, for a devoted mother, a newspaper remained available for tiny, soft chicks. And with parents' help, a small profit developed for Doug.

## More Math Problems

The beer Max received disappeared. No sense letting it go stale, or storing it in the cellar like vintage wine. Doug's chicks lasted longer. But the newspaper company had to be paid and how do schoolboys of 7,10, 12 years of age switch bunches of collard greens and beets, beer, and bantam chicks into coins?

It was a challenge to learn each coin, and then progress to addition, subtraction, and those multiplication tables. Next, the paperboy was to figure math word-problems. How does the life span of chicks being fed, minus the energy to cook vegetables convert into cash? Collecting was exact: specific number of customers and specific cost of the paper. For two cents, five cents, a dime on Sunday, a quarter a week, the agreement was precise. But what monetary worth is assigned to the pleasure of eating ice cream, the enjoyment of pleasing dad with beer, the long-range lesson in understanding people's pride? Though confounded with math conversions, the problems surpassed being avoided or cheated.

Destitute financial conditions were not a customer's choice, nor the carrier's. From Virginia to Alaska, people utilized the barter system when work was limited or non-existent. With beer flowing, with bantam chicks growing, could collecting be any better? Yes, floating.

## Hated More Than Collecting

Two brothers accomplished a profitable conversion. Burnie Dunphy and his little brother, Barry, really hustled to make money in Ketchikan. When Burnie sold a copy of the *Ketchikan Chronicle*, the only daily paper in the southeast hill town, he earned a nickel. This was a higher return for children, in 1940, than offered by many daily newspapers in the Lower 48.

The boys, selling papers, approached a possible customer. The man wanted the *Chronicle*, but he suffered financially with a slack fishing year. He knew Burnie and Barry were not trudging in Alaska weather to hand over papers as a charity. They worked for the same things other paperboys wanted: baked goods, games, comics, a movie (if the Ketchikan theater wasn't flooded with high tide).

For folks who desired the paper, it meant paying, but this "one red-faced, old fisherman down at the Tongass Basin" didn't have spare change. He just owned spare rowboats. The old man out by the sea offered Burnie and Barry boats "for a few free newspapers." He'd donate not one boat for each brother, not two and an extra, but five rowboats, his being considerate and all. The little merchants enthusiastically agreed to a deal.

However, a large, long dock space at the marina for the fleet of five boats was un-necessary. Three boats were hopelessly rotted and impossible to move even by energetic boys. They tried the fourth one. Climbing into it, rowing away from town, the two almost drowned as it "started to sink out in the middle of the harbor." The boat sank faster than ice cream melts, and in Alaska the waters left them colder than ice cream. They surfaced. Fortunately, the man had been generous to give five boats, so the brothers acquired one useable boat and the fisherman received free newspapers.

Captain Burnie and his first mate, Barry, set sail. Rowing was fun, though maybe not as satisfying as a daily treat. Would the boat expand money-making ventures as fast as a trolley ride? The boys didn't require a huge profit, but enough steady, reliable results to make it worthwhile to row in the rain. After changing from cold, sopping-wet clothes to warm, dry protective gear, an old rickety, patched boat became worthwhile. A profit even appeared.

The excited entrepreneurial mind of Burnie made one boat out of five financially viable. The fellows spent time fishing. Catching dogfish, bottom fish, and "selling their livers to the local canary to make cod liver oil," they happily enlarged the meager newspaper profits.

Others felt differently---even veggies are better than cod liver oil. Children hated a fishy spoonful of oil. Yet, that slurp each morning was beneficial. Dick Kalivoda's mother gave him a dose in orange juice every morning. Delivering the shopper guides at age 8, maintaining a full route by age 12, and becoming a station manager by 13, Dick never missed a delivery day during nine years in drippy northwest weather. And his mom never missed spooning out cod liver oil. No wonder Barry and Burnie's fishing business was profitable.

As beer kept benefits flowing, so boats---make that a single boat--- kept the brothers' financial plan floating. In the spring of 1942, World War II opened Alaska through the Alcan highway construction. Burnie took his savings from his newspaper earnings and the fish oil money and bought an old (but not as old as the four rotten rowboats), sixteen-foot runabout for $125. With dad's help, the three caulked and painted the boat. Then dad's Coast Guard friends, mechanics, overhauled the engine. The new captain and his first mate patrolled the waters off Ketchikan, when they weren't casting fish lines or donning gas masks.

The Japanese "took Attu and Kiska in the Aleutians and bombed Dutch Harbor." The school boys' selling and fun routine was altered. The black outs at night and the air raid drills in the day interrupted business. When sirens blared, the kids joined town folks and evacuated to concealed "makeshift wooden shelters in the woods to practice hiding out when the Japs came." Before hurrying to hide, the boys quickly changed clothes.

Why? Well, when "Dad came home on leave from the Aleutians, he said that Japanese soldiers had no respect for civilians, but respected uniforms of any kind." He told his sons to wear their scout troop uniform, "Burnie in his Boy Scout uniform and Barrie in his Cub Scout uniform." Along with protective attire, they included their Navy issued blue bag hung from a shoulder strap. However, they "were not to tell what was in the bag because there were not enough masks for everyone." Silently the sons and their mother scurried to the shelter. Barrie felt strange "in my Cub Scout uniform with my gas mask bag and saying, 'Oh nothing much' when asked what was in my bag." Hopefully the mask stayed tucked away. Masks smell when covering a small pug nose, though never as smelly as fish, especially dead ones left in the sun for a day. But the Dunphy boys' procedure with their catch, and not seeing sun in rainy Ketchikan, couldn't possibly have any smell as bad as the situation Bob found himself in.

## Collecting Stinks

Bob Brink's route required considerable collecting time. But he stayed motivated, since he wanted his profit for Boy Scout activities. With the company to pay, plus paying rent for the route, and subtracting money lost when folks weren't around, Bob needed as much money as possible to pay for sports and scouts. However, collecting from one seemed impossible.

Bob's slow customer, the very slowest of his 400 afternoon subscribers, kept him waiting and literally holding his breath. His method before entering her home: inhale a deep breath and hold it as long as possible through the Augean task. Smelling the strong odors from animal excretions in the confines of a house nauseated him.

First, the elderly woman shuffled slowly to the other room because of "her infirmities." She needed to locate her purse, find a small coin bag inside the cluttered container, and with arthritic fingers, count the right amount. All the while, Bob held his breath. The old lady lived in the most obnoxious house, "with the worst imaginable odors all around and inside her home." Of course, a powerful stench did nothing to ease her aches.

Residing with her were, "more cats than anyone could ever count." Bob stood in the repugnant setting amidst scraggly kittens, feisty felines with crusted eyes, cats with matted fur, and others, hissing and ear-tattered, that produced more litters than stray dogs created. It was worse than mice populations.

The daily newspapers delivered to the house never soaked up the cat urine and offensive brown piles. Waiting in the hallway was like standing by an outhouse. No, like standing down *in* an outhouse. Apparently, the woman's olfactory sensors worked even worse than her hobbling legs. Bob's nasal passages suffocated from the noisome caked stains. His stomach juices reversed. The place stunk. Better to cross paths with a skunk. Oh, the price of being a persistent paperboy. A decision: should he absorb the loss or absorb the putrid conditions?

Bob, be of good cheer. Christmas rewards from normal people are offered. Only first,...

## Trick or Treat, or Both

By late October, bets on the Yankees capturing another World Series became old news, stylish new cars arrived at the dealership, and aromas of hearty, hot stew and tantalizing, crusty casseroles seeped out the kitchen door. Cider was still sweet. By December the taste would have the crisp sting of hard cider.

For now, a paper route was pleasant in the cool autumn air, infused with smoke from wood-burning stoves and piles of burned leaves. Days of Indian summer dried the corn shucks. Pumpkins ripened to golden orange, and best of all, the last red balls fell under withered vines.

With a long rain and a hard frost, tomatoes turned just right for a devilish boy. A soft, smelly, worm-eaten cabbage head rotted. Keep it. Halloween was coming. Tricksters prepared to toss the garden messes. Soap wasn't being used to wash hands, but was saved for one special night a year. The stash grew larger. Kids bought a short black mask, which always scratched soft cheeks, noses and eyes, plus it hid the wearer's vision more than hiding his recognition.

To a paperboy, the best night to collect was approaching. Porch lights on, folks answered the doorbell to darling fairies, little ghosts, black witches. And the dog was tied around back. A hand offered a Milky Way, Hershey bars, apples, Mars Bar, popcorn balls. On the traditional night of tricks, folks did not avoid answering the knock by a paper carrier.

Paperboys collected, received treats, and still had time that evening to grab dark costumes and do tricks to level the complaints inflicted months before by customers. A boy just had to be sure to leave his identifying canvas newspaper bag tucked out of sight. He and friends soaped screens, windows, storm windows, stuck the car horn with a straight pin, offset the outhouse, greased the door knobs with lard, tossed fish heads on the back floor of a car, and turned over trash cans. Whew, a busy night.

October 31, a great day to successfully close the tenth month of the year. And carriers were on the way to their best week for closing the year with significant profits. Even better than the one night of Halloween was the week leading into Christmas.

## Dreaming of a Green Christmas

In the approaching season of giving, a paperboy improved his behavior as he sped along his route, making certain the paper landed right beside the door or he placed it inside the storm door. As the Christmas lights appeared, his polished manners sparkled bright enough to light candles. Possibly that jolly fat man in a red suit knew who had been naughty and who was nice. Customers remembered. Fortunately, people didn't stand in open doorways in the line of a stiff paper trajectory during cold winter days. Even without snow, carriers stoked the spirit of the season to enhance their green Christmas. Not wishing for cookies and candy, paperboys gave cards and calendars hoping for cash instead. The customers understood his message.

A long tradition, extending from Ben Franklin's days as a paperboy into the current times, brought results when a child penned a poem for his carrier's address. Professor John Long of Roanoke College, once a paperboy, wrote an article about the Salem Museum exhibit in Salem, Virginia. The Museum houses a collection of newsey cards from 1854 to 1904. If little rascals were not to be heard, at least seeing a greeting card encouraged people to give money.

John Nicon, delivering in the center of the University District in Seattle, "made Christmas cards each year," for his *Seattle Times* customers and "got a few more tips that way." Not just the nickel or dime tip with his monthly collection but a substantial holiday offering. "The biggest tip: five dollars." In 1950, a $5 bill made him ecstatic. Creating cards was worth the effort.

Joan Kopczynski's dark morning route during December didn't lessen her excitement for the Christmas season, nor reduce her efforts to make cards. "I gave each of my customers a Christmas card." Customers responded. Her sister and brothers "accused me of having the best territory because I collected the most candy and tips from customers on holidays. I remember getting chocolate covered cherries, something I'd never buy for myself. They weren't my favorites but I was grateful. My bag would be loaded full of treats. I had difficulty carrying it."

## Brown and Green Surpasses White

When was difficult weather welcomed? The Christmas season. The white hillside, the evergreens bowing in white skirts, lawns sparkling, these conditions stirred folks to expand their Christmas cheer and generously care about others. People in the neighborhood knew which carriers were fatherless, and especially enjoyed giving to these kids as the spirit of Christmas radiated through the community. Carriers were greeted with a brightly lit tree in the middle of the window, with strings of porch lights, a fresh aromatic wreath, and spicy, baking aromas.

Better than cod liver oil, most any child would agree, were the Christmas cookies and chocolates that carriers received during the festive season, along with the really desired cash, which made a brown and green Christmas terrific. A carrier's attitude sparkled. School closed for the holiday break and lessened his tension to be on schedule. However, he had not wished for so many cookies and boxes of candy. To counter the sweets, there were carriers who gave calendars for the desired cash.

Cards handed to customers evolved into 12 pages distributed in December. With the help of newspaper company presses, many carriers were provided bundles of calendars for the New Year. The company printed and sold them to carriers at wholesale cost. The children decided whether to give or to sell a calendar to each customer. A paperboy's low cost for calendars only appeared once a year in his debit column. The investment quickly rolled over to the cash column.

Instead of ringing bells on a street corner, a youngster rang the doorbell and politely handed a calendar to his subscribers. The customers offered cash. While the long Sunday list of subscribers caused a heavy load, during Christmas week the large number paid off.

In New York, *The Binghamton Press* company sold calendars to their carriers, and the boys then sold or gave the "tip prompter" to their customers. In 1947 Frank Gennarelli gave his away. When he was handed a $5 tip from a doctor, Frank knew he had approached the holy season of giving with the right plan.

In the mid 1950s, Ron Haringa's total amount in Christmas tips accumulated to $100, more than enough for his daily afternoon chocolate. And many customers gave him chocolate.

Delivering 200 papers each morning and 400 in the evening, Bob Brink had a sufficient number of customers who might tip him at Christmas. Furthermore, "the news company sold the carriers cardboard calendars with a small page for each month and our name and phone number printed on it. After we paid for these, we were to give one to each of our customers. They understood there was some expectation." By the end of six Christmases, Bob learned the differences in the nature of people. "Some customers would give me a whopping $5 and others a whopping 50 cents. Kinda like a slot machine. I felt quite rich by the time all of my calendar gifts had been exchanged for real money!"

Calendars brought the desired cash but the season also brought quantities of cookies and boxes of candy. The children's bike basket overflowed with cartons of sweets, rainbow colored book-style life saver boxes, gifts of gloves, hankies, a billfold, an adventure book, and more.

# No Thank You

Closed against the frigid winter air, kitchens filled with an aromatic stew from baking holiday specialties of stollen, lebkuchen, gingerbread, and krumkake. And the sweets were accented with simmering spiced cider, steaming cocoa with cream, perhaps cinnamon toast.

Rather than left standing in the cold while collecting, Max was welcomed into a kitchen with baked goods fresh from the oven. The wife looked for change to meet the 50 cent cost. These considerate, friendly folks, made Max Fisk feel comfortable.

Waiting patiently, shifting on his feet, his wet cap in hand dripping on the linoleum, he stared at the center of the cluttered kitchen table. Set in the middle of the large wooden surface stood a small, live Christmas tree with colorful ornaments---that moved. The evergreen held roosting baby chickens and fluffy ducklings. His eyes followed the jiggling, delicate glass balls down the green boughs to the space under the tree, where a platter of Christmas goodies rested.

Seeing Max focused on the holiday arrangement, the owner offered a treat, "Help yourself."

Max declined with a polite, "No thank you." He kept his hands in his pockets. He really hoped his stomach wouldn't growl.

"Aww, have a piece."

Thinking of mother's admonitions: don't eat candy it causes tooth decay, don't spoil your supper with sweets, wash your hands before eating---all rules by a mother who knows best. Max intended to mind his mother. He'd avoid eating sweets.

He again refused any of the pieces. No handy wipes readily available in the 1930s. More than scrubbing his hands, he'd have to wash his mouth if he ate the morsels. They'd slide down the throat as easily as cod liver oil, though without beneficial attributes. Every so often the chicks and ducks whitish-yellow, gooey plops landed on the chocolate candy like frosting decoration.

# CHAPTER 16
## SENSUOUS SIGHTINGS AND CONFUSED SILENCE

With Christmas packages unwrapped, thanks repeatedly expressed, cookie tins holding only a few crumbs, and the decorated tree dropping piles of needles, a carrier counted and re-counted his Christmas money, with bills that were greener than the dry tinder tree.

Closing out the year, how did the cost column balance against the profit column? In a dreary, dismal January would his money stack any higher? Perhaps he'd look for another job, now that Christmas benefits were in.

With New Year's Eve arriving, instead of calendars it would be better to hand out a list of resolutions to the irritating customers. A list that read: *Leave the porch light on; answer the persistent knocking on your door; securely chain the dog in the back yard; keep track of my phone number. If you have a complaint, call me at this number.*

### Terrific

Much like the lighted houses on Halloween, a house with porch lights shining on New Year's Eve would signal a sensible time to collect. Though he had no written resolutions to distribute, Jim still needed to finish collecting for the month. Stuffing a roll of Life Savers from his Christmas stash into his pocket, Jim Rudy figured he could complete the collection rounds for December before midnight of another year in Colorado. With over 100 customers on his morning route, and the monthly subscription fees raised from $1.25 to $1.75, plus Christmas tips, he'd end the month earning above $60. And the best part, no broken storm windows costing more than a week's pay. He passed quiet, dark homes on deserted streets figuring people weren't planning to be awake at midnight.

Ahh, finally, a house well lit, a lively place with a party ready to ring in the New Year. Jim knocked. His customer tottered to the door a "little tipsy." The guy was cheerfully cognizant and called out, "Hey, it's our paperboy, pass the hat around. He's a good kid."

Jim didn't mind being called a kid since the adults were acting like kids. They passed the hat as if playing a grade-school game. After they fumbled in pockets and purses, the man weaved back to the door and through his spirited, warm breath, smiled and handed Jim the tips.

Liquid spirits toasting the New Year were not the cause of his intoxicated happiness. The money was "to this day the largest tip I ever received. I went straight home, shaking. I was so excited." Any further collecting for the end of the month would wait. Jim pocketed an $18 tip. All his. He counted and recounted the tip. The money even felt good. Was this a portend to another good year of delivering the *Rocky Mountain News?*

## Better Than Money?

Sunday morning, the first morning of 1956, and Mike Rhodes was out before sunrise, ready to deliver heavy papers to 125 customers. Though it was a national holiday, he needed to complete his rounds in a timely fashion. The weather in San Jose, California was reasonable for the first of January, so why couldn't the bundles arrive on time?

"It was 5:00 a.m. Sunday, New Year's Day and the papers were late." The teenager fiddled around in front of a house where he always waited. Shivering in the dark, he saw lights, "where a large New Year's Eve party was still lingering. I saw people inside celebrating."

At last, his *San Jose Mercury* papers arrived and Mike began preparing them ready to hurry through his rounds. Unexpectedly, "a rather striking young inebriated woman emerged from the house and slithered over to me." Surprising Mike, she reached out to grab one of his newspapers. *Was she clear-headed enough to read any of the news?*

His concern instantly disappeared. As she leaned over in her party dress for the paper, she gave him "a kiss on the side of the cheek." A whispering air of ethereal bliss bathed his face. Her spirited, "Happy New Year," mixed with perfume, intoxicating spirits and a more intoxicating sensation, left as sudden as evaporating alcohol.

A subscriber's paper was gone. Mike, "didn't care. I liked what had transpired." She was not a customer, not a resident of the house, and though he watched, she didn't appear again except in sweet memory. He held a taste of warm pleasure as she "traded a kiss for a paper." At his age, the trade was better than an ice cream cone. Her soft sensuous kiss computed higher than the worth of a 35-cent Sunday paper. Mike smiled, spinning through his route.

# Titillating Smiles and Tips

Women caused paperboys to smile any number of days as boys encountered ladies---not with a quick kiss and then never again---but in the weekly rounds. Such women were more than Coby Lamb's nice elderly lady with hot chocolate or Paul Meyer's long-winded chatterers. And far more appealing than the woman Bob Brink tolerated at that stinky house of cats, a place in complete contrast to bordellos.

Fragrant bordellos with reliable residents offered no particular surprises. Carriers knew their community, knew the streets and houses, the occupants, and were aware that prostitutes were good customers. Just as the working class paid their bills, so the working ladies paid theirs.

The houses of ill repute offered a different respite for paperboys. A woman opened the door with a smile. Her lacy blouse and tightly clothed hips seemed in place. He encountered whiffs of Tabu perfume, an inviting lingering scent, surrounding her curvaceous body. She created a stimulating delight, though the boy hoped his nose wasn't too stimulated by the perfume causing him to sneeze. With no avoidance or arguing, the ladies paid on the first request. And the best part: they gave frequent tips and gifts.

Whether in Cordova, Ketchikan, Everett, Seattle, Lewiston, Oklahoma City, Wenatchee or down the pike or in the next seaport, the naughty streets of town, where houses of pleasure were woven into the city's fabric, were simply part of the communities. Houses of prostitution functioned in logging towns, mill towns, mining areas, and business centers where robust men had money. Not scary like dogs, drunks, dark spooky houses, these places, seemed acceptable. Their inhabitants wanted and paid for the latest news. Innocent boys delivered without guilt.

## The Profit Line with "girls on the line"

Unlike the Greek card parlor built on the dangerous City Dock, the four houses of prostitutes on a street in Cordova added an excellent stop for Ruth. Her best days on the route occurred when she collected. The friendly ladies paid and even better, "were good tippers." Besides money, they also gave their papergirl "gifts of sweaters and such." Ruth was considerate about her time for collecting, being sure not to bother the "girls on the line" when they hosted a line of male customers on pay day.

Though the Depression made it difficult for some customers to meet the newspaper subscription cost, the prostitution business still profited. In 1937, Wenatchee city leaders launched "a yearlong campaign to clean up the prostitution" and other related social businesses. However, "the campaign had little effect."

In Washington, Idaho, Oklahoma, or any of the states, ladies' business provided reliable customers for a route. A striptease image and a tee-hee if prostitutes are mentioned conjures a mistaken opinion. In Sedro Woolley, by Washington's Cascade Mountains, Jack Deirlein's carrier buddy was "who got the ladies in silk and they always paid."

In Clarkston, Idaho, Orin fared better than Jack. Like most boys, the 10-year-old met a few annoying customers who stalled on his Saturday morning collections. But at the "houses of ill repute" no stalling. Located in apartments on the floor above larger commercial layouts, the ladies' private business provided him with good results. The girls subscribed to six copies of the *Spokane Daily Chronicle*, consistently paid their bill, and the best part, the "girls really tipped."

Young Barry, trying to sell the *Fishing News* in Ketchikan, skipped venturing along the boardwalk on Creek Street since the prostitutes weren't into ocean fishing. However, the pretty houses with flowers growing in front of the red light area offered a better scene than ghastly rats in the warehouse hit with ball bats. Rain seeped in everywhere, rats scurried across the dock, but the red light district caused no problem. Barry was unconcerned. He knew exactly where the red light district extended, just as boys in other towns shared the information with new paperboys.

The Bennett brothers understood which "houses the pretty girls lived in" on their Everett routes. "One customer always paid promptly." She resided upstairs in a brothel on Hewitt Avenue and when a shoe landed on the fourth step of the outside stairs, "a loud buzzer sounded." The brothers collected each Saturday morning. When a boy heading upstairs pressed the 4th board, a lady appeared. She met him "with a sleepy smile and gave him the 15 cents."

From decade to decade, information passed to new carriers. Busy boys covering a town should know their way around. They learned where the cafes, card rooms, hotels, houses with pretty ladies, and the entertaining theater were located. Like prostitute houses, risqué burlesque theater was part of city society through which the paperboy traversed.

In the 1940s, the *Hudson Dispatch* newspaper office was located on 38th Street in Union City, New Jersey, right next to a lively burlesque theater, complete with a marquee and a window display of life-size enticing entertainers. The boys could window shop but not enter. For Ed White, a fourth grader scurrying on his morning route, passing produce peddlers arranging their displays for the day, he saw only a quiet, still theater at 5:00 a.m. But on Friday evening, his time to collect within his community, the theater was lit and folks were in the ticket line for the nightly performance. While the dreary Depression years receded, the vaudeville acts and the scintillating striptease dances continued through the 1940s, before bowing to enhanced movies and expanding TV entertainment of the 1950s.

From visiting the establishments of prostitutes, who were regular newspaper customers, to the homes of proper housewives, the youngster routinely did his rounds. A boy focused on collecting, not cohabitating. That is until his focus was spun off-balance. A page turned in his young life. Seeing the lady of the house, or more of the lady than the carrier expected, was disrupting. Regardless if he stood under a red light or a porch light, his insides lit up. At least he was not facing a closed door. But, oops! The housecoat wasn't closed.

## Exposed

An adolescent boy blushed and squirmed in front of a housewife in an unbuttoned robe, in sheer lingerie, or only in the buff. While a woman might inadvertently let her robe slip open revealing a forbidden view, for the paperboy such a flash was more significant than the exposed woman considered. As she handed him a tip, his stammered "Thank you ma'am" covered a lot more than her robe covered. And the risqué lady of the house wasn't a madam.

To a developing boy used to pumping the bike pedals, with blood pumping, his hormones continued pumping hours after his bicycle stopped.

## Look. For Sure!

Gerald Horna was not concerned with a customer's Great Dane. He knew the mild-mannered, huge dog weighed over 100 pounds, around 20 pounds past a 12-year old's weight. However, the imposing muscular pet liked people and the massive dog was much better than that nasty rooster that flew menacingly at him. "A big rooster chased me," and chased him often.

Instead, the Great Dane blinked his soft inquisitive eyes displaying the look of friendship. His loose jowls wet with slobbering saliva made him comical as he lumbered out to greet Gerald, who stared directly into the calm eyes.

Similarly, watchful eyes met Bill Gamel as he rounded a path, heard branches snapping and heard the worrisome snort. He was staring directly at a moose. Bill tilted his head upward to scan the animal, whose shoulder height averaged seven feet and whose weight measured well over 1,000 pounds, ten times larger than Bill's frame. The eyes watching the intruder were small compared to its thick, oblong, comical head, and long, awkward legs. Only briefly startled, Bill, knew that moose often wandered around the streets in Anchorage, annoying home owners, disrupting traffic. He had learned that a moose is actually rather tolerant if granted undisturbed space, so he wasn't concerned. Bill looked at the moose, stood still and sighed.

When learning "look" in the first *Dick & Jane Reader,* there was no explanation in reading circle about what to say with what is seen! Look a Great Dane in the eye, look an immense moose in the eye, or look a soft round white...Oh my gosh!

A paperboy stared at a bare navel as blood rushed to his cheeks, upper and lower ones.

## Not Allowed

Before the 1960s, people spoke discretely about topics of a sensual nature. Hanging wet laundry on the triple clothesline, housewives hung their lingerie on the inside cord or under the wide bed sheets. If men were near, women stepping into a bathroom turned on the sink water before sitting on the toilet. Chicken was, "White meat, please." Ladies never mentioned breast at the meat market. The ineffable word "prostitute," or heaven forbid, the precise term "pregnant" was forbidden at the supper table. A wife over on Elm Street was "in a family way."

The immense movie industry censored bedroom scenes with undressing limited to removing shoes and unbuttoning shirts. Actresses did not strip. Sensual scenes stayed concealed, which became more enticing. As television expanded, changes inched into society's sexual expression. In the long-running TV series, *I Love Lucy,* Desi and Lucy were married yet never appeared together in the same bed. In the 1952 season, Lucy's pregnant status was discussed as "expecting." The hilarious black and white series barely challenged the prim status of viewers.

With *I Love Lucy,* youngsters were left to wonder if Lucy was expecting the way mama told papa they were expecting Aunt Ethel to arrive. Mrs. O'Leary and Mrs. Italiano were always in a family way, so seeing Lucille Ball pregnant didn't seem different. Emulating Mrs. Nelson, Ozzie's wife, housewives wore a plain housedress, protected with a gingham apron, all very proper. The carriers, swinging between forbidden sayings and factual sightings, tried to balance their response and obey the rules.

## Not There

Starting in 1947, nine-year-old Ed Boblitt delivered the daily *Bellefontaine Examiner.* The end of his route included selling 25 newspapers to patients in the Mary Rutan Hospital, located on Palmer Road. The hospital, the only one in Logan County, Ohio, was in the parameter of Ed's route and therefore his responsibility.

Patients appreciated his visit and their *Examiner* companion. He sold the local paper for a nickel and pocketed two cents, earning $3 a week on just hospital sales, a fine steady profit, minus a few coins spent frequently for a soda pop and a bag of peanuts.

Not restricted to visiting hours, he scurried from room to room, stepped past the separating curtain, hurried to the next floor. He was company for a person confined with a broken leg, or someone connected to an oxygen tank after a heart attack. He smiled for people though they grimaced with pain. He saw bed pans, noticed a patient trying to fit a hospital gown over her body, and smelled meal trays that would soon be served. In the small town, he knew his customers very well and everyone knew he was George Boblitt's son.

He continued delivering and abiding by hospital rules for eight years. "My only restriction was that I was not allowed in the maternity ward." The mothers, whom he knew, had to wait until they were home to read their child's birth announcement in the newspaper.

# Wide Open

Living with discrete behavior, it was far from normal for a housewife to casually expose her breasts and genitals, those "private parts." A fellow with an active curiosity, and developing hormones zinging through his blood, had rapid reactions when hidden flesh was revealed. From a buttoned housedress to an open house coat, adolescents were confused. With classes in economics, physics, and sociology, *Main Street School* now taught lessons in sex-education.

A boy entering his teenage years expected to leave the boys' choir with his altered voice, and he tolerated teasing about facial fuzz. But his first encounter with a full, sexual view lit an internal reaction to the external display. His mild response to the houses of ill-repute switched significantly at the houses of the ill clothed.

A housewife in a baggy, purple robe, her worn, green slippers and large, pink cylinder hair curlers that bobbed to her animated chatter, left a carrier thinking her comical, sloppy items could be a Halloween costume; but, year-round she wore disheveled, blousy attire.

By contrast, an open robe, that a woman of the house considered an inconsequential slip, startled a child. Private respect was shattered. The shell of protection dutifully taught by mothers, grandmothers, and Sunday school teachers was instantly cracked, as a woman's careless exposure made him flustered. The attractive housewives were not femmes fatales, but they certainly created a disturbance for a young fellow coming of age. Did the census taker distinguish between the advertised houses and the inadvertent houses?

# Look At the Details

Paul Fellows managed his route in Pipestone, Minnesota, where he first delivered the *Minneapolis Star* and then changed to the *Minneapolis Tribune*. He knew his customers, among them a school teacher, the minister, his dentist and a variety of people active in his modest hometown of about 5,000 citizens. And subscribers who owned a television by the mid 1950s didn't complain when Paul lingered to watch their TV as he stopped in to collect.

However, on Fridays after school, his regular time to collect, a different view might appear. "Sometimes the lady of the house was not completely dressed when answering the door. I can remember being greeted by ladies in a bathrobe or slip." They showed a semblance of cover over delicate underclothes, the ones usually "hidden" on the clothesline.

Finishing his collection rounds for the *Minneapolis Star,* one afternoon he had a view not seen on TV programs. "A lady came to the door dressed only in her underwear. She seemed nonchalant as she handed me her money." Paul was quickly intrigued with an interesting coin.

His father, a coin collector, influenced Paul's interest in special coins. In the mid 1950s his collections sometimes included late nineteenth and early twentieth century nickels, dimes, quarters and half dollars, though "never once an Indian head penny." The treasury stopped minting the Indian head one-cent piece in 1908. Those special pennies had been collected.

Well, this one cold winter afternoon in Minnesota, "I received a Booker T. Washington commemorative half dollar." It wasn't until Paul returned home and showed his father "that I knew what it was." He learned to look for details. So when the lady, in only her underwear, gave him an early twentieth century half dollar, he recognized he should check it out. She also gave him a scene to remember along with her 50 cent subscription fee.

## In Full View

In Columbia, Missouri, with over 175 customers for the *Columbia Tribune*, Jim Ausmus spent an extensive time collecting. Though it was a tiresome routine, he recorded one specific collection among many hundreds over his three years. "I vividly recall one particularly attractive young lady who, when she opened her door to pay, inadvertently allowed her robe to, shall we say, open. It made quite an impression on me. I owe the *Tribune* quite a lot." Not in back payments. Jim was conscientious and always paid his bill.

Bruce Dodson's best moment in collecting occurred early in the day, resulting in a wide-awake morning. The "front door was answered by a beautiful woman in a bathrobe. When she reached for her purse the robe came open." Maybe another inadvertent happening. Bruce didn't pause to judge. For him it was the "first time I had ever seen the secrets of a female body. Wow!" Hollywood came alive in his small Illinois town of Wood River. It was difficult for the newspaper, even with sensational headlines and photos, or the entertaining comic strips to compete for Bruce's attention.

Paperboys raced past houses where residents, busy with their schedule and activities, were oblivious to small eyes scanning bodies. Yes, broken windows were costly, as Doug Larson learned after breaking five in three years. But windows held pleasurable experiences for boys, who felt no hesitation to view adult figures standing in a transparent space.

Delivering the *Daily News Miner*, heralded as "America's Farthest North Daily Newspaper" in Fairbanks, Alaska, Kent Sturgis experienced a wide range of adventures. He carried papers in icy -50° F. as well as enduring sunny 90° F., a 140 degree range. Like other paperboys, Kent lined up for the first come, first serve system to hawk papers. He wanted to be first because he'd sell in the eight or so bars along a two block stretch. Selling the 25 cent paper, he often pocketed a 75 cent profit because the drinkers gave him a dollar for a paper.

And one day he pocketed a nice memory. On a bright afternoon, not bitter cold with solid frost coating the window, Kent viewed a living *Playboy* center-spread. Standing near the transparent glass, a nude woman was inadvertently seen. He grinned, sighed, and whistled down the street, his delight unknown to his model.

Gordon Labuhn's model, who was actually an actress, was aware that he stood at the door with his collection list and she stood naked. To conceal her predicament, she had discreetly peeked around the door. While Gordon waited and watched, she counted out her subscription fee to the *Detroit Times*, staying behind a curtain of solid front door that remained ajar. He didn't mind if she took her time.

Even though he wore glasses, he wasn't Superman. Gordon couldn't see through the door that screened her lovely nude body. Then how did he know she was naked? The grade-schooler, wearing glasses, as he had since he was six, was having a fine time studying the full length mirror beside the door. He kept his sighting of her body reflection discrete. She paid him, closed off the view and he continued on, happy that his glasses weren't too steamed to stroll down the steps.

# On Display

Klamath Falls, like other working towns, offered houses of ill repute. Bob Barr took that in stride. In 1936 he had his own business to operate. Making the rounds, he walked up to the front of another house and waited for his knock to bring results. He mentally ran through how many collections he had left to complete. The door creaked.

"The lady came to the door stark naked." The word lady has a broad meaning.

She was not in a robe that dropped open. She was disrobed. And she looked at Bob "unconcerned." Inadvertently or deliberately, her appearance stunned him. Self conscious and embarrassed, he stood "red faced looking at a nude woman." Should he keep his eyes on her navel? The circulation manager said to look the customer in the eye but his eyes were really blinking. Should he say "Thank you."? Ahh, did she pay?

Regardless of the decade or the region, boys consistently stammered in response to female showings. For Grant Wise, carrying or collecting resulted in views not routinely permitted on the porches of Hodgenville. His stack of Sunday papers were dropped at the post office, " around 3:00 a.m. That early in the morning I saw a lot of sights that a young teen shouldn't see. After a Saturday night of partying, nude folks would be outside. Or appear at their door totally nude. A boy really didn't mind a lady appearing like that." Grant figured his circumstances were "an education in the real world."

Children weren't allowed to say pregnant or chicken breast, forbidden to buy a ticket to the burlesque theater. But all alone, a boy saw nudity. In a silent era of "don't talk about that," he certainly could not go home to mother and share how the customer's body appeared different from his family members.

Completely unexpected, the housewife experiences were the opposite of the common knowledge about bordellos. No one told the paper carriers to collect at bordellos, tobacco cigar stores, bookie joints, pool halls, card parlors, saloons and taverns. Sometimes they were told to "Get out!" But common sense led them to collect where money changed hands.

## An Excellent Place

When collecting was not up to speed, or was significantly disrupted, carriers moved toward dependable money. Prostitute houses were fine compared to the fetid saloons with their dark interiors and rank smells. Yet stopping in the tavern made sense when trying to finish the required collection task. They persisted to collect the week's fee, the back fees, facing the no pay, listening to the slow pay, smelling the soused, in order to successfully pay themselves.

Through a range of situations, collection finished, carrying piles of coins, carriers headed to the bank to purchase a money order. Ed White took his sack of coins to the grocery store for dollars. Bill Malone scooted in the back door of the pool hall and the owner converted the heavy coins to dollars. Circulation managers pressed the boys to pay on time on Saturday morning, just not with hundreds of coins.

When the system changed to monthly payments, the company tried incentives to receive the cash in a timely manner, using prompt payment in contest rules for winning prizes and trips.

The *Seattle Times* featured a display that recognized all the carriers' bills were paid by the 5th of the month. Hanging on the substation door, a large red A pleased the paperboys and delighted the district manager even more. If every kid stayed on the Honor Roll for 12 months, the red letter was replaced with a prominent gold A. Wanting to win, the youngsters prodded each other to collect, so no one could be the kid blamed for losing the gold A. More so, the children wanted the hamburgers, fries and cola provided as a reward.

Managing a paper route required order. Keep the right order: pay the company and *then* spend. Don't reverse the pattern. With a lot to learn, many were tempted to relax from the responsibility and go fishing. Except a young paperboy would need to buy fishing gear. He might stop by the carnival for fun. He had watched carnival activities, smelled cotton candy, caramel apples, sausage sizzling. He wanted to eat. Maybe he'd spend just a dime.

# PART III
# SOAR

## Celebrating

Paperboys carrying a load every day, collecting from customers every week, covering miles through four, seven, nine years, earned the right to celebrate their reliability and accountability. These enterprising children were the soil of the earth: productive.

A boy's awkward struggles declined with his agile, taller body. Forget that first fearful morning, or at least control any concern now that confidence prevailed. His biological clock had adjusted; mistakes had improved his capability. Errors diminished after the lasting lessons were instilled, especially first mistakes that brought swift consequences.

## The Price of Fun

Seeing the carnival come to town and fingering empty pockets felt similar to staring at a dry, empty swimming pool. A carnival, the county fair, the circus, any of these events drew boys more than honey draws flies. Oh, to spend nickels and dimes for waffles, hot dogs, a Ferris wheel ride, ring tosses for prizes. To wander past the mid-way glitz and hear a barker call louder than little newspaper hawkers ever managed. A carnival rose above their earlier longing when looking in a candy store window.

## A Primary Lesson Instilled

John Dappen didn't have an easy time in a northern climate, skidding on ice, and also being scared of vicious dogs in the early morning. He started at age 10 delivering the *Sioux City Journal* or the *Des Moines Register* to folks he knew in Graettinger, Iowa. From 1930 to 1938 he worked to collect in the heart of farm country. Farm families had struggled well before the Depression cut through the nation. Yet, the people reliably paid so he reliably managed his route and collections. After he learned a primary lesson.

Enjoying the new sensation of coins jingling in his pocket, John fingered the pennies, nickels, dimes. Wow, quarters. He advanced from zero to a hand filled with change, and his collecting time was right. Graettinger, settled by German immigrants with discipline, offered a respite from daily toiling: the carnival arrived.

John entered the carnival, that vibrated with laughter and lively music, enticed with a variety of sweet and spicy aromas. He played, he ate with nary a thought beyond the immediate fun. Then his finite funds ran out. The fate from the temptation struck him. With all his money lost, he learned to hence forth stay on the straight path, which directed him straight from the customers' doors to quickly pay the company. John did not stray, again, from his responsibility.

In 1948 when Mr. and Mrs. Hubbard drove to Spokane, to enjoy more than the hometown view of Grand Coulee Dam, their sons stayed home. The parents left, Don, a middle-schooler, with his younger brother for a couple of days. "There was a carnival in town on that weekend. We really wanted to go and on top of my dresser was a whole bag of money." With his collection coins readily available, "We had a great time at the carnival."

Great until Don's stomach churned worse than when he ate waffles, cotton candy, buttery popcorn, caramel apples, corn dogs slathered with mustard, followed by riding the Ferris wheel, the fast whirly gig, and weaving in front of the weird mirror exhibit. Well, maybe not worse. But Don felt awful facing the consequences. "Dad had to pay for the papers that month, but I had the embarrassing job of telling the newspaper manager what I had done." Face dad, face the manager and face paying dad back for a month's worth of collections, casually spent fast at the carnival.

Orin Smith started his paper route on foot. Collecting each Saturday morning, he managed his expenses and purchases, to include, before long, a bicycle. Though he saved for a bike, since his bundles were dropped at a mom & pop family grocery in Clarkston, Idaho, he conveniently drank colas, ate candy and lots of doughnuts. He also tried cigarettes, but dad caught him. Dad kept Orin smoking, coughing, until he turned grey. He was ill. Certainly learned that lesson: don't buy nor smoke cigarettes. A colorful carnival was more tempting and not sickening, because afterwards his mother bailed him out from over-spending, way over.

After his spending trouble, Orin settled into saving for speed. By 1950 he bought a motor scooter. In awhile he sold the scooter and bought a car. Four years on the route taught him quick lessons, with a few short, sick feelings, and then he advanced to long satisfying rides.

For paper carriers everywhere, successfully collecting meant managing money. Their intent was to make money, though they did not become hoarders. The funds and the freedom expanded into fun celebrations *after* all their struggles and endurances. A boy spent dimes, yet at the same time saved dollars. As the dollars accumulated, his satisfaction with success rose. Through stellar reliability and accountability, he soon shared funds that created an even higher level of exhilaration. Paperboys soared forward, even upward.

## Excitement

Through the terrible times in the twentieth century, with horrific events beyond what the world had ever witnessed, paper carriers also delivered uplifting news in the century of airplane development. Trains continued to crisscross the country and ships crossed the waters, but important travel steadily ascended.

Congressional members, in 1924, developed an amendment for the Constitution that could prohibit youngsters from working. In Ellensburg, David Bowles walked his route; second-grader John James crossed the streets in Hazleton with his heavy bag; 10-year-old Dick Irvin completed his second route in Des Moines. And in Seattle, four airplanes left in April, 1924, flying above Alaska, across the Pacific Ocean to Japan, past Asia, the Middle East and Europe. Two of the planes continued over the Atlantic Ocean, past Newfoundland, into Boston and finally back to Seattle on September 28. An around-the-world flight was completed in 175 days. The stage was set; pilots kept vying for more competitive firsts in challenging airplane flights.

With few radios in 1927, all the newspapers headlined the details of Charles Lindbergh's solo crossing of the Atlantic in his single engine, *Spirit of St. Louis*. He elated the nation with his successful 33-hour flight that landed in France on May 21.The electrifying event provided rapid, special-edition sales for local newspaper hawkers. Running, shouting the stupendous headline, John James sold stacks of papers in Hazelton and rushed for more bundles. It boosted the spirit of little merchants until they nearly soared off the ground.

Just over four years later, 1931, a nonstop flight left Japan and crossed the Pacific Ocean, again capturing front-page news. Two pilots, Clyde Pangborn and Hugh Herndon, landed their monoplane, successfully, without landing gear. Forty-one hours after takeoff, they arrived in Wenatchee on Monday, October 5. In spite of people's difficulty to find pennies in the growing Depression, Vernon Franze quickly sold the *Wenatchee World*.

Citizens stoically faced desperate economic conditions, horrific war battles, polio epidemics, and yet decade into decade Americans soared ahead, faster and further in the age of airplane advancement. A carrier escaped his monotonous delivery when the roar of a plane drew his eyes upward, searching for it to emerge. Circulation managers soon knew the best reward to offer competing paperboys: an airplane ride.

David Janecke savored a brief respite from two *Seattle Star* routes when he won a ride in a Stinson Voyager airplane. Rising above Puget Sound, looking at the imposing Mount Rainier, his life became bigger. And at 100 mph, faster. The sound and vibrations were ringing through him, while he saw his world recede to his size. Just watching a plane, the exhilaration left boys flying high, head in the clouds, feet skimming the sidewalk.

Superman, his cape flowing, flew aloft. Released from the confines of home and school, a carrier's euphoria with his freedom was often expressed in a fast downhill bicycle flight. Pedaling hard, he'd fly aloft as though Superman. Securing his folded canvas bag on the rear bike rack, he bent low, gripped the handles, head and neck stretched forward over the handlebars, shoulders squared, feet pumped in one continuous spin. He gained speed, his shirt sleeves billowed, legs turned like pistons as wind swooshed over his ears creating a motor-like hum. Splotches of sunlight blinked through tree limbs and trees flew past as if a hedge; the houses flattened into one continuous building. On a dip in the hill he gulped but quickly leaned to the left on the curve, then moved into the center of the street, his body and bike flowing through the wind tunnel he created, finishing as though a salvo fired over the stadium wall. *Wait'll the guys at the shack hear this one. A record flight and I'll pass that tomorrow.*

A paperboy's scrapes healed, the scars diminished, mistakes subsided, and his spirit soared, particularly when fast speed energized him. Fun trumped fear and frustrations. The small kids at the paper shack appeared sillier and less reliable than he and his big buddies. Misdeeds had disappeared with maturity. Replacing bike pedals with an accelerator pedal in his first car, he focused on plans for future accomplishments.

A child tripping along the street, unsure if he'd keep his route until his self doubt was trampled, had replaced that doubt with confidence because he wasn't fired, didn't fail but absorbed a couple of fines that directed him to correct errors. He learned how to cope and his common sense handled most incidents. His outlook rose to an even higher altitude

## Flying Forward

Russ Tobey's feet were off the ground, though his head didn't reach the clouds in his first flight lesson. He was focused. His feelings carried him upward soaring more smoothly than the small bi-plane. The vast sky above Tulsa spread dramatically over the flat windswept earth as the airy, blue expanse dominated the brown, dull ground of Oklahoma. In perilous weather, when Russ was unable to fly, he felt the power of the atmosphere in the rip of lightning, the roar of thunder. The wind-swirling rain spit on the dirt as he threw newspapers, dodged dogs that scared him, and earned more money toward his next flight lesson. Into five years, Russ delivered every single day, morning and afternoon, collected regularly, and saved for another quick lesson. The United States entered World War II. On the west coast fear gripped people, and blackouts were ordered around the nation. But on January 3, 1942, Russ passed his solo flight in a clear, bright sky. Thrilled, the 16-year-old flew forward and upward.

## The Significant Morning

Each morning Roger Hagen walked his route to 100 customers, all of whom he knew in the small town of Parker, South Dakota, with slightly more than 1,000 residents. Driving a car, which he had since about age 10, was inconvenient when going porch to porch. His bundles of the *Argus Leader* had arrived early from Sioux Falls, 30 miles northeast. Even with -20° F. and blowing snow drifts deep enough to shorten telephone poles, Roger punctually reached his customers plodding in his double boots. He shoved rubber boots inside surplus army boots, which were readily available since World War II ended. During summer months, biking in the morning he avoided the intense, miserable afternoon temperatures that climbed to 110° F. All the while his mind circled the wide open sky.

Weather extremes seldom interfered with frequent enjoyment: movies for 5 cents, building model airplanes, reading comics, being active in scouts. On Saturdays folks came to town, enlivening the two hardware stores and crowding the two taverns. And then in late summer, Parker, as the county seat, hosted the Turner County Fair, the oldest fair in South Dakota. In his friendly town and with lenient parents, Roger had few restrictions.

He did have one restriction, which required he be age 16. In 1947, on the morning of his sixteenth birthday (before he completed his Eagle Scout ranking, and seven years before he held his first actual driver's license at age 23, a perfunctory step), he soared forward and upward alone. His significant solo flight accomplished.

## In Control

Spending controlled, a paperboy's funds accumulated for more substantive buys than cheap carnival trinkets and thrills. Better than pocket change, though the money mattered, was the accumulation of friends at the newspaper station and around his route. His customers recognized him. Though he had struggled, he soon struck a balanced stride. Showing neither an arrogant nor an aloof attitude, the carrier developed a controlled certainty.

He worked, earned, and received rewards from his paper route, a short flight in a boy's lifetime. Nevertheless, short flights take off. And parallel with his youthful years, the news he carried told of a nation soaring. Looking at a jet, with the contrail accenting the atmosphere, he too could dream of soaring with mankind. Furthermore, carriers looked skyward as sonic booms from 45,000 feet blasted over their route, after Air Force Captain Charles Yeager flew faster than the speed of sound in October, 1947.

Ron Petersen rushed each morning delivering his *Salt Lake Tribune* papers from his American Flyer bike. His monotony broke hearing the unique B-36 sound sweeping across the Utah sky. Even if he needed to rush, the moment he heard the distinct sound he followed the flight until the speck disappeared and any contrail evaporated, but the thrill stayed with him. Further, he absorbed news when headlines on March 2, 1949, announced the first around-the-world nonstop airplane trip. In 94 hours the Boeing Lucky Lady II landed, a quarter of a century after the first 175 day flight stopped around the world. Jesse Montoya had exciting news to sell, in the *Wenatchee World*, as did thousands of other newsboys across the nation.

## More Than Constellations

Then in the late 1950s paperboys added another search: trying to spot an orbiting satellite. On clear winter nights, Kent Sturgis, covering his freezing route in Fairbanks, looked skyward fascinated with shimmering, fluorescent-green northern lights. Watching the dancing eerie glow intrigued him. In early March, 1957, he was transfixed by "a very rare, all-red Aurora Borealis." Few people had seen gossamer streamers of red northern lights. Mesmerized, his stride became slower as he watched the amazing red-sky scene. Then he had an additional watch.

The day after October 4, 1957, when Americans were alarmed by a successful Russian satellite launch, Kent searched skyward for Sputnik. Soon the American satellite, Explorer I, launched January 31, 1958, less than four months after Sputnik, stirred carriers, like Kent, running a dark route, to look for the source in the new Space Age.

Though American confidence shook when Russia heralded their space program, in just five years, on February 20, 1962, Americans were ecstatic as headlines and televisions broadcast the news: our first astronaut orbited the earth. John Glenn successfully orbited the planet three times. His capsule traveled far above the little town of New Concord, Ohio, where, as a school boy, he first circled the streets throwing the *Columbus Citizen Journal*.

Even more customers collected extra papers as the historic newspaper headline announced the moon landing. Neil Armstrong, on July 20, 1969, took his famous *giant leap for mankind*. The tumultuous 60s decade closed with stupendous awe. Young paper carriers could see the moon in a different light, seeing their life heading forward in a different light.

## Forward and Upward

Newspaper carrier's first, year-round job led his parade of other firsts; first new set of clothes, first love trial, first car, first in the family to enter college. The short steps along the sidewalk, which laced just a few years in an overall lifetime, provided leaps into future ventures as he tackled opportunities. He built a savings account that accompanied his stock of common sense secured with confidence. He received rewards and recognition. Starting on the bottom of the paper shack hierarchy, his dogged efforts took him upward and onward, as ambition let his lofty thoughts rise, his dreams ascend.

With no pretention, the pride, or as Vernon Franze expressed it, "A feeling of juvenile prestige" grew with personal development that tipped the experiences to positive. Fun? Not always. Not the binding routine, the accidents or the blame from some crank, nor the mean dogs. Yet carriers captured adventures and independence.

Kids possess an innate desire for fun, dosed with competition and curiosity. Quite inquisitive, the newspaper route helped feed his curious nature. Within the parameter of the local community, the route supported his needs and wants, along with a surplus to share.

For circulation managers, in spite of frequent frustrations and aggravations with droves of kids, and the accusations hurled at the newspaper industry by reformers, the managers cared about their carriers and expressed it with more than a platitude of words. Children loved receiving. And the opportunities to win prizes, tickets, and trips abounded. A carrier expected better results, better prizes than with three balls tossed at a carnival.

Winning incentive contests for trips to ball parks and amusement parks, winning a train trip across the county line, sailing to Canada or the Caribbean, or just sailing on a lake with other very novice sailors sent his enthusiasm soaring, especially if an airplane trip was involved.

# CHAPTER 17
## DIMES FOR SWEETS, DOLLARS FOR SUCCESS

### Money is the root of all evil.

Dour adults proclaimed such words, the way they exclaimed "Exploited!" However, from grandparents, parents, and individual experiences, carriers knew that money was the root of existence and a road to occasional enjoyment. Earning on their own, paperboys savored snacks, feeding the stomach and the feeling of independence. Spending allowed a small fling against the restrictions lashed by continual discipline.

All the effort to acquire a route, wait on bundles, commit to daily delivery, tolerate customers like Mrs. Stink's tardiness in paying, and then, in a perfunctory manner, meet the obligation to the newspaper company every Saturday morning. A carrier absorbed complaint fines, subtracted deadbeat costs, covered other expenses and the weekly lay-away amount for a bike until finally, he was ready to spend money---the very reason for a route. With coins tumbling in his pocket, he intended to treat himself.

### Spending

The responsible paperboy earned what he purchased, unlike some privileged, protected children with possessions to spare. Dad might assist by bargaining down the price of a cart, or signing for his son's debt balance on a bicycle or a lawn mower, but the paperboy, through his job, paid his way, step by step.

### Available

Breakfast or supper aromas drifting to the street stimulated the paperboy's taste buds as he hurried along. The air was redolent from customers' kitchens and the exhaust fan blowing out from the corner café. The German, French, or Scandinavian bakeries tantalized a perpetually hungry youngster. Convenient Mom & Pop corner groceries were attractive with tempting foods beckoning him to spend. Why not balance the rush of the route with a treat? A boy reached into a large, red cooler chest for a cola or spent a nickel for candy, appreciating each small purchase.

In 1934, when Bud Dreyfus was "free to keep 50 cents to spend," he chose the movies at the Five Points Theater each Saturday, seeing features like King Kong , Duck Soup and best of all the cartoons featuring the hilarious Donald Duck. He giggled and munched popcorn with other paper carriers. The group sat in a dark, air-conditioned theater, letting their imagination soar. With 25 cents remaining, Bud spent a nickel a day "for a huge Butterfinger candy bar." He portioned money the same as he portioned time.

## Late Snack. Or Early Breakfast?

"Jumping out of bed at 3:00 a.m. I pedaled my bike downtown to the press to take papers for my 110 customers." Tillman Houser, riding on the sidewalks in Salem, covered the top of Nob Hill to deliver the *Oregon Statesman* before the sun lit the snowy Cascade Mountains. "After I finished my route, I often stopped at the bakery to buy a small sack of day-old pastry for a dime, washed down with cold milk from a pint glass bottle bought at the creamery for a nickel." His stomach satisfied by a late night snack, or since it was pre-dawn, an early breakfast, he returned to bed at 6:30 a.m. catching a quick snooze before school.

For an extra special treat on a hot summer day, he bought "a delicious five-cent Siberian soft ice cream cone." In 1936, collecting 65 cents a month from each customer was a challenge. But to buy treats, he needed to collect a sufficient amount for a profit. He also saved for a Schwinn bike. With a goal, he worked at earning.

The same for carriers anywhere: eat chocolates, drink a cola, read the comics---snacks for the body with laughs and adventures for the mind. Life was terrific when sweets coated the taste buds and teeth, ignoring whether the morsels contributed to healthy development. The youngster met his responsibility and afterwards rewarded himself at candy and ice cream counters.

## Confiscated Coupons

On a hot San Jose afternoon with over 100 deliveries waiting, Mike Rhodes took a minute for his usual glance at the *Mercury News* before starting his sweaty routine. His attention was captured when he saw "a coupon for a free Shasta soda." Instead of paying for a 10 cent drink, he'd enjoy a free one. "Coupons in the paper were very much a novelty. Like lightning, the thought of having a cold soda every day provided the temptation to take action. I reasoned that one coupon ripped out of one customer's paper probably wouldn't be noticed."

Perhaps that rationalization might work. However, "this error in judgment prompted me to rip every coupon out of all 125 papers." Over four months, in the heat of summer "I would be enjoying a cold soda for free." Rather than spending $12.50, he imagined being refreshed without a dime spent. His first year on the route was certainly offering unexpected benefits.

Until...his miscalculation from "89 of the 125 customers who noticed the missing coupon and called the newspaper to complain." The complaint was not "where's that paperboy", but "where's my small missing section." Customers were precise about time and coupons.

Mr. Blank, the district manager, made Mike "redeliver all 89 papers and confiscated the coupons." Carnivals, coupons, money caused transgressions, but only once. The complaint system operated because of coupons, the comics, and because customers clocked the carrier to be on time. They expected their demands be met.

## Extra Requests

Besides sharing bites of candy or sips of cola with others at the paper shack, and not prone to just think of themselves, carriers thought of their helpers. Yes, the substitute liked a candy bar for his effort, but a paperboy's companion also wanted treats.

In 1924 David Bowles collected on Saturday riding his horse, Ted, through Ellensburg and on to the outlying customers. Finishing his task, "when I got in about noon, I'd buy him [Ted] a candy maple bar, ice cream cone or a bottle of pop. He liked strawberry pop. I'd put it in the side of his mouth and raise his head so he could swallow and not bite the bottle. He was good to hold his head up. When it was all gone he'd nicker and nudge me for more." Routinely collecting, David faithfully remembered his horse.

In 1947, Dwayne Lane rode his bike over the two mile paper route near Beverly Lake south of Everett. Unless the lake froze and a couple of feet of snow covered the area, then he rode his horse, Starlight, since the four hooves managed well in the snow. Completing his rounds, Dwayne bought a candy bar. His horse wanted one, too. Starlight didn't intend to be left out and his owner obliged his request.

## More Than the Stomach

Children harbored an innate ability to create fun, often without effort. They entertained themselves making shadow figures with finger gestures, playing with a loose tooth, unraveling a knitted sweater. Childish actions mixed with stern adult positions led comic strip creators to simply reflect everyday life. Following church, after a long sermon with dire warnings about burning in hell, the Sunday comics particularly brightened a kid's day.

In 1920, the return of the Katzenjammer Kids in the newspaper funnies accented the shift to a better decade. In the Roaring Twenties, the German twins, Hans & Fritz, who were switched to Mike and Aleck during the horrors of World War I, reappeared in American comic strips. Paper carriers absorbed the cartoon, laughing with the twins' rebellions against authority. Their creative, mischievous pranks reflected those committed by carriers. Handling daily newspapers, the children relished reading the funnies, chewing on a chocolate bar before they delivered to customers. Through the decades boys like Sam, Jim, John, Ron, Tom, and Roger enhanced their days with a good laugh at Major Hoople, Barney Google, Blondie, and Alley Oop. A child sat a spell and absorbed the thrilling adventures of Terry & the Pirates, Dick Tracy, Buck Rogers, Steve Canyon, Superman or the Prince Valiant strip. Paperboys needed to rush, but snagged time to check the funnies every day.

There were no funnies in the *Ketchikan Fishing News*, which may have explained part of Barry Dunphy's trouble in selling it. People checked the comics first, then the sports page, before settling into the rest of the news columns, features, and ads. One carrier learned he could control collecting using the page of comics. Bill Malone issued a simple rule: "no pay, no funnies." His customers in Memphis consistently paid for their *Commercial Appeal* subscription.

A daily reading of the comics broadened when a paperboy found an opportunity to purchase a new publication. In 1934, a company called Famous Funnies began publishing comic books. For 10 cents a kid entertained himself while waiting for his bundles or he passed the entertainment around at the newspaper shack. When he left he stuffed his reading material in his back pocket. That way he was prepared to fit the thin magazine inside his English school book, to enjoy during an hour-long Shakespeare lesson.

The world roiled in war horrors and America's contributing strength was reflected in Superman comic books, starting in 1940. As a little paperboy plodded his route, daydreaming, he pictured himself in Superman stunts. And even more so with Superman movies.

In addition to buying comic books, carriers attended the Saturday movie matinee, which brought more laughter with boisterous cartoons. Held to monotonous routines, occasionally caught in harsh conditions, the animated world of Bugs Bunny delighted carriers. The weather in Fairbanks ranged from miserably cold to uncomfortably hot, but Kent

Sturgis and other paperboys escaped the Alaskan climate, as they reveled with the movies watching special showings reserved just for carriers.

Items beyond food, comic books, and movies captured a paperboy's attention. He bought tools, fishing gear, baseball gloves and bats. Paperboys paid for bike attachments, a yo-yo, a slinky, 45 rpm phonographs, balsa airplane models, and played the pinball machines, lit firecrackers, and lit cigarettes. From every direction came temptations to drop a dime, squander a quarter, spend 50 cents and clean the pockets of change. Yet with frivolous spending, the boys' earnings still accumulated. Their attention turned to saving dollars for major purchases.

## The Path to More

With the collection of $60, $85, $100 a month, a boy's profits rose. Once a month, Bill Gamel counted $200 or higher in change from his money bag that weighed him down as he headed to the newspaper office. Kent Sturgis, with 90 customers, regularly collected over $240 a month. He acquired dollars when a dime was significant.

Excited about the prospect of having additional money, paperboys signed on more subscribers. Jim Ruck determined that with apartment houses in his compact route, he could handle a second run covering a further distance across Tacoma. Having two routes raised his number of subscribers to 188, which improved his profit margin.

Opening the 1950s decade, Paul Meyer obtained a *Tacoma Tribune* route, near the military bases at Fort Lewis and the McChord Air Force Base. He switched from a long, rural run to a compact distance. Even better, he built this route to 200 customers. And his profits grew significantly when he added a subscriber, because the *Tribune* paid a dollar bonus for each new customer. Another bonus---located near military families, his route had frequent turnover.

Beginning in 1949, with 32 customers, Gerald Horna worked to acquire a greater number of subscribers. Covering 10 miles to deliver the *Chester Times*, the *Philadelphia Bulletin and Inquirer*, and a few *New York Times*, his business rose to 400 customers. By the edge of a rapidly developing suburb, Gerald watched for opportunities and was quick to sign on new residents.

Whether or not an area afforded new customers, a carrier increased his income when he was selected as the station manager. Given a key to the "paper shack," the boy manager was responsible for distributing the bundles, being certain all the routes were delivered, and maintaining some semblance of order. For this additional responsibility, the newspaper company paid him an extra monthly amount for the sub-station tasks, and problems.

Starting his route slightly before age 12, by age 14 Tom Sherrill was tapped to be a route captain for the *Tampa Daily Times*. He supervised 20 to 27 carriers in four locations. Boys in this role were supposed to be 16, but in 1944 older fellows left for the service or worked in the shipyards. Youth stepped forward. Tall and thin as a teenager, Tom responsibly managed his position after school, checking stations to be certain carriers picked up bundles. At 5:00 p.m. he answered complaints in the newspaper office, and finished with delivering missed papers to disgruntled customers. He may have already covered a route for an absent carrier. Another responsibility meant an afternoon or Saturday stop at each carrier's home for the weekly collection. Tom moved along handling the steadily expanding bag of money. He earned $16.20 a week for his captain position.

Loren Day learned from his shack manager, Ron Cameron, how to be a model of fairness and efficiency. In 1956, Loren was promoted to shack manager, earning an extra $20 a month. He put the money to good use buying his clothes and anything else he needed. However, paying his brother's newspaper bill, after the kid bought fishing gear with his collection sum, was not what Loren wanted to do. Nevertheless, he felt obliged.

## Carefully Calculated

When Dick Kalivoda wanted a bicycle, his dad told him, "Get a route. Buy your bike." Starting at age 8 with delivering the shoppers' guide, in three years he owned a bicycle. He also took on lawn mowing jobs for which he bought a lawn mower. His father signed for his purchase, but Dick never questioned his responsibility to meet the payments. A daily paper route kept a boy's credit line stable. Dad made certain of that.

At just 13, Dick managed his *Seattle Times* route of 115 customers and managed the paper station. There were 18 routes and boys that he was responsible for seven days a week.

But his parents didn't anticipate how their son's mind planned. Making $15 to $18 as the shack manager, along with income from his route and extra jobs, Dick was buying savings bonds by age 15. Not just the small $25 ones, he bought two $100 bonds and then a $1,000 bond. He liked the $1,000 one because if he bought 999 more, he determined, "I'd be a millionaire." In 1953, he was consistently earning $80 a month, $960 a year. His money management and his setup with the *Seattle Times* made a difference.

Dick signed for the *Times* to automatically deduct $5 monthly toward a bond. When his account reached $65, the company added $10, which bought a $100 bond. Of his monthly $80 profit, with $5 put aside, he gave Hope Lutheran Church $5, deposited $50 in his own bank account (maybe toward another $1,000 bond), and paid the dentist $10. He pocketed $10 to spend independently on needs or wants, probably some sweets.

Selected as station manager, a young merchant gained additional money, and best of all the recognition by his manager that he was a responsible, maturing adolescent. His self-esteem expanded along with his wallet.

## Wearing Additional Hats

Hired to be a station manager, customers also recognized a quality carrier and asked him to mow lawns, rake leaves, or shovel snow off the sidewalks. Seasonal jobs were plentiful.

Tasks became a natural part of boys' routines. By age 9, Francis Walsh in 1932 held a *Columbus Citizen Journal* morning route seven days a week. Even with steady earning, he needed to put more "money on the table" to help his mother, so he sold "Extras," set bowling pins, mowed lawns, served in the school cafeteria for his lunch, and in the approaching cold Ohio weather found more work. When Francis saw a truck load of coal dumped at the curb, he asked for a job. He and his brother used a large basket to move the huge pile from the street into the basement coal bin. He earned an additional 25 cents for his fatherless family.

Mowing lawns was less strenuous on shoulders than shoveling a load of sawdust. Like Francis, Jim Kavanaugh worked extra as a kid in the 1940s. With an abundance of forests and several sawmills near Lewiston, people ordered shavings before the Idaho winter arrived. Jim saw the truck load dumped and asked for the job of shoveling sawdust into the chute, same as a coal chute, ready for people to burn the wood dust in their furnace.

At age 12, Harry Peifer began a *Seattle Star* route in 1942, one more responsibility in a list of work experiences. He mowed grass, milked the cow, and worked in a farm supply store. Just 7, he earned 10 cents a week "loading coal into a big stoker." Each dumped load didn't seem very large compared to the fiery furnace, which was enormous to a second grader. But the job was inside, instead of out in pouring Northwest rain. Learning to hustle, Harry "always worked."

To some youngsters, tossed out meant money. Willing to haul trash, Frank Gennarelli supplemented his paper route with an extra job. A doctor hired Frank to carry "the rubbish to the curb twice a week," 104 times a year. This money delighted him.

Every day around the neighborhood, kids watched for any sources that led to earning, such as collecting empty bottles. They put the ubiquitous red wagon to productive use rather than just enjoying a fast ride down hill. In 1947, along with school, Tom Lewis participated in scouts, delivered the *Seattle Times*, hawked dozens of "Extras" at the University of Washington football stadium, and picked berries in seasonal jobs. However, when the whole day wasn't scheduled, he collected empty bottles to receive the deposit. Pulling a wagon, wheels rattling along the street, glass clinking, he filled his mode of transport until bottles tumbled out. He was ready to earn dimes, and did accumulate a stack. With dad's guidance, Tom started investing his profits, $1,000, into stocks, learning about investments as he earned more.

The same as Tom, Jim Root learned that grocery stores paid for empty glass soda bottles, so in the 1940s he and friends went apartment to apartment in their housing-project residence, "begging for bottles. We filled a wagon and went to the store to redeem the empties for pennies."

## A List of Jobs

Working inside for bowling teams and tournaments, boys hustled to set pins through the loud cracking noises in the smoky bowling alleys. In 1960 John Wilson acquired a job learning to clean the newspaper press. He earned $1 an hour in a job that required speed plus dexterity.

In the quiet outdoors, when weather was nice, boys with arms and backs strengthened from carrying a stuffed canvas bag, increased their income carrying a golf bag. Though Ed Schroth was busy with morning and evening routes, he filled time between deliveries by serving as a golf caddy earning 50 cents a game, in a clean, colorless job. For others, picking spring asparagus and summer beans turned grey hands to green, or to red from gathering berries. Mike Rhodes' hands were dark. In California, he picked walnuts and walnut oil stained his hands black, similar to kids who handled coal. The grey from newspaper bundles went unnoticed.

Through both customer generated opportunities and on their own, enterprising youngsters created business. In 1942, Jack Gahan raised 12 chickens, caring for them and collecting the eggs, which he sold. Roger Hagen, in 1945, worked inside part of the time, away from the extremes on his route in South Dakota weather. Using thin slats of wood, which the local creamery provided, he earned two cents for each egg crate he constructed. Frances Grab, living on a large dairy farm, helped her father clean the barn for $10 a month.

## Saving, to Spend Later

Active and energetic, with an entrepreneurial attitude, children earned and saved to reach rewards beyond snacks and toys. Advancing in school and with brothers moving into the grade levels behind him, a paperboy's profit paid for his school tuition, school clothes and supplies.

Pocketing more than mere pennies, a carrier spent a dime with a child's eye and saved dollars as a young businessman. Like delivery, spending dimes was quick; like collecting, saving dollars took longer for the profit column to grow. But it did grow. And then he had the funds for more significant purchases or investments.

# Earnings

The amount of money a carrier gained each week or each month was determined by variables, including the decade in which he worked. In the 1920s, a two cent edition provided the paperboy a profit of less than one cent a paper, with nearly all the money handed to Mother for family use. However, a penny or nickel meant more in the '20s than it did in 1950 when the daily newspaper cost had risen to five cents. No matter the year or decade, the well-prepared carriers figured on profits based on:

1. Number of Customers: If a boy only listed 28 customers, his profit was obviously less than for Bill Bates with 175 customers, rising to 200. In the close of the 1930s into the 1940s, Bill regularly earned $40 a month in a job requiring only a few hours a day.

2. Economics of the Neighborhood: In 1938, Bill collected in the exclusive Broadmoor neighborhood of Seattle. This provided more in tips than a paperboy made in a lesser neighborhood on the south side in the Hooverville camp. However, working class folks paid their bill just as well as owners of any business or mansion.

3. Sunday Paper: Since the Sunday edition usually drew the largest number of customers and cost more than the week-day paper, a boy's profit increased, helping to compensate for the need to rise so early on the traditional day of rest.

4. Tips: This added considerably to the profit column, especially during Christmas, and higher as calendars were distributed. In the '50s, Ron Haringa received $100 in Christmas tips.

Beyond these four, the most critical element in making money---

5. Self Discipline: A carrier who collected consistently, whether he liked doing it or not, the strong persistence made the essential difference. If a paperboy disciplined himself, he enjoyed an income. And more, when he supplemented his route earnings by hawking special editions and being selected as the shack manager.

Bob Barr with 100 customers in 1938 made $25 month. Less subscribers than Bill Bates and the tips were not $5 because most of his customers were mill workers who struggled for every penny in the Depression, yet they paid their bill regularly.

By the 1940s and with the Depression declining, Ed White made $10 to $12 a week, with 128 customers, money he used for school tuition.

Jim Ruck's route covering 188 Tacoma residents netted him $50 a month in 1942.

In 1942 Harry Peifer increased his 70 subscribers to 144, and doing so his profits reached $40 a month. In the summer he supplemented his earnings with lawn mowing at 25 cents a lawn. Dad bought him a bike for $5 and Harry was under way each day on a 12-mile route. Carefully saving, before long he bought a heavier bike for $35.

Collecting wasn't always perfect, and sporadic spending sliced into savings. Yes, a boy slipped a little, ate lots, but interspersed his daily buying with weekly saving. The harsh, deep lessons from the Depression led adults around him to expect investing in a serious savings plan.

## Growing Faster than a Boy

Paper route money accumulated, whether carriers kept it at home, in a local bank savings account, or in a school savings program. Paperboys were encouraged by parents, grandmothers, and school leaders because this wasn't just mindless saving, like acquiring the biggest bag of marbles. Youth saved first for school necessities, then to slowly gain funds for the first car, and finally college tuition. They were not obsessed with money and did not greedily hoard it or brag about it. Their focus was aimed at meeting current needs and expanding future plans.

Starting at the *Tacoma Tribune*, Jack Gahan bought United States savings bonds. When the family moved to Seattle, he signed onto a new route and became a charter member of the *Seattle Times* Newspaperboys' Thrift Club, which helped him save for college. The account grew, providing the funds to enter Seattle University.

Harry Peifer's $40 in monthly earnings allowed him to save dimes weekly in his school savings plan. Such school plans also served Jim Kavanaugh, Ron Richardson, Jim McArthur and thousands of other dedicated savers. In 1950 Leroy Modine built his route from 55 to 85 customers and began participating in his school savings program, carrying his dimes to school. Leroy saved $4 a month and with the accumulated dimes, bought stamps for a savings bond.

Funds from routes provided a used bike, then a new bicycle, and bicycle extras, along with necessities such as a double canvas bag, or a cart for Sunday loads. Yet, money still grew in the savings account, whether at the bank or the school, accumulating for special purchases.

## Accumulations for Clothes, Cars, College

The annual selection of a school outfit broadened into other items for outings beyond just school and work activities. Appearance captured some carriers' interests as much as the practical protection allotted from clothes and coats.

In 1945, Beverly Brunner, with her Christmas tips from the *Syracuse Post Standard* route bought a grey, princess-style coat with a fur collar, and black, fur-trimmed high heeled snow boots. Looking like a fashionable model, the capable 16-year-old sparkled like her attitude. The beautiful, tailored, grey cloak never showed a grey smear from any printer's ink.

Clothes mattered to boys, as well as the girls. Department stores continually used newspapers to promote the importance of appearance. More poignant than simply following the latest fashion pictures, children in large families, like Jesse Montoya's, felt proud to buy clothes that fit. Once a youngster gained a paper route, he acquired school clothes. And with a steady job, he purchased stylish shoes, his first suit, or a sweater in school colors, happy to improve his tattered looks and forgo the hand-me-downs.

Before school started in September, Don Hubbard sat beside his mother as the two perused the thick Sears & Roebuck Catalog. With her guidance, Don selected an outfit for the school year and using his own money, he ordered the new clothes from Sears.

Leroy Modine "wore bib overalls" when he started school. And the same as Jesse, school mates commented on his apparel. A few taunted him. Leroy's mother shortened the strap of his large canvas bag, but she didn't change the straps of the bib overalls. So he kept delivering papers. After two years, before another school year of being teased for looking like a comic book character, he used his earned money. Mom guided him in buying trousers like other boys wore.

## Forward Faster, When It Runs

In 1920, while the population of nearly 107 million people in the United States shifted from rural to urban, folks were also on the move using automobiles and trucks. With 7.5 million cars and trucks on dirt roads, the use of motor vehicles spread, the way electric lights and jazz music arrived to enliven communities. By 1930 one in every five Americans drove an automobile. But the increased production and sales sharply decreased in the Depression and almost totally stopped between 1942 and 1946 for war production. With prosperity, an explosion in the number of automobiles shaped the last half of the American century, influencing where people lived, their home's architecture with attached front garages, location of shopping centers. Vehicles rolled into drive-ins. Pedaling a bike past the subscribers' driveways, seeing their automobiles, the paperboy formed a goal: purchasing his first car.

Living the common line: as American as apple pie, baseball and Chevrolet, paperboys were also a common American identity, who favored apple pie and baseball. And for many, their first car was a Chevrolet.

# In Style

In 1932, only nine years old and earning $2.50 a week, Bud Dreyfus managed his route on foot for over a year, before he had the help of wheels to deliver 125 newspapers. The used bike that he purchased made the routine more fun. He continued to provide funds for the family while he increased his earnings with hawking special editions and sports copy. "I sold extras with the Lindbergh kidnapping, the Joe Louis win over Braddock, and the Hindenburg disaster." Whenever the University of Alabama hosted football games, Bud spent his Saturday time at the Birmingham Legion Field. He sold "football editions with the teams' line-ups, statistics, school record and thus got to see the game free." Earning and free, a winning attraction for a paperboy.

In the mid 1930s, Bud's family moved and he changed to a new route, new customers, in a new town. He was delivering the *Nashville Banner* in Tennessee in 1935. Finally meeting the stated Newspaper Code, age 12, he became the junior district manager of 10 other carriers. He made sure they delivered each day, and issued starts, stops and complaint slips. Plus, "every Saturday collect their newspaper bills" and then head directly to the circulation department.

Four years later, in 1939, with seven years of delivering after school, Bud was in another city, on a new route and the new experience of delivering at 3:30 a.m. His *Indianapolis Star* route brought in $9 a week. He had advanced from earning $10 a month to $36 a month in the Depression years, and went from two wheels to four wheels. At age 16 he bought his first car, "a 1933 Chevy for $65, a big help on Sunday" when he had 125 subscribers for the heavy edition. Furthermore, he looked spiffy in his car with new clothes, to include the purchase of his "first tuxedo" that he wore as he gave his date her corsage.

A boy's first car was a stick shift. He poured water over the windshield when bugs collected, hand cranked the window for instant air conditioning. He made time to wash and wax his prized possession, weekly, if not daily. And, like costs in managing a route, owning a car meant money for gas, tires, and eventually a driver's license, when old enough to apply for one.

# Try Again

Ron Haringa rolled forward through his *Seattle Times* routes whizzing down the streets on his bicycle. But speed disappeared with his car. In 1953, Ron at 13, bought his first automobile, an all-American Chevrolet. With help he towed his purchase home. The 1930 Chevy roadster cost him $8.50. It didn't run. That was okay because Ron needed to learn how to drive. The car certainly provided plenty of learning.

Having passed the age when tinker toys and the erector sets were fun, he took his car apart, tinkered, and worked on the greasy engine with tools he bought from Sears & Roebuck. Despite his efforts, he decided to try another car. At 14 he bought a 1936 Chevrolet, which he drove up and down the Seattle hills.

## Also a Ford

Like selecting a favorite baseball team from many teams, the choice of an automobile was not limited to the classic Chevy. Particularly in the 1930s when a vast number of Henry Ford's assembly line cars remained available and operational.

Walking a paper route during the Depression was common. However, foot power wasn't necessarily an economic issue; sometimes routes were easily managed on foot. Vernon Franze delivered to 160 customers striding along the streets in Wenatchee. He made about $6 a week, without a Sunday edition. Trying to collect the weekly 15 cents, especially with folks out of work, was a slow challenge. He persisted, earned, supported himself and saved until he bought a Model A Ford. He was justifiably proud. The heavy black car with running boards took him around town. He enjoyed the recognition he received. Then, darn, a drunk ran into his car.

As the United States entered World War II, William Stoebuck managed his #812 *Wichita Beacon* route, making $7 a week. He was glad he delivered in apartment centers protecting him from the Kansas weather. Scurrying quickly through the buildings, the advantage of less time hefting weight turned to a disadvantage at collection time. It was "harder to collect from apartment dwellers." He faced "work for little pay" but with persistent effort from 1941 to 1945 he accumulated enough money to buy a 1929 Model A Ford.

Starting in 1940, Don and Gene Chiodo delivered morning and evening, Sunday too, keeping customers informed of the war news. Helping to promote the sale of defense bonds, they encouraged customers to pay dimes for the patriotic stamps, as well as pay for the *Des Moines Register* and the *Des Moines Tribune*. Working in challenging Iowa conditions, the brothers nevertheless had "fun," particularly when Don found time to drive their secret car. Buying a "Model A Ford coupe with the rumble seat" he kept it "hidden in the country so his parents didn't know." Out of sight, and occasionally out of gas, until the monthly gas ration coupons were available, the secretive vehicle brought them excitement.

With victory, the production of automobiles resumed. Assembled at the new, high production rates, developed in critical war necessity, cars rolled out of Detroit. Working men purchased new models, creating a glut of used models for paperboys to purchase as their first car. After pumping pedals on two wheels, a carrier now pumped gas and pushed the pedal to accelerate. Having purchased bike parts, he switched to paying for replacement of auto parts.

Cathi Vannice and her younger brother, who helped her with the route in 1957, managed to buy a 1939 Dodge. It was in good condition so the $75 purchase was acceptable and useful. But 14-year-old Ray Poletti's first auto, purchased in 1963, was not as sound. The 1936 black Plymouth sedan didn't run in spite of his tinkering. He made another purchase, and many more.

The key to a first car became a key to another automobile, another job. Owning a vehicle, the carrier advanced to longer, more involved positions, but it was his first job as a newspaper carrier, which paid for the first car that helped move him upward on the productive scale.

## Future Plans

Savings accounts did not completely disappear into clothes and cars, to scout jamborees and soapbox derby finals. Carriers looked to the future. With the GI Bill impact (signed in June, 1944) and the increasing population, college campuses greatly expanded and a child's confidence in the future swelled. Conscientious children saved for college, and from time to time their savings plan was further augmented by newspaper company gifts, like the *Marietta Times* in the 1950s presenting a $5,000 scholarship to a senior carrier.

But ahead of scholarships, the carrier saved month by month. Bill Miller spent 50 cents a week for another boy to help make collections, and Bill's stash of earnings grew to $600. He was ready to enter college in 1949 because of funds he saved for his tuition. The same with Jack Gahan who delivered through the 1940s until 1952. His savings account gave him the opportunity to enroll in Seattle University. At the same time, the savings from Paul Meyer's route allowed him to enter the University of Washington, decked out in collegiate clothes and a sufficient savings account for tuition.

Though mother occasionally needed to borrow a little from Mike Rhodes' growing account, she carefully repaid the money and continued to guide his savings plan. Mike earned and his mother encouraged saving, enabling him to enroll in San Jose State University in 1962. His accumulated $1,000 put him on his way to pay for his diploma.

Like other carriers, Tom Rockne knew he was "expected to go to college." Year by year, staying on the direct path, reaching Eagle Scout, Tom saved for his major goal. Though the funds slipped back ever so slightly, like the times Dad needed to borrow money but was always paid back with interest, Tom accumulated his tuition for Iowa State University and fulfilled his parents' request. He received his degree.

Paperboys' dedication to their routes made them ideal candidates for saving money. Fortitude, resilience, discipline, all qualities that benefitted managing a route, also empowered children to save significant amounts that changed the trajectory of their lives.

## Sharing

Carriers were well aware of giving in the community, what with service clubs and the church guilds, with March of Dimes cards filled with dimes. They also appreciated, on a personal basis, customers giving a cold drink in the heat of the afternoon, or a hot cocoa on a blustery bitter day, plus Christmas gifts galore.

And the newspaper industry contributed greatly to this spirit of giving. For a carrier who did not hold the full status of the family bread winner, he felt important when the big turkey, ham or goose rested on the holiday platter. He sat taller at the table. His pride in his ability to contribute to a family feast cast a spell wider than his smile. Mistakes, misdeeds, immaturity all diminished when thanked for providing the family's turkey.

Happy with coins to spend, happier with accumulated savings that led to a bike, a jacket, or the first car, the carrier's sharing in an honorable act created the greatest happiness.

## The Happiest

With all the rapid changes in the 1920s, certain acts continued unchanged. Actual money was not the specific problem; money solved the problems and a paperboy was determined to use earnings to help solve problems. A large route eased family needs when working children regularly brought their coins home to mother. The Roaring Twenties was actually the Gnashing Twenties for most. No long raccoon coats at college football games or huge Studebaker cars for the mass of ordinary, struggling families who accounted for each penny.

Across the decades of the paperboys' golden era, from 1920 through the 1970s, the dire need by families for the children's earnings began to subside when the Depression finally ended, though individual families often needed assistance into the 1940s and '50s.

Acquiring a route in 1932, Bud Dreyfus shared 4/5th's of his earnings with his family. Handing mother $2 a week, he helped her be able to purchase 10 pounds of sugar for 38 cents, one pound of lard for 5 cents, a pound of coffee for 32 cents and two packages of Wheaties for 25 cents. She used the remaining half of the money for eggs, meat, and rice.

With a wagon, and when necessary a sled, Don Fraits managed his *Providence Journal* route in Cranston, Rhode Island, during many a rugged evening in New England weather. In 1940 with 200 customers, Sunday too, he earned enough to give his family $10 a week, over $500 a year, plus he saved for his eventual college tuition.

Ron Park's modest yet stable family situation plummeted when his father was killed in a construction accident in 1941.Through four years on a paper route, all of Ron's earnings went to the family. Living in Niles, Michigan, he had limited opportunity to accumulate dollars by his *Niles Daily Star*, more limited without a Sunday edition. Challenged to run a route with no bike, because all his money was handed to mother, regardless, Ron declared his paper route "fun."

## For Mother

In 1951, Eugene Gatterman needed a steady way to earn money for his necessities. An *Everett Daily Herald* route became available, though not much of one. No Sunday edition, only 63 customers netting $20 a month, in a small town of 750 residents. Nevertheless, Eugene tackled his task. With a dogged effort he developed a four mile route for 216 customers in the south end of Monroe, a close-knit community.

Bicycling four miles on flat streets would be quick, but his bike was a bother since he dismounted and placed the paper inside the screen doors, so he covered most of the distance, on foot. He repeated the walk to collect. Eugene knew his customers, and they knew Mr. Gatterman had died. The family struggled. However, Eugene pushed aside his struggles to assist his mother. He also saved $10 a month, matched by $10 from the *Herald*. He supplemented his profit with lawn mowing jobs. A controlled plan allowed him to provide mother $50 a month. He stayed centered. Dependable, the customers appreciated his consistent delivery. His subscribers paid, all except for Dike. Forget waiting on that deadbeat, Eugene paid his bill before the tenth of the month. The circulation manager had no challenges from Eugene. Mother had $50 a month.

But his functioning plan would be disrupted; his route was to be split in half, the one he developed and managed with excellent service. Why? Were there complaints? If any, Eugene addressed the problem.

With heavy steps, he walked his route, thinking, questioning, studying the situation. Finished with his afternoon delivery, Eugene reached Main Street and boarded the bus for Everett. Knowing the county seat was about 18 miles to the west, bus transportation was essential. Though he was in shape from walking every day, the distance required too much time to reach the newspaper office before dark.

Entering the lobby of the *Everett Daily Herald*, he stated his purpose to the receptionist. She said the publisher was not in. Eugene said, "I'll wait." He sat. Folks came in, finished their business and left. The sun dipped below Puget Sound. He visited the restroom. His stomach growled. He stretched and repositioned his feet. The street light shone through the window.

The receptionist made a phone call. Again she said, "The publisher won't be in." Eugene simply stated, "I'm not leaving." Restless, he wondered if someone complained about his delivering and collecting. Did Dike? No, a complaint required effort. Dike never made an effort. Eugene glanced at the other chairs. Yes, he'd rest across two of them for the night. Waiting strengthened his determination. By the time he finally gained a meeting with the manager, his voice was clear and controlled.

Yes, the gentleman agreed, all was in order. No complaints. No concerns. Eugene demonstrated exemplary characteristics that a newspaper company needed in a carrier. High earnings in the savings plan. Did he plan to buy a car, a hotrod?

No, he needed money for his widowed mother, and for his future.

The route remained un-split. Eugene retained his 216 familiar customers and mother continued to receive necessary money. The wait was worth it.

The last bus headed east to Monroe that night had already left Everett making for a long night. Not a problem. He was given a ride to his home. Furthermore, after four years, 1951 through 1954, he was presented a Paperboy of the Year award in 1955, with a $500 bond.

## Responsible

There was nothing simple for a single mother. The everyday strain required considerable strength. Dave Mushen's father died when Dave was nine. Under an age restriction for a *Detroit News* route, he earned, sporadically, by mowing lawns and shoveling wet, heavy snow, tough jobs for a grade school boy. At last, he acquired a route in 1959, when he turned 12, though it only served 45 customers. Dave built his business to 98 daily with 108 on Sunday. Providing money for Mother each week, he also paid his parochial school tuition and met personal expenses. At a young age he was independent but never separated from family responsibility.

Paperboys weren't necessarily pious cherubs, saints, or angels; nevertheless, they certainly didn't deserve to be classed as heathens or demons, so labeled in earlier testimony by child labor reformers. Conscientious children cared about their family and worked incredibly hard to actively help out.

# Worthy of a Papal Blessing

Brothers teased, tumbled, outright battled, yet, were there for one another, as when Ed Schroth needed out of his predicament. A small boy, Ed began with just 30 customers for the afternoon *Cleveland Press*. With tough competition, he appreciated his opportunity, felt "lucky to have a route." This was steady income, rather than the intermittent money he made mowing lawns with a hand mower, shoveling snow from the storms off Lake Erie, to include the horrific 1950 Buckeye blizzard, and serving as a golf caddy for 50 cents. Ed worked. He also sold extra papers to a Mom & Pop store, where he allowed himself an occasional treat.

And then another opportunity: a morning *Cleveland Plain Dealer* route, including Sunday. Managing a morning and an afternoon job, he earned enough to buy a bicycle. On a roll, he added the *Cleveland News* delivery. His subscribers topped 300.

In spite of bike spills, brought about because his used bike didn't have a chain guard, his painful earaches in winter, and plagued by unleashed dogs, Ed still managed three routes, with his school schedule, until...

# Trouble!

He was caught. Competing newspapers refused to allow paperboys to deliver for the competition. Running both a *Cleveland Press* and a *Cleveland News* route after school, he collided with management's rule. The small boy squirmed under the criticism. The weight of papers felt better than the weight of regulations.

Undeterred, and knowing the limited family income, he turned to a brother for help. The oldest of four boys, Ed quickly assigned one route to a brother and solved his predicament.

What he didn't do was replace his used bike. Though he wanted a new bicycle, worked enough for one and certainly could have used a better bike, he coped with his current means. Making headway with extra earnings, he finally spent money on a new bicycle. Oh, not for himself, but for his younger brother who helped with the routes. "Just the way it was."

# The Best Ever.

Dugg understood the difficult times. Sliding deeper into the Depression, Dugg Holmes and his brother, Richard, bought only necessary clothes and essentials after they contributed to the family's needs. The parents had lost their home in Denver, so the family moved to the south edge of the city. Richard obtained a *Rocky Mountain News* route on rough rural roads. With his little brother's help, the two delivered seven days a week, often on dark, cold Colorado mornings.

By 1935, Richard moved ahead to a longer job, and Dugg took over the route, managing the challenges every day by himself. He "couldn't afford to be sick." Though a small tyke, he toughed it out and sped along. He was 13 now. No baby teeth left. Like the big boys, he began smoking. What demonstrated his older status in a better way was that he could, "just touch the bike pedals" on his special bicycle. For Christmas, Richard had given his bike to Dugg. Tears filled the eyes of a "big" boy over his brother's surprise Christmas gift, "the best present ever." The used bike was wonderful as well as the salute by an older brother to Dugg's strength and resourcefulness.

Like Dugg, Paul West delivered in the early morning hours and also in a rural area, but north of Seattle. The same as other morning carriers, Paul faced the tests in rising early to finish a long, rough route by 6 a.m. Though prosperity was flowing through America in the 1950s, it did not flood the West family. Paul, the youngest of nine boys in a family of 12 children tried to help with collecting empty bottles for the deposit money. Every coin mattered. When he acquired a *Seattle PI* route there would be more money, enough for necessities.

Proud of his little brother's efforts, Paul's brother, who was home from the Korean War, bought Paul a three-speed English bicycle. The used bike made morning rounds much better.

## Covers One

John understood the need to think of others in the family. He and his brother, Walter, pooled their earnings from delivering the *Indianapolis Times* and bought the family Christmas gifts. In the 1950s, with prosperity increasing, they heard school kids excited over family Christmas surprises, so John and Walter provided holiday cheer in their home.

But John realized a way to give more than a wrapped package. Walter was a special big brother who helped fill the void in being fatherless. His efforts didn't take the place of Dad, but John was grateful for Walter's guidance. Just little tykes when their Father was killed in World War II, they struggled in school years, staying the best of buddies, playing and working.

And now, hustling to acquire additional subscriptions in an already saturated route, they simply couldn't find 40 new subscriptions, 20 each, to both earn the all-expenses-paid carriers' trip to Niagara Falls. Recognizing they were short of their goal, John assigned his new customers to Walter for his 20.

Walt left Indianapolis in the evening aboard a train car filled with lively carriers and lots of laughter. On his first long train ride, first time to stay in a big hotel, first time to see, hear, and feel the power of Niagara Falls, he recognized the profound power of brotherly love.

## Feeling Warm

Located on Lake Michigan, north of Milwaukee, the town of Manitowoc, Wisconsin regularly endured long, bitter winter weather. And in the last half of the 1930s, like everywhere, the Hansen family felt the cold reality of the Depression. Fortunately, in 1935 Ben Hansen obtained a *Manitowoc Herald Times* route to help with his own expenses. Though he knew his customers "very well," in such hard times he often had to return to a house three times before he collected the weekly fee.

Ben worked the route, worked at collecting and worked to save $39. He delivered on foot and soon reached the age to drive a car, like his friends. But the money he accumulated was not for a bicycle, a car, or his own needs. Ben spent the $39 to buy his mother a winter coat. She could sew a cotton housedress and make a gingham apron which covered a faded or worn part of a dress. But tailoring a heavy coat was difficult. His purchase was not a full-length fur coat for Mom to imitate movie stars. However, appearing in public her new coat provided warm protection amplified by a Mother's pride.

Mothers didn't ask for recognition or gifts but children recognized how much mom gave to the family, and cherished  an opportunity to make life a little better for her. While it's remarkable that Ed Schroth managed three paper routes and worked extra jobs, his awe was reserved for his mother. He felt "amazed how maw managed."

## Purchasing Appreciation

Whether standing at the door or stepping inside to wait for the customer to find money to pay the subscription, carriers began to see consoles showing a grainy white and black picture. Crossing up and down the streets, kids saw new poles appear. By 1950 roof tops sported TV antennas. Boys entered taverns with papers to hawk and view the TV, or watched through a customer's front window. School mates made a point to inform friends when the family bought a television. Their TV room now competed with the front porch as a place to sit a spell.

Families who had been hard pressed through the Depression were not prone to buy items of pleasure for themselves. Cliff Benson understood the attitude in Everett, a working mill town. Never handed an allowance, he paid his school expenses, and helped his parents with groceries and incidentals as he mastered fiscal responsibility. Increasing his routes and then advancing into the *Everett Daily Herald* mail room, Cliff saved for future college costs. However, he included his family in his widening benefits and bought them their first television.

Once Mary Ann and Phyllis, the first Grab daughters, established the newspaper delivery for their seven sisters, the older two moved beyond picking berries, delivering papers, milking cows and working the hay field. Knowing their sisters earned money for school clothes, and knowing their parents worked endlessly to care for the family, Mary Ann and Phyllis brought enjoyment into the home by purchasing a television. They tried to have mom and dad rest with occasional TV programs.

Televisions increased and so did automobiles. Kids on a paper route noticed each new auto in the neighborhood. By the 1960s many families became a two-car unit, while the paperboy saved for his first used car.

## A New Vehicle

In the small town of Cottonwood, the Kopczynski children had continued walking their routes and continued to benefit from Mother's endless work to maintain a nice home. But after five years of delivering every morning, from age 8 to13, Joan quit the route, stopping at the same time as her sister and brothers. When they finished their jobs, the *Lewiston Tribune* company returned the bond money, it held, to the carriers. Money in hand and with so much to buy in the late '60s, four teenagers with a large stash of bills possessed a larger heart. The bonds provided a collected profit from their routes, and with other money saved from extra jobs, Allan, Connie, Don and Joan pooled their savings to help mother.

They bought her a car, her first automobile. Not a fancy Detroit-latest-model from the 1968 automobile show pumping the power of the 1960s large "muscular cars." No, just like Joan's scruffy snowsuit appearance, the superficiality was insignificant. Instead of reaching in their pockets for dimes to spend, they reached out with dollars and bought a car. This meant less rides in the back of dad's blue pickup truck for his business. Mom's car showed considerable use and was about to be used considerably more.

Her " snow-green Ford, our first car." came with a defroster, which functioned in the summertime. The automobile's air conditioning worked year-round. That's because it was serviced by Mother Nature through a hole in the backseat floor. The worn upholstery on the front seat was covered with a piece of carpet. Joan named the vehicle, "the rattletrap." It rattled, but, "we loved it and words cannot convey how grateful we were." The seven sisters appreciated it because their skirts only fluttered in the air conditioning system, rather than billow in dad's open pickup. And mother sped along fueled and powered by her children's wonderful thoughtfulness.

# Happy at Home

Growing up in a rental house, someone else's property, children became determined to someday own a home. David Bowles moved frequently with his family, but he always wanted a home, his own place. In the 1930s parents lost their residences and farms in the severe Depression. Such circumstances sealed a child's desire to someday own a home.

Starting in grade school, Jesse Montoya provided excellent service with a winning grin. His spirit smiled. Jesse and his siblings worked. Living in the Apple Capital of the World, the brothers were on hand each year to pick apple crops. Earlier in the growing season, they picked asparagus and other produce, besides hawking the *Wenatchee World*. They all delivered routes, and worked in the newspaper mail room. Many days, the *World* newspaper defined their world.

Though their father labored in logging, then in maintenance, his income remained thin. And with 12 children, mother toiled seven days from dawn to dusk. Their finances were limited but the parents gave unlimited love. Not hugging, hovering, spouting words of praise, but the certain love of being there with care and comfort. The parents provided plentiful food; however, dad just couldn't provide a home beyond a rental place.

In 1954, now a 14-year-old, Jesse Montoya continued his route into the fourth year. Committed to harvesting jobs, wedged into school and delivery time, he combined his earnings with the accumulation of his brothers' money. The boys' year-round work netted a pool of $3,500. This became the down payment for the Montoya's first owned house, an inviting two-story home. Mom settled into her own kitchen, the family center, cooking for14. She treasured her world, often making homemade bread for Jesse and his friends. The boys continued working, preparing for college costs, and Mother stayed in her home into the new millennium.

It wasn't how extensive or how expensive nor even how exceptional the children's gifts. They gave without an expectation for recognition. They gave with unconditional love for a brother, a mother, their family. Yes, the kids spent dimes for minor rewards of ice cream and movies, but they saved dollars toward the most significant purchases. For these paper carriers, like many others, their reliability and accountability were exemplary. However, the children's most commendable ability, worthy of papal praise, reigned in their nobility.

# CHAPTER 18
## REWARDS

Responsible, often right, other times wrong, the remarkable effort of paper carriers brought both rewards and recognition.

From collecting, money trickled in like a spring on the hillside, with Christmas week flowing. Paperboys bought detailed toy models, music records, silly putty, a slinky, increasing to a bicycle and clothes. In addition, circulation managers devised ways to reward carriers by providing different incentives. The annual newsboy banquet remained important, but all the months in between offered an opportunity for prizes and outings.

Children have an innate ability to have fun and circulation managers used prizes to enhance their childhood play. If a small Cracker Jack toy delighted boys, a manager tried to top it. And the winnings were inevitably better than cheap trinkets won at the carnival, plus a guy kept his collection coins. Being a winner was often better than the prize itself. The sense of pride when being recognized snapped off discouragement from customers' complaints.

Without a closet of his own in his shared bedroom, a youngster didn't shove boyish treasures into a jammed Fibber McGee closet. From the paper carriers' catalog, items abounded: win a flashlight, pocket knife, baseball, bat, glove, a wrist watch, radio. For awhile, the *Seattle Times* provided a competition each week. Using a standing clown model with a long, curved hook nose, Bopo the clown was a wild hit as the boys tossed rings over his nose for a prize.

Since Jim McArthur quit throwing away the Shoppers' Guide and advanced to a full time route, he worked hard every day. So when the *Seattle Times* ran a final contest at their large publishing headquarters on Fairview Avenue and John Street, he made his way off Beacon Hill crossed city blocks to the contest center. Trying to quickly unscramble the name of a city or town in Washington State, youngsters tested their spelling and geography skills to become the top winner. Jim, however, "was not the best but I won a red coat." His excitement, along with a practical and recognizable prize, made him a winner, without being the single finalist.

## Drinking and Selling

Jim Mack won a wagon from a *Detroit News* challenge, a sensible reward. He used it weekly through his seven years as a paperboy, making it easier to handle a large Sunday edition, and the twice weekly addition of extra weight from hundreds of *Detroit Shopping News* papers. Then he found another use for it: hauling a case of soda pop, a heavy load for a grade-schooler.

A whole case rather than only a bottle?

Sure. Competing against 20 other paperboys, Jim won a case and needed to manage the bulky load until he sold or consumed the sweet contents. The active center where the gang of boys picked up their *Detroit News* bundles was located next to a gasoline station, which naturally sold pop from a large, red cooling machine. Coca-Cola came in six ounce bottles with the name of the bottling city stamped into the glass bottom. To encourage boys to spend nickels, and for competition fun, the gas station manager created a contest. Each week he would "give a case of cola to the person with a bottle filled furthest from Detroit. Of course we drank a lot of Coke." Enjoy the tasty drink once the purchase is out of the machine and the bottling city identified.

Boys wanted to win, even during a cold, icy Detroit winter. When a kid won, he owned 24 free colas. Always enterprising, the winner sold bottles to the others. A carrier didn't transport the case home so mother learned he was drinking so much soda. Have to be sensible.

More than a cola, newspaper companies offered paperboys coupons for hamburgers and milk shakes, which were cashed fast. And these coupons weren't torn from customers' papers.

## Crash! Cancel

To motivate carriers to pay their collection on time and most important, sign on new subscribers, the *Seattle Times* was offering a prize that excited Jim Root. His coveted win wouldn't be a balsawood airplane model, one he could easily buy. He intended to win a more substantive model airplane that zoomed. He watched planes take off from Boeing Field, saw photos of planes in *Life* magazine winning the war in Europe and Asia. Fast airplanes.

His past frustrating results---broken front teeth that a dentist wanted to yank, trying to collect from a deceased customer---those incidents lapsed behind this wonderful opportunity. But he "fell short of getting the required number of new subscribers." Jim figured out how to win what he "really wanted," by turning in "two or three addresses." He met the requirements. He flew his brand new, gasoline engine model.

Darn! The stars weren't aligned right. His airplane crashed. It shattered. He tossed the broken pieces into the trash. Yet, a daily reminder of his model plane resonated as he handled his stack of papers, which included the extra subscribers he created for winning. "I still had to pay the subscriptions for a few months until I finally cancelled them."

Prizes consumed, prizes crumbled. Offering something that lasted a bit longer, to enliven the boys' routine, circulation managers distributed tickets for the Saturday movie. Rows of paperboys howled at the cartoons, shouted at the bad guys, threw spitballs, crunched popcorn. Their Saturday afternoon surpassed Saturday morning collecting, and in the theater no one filed a complaint for their noisy laughter and yells.

Boys spent an entire day at the county fair or attended ball games. Like many carriers, Jim McArthur captured the opportunity to be a guest as a paperboy and "see the Seattle Rainiers play baseball at the Seattle Sicks' Stadium," on Rainier Avenue.

Delivering St. Louis papers, along with his 240 *Columbia Tribune* customers, Joe Forsee made certain the people received the latest sports pages. Then Joe won chances to watch the big league baseball and football games in Kansas City and in St. Louis. In 1940, he couldn't afford a long trip from Columbia, Missouri, to St. Louis, but with his paper route he earned trips and stadium admission tickets.

Reading sports pages after a fantastic time at the ball park, a paperboy didn't just scan the story of the game. He read every single line recalling the shouts, thunderous claps, loud boos, and the delicious hot dog, or two. Attending a sports event was the real thing, not a radio version.

Circulations managers recognized the need for exceptional prizes, for excitement to keep boys selling. A first airplane ride certainly met the sales promotion. Not simply a school-class visit to an airplane company to look and wish, but an actual ride. Feeling the vibration, the surge upward, and then below him the shrinking houses and streets, ones he crossed every day.

## Tank of Gasoline

The young Kopczynski carriers, Connie, Allan, Don and Joan, rode in the bed of dad's blue pickup, with no fussing, not even a thought of it. As they bumped over the back roads of Idaho, the siblings focused on fun. Dad drove them from Cottonwood to Lewiston, an hour away, to participate in the annual Carrier Picnic at Spalding Park sponsored by the *Lewiston Tribune*. The four qualified to attend, but had to provide their own transportation.

In America's turbulent times in the last half of the 1960s, these children were enjoying time to eat and play all day. It was an incredible diversion from their usual Saturday chores. In comfy, non-binding play clothes, the kids competed on green play fields in good, old-fashioned, community-style picnic games.

Their speed to complete a morning route every day gave little advantage as the kids tried to race inside a tough gunnysack, hopping toward the finish line. And tossing newspapers was different than catching a fresh egg tossed between competitors. But running! Watch out. Girls were separated from boys for the contest. Fellows didn't want a girl to outrun them. Connie outran other girl carriers. First to cross the finish line, declared the winner, she won a football.

Hungry from a variety of games, they ate grilled hamburgers and hot dogs, which always tasted better sitting outside. And a special treat: potato chips and pop, since these "luxuries" were not available at home..

Then in September, the children received free Lewiston Roundup tickets so they asked dad to fill the truck with gasoline, again, for a drive to and from Lewiston. The well-known rodeo began 30 years earlier, in 1935, drawing folks from around the area, and even further away. Joan felt natural and comfortable in a picnic crowd. But the large rodeo was very new to a grade school girl. "My eyes widened to see such strange sights---calf roping, bull riding and bronco busting." A lot rougher and more vigorous than a gunnysack race. The dusty, tough and tumble acts were terrific, however, "I loved the rodeo clowns." Silly devilish acts, ridiculous clothes, pure slapstick and pure fun for the audience, yet an incredible challenge for the clowns avoiding a bull. In a struggling family with 10 children, the luxury of a day-long event just for entertainment was one the family could not afford. It was beyond their wildest dreams.

Picnics, movie passes, ballgame outings, one circulation manager in 1953 decided to extend fun for more than a day, a week or a month. When Virgil Fassio served as a paperboy making $2 a week in Pittsburgh, he missed out on frequent ball play. He decided as an adult, managing over 300 carriers, that all his boys receive membership in the YMCA. They'd use their excess energy to play basketball, swim, belong to teams with fellow paperboys.

A circulation manager developed more reward ideas than his troops created ideas for mischievous deeds---almost more. The seasons helped. With baseball in the summer, then the round-up rodeo and county fairs at the close of harvest, followed by football games, a Thanksgiving banquet, Christmas party, skiing trips, a full calendar of events played out.

Prizes could be practical like winning a wagon, a bike, a jacket, or simply playful. If tickets for a day at the ball park or amusement park excited, and they certainly did, then winning overnight trips or week-long excursions was the pinnacle of prizes.

# Set Sail

Qualifying for a *Columbia Tribune* route under Mr. Pike was a challenge and a privilege. Once acquired, the carriers held onto the job. The asset of earned money was surpassed with the joy of team involvement. The manager made certain his paperboys stayed actively involved.

An experienced gentleman, Mr. Pike established orderly procedures. He knew the newspaper business from experience, and combined that with a degree in journalism from the University of Missouri. He spent 75 of his 100 years of life with the *Columbia Daily Tribune*. In his quiet approach, he set standards, instituting requirements in a fair manner.

Mr. Pike, who was never less than Mister to his carriers, met his lively charges as they arrived at the *Tribune* office after school. Supervising and shaping the boys, he molded their role since he understood that delivering newspapers was serious business. Miss a paper, mess up, and the subscriber made the seriousness known.

For some carriers, home life was less than ideal, but under Mr. Pike they had a place after school where they belonged, where they were recognized , and also earned money. He valued his boys. They trusted him. The soil of the earth, these productive children, under his guidance consistently produced. And he provided his carriers with sports and scouts. He formed softball teams in the summer and in the winter the boys enjoyed basketball teams, playing at the YMCA. The children also belonged to a  special Boy Scout troop, which spent a week of summer recreation on a sailing adventure.

Sailing? In the center of Missouri, far from either ocean?

The state had just the place for boys to camp and to sail. Through the Boy Scouts of America, Mr. Pike formed the carriers' Sea Scout Troop with the *SSS Tribune* as the scout ship. From the calm town of Columbia, the group was transported past the state capital, at Jefferson City, into the heart of Missouri, to the immense Lake of the Ozarks.

Constructed for hydro electric power, the Bagnell Dam created a 90-mile long reservoir holding water from the Osage River and large creeks. Built for electricity, not flood control or vital irrigation lines in a desert, the long lake has over 1,150 miles of shoreline.

Mr. Pike's regatta was the highlight of summer for his carriers. Awkward, gangly, landlubber kids enjoyed a whole week to swim, canoe, and sail, with a few dunkings in the lake. One of his carriers, Luke Chase said, "What kid would pass up on adventures like that?" On Sunday they were required to attend a church of their faith. Never a thought of mutiny with the revered Mr. Pike. Luke stated, "He truly had the interests of his carrier force at heart." Struggle for a route, struggle through ice storms that pull power lines down, hurry in sweltering summer heat, it was worth the trouble.

Cary Thorp definitely valued the effort. He was raised in a small home where both grandmothers lived with his family. Grandmothers, mother, sister, golly, Cary and dad were outnumbered. His bedroom, small like the house, shared foot traffic since it was the utility room. Once he acquired his paper route, #33, he savored the large, outside space for weeks on end, for six years. With 130 customers he earned money, and with good service enjoyed the canoeing time and a variety of adventures including trips to the St. Louis baseball games. Mr. Pike was a "marvelous role model" who influenced Cary to continue his education. Saving route profits for tuition, he entered college, succeeded and progressed to a Ph.D.

## A Trip for Kings

Don Hubbard's biologic clock almost adjusted to his early morning route. He napped less often, curled by the construction lamp, since the road work was nearly finished. Living in the government housing project by Grand Coulee Dam, Don watched tourists visit the area, so along with his route he sold papers at the tourist center. With good delivery techniques and selling subscriptions his route reached 150 people during the week and 200 on Sunday. He bought a bike. And in one of the many contests offered by the *Spokesman Review,* he won "a nice race car with a remote control, small electric motor."

Then he won a contest, even better than the electric car model. He'd be like the tourists visiting his town, only his destination would be fancier than an immense construction site full of rocks, concrete and sand.

The *Spokesman Review* awarded him a complete trip, "staying in a real nice hotel for a couple of days and being treated with good times around the city." Large numbers of carriers stayed in the renowned Davenport Hotel and Tower in Spokane, with the air conditioning and a ballroom gilded in gold and sparkling crystal. The sky lights were bright again, no longer tarred over for the World War II blackout necessity. The hotel was as grand as an ocean liner and it was docked in the Inland Empire, in the city center by the wild, tumbling famous Spokane waterfalls.

Staying at the Davenport, the carriers were "treated almost like kings." At the closing, an elegant banquet was served, and the boys "received award plaques for getting so many new customers. A fun trip for a young boy." And a very memorable one.

Circulation managers expanded their carriers' horizons, offering trips and transporting them to corners unavailable to a child of working-class status. A family only traveled to Saturday market, Sunday church, or to relatives in the next county. Mike Hall, who delivered the *Spokane Daily Chronicle* in the 1950s, said, "I could never have taken the trips without a route." Whether it was the 1930s, '50s or '60s, carriers appreciated the excitement in crossing the state line.

## Christmas Like No Other

Dad's labor in the Butte mines provided for the family, just provided. Immigrating before age 16 from a mining life in Wales, John Rodda endured strenuous work in the mines of Montana. His son, Jack, helped financially by delivering the evening paper. Along with regular necessities, Jack wanted the family to be up-to-date and bought their first console radio. Acquaintances, neighbors, miners, they all knew the paper carrier was Mr. Rodda's boy. And so the parents felt extra proud when their son's photo and the column caption "Wins High Honor" was featured on the front page of the *Butte Daily Post*.

Right there on December 15, 1930, appeared the breaking news story that a junior at Butte High School had won an all-expenses-paid trip to Washington, D.C. His parent's pleasure far exceeded radio news, sports casts, or entertainment programs. Their son won the opportunity to be the Butte representative for the First Annual Patriotic Pilgrimage of the Newspaper Boys of America. Folks throughout the depressed mining town felt a part of the honor.

On December 20, in the cold morning air, Jack arrived at the train station ready to board the Union Pacific rail line. He was amazed to hear his high school band saluting him. The classmates, in full band uniform, played the rousing tune "For He's a Jolly Good Fellow." Jack, being respected as a fellow, stepped from childhood to adulthood. Standing tall in his hat and coat, a poor miner's son realized he represented more than the *Butte Daily Post*.

The 2,171 mile train ride transported him across state lines, which he had never crossed. The train chugged into the mighty Chicago railroad station after three days. There he transferred to a Baltimore and Ohio line. To working folks back home, as the severe uncertainty of the stock market crash slowly unfolded, Jack's 1930 trip became even more incredible.

Jack had repeatedly explained to the local people why he was exerting himself to sell subscriptions and win the reward. What thrilled his supporters was that once he qualified, Jack, unbeknownst as he added customers, was chosen from hundreds of paperboys for a special honor. Out of all the thousands of towns through the United States, Butte's hometown boy was selected to place a wreath at the Tomb of the Unknown Soldier in Arlington, Virginia.

His trip on December 23, 24 and 25, followed a tight schedule in order to include the many important sights in and around the capital. The large group was granted a Potomac River cruise on a coast guard cutter to Washington's Mount Vernon estate; was hosted at a reception with Vice-President Charles Curtis and the President's cabinet; listened to Christmas services at a cathedral; and marched in a parade down Pennsylvania Avenue, led by the United States Marine Band. Oh, if only he could share this spirited music with his school's band members.

On Wednesday, December 24, the Marine Band was also present as part of the service at the Tomb of the Unknown Soldier. In temperatures hovering near the freezing level, with his newsey cap in hand, like the rest of the crowd of carriers in the background, Jack respectfully placed a wreath at the Memorial. He stood extra tall before the sacred site, awed as well as humbled at being the one selected for the important tribute.

Thursday opened with Christmas breakfast at the renowned Willard Hotel, where for decades  national and international quests were often feted. In the afternoon, the winners were received at a special Christmas reception in the White House with President Herbert Hoover. Yes, a poor kid from Butte, who reliably delivered papers to earn money to help his family, stood in the presence of the nation's leader, a world figure, "for a Christmas like no other, ever."

## A Fair, with Feather Fans

Walter was rolling on the rails past modest frame homes with wide porches that protected residents from the heat. He watched trees, houses, barns flash by faster than when his bike rolled down hill. The train passed fields plowed by mules, small dusty towns with idle businesses, crossed the county line, the Alabama state line, heading out of the sunny south.

Walter (Bud) Dreyfus was riding a powerful train that demanded the right of way. His trip in 1934 continued for hours. "I got to sleep in an upper berth! Very exciting!" If he slept at all. His limited daily routine broke away to open space, to a world distant from his family. Bud was headed to skyscrapers, to a city of steam and smoke, smelly bawling stockyards. A big city holding a big reputation for brawn, speed, and hard working immigrants. He absorbed it all from his cushioned seat as the train belched and moved through a gateway to the future, into the giant hub of railroad lines. He arrived in Chicago.

The young son, along with 25 other boys, all bursting with wonder and uncertainty, headed for a big city. Bud was close to 12, to the age rule in the newspaper code. Fortunately, he began at age 9, so by 11 he was quite experienced, at least on his familiar streets. He attended the local county fair with neighbors, watched the sulky horse races, and ate cotton candy made by the church league. The Chicago trip was an immense leap, as if going from foot power to driving a locomotive. This was a World's Fair, the *Century of Progress: International Exposition*, when progress in the Depression was terribly slow. In spite of the devastating economy, over 20 million visitors were awed at the 1934 World's Fair and Walter was among the crowds.

The boys and their chaperones stayed at the YMCA, a safe well-known facility, unlike the steel structures and noise of the immense railroad yards. After quite a train trip, the youngsters clamored for another ride, slower paced and open to the full view of the Exposition. They rode the Skyride, an aerial cable car that ran for acres from one end of the fairgrounds to the other. Wow, nothing like that back in Birmingham.

With a little money in his pocket, but not much since the family needed help with basic groceries, Walter bought a "keychain that had the emblem of the Fair on it." Maybe he'd need a keychain, like big men carried, when he bought a car. Though his auto would be simpler than the streamlined futuristic cars displayed at the World's Fair.

For all the pavilions and ultra-modern displays, "the big attraction was a star, Sally Rand. We boys were not allowed to see THAT!" Naturally, with her extensive promotion and being told, "No," their interest peaked. Sally was a fan dancer. Oh, not little cardboard fans like those used on Sunday in a hot church, ones which spread open for an advertisement of the Friends' Funeral Home. And unlike the church organ's slow hymnal music, Sally's long ostrich feather fans waved and revealed to stimulating music.

A fair was a family place, not a place of prostitution. Sally wasn't a prostitute; she was a dancer and the World's Fair changed her world. The stirring act made her famous in a time when burlesque dancing was sensational.

No possibility of sneaking a peek in the Paris pavilion, like under a tent at the county fair. Still, boys found ample excitement with so much to see and to eat from morning to night. Then they rode home, returning to their daily routines. Except Bud's youthful world looked different, filtered through an incredible, magnified view of the future, unadorned by fluttering fans.

## Fish Fun

The state capital in Columbus provided an important field trip for school classes. Located in the middle of Ohio, each year students leaped off yellow school buses and tramped up the high stone steps delighted to be out of the classroom for a day.

For Dante Guzzo, visiting a capital expanded beyond a one-day trip. He delivered the *Columbus Citizen* every evening plus Sunday morning. Holding to a strict routine, or rather strictly held to tasks by the nuns at

St. Peters Catholic School, he served as an altar boy for 6:00 a.m. mass, walked back the mile from church, arrived at school on time, delivered and collected for his route. He was responsible, particularly since his customers knew him, and his parents. So Dante set his sights on selling subscriptions to win a trip to the East Coast and leave the landlocked city in the middle of farm fields. Selling 20 subscriptions, he'd be "sell-ebrating."

He added five, eight, eleven new customers. Over halfway. Another one. Just eight to go and Dante would travel to the Potomac, the ultimate visit to the nation's capital. The deadline approached. Dante turned in the final eight subscriptions.

His substitute arranged, his little satchel packed, he rode the train out of Union Station, headed east across the Franklin County line, the Ohio State line, over the Alleghany Mountains into the Potomac River Valley, into a capital known to the world: Washington, D.C. He arrived in the quiet, southern city designed with wide boulevards, large hotels, and immense government buildings. Wow, the sights: monuments, the Smithsonian Museum, Library of Congress, the White House, except these paperboys didn't wave to or dine with FDR.

Twenty boys of the Columbus contingency dined with numerous carriers in an elegant grand hotel dining room. This was Dante's and the others' first time sitting in a stately, carpeted room with chandeliers, linen table cloths, and China plates. For immigrant families in the Depression era, they had yet to rise to this formal status.

The boys gawked and squirmed until their dinner arrived. A proper waiter in formal attire set a large dinner plate with the steaming supper before every guest. The fellows smelled the fish, stared at the fancy fish and two shiny, round, lifeless eyes looked at them.

No way! Yep, the city chef served fish with the whole head and those cooked eyes.

They giggled. These youngsters weren't quite ready for the expansive changes in the metropolitan hotel. They were more comfortable just being boys, behaving the way they did each day. Paperboys are conditioned to throw. One threw.

Lopping gelatinous fish eyes across the table, one direct shot landed against a forehead. Laughing hard, when all the squishy fish eyes were thrown, they threw rolls. Dante's school lunch room wasn't this much fun, since the stern nuns never allowed fantastic food fights. Through the following weeks, as he paid for the eight extra subscriptions, his ticket price to a fantastic trip, he laughed about that dinner complete with more eyes than appear in a potato field.

Behaving with fans, misbehaving with fish eyes, boys remember first encounters. The carrier incentive trips of a week or two were a mere blink in the length of a paperboy's lifetime, yet the memory and influence lasted a lifetime.

## Fun Anywhere

Newspaper companies offered their youth carriers incredible travel to the north, south, east and west. They toured Boston, Niagara Falls, New York City, Philadelphia, New Orleans, Puerto Rico, Mexico City, the Indy 500, dude ranches, white-water rafting, the destinations were endless. From Alaska adventures to the balmy Caribbean, from the beautiful Ozarks to Victoria, Canada, and the top spot: Disneyland. The kids wanted action, speed, complex outings. An immense city, a fast train, a ship, the rugged deep Grand Canyon thrilled them.

Winning a contest required: 1. excellent service, no justified complaints; 2. subscription fees paid on time and not lingering until the 10th of the month. Most of all, 3. sign on new subscribers, the most important element. Retain customers but raise the circulation figures.

The shift from hawkers shouting headlines on a corner to delivering in residential neighborhoods did not eliminate selling. In the severely depressed 1930s, newspaper advertising dollars decreased. Circulation managers needed to increase subscriptions. The local managers were encouraged and supported from their national circulation meetings through the International Circulation Managers Association (ICMA), to establish weekly sales training programs for paperboys, who composed 70 percent of the route carriers.

A paper route consisted of three requirements: carrying which was what the customers expected; collecting (though they disliked the task) which was what the carriers desired; and selling which was what circulation wanted. Paperboys committed to the carrying and collecting. Now the manager should convince youth to sell. The ICMA conventions provided role playing sessions showing how to have children sell subscriptions. In 1936, ICMA reported that "more than 300 circulation departments in the United States were conducting carrier sales programs."

## A Better Way

Tillman Houser in 1936 was under way with his first paper route in West Salem, Oregon. The paper arrived from Portland for an after-school delivery. The circulation manager, from Portland, joined Tillman and "spending a couple of hours knocking on doors" the manager repeatedly gave his sales pitch. In a friendly manner he greeted the occupant and stated, "We represent the *News-Telegram*. This young man is the carrier. His father is in the hospital as a result of a very serious accident. He broke his leg, pelvis, nose, ribs and will be out of work for a long period. I know you would like to have the paper delivered right to your door each evening. The cost is only 65 cents for the month. You would be aiding a worthy boy whose family desperately needs help." With 30 new subscriptions, Tillman was busy at collection time that month. Yet, 29 cancelled in one month. "Only one continued the paper."

Rather than rely on a sad family situation, and in need of income, Tillman applied for a route with the *Oregon Statesman,* published in Salem. His major switch from 3:00 p.m. to 3:00 a.m. for the new route, with 110 customers who preferred the local news, supported his job.

## Keep Selling

To convince boys to canvas for subscriptions, a company had to entice them. Beyond emotional appeals to potential customers, more attractive than higher earnings for the carrier, the company offered extensive prizes and trips. Even if a lad was an extrovert around his gang, some became introverts when asking residents to subscribe. But if the rewards could motivate him, he'd stammer through his pitch to gain new subscriptions, and then he'd "sell-ebrate."

Paul West wanted to win a trip to Victoria, British Columbia, so he made certain the exacting customer who consistently timed him had no opportunity to call in a complaint. In addition, still needing four new subscribers, he hustled and acquired ten. The trip to Canada and the increased earnings from specific new customers belonged to Paul. The same for Tom Rockne. If he acquired 25 subscriptions, he would enjoy a trip from North Dakota to Minnesota. With his dad's guidance as a successful salesman and Tom's determination, he traveled to Minneapolis. Carrier selling occurred, though less frequently than carrying and collecting.

## Ready. Go

Gaining subscriptions and winning a coveted adventure, the paperboy had to arrange for a substitute, one who would continue through the length of the trip. Probably better to offer more than a candy bar. Maybe a younger brother could be prepped. Gee, mom's pleased with the contest. Would she help out delivering every morning?

Children didn't need lavish trips to be awed. If fish eyes entertained kids, they'll pursue fun in simple places, particularly with a first experience. Of course, varsity winners convinced novices to play all kinds of tricks. The 10, 12, 20 rascals at a paper shack created devilment. With 100 or 1,000 noisy paper carriers, the shouts and trouble became an active part of a trip.

This wasn't a field trip where school children walked in lines two by two, nor when the travel was over, wrote a required essay listing facts and favorite things. No, this was excitement. For the carriers' outings, their purpose was rambunctious fun. *Main Street School* offered a diversion from rote learning. Each antic expanded into ever greater acts. Circus clowns creating new roles should have traveled with the boys, whose actions outclassed the Keystone Kops. Slapstick at its best.

Before leaving home, mother stated:

Don't swipe your nose on your sleeve. "What if it's dripping?" No

Don't pick your teeth. "What if I get a strip of green bean caught?" No

Keep elbows off the table, use your napkin, don't talk with your mouth full.

All of mother's instructions receded before the group's actions. Without parental restrictions close at hand and no teachers present with paddles, just free for the day, the roustabouts tested the turf. Their horseplay raced chaperones from one group to the next.

## A World Away

Managing hundreds of paperboys on 10 large buses from Seattle to Vancouver, British Columbia, past the tall white Peace Arch at the international border, the drivers pulled to the side. Police entered each bus to search the little, and big, ruffians. The authorities confiscated fireworks, since experience forewarned adults that kids threw explosives, especially down ventilator shafts. And also threw stink bombs. Some sent a large pumpkin down an escalator that split piece by smashed piece as it rolled down each step scattering pulpy seeds, which stuck in crevices. The chaperones skipped smoking control since cigarette searches drove boys to the trash can. If a kid's about to be caught, he hastily threw his lighted cigarette into a waste receptacle, which burned the trash. A fire ensued. This excited the rowdies and encouraged more fires. Anyway, adults were smoking.

Buses rolled out plenty of fun and devilry as did full trains. Ron Haringa recalled joining "a whole train of carriers from Seattle to Portland, with a fancy meal." The *Seattle Times* filled the plush seats with energetic boys. The trip became too long to just sit still and watch trees flash past, so the restless rogues checked out the privy. *Whoa, pull the chain for the toilet, not the emergency cord to stop the train.*

*Hey, a discovery.* In the last coach, stored on the shelves, sat the large supply of toilet paper. In seconds, rolls of white streamers unwound from the fast train. Then the boys wandered to another section. As the train traveled down the tracks, they joined the crowd in the reserved smoking car. It was packed, though paperboys were not to be in the smoking car.

# Adding Color

Spending several hours on a ship crossing the Straits of Juan de Fuca between Washington State and British Columbia, youngsters had ample time and opportunity to entertain the gang. Away from the dull routines, carriers committed silly and serious acts. With large numbers to impress, which accelerated competition, their excess energy escalated into various levels of trouble. Sure, the 100 chaperones planned games, music, and food for the 1,000 boys, with lunch boxes handed to each carrier.

A menace decided what to do and the others quickly joined him. Kids just can't let that idle arm rest while on a trip. During delivery, carriers raised their arm, ready, aim. Why should adults be surprised when youth practiced what came naturally? Throwing. Their hand went up, shirttails pulled out, hair flopped across the forehead as robust boys kept aiming. Playing on ball teams, fellows were good at handling balls, at sustaining games. They were seasoned throwers.

And so with lunch boxes distributed, hundreds of hungry boys opened the lid and swiftly spied a round, red fruit in one corner. A grown-up actually packed a tomato in each box. The gleaming white ship was soon shiny wet and slick with bright tomato pulp.

Breaking out of the rigid shell in daily routines, paperboys got even with the gang at the Hill Street Station. Splat across the face. Bull's eye. The rowdy's hair, face, shirt, and trousers were adorned with yellow seeds and drippy bits of red skin. The blue sky accented with white clouds, the blue ocean water topped with white caps, a grand white ship adorned with red circles around the deck---such a colorful time.

# Fun Anywhere, Anytime

In the wider world, for many children their angel wings folded beneath a shirt. Enjoying an elaborate hotel in Washington, D.C., carriers weren't concerned with sleeping, like their exhausted chaperones. Kids stayed awake leaning out the window, dropping water balloons. With careful aim, practiced on their route, they now kept ladies of the street alert as the water container burst. Yes, right on target. Oh darn, the street women reported the splats. The police stopped the fun, even if the patrolmen had assistance relocating the women to less respectable business locations. The police and circulation manager sent the little cherubs to dreamland.

Water balloons, smoking material, firecrackers, managers tried to strip the imps of any troublesome items and curb the boisterous, bragging sex talk when they passed within earshot. Dick Kalivoda, working as one of many chaperones on the grand ship to Vancouver Island, even served on "anti-spit patrol." With nothing to toss, the rascals used what they had:

blobs of frothy spit shot from the upper deck. Or they turned to readily available safety provisions placed in a variety of locations. Boys caused fast reaction after breaking a fire alarm box.

In Victoria, British Columbia, at the magnificent Empress Hotel, designed for the elite of the British Empire, ladies sat in the elegant lobby properly partaking of high tea. Until, a mob of wild paperboys came screeching through the room. *Those horrible heathens from the rebel colonies.* The orderly staff of the Empress closed tea time when American paperboys arrived.

As a trip ended, youngsters returned to the ship, the bus, or the train. Should an adult take back a stolen street sign? Why would a boy want a street sign? *Oh heck, just confiscate it.* At least chaperones weren't stuck with returning any horses to a rodeo. Allowed by the ship company, or by a train line to travel the next year with another cadre of carriers, the newspaper company was required to reserve a train line or a separate ship just for lively newspaper boys. However, sometimes children were not the cause of a problem.

## Another Wait

Before the gang plank of the 115 foot Virginia V boat was lowered releasing passengers for Blake Island, the *Seattle Times* paperboys were issued an order: Return to the boat dock on time. No late arrivals. The warning sounded absolute.

After an all-day outing, the carriers had enjoyed enough of the Island and Puget Sound waters, so they obeyed their instructions. Chaperones counted heads. On a pleasant Sunday in June, 1961, without Northwest rain, the youngsters stood in groups ready to board for home. Tired, they sat on the ground, talked, laughed and waited for an hour. *Gee, what are parents saying at home? Anyone doing the household chores?*

Restless, they waited another hour. Try keeping a school class of 25 settled if an assembly program starts quite late. With 250 active carriers and no kites to fly, no bicycles to ride, no drive-ins to serve perpetually hungry stomachs, the adults faced frustration.

A stuck boat in thick mud, regardless of the energy thrust of 250 boys, will not move in a minus tide. The unusually low tide challenged everyone's patience. The Coast Guard arrived with a 56 foot boat and a 40 foot boat. Betting on whether the Coast Guard boats would succeed, this entertained the young gamblers as the white patrol boats tugged but failed to pull the Virginia V free. People managed, sort of, while the record low tide, changing at the speed of the moon's pull, slowly raised the water level of Puget Sound. In the meantime, Seattle's KJR radio broadcast news of the stranded boaters in an effort to notify parents. In the dark, at 10:30 p.m. the restless children finally returned home, though late.

For most carriers, trips became an awesome experience. They followed mother's rules, making parents proud of their sons, who likewise wanted their fine upbringing represented. Through the decades, as society's class of paperboys transformed from the nineteenth century ragged street urchins to well-mannered, middle-class carriers, the children were individually transformed as they matured over months, into years of delivering a local paper.

## First, First, First, and His First

Jim Kavanaugh slept on an alarm clock to be certain he was underway by 4:30 a.m. In the winter he tugged on long underwear, which felt good in a bedroom with no central heat. Outside on a bitter cold Idaho morning, wearing an airplane style hat with flaps over his ears, Jim wrapped a scarf across his face to protect against the -10°, -20°F. The soft, warm cover helped. Then breathing out moist air, ice soon formed on the material. Wool fibers "froze to the lips." His chapped, cracked skin pulled away, leaving tissue on the stiff scarf.

Riding his bike in the dark, even darker than usual during war blackouts, he often wrecked on icy, steep hills in Lewiston, like the four-block-long 5th Avenue. He limped into the paper shack. The cozy potbelly stove thawed his frozen clothes, and several friendly carriers warmed the atmosphere. But once the bus arrived from Spokane with *Spokesman Review* bundles, the boys hastily left for their routes.

Like his older brothers, he was a responsible paperboy, though he "didn't like to collect." The small tyke soon enjoyed adventures that dismissed all his tough adversity. Jim was headed to more than a Lewiston Round Up, more than a nice trip to a large hotel in Spokane. He was ready for a few days without carrying papers, serving as an altar boy, or working on Boy Scout badges.

Trip winners left the county seat on the Snake and the Clearwater River, left the familiar hills in Nez Perce country, the Port of Lewiston, the farthest inland port for the West Coast and Idaho's only seaport. That was behind them. The excited carriers passed through the Inland Empire, crossed the great Columbia River, chugged over the Cascade Mountains to Seattle. By train, Jim had crossed 316 miles from Lewiston to Seattle, widening his world.

After covering the sights around Seattle, the group boarded a ship, the stately SS Princess Marguerite, headed across the international straits of Juan de Fuca, into another universe. The travels unfolded like a movie. While the growing World War II events were lost in thousands of miles across the ocean, the boys realized war intervened in their travel. Expecting to port in the grand provincial Canadian capital, English-style Victoria, instead the ship detoured into Vancouver's port, because of

Canada's war commitment and the military rules with Great Britain. That didn't matter. Victoria or Vancouver were fine with Jim, since this was his, "first time on a train, first time on a ship, first time more than 100 miles from home." He enjoyed the thriving city with his "first cigarette."

## Livelier than North Dakota

Tom Rockne carefully managed his *Minneapolis Tribune* delivery. Using his bicycle, his wagon, a sled when necessary, every morning in Jamestown, North Dakota, he placed papers inside the doors before 6:00 a.m. Collecting fees in the dark, with cold hands, he considered the frost bite on his fingers and toes as "nothing serious." Tom tolerated a lot to save for college.

When the family moved to Bismarck, he obtained another *Tribune* route. He continued to serve as an altar boy, participated in Boy Scouts, rising to Eagle Scout, and collected. "Told from a very young age I was going to college and needed to prepare financially," Tom did. At times Dad borrowed from the route savings, but Mr. Rockne repaid with interest.

Signing on 25 new subscriptions, an extensive challenge, Tom won an incentive trip. Traveling by train, for 427 miles from Bismarck to Minneapolis, his "first time on a train and his first time outside of North Dakota," the 1960s decade came alive for the school boy. The group of carriers toured the big city of Minneapolis, ate in large restaurants, visited the production sections of the *Tribune* company, and saw a Minnesota Twins baseball game. They were visiting terrific scenes beyond anything in their sparse Dakota countryside.

## Partial Pay Paves the Way

Nathan Everett reliably delivered his four-mile route every morning before 6:30, winning carrier of the month more than once. He reached his customers even in northern Indiana winters and the severe snow. Living in the country, his bundles were dropped at his home, except when the residential country road was impassable with drifts. Then Nathan hiked the mile to a gas station where his papers were left. He owned a "huge, heavy duty bike with shock absorbers on the front and big fat tires;" however, in deep snow the bike was a disadvantage.

His advantages occurred with winning points, which converted to cash at local stores in Mishawaka, so he obtained a "good quality reel-to-reel tape recorder and a five-band transistor radio." Nathan felt proud to acquire extras in the 1960s, things "other kids were given by their parents." His mother and father provided, but even with both parents working, the family of four girls and a son faced limited funds. His dad worked at the Studebaker plant in Mishawaka, Indiana, and "was often laid-off or out of work for months at a time." Finally, off permanently.

The factory closed. In Lyndon Johnson's war on poverty, the President declared the South Bend region "an economic disaster when Studebaker closed."

For Nathan "carrying papers gave me a sense of independence," handling his own expenses for necessities, lunches at school, clothes, entertainment costs. He had fun seeing the Chicago White Sox play, whether they scored or not. He also won a trip to the 1964 New York World's Fair that showcased American technology for 51 million attendees. And an exciting, robust adventure at a dude ranch. And then, the pinnacle.

Nathan could win a trip to the West Indies. Meeting the requirements, paperboys would cruise the warm waters around the Bahamas, sail into the port of Nassau, dine, explore, and play. From the working-class economy of Mishawaka to a cruise in the Caribbean, why, it was like being cast in a Hollywood movie. This was the style of travel that city newspapers featured in the society pages about wealthy honeymooners. Nathan planned how he would "sell-ebrate." Problem, he had to sell new subscriptions when folks were strapped for money. It would be great to give a good paperboy a trip; however, his sailing in blue waters didn't lift their needs.

He thought of an advantage. On Saturday mornings, at a considerate hour, he collected 65 cents a week from each subscriber. As an independent little merchant, meeting the wholesale price of the papers was his responsibility. For folks to sign on, he offered a 50 cent subscription cost. Just like kids winning a prize, people liked a deal. Nathan met his contest requirements, met his weekly bill managing the 15 cent difference for three months. Paying his portion for Nassau was worth those nickels and dimes.

## Young Columbus

The newspaper industry heightened trips for winners to grand destinations with the crème de la crème expanding beyond the shores of America. An especially excellent contest was offered everywhere in the United States that local newspaper companies added the Sunday *Parade* magazine. Like the great discoverer, Christopher Columbus, paperboys had the opportunity to discover famous locations beyond the U.S.A. through the fabulous Young Columbus trips. The requirements were based on consistent route excellence, scholarship standing, citizenship traits, and subscription sales. With 600,000 newspaper carriers throughout the country (though a number of newspaper companies did not include the sponsor, *Parade Magazine,* thus reducing the number of competitors) and a limit of less than a hundred winners on the trip, the competition became intense.

## Tales From Two Cities

Opportunities increased as Mike Rhodes settled into a smoother routine, after his first year of both struggles and troubles on his San Jose route. Each year, from 1955 on, he improved and each year he added new subscribers who moved into housing developments around his route. This helped him win prizes: baseball gear, a radio, fun trips to Disneyland, and deep sea fishing. Then in 1960, he won the ultimate two-week reward. On a TWA flight from California to New York, slow because of frequent stops to board other participants, paperboys began a long trans-Atlantic flight to Europe. Attended by stylish, slim airline stewardesses, the young passengers enjoyed meals and snacks, which topped the treats bought on a paper route. Sitting in a tight airline seat left Mike ready to disembark and be a tourist in London and Paris.

High school classes in European history seemed elementary compared to the centuries-old historic sites the group visited. And the exotic French lady. Mike had been attracted to several cute girls on his route, particularly a wealthy young lady who lived in a mansion at the end of a long curving driveway that he walked up in hopes of seeing her. And the phantom lady with her New Year's kiss. Yet none of these gals was as intoxicating as a French movie star. The sensuous pleasure of her perfume, Parisian dress, coiffured hair, her French accent captured him. He was mesmerized. Of course the 16-year-old was also interested in the grand British pageantry, immense museums, exceptional French cuisine, Eifel Tower, and more. His "trip of a lifetime" was the culmination of Mike's paper route years, closing childhood and introducing him to a stunning world stage and all that adulthood offered.

## A Papal Blessing Missed Denver

As Mike completed his six wondrous years as a paperboy, Jim Rudy adjusted to his daily route in Denver, to everything except the early hour. His *Rocky Mountain News* bundles were dropped at 4 a.m. providing time to race on his route, serve as altar boy for 6 a.m. mass at St. James Catholic Church, and consistently sit in his school seat before the tardy bell.

Tired or not, facing erratic Colorado weather, distractions or not, Jim dependably served his 100 customers, up to 120 on Sunday. With steady delivery, he earned a profit to meet his expenses that included an annual $500 school tuition, and the occasional cost for broken windows from the rush to porch his papers. Nevertheless, his quality performance allotted him a few regional trips, leading to the 1964 competition for the ultimate paperboy adventure.

And like Jack Rhodes photo and story in the *Butte Daily Post*, Jim was photographed and featured for winning a trip in April, 1964. He had never been out of the country, and now he would spend Easter in Italy. Faithfully serving as altar boy, any possibility of visiting the holiest of Catholic sites, the Basilica of Saint Peter in Vatican City, rose beyond his hopes.

All dressed in ties, stylish blazers with emblems, and grey slacks, the group of 88 top carriers began an exciting TWA flight with terrific chaperones: members of the All-American football team. The stewardesses managed the competition for attention. Or maybe the boys declined competing with robust football stars.

Anyway, by the time they arrived in Italy the fellows were ready to focus on the incredible pasta and bread, along with the tours of historic Rome, Milan, Venice, Florence, which included fun Italian street vendors. At a dignified reception, Jim met the American ambassador to Italy, which included the memorable pleasure of meeting his chic, charming 16-year-old daughter. Wow, that day was wonderful. Though swirling with excitement in the myriad of experiences, Jim remembered mom and bought her a piece of Venetian glass, which she always treasured. However, the most impressive, an audience in St Peter's Basilica with Pope Paul VI, culminated Jim's "most terrific two weeks of my life."

From a devilish newsey to a world traveling newspaperboy in an elite coat and tie, he was transformed from an adolescent to a young adult. Though Pope Paul VI in his address and blessing referred to the carriers as "dear boys." The Pope encouraged them to follow a route of "perseverance and good will" emphasizing "be cheerful and helpful to others." The trip and their audience with the Pope elevated them past boyhood.

When the "most terrific" trip came to a close and he was back to his routines, back to St. Regis School, Jim learned more, because of his time in Italy rather than in school.

Enjoying the attention of his classmates asking about his experiences, Jim's attitude was quite cheerful, just as the Pope emphasized. Students in his school knew him since he had attended for several years, was an excellent student and an outstanding athlete. In other words, an all-around American guy, the kind schools endeavored to develop. When he was summoned to the principal's office, he expected more interest and questions about his 12 days in Italy, his experiences, his fantastic trip to the Vatican.

Jim had missed school on an unexcused absence. The long travel time was other than for a death in his immediate family, the only acceptable reason to be briefly absent. The Jesuit father was very explicit: "Expelled."

It's so difficult to be cheerful when expelled. Jim could not graduate with his school friends. In the years ahead as his class held reunions reminiscing about "the class of 1965," he would not be included in "the class." The Denver leaders were familiar with the fine young man and his story that was featured in the newspaper. The Chamber of Commerce president, the mayor, the governor of Colorado intervened, writing letters of appeal.

Response: Standards have a purpose. Obey regulations. Though the rule was clear, its application was insensible. As extreme as prohibiting children under age 18 from working, the strict policy to expel demonstrated no balance in educating a productive citizen.

Undeterred, Jim followed the Pope's advice to persevere. He switched for his senior months to graduate from the public school, George Washington High School. In spite of a sharp detour, he continued a route to success.

# CHAPTER 19
## RECOGNITION

### Statues

Centuries before newspapers, long before machines were invented that created news sheets, statues were built to proclaim the accomplishments of an emperor, a victorious general, a deity. Grand memorials abound in countries, honoring greatness. Michelangelo's larger than life sculpture of David, the imposing Abraham Lincoln memorial, or in South Dakota, the likenesses of Washington, Jefferson, Lincoln and Theodore Roosevelt carved into Mount Rushmore, all magnificent structures impressing tourists as they gaze upward. Whether it's local or national, simple or sacred, viewers pause to praise the figures. In 1930, Jack Rodda, with respectful awe, placed a wreath to honor the nation's Tomb of the Unknown Soldier.

Establishing monuments to formally recognize greatness happens with frequency. But an unusual salute occurred with statues honoring newsboys, ones that acknowledged an ordinary class of working children, resourceful kids who exerted themselves every day, regardless of conditions or their constitution. Contributions to communities and to newspaper companies were heralded in paperboy statues.

In 1895, in the independent New England spirit, a newsboy statue was unveiled that reflected the Puritan work ethic. A Civil War veteran, Col. William L. Brown had become the successful publisher of the one cent *New York Daily News*. Newsboys, though not single handedly but very significantly, made Brown's paper a success in the 1880s and '90s. Col. Brown knew the small salesboys' efforts were crucial to the survival of penny papers. With appreciation, he gave a gift to Great Barrington, Massachusetts, near his residential farm. Larger than a child-size newsboy, the statue, centered in a fountain in a tree-shaded, quiet park, was created at the time hawkers led the sales force. No fishing pole over the shoulder but a canvas strap, a rumpled cap, the simple, plain appearance easily identifiable as a newsboy.

Barrie Hughes, a paperboy in 1949 for *The Calgary Herald* in Calgary, Canada, later wrote, *The World Honors the News Carrier,* in which he identified Col. Brown's gift as the oldest known paperboy statue. Mr. Hughes also included details of other leading newspaper centers, where ever-increasing circulation was often accomplished through children. Publishing companies erected statues in Detroit, Los Angeles, Portugal, Brazil, Anchorage...

Anchorage?

Over the years, Alaskan leaders argued fervently for their territory to be admitted as a state. Always energizing the group, Mr. Robert Atwood, owner of the *Anchorage Daily Times,* served as the chairman of the Alaska Statehood Committee. He traveled the region, and in addition made arduous 3,370 mile trips from Anchorage into the halls of Congress. Year after year the determined committee men pressed forward for statehood.

Alaskans are used to challenges as big as their gargantuan territory. Alaska could be named the "challenge state." And the newsboys verified this label when faced with incredible conditions. The paper carriers' persistence was a reflection of the dedicated residents, political and business leaders, who faced long struggles to move the United States Congress to act for acceptance. Alaskans persisted.

On June 30, 1958 the United States Senate passed the Alaska Statehood Act. Alaska would be a state on January 3, 1959. Far to the north in Fairbanks, Kent Sturgis hawked the town's special edition, appreciating his exceptional sales for the collector's edition. The *Daily News-Miner* published pages of details for the 49th state. The nation's stripes and forty-eight stars had flown since 1912 when Arizona and New Mexico, in the desert region of the Southwest, were granted statehood. Now, nearly five decades later, Congress turned north.

And being sensible, folks in Fairbanks celebrated in the summer, rather than in January when Kent carried papers at minus, yes, -50° F. The town reveled in the news. Sirens hailed the new status, fire trucks slowly eased through the streets with children climbing on and off the vehicles, jubilant crowds gathered. Excitement rose on every street, in every store, every saloon.

To commemorate the national event, which changed "*Old Glory*" from 48 to 49 stars, the *Anchorage Daily Times* ran a six-inch headline: *WE'RE IN.* The celebratory words were spread by children's hands to inform everyone about the news. To further herald the win, Mr. Atwood commissioned the creation of a standing icon. The engraved statue of a newsboy, his arm raised, a hand extended holding a newspaper for citizens, proclaimed the important change, *We're In.*

To some, producing a paperboy statue may seem insignificant, but to those who valued the service and the dependability of young paper carriers, recognition through statues was quite significant. Small models of paperboy statues stood on desks in many newspaper offices and were respected gifts given to professional newspaper personnel. However, statues were not broadly sufficient to reach the majority of carriers and the general public.

## Salute

Newspaper managers lauded their paperboys by offering programs that applauded the children's work. Of the 365 days that carriers delivered papers, one day was to be officially proclaimed Newspaperboy Day.

The rough, ragged urchins of a nineteenth century image, and most were fighters struggling to survive, declined on city corners by the 1930s. The newsboy lodges in New York City had long since closed, knickers ceased to be fashionable by 1940, the newsie cap was replaced by a popular ball cap. Even the common label "newsie" or "newsey" disappeared. The status of paper carriers, from middle-class families, in respectable community jobs, steadily rose.

Men in the newspaper business appreciated what the carriers contributed by the fast distribution of each day's news. Children rushed on their paper routes to reach customers' homes, strengthening the essential link that connected the latest printed news conveniently to the consumer. And paperboys increased business with selling additional subscriptions,

Howard Stodghill, a prominent leader in the circulation service, held a strong belief that the newspaper industry benefitted by selecting boys to distribute papers. He believed just as strongly that the youth also benefitted. Howard organized his fellow leaders to enlarge the already acclaimed National Newspaper Week. The Saturday of Newspaper Week would be identified as an official day for newsboys. When it was launched in 1932, Howard's nascent plan for this special day did not flourish. But early on he learned a basic attribute when he sold papers: persistence. His idea grew exponentially as if Santa Ana winds blew the plan through the United States. He lit the energy to establish Newspaperboy Day.

Recognizing Mr. Stodghill's strong commitment, the committee and colleagues in the International Circulation Manager's Association (ICMA) supported his stand. They pressed to enhance and elevate the status of paperboys, even if they were inexperienced rascals. Yes, youngsters made mistakes, committed misdeeds, but their contribution to society was praised and their daily commitment deserved to be acknowledged and celebrated. The ICMA efforts gained momentum and by 1940 the national observance of Newspaperboy Day broadened.

Carriers, their parents, school principals, the press, business leaders, service clubs like the Kiwanis and the Elks, entire communities expressed pride in the boys on their designated day. Prominent politicians from the local to the state and on to the national level lent their voice. Public recognition was granted with full-page newspaper ads. Radio stations broadcast the tribute. Newspaper companies hailed the little merchants' accomplishments and promoted co-operation, quite contrary to past voices condemning the rascals.

## His Day

Not wanting to limit appreciation to one day a year, circulation managers advanced a step further and selected a carrier of the month. Starting as a substitute, Ed Dulaney became responsible for his first job in 1939. His route grew to 225 subscribers, a large number of customers who could register complaints, and a long list from whom to collect weekly. Ed stayed with the system, worked to be accountable and, sure enough, felt a strong sense of accomplishment when his picture appeared in the *Columbia Tribune* as carrier of the month. With a record of reliably picking up his bundles, no "kicks" (complaints), his bill paid in full, he enjoyed the deserved recognition, the same as thousands of similar carriers across the country. Mention paperboy and people connected the picture of a young merchant with a purpose.

## Twice as Good

To further recognize these young boys, a city's newspaper manager selected a carrier of the year. Kent Sturgis started his experience in Fairbanks at age 10, hawking in bars. Once assigned a full-time *Daily News-Miner* route, he performed his duties whether he intersected with bar patrons, old turn-of-the-century sour-dough Alaska miners, or a nude lady. Focused on the job, he delivered through the sloppy spring break-up of ice, the summer heat, and the icy winter when temperatures descended below -40° F., exceptionally challenging conditions. He had every reason to feel proud when selected as the Outstanding Carrier of the Year. With his picture in the newspaper, the customers, other carriers, teachers, and friends, all noticed. Along with his proud mom. His world heralded his service. Not a chance designation, Kent continued to excel and earned the title, Outstanding Carrier, again the next year.

## Lunch is Served.

In 1942, 10-year old Jack Gahan, began delivering the *Tacoma Tribune*. He was awarded savings bonds from the *Tribune* for being an outstanding carrier. Then his family moved from Tacoma to Seattle and he continued to manage a route with the *Seattle Times*. His earnings increased and so did his self-confidence, and soon was selected as a station manager. He was stoic during customer complaints because the paper cost changed from 3 cents to 5 cents. Why adults thought he had anything to do with pricing, baffles the mind. He persevered.

Jack was selected as the Hall of Fame Ace Carrier for 1949. Winning the *Seattle Times* "Carrier of the Year" meant an opportunity for lunch with Washington Governor Arthur Langlie. Standing with Governor Langlie, the slim, tall teenage boy, sporting a suit and tie, appeared even taller, elevated with pride.

He joined three other spruced-up fellows from Yakima, Everett and Tacoma, for a special delivery at the luncheon. The four carriers presented Governor Langlie a canvas newspaper bag, the identifying apparel of paperboys everywhere. However, it was a clean, unused bag. Governor Langlie was acclaimed Honorary Newspaperboy for Washington State.

## In the News

A generation of fathers, who delivered papers in the 1920s and '30s, revved up paper route promotions after total victory in World War II, and they now worked with circulation rewards. Newspapers reached everywhere in the energized, prosperity boom. The circulation managers associations and individual newspaper companies produced books, booklets, and films for conducting sales meetings to further develop the salesmanship and service of Little Merchants. In 1948, the California Newspaper Association, with the support of Bob Hope (who once sold newspapers), released a training and motivation film, which was especially effective with newspaperboy movie-enthusiasts.

Supreme Court Justice William Douglas and J. Edgar Hoover, Director of the Federal Bureau of Investigation (FBI), made emphatic statements saluting paperboys, with their words carried by papers across the nation on Newspaperboy Day. Acknowledgments were broadcast on radio stations. Over the years, Treasury Secretary, John Snyder, and then President Harry Truman, followed by President Dwight Eisenhower, signed salutes to the youth carriers. Child-labor reformers, social reformers, and juvenile detention activists were bombarded as the syndicate writers, along with favorite national cartoonists, conveyed more positive messages about the rewards of being a paperboy. Recognizing the perpetual interest in food, news companies also continued hosting feasts for their young charges.

## Only an Initial

Though lunch with a governor was limited to only a few, thousands of other carriers were not ignored or left unfed. Large newspaper companies held recognition banquets, as they had for decades, with complete dinner for their enterprising paperboys, and a very small number of girls.

Frankie Grab, her jaw healed from the terrible bike accident, loved "the honor of going to the banquet. Imagine being almost the only girl with about 200 boys, age 12 and the hormones kicking in." The guys certainly encountered competition for a smile from a cute girl.

In 1962, the *Tacoma News Tribune* again held more than one banquet around Newspaperboy Day to celebrate their 1,050 carriers. Dinner was served at the Top of the Ocean restaurant for the city boys, then another dinner at the restaurant for the youngsters who delivered in the towns and villages nearby. Amidst an evening of laughter, chatter and plenty of food, the children enjoyed an October evening away from the daily rut of delivery. Starting with music and door prizes, the circulation managers addressed the carriers with a welcome and expressed appreciation for their service. The printed program recognized employees, listing the circulation managers and supervisor, the city district managers, the suburban district managers, night crew, even the full name of staff women in the *Tribune* office.

Next, the program stated the accomplishments for junior carriers who delivered the *Tribune* with *SIX or more years of continuous service*; then a paragraph with *FIVE years or more of continuous service;* and the longest list featured the full name of all the junior dealers *With FOUR years or more of continuous service.* Well, almost the "full name" for each. The fourth carrier on the alphabetical list was printed only as K. Was the K. for Ken, Karl, Kurt?

The K's last name stated Grabb, typed with an extra b. Starting in 1950, Mary Ann and Phyllis Grab reliably delivered the route for South Prairie. Frankie Grab attended a banquet during her more than six years of delivering the *Tribune*. By 1962, into the twelfth year of Grab sisters running the route, Kathy, had capably managed it the last four years. Maybe when Patricia and Frances carried the paper before Kathy, their listed name of Pat or Frankie was acceptable, but Kathy was designated only as K. This was the Newspaper*boy* Banquet.

## Stamps

Every day, one customer at a time, paperboys and girls served communities. And during the World War II years, carriers served the country. Beyond statues or special salutes, a federal office in conjunction with cabinet members and circulation leaders would later present a national tribute through a stamp for their extensive youth service during war years.

By age 10, Sam Rarig was delivering the *Shamokin News-Dispatch*. When winter enveloped Catawissa in the Alleghany Mountains of Pennsylvania, he walked in three to four feet of snow or used skis to maneuver the streets. With exertion, Sam gained strength by working his route and participating in sports. In 1941, now age 16, he added another activity to his busy schedule of school, Boy Scouts, sports, and route. Never a slacker, as demonstrated by his rise to Eagle Scout, Sam determined to "provide a meaningful service as a block captain's aide with blackout monitoring, and by collecting scrap metal on Saturdays," for the war effort. Upon completing high school as the valedictorian and finishing his paper route after eight years, Sam left Catawissa to serve in the U.S. Navy. Many paperboys signed on for military service.

Near Johnstown, Pennsylvania, the Ruth brothers also ended their route, which they held since 1928, and entered the military: Robert served in the Philippines with the army, Paul joined the navy in the Pacific, and Bill fought in the army across Europe. Dick and Bede Irvin left Des Moines for the front, with Bede as a photo journalist for the AP press and Dick in the army. Dick came home to a long productive life. However, his brother, his close pal through the cold snowy treks delivering Des Moines papers, remained in Normandy. Bede, struck down in the horrific battle at St. Lo, was the first AP journalist killed in the European theater. He rests among military members in the Normandy American Cemetery in France.

Bill Nolting collected his pay, not a large amount for the terrible battles he endured, but not turned away, as a paperboy, for two cents. Dante Guzzo didn't waste food thrown from a foxhole. No fish eyes (like at the hotel) in the C-rations. Francis Walsh hefted his rifle without effort after hefting baskets of coal as a child. Ray Bloomer had army marching strength in his legs, developed early by running hills and steps in Cincinnati. Ed Norlin, after five years of walking every morning and evening to deliver 150 papers, now mixed walking and riding with his armored division. The youthful Dugg Holmes set aside his used bike, gave another guy's name and older birth date to enlist in the army. Across America, mature paperboys left their canvas bag and hoisted the heavier GI issued duffle bags.

## On the Home Front

Children, sometimes little brothers, served as the messenger of papers reporting the sacrifices, the horrific battle struggles, and the losses of local soldiers. The large posters in the library, the post office, city hall, conveyed the importance of raising funds to support the troops.

When planning the fund drives, organizers looked immediately to the paperboys. Who in American towns and cities had the endurance and the outdoor stamina along with the knowledge of the streets and neighbors? And who knew how to collect and to keep correct records? No force could be more powerful than the extensive web of paperboys.

These legions of paperboys sold stamps based on their local publisher's participation. Not three-cent postage stamps but ten-cent stamps, which citizens attached to a book to accumulate for a war bond. If a town's newspaper enrolled in the federal program, the experienced salesboys added a patriotic service: sell defense stamps. And they sold. Sold, and sold more: A million. Two million. Twenty million. Then on to 100, to 500 million. As older carriers left for all branches of military service, their replacements kept selling stamps. By the completion of World War II, newspaper carriers sold just under two billion stamps for defense bonds. Yes, Billion.

Don Fraits' route of 200 customers in Cranston, Rhode Island, taxed his strength. He kept his pay records correct for the daily subscribers, the daily and Sunday, the Sunday only customers, for the amount owed to the *Providence Journal*. As his family struggled out of the Depression years, his weekly $10 contribution remained important. Like Sam Rarig, Don took on another responsibility by helping the war effort. Along with his collection for the *Journal*, Don jingled down the street each week with an additional $60 to $75 for stamps. At home he stacked 600 dimes, 700 dimes on the table ready to turn in. He conscientiously helped, knowing his older brother served as a marine on Guadalcanal.

Jim Birchman, after buying his afternoon Detroit route in 1941 and successfully managing it, sold bond stamps, sold and sold. Each week he collected three cents a paper, which increased to four cents, kept his Sunday-only subscribers correct and turned all the war stamp money in with his newspaper bill. For his outstanding sales, he received "three awards designated on a minute man pin."

Like Jim in Detroit, Jack Gahan sold bond stamps in Tacoma and bought his own savings stamps for bonds. Plus newspaper managers awarded carriers savings bonds because of outstanding service. In 1942 Gene Reiber was awarded a bond from the *Tacoma Times* for a year without a single complaint. However, a complaint was close when an elderly customer thought her newspaper missile would explode as an incendiary bomb.

The war ended. The stamp-selling paperboys graduated to more involved jobs. Home from serving in World War II, a number of military personnel were accepted into positions for government service. Five years after the national victory, help from paperboys was requested, again. In 1950, the U.S. Treasury promoted a drive for the purchase of Independence Savings Bonds. This time, rather than collecting dimes each week from customers to buy defense bonds, the boys distributed information on how citizens could and should participate in the drive.

Carriers delivered 15 million leaflets to newspaper subscribers. The next year children repeated the task, but with 25 million leaflets and pledge cards circulated to residents, who committed to purchase Defense Bonds. The citizens signed an agreement to buy a bond or bonds, then bought bonds at banks, the post office, in their business of employment through payroll deduction plans.

For the boys' efforts, local circulation departments offered a summer incentive trip to be awarded to their top salesboy: a two-day trip to Washington, D.C with visits to monuments, the Treasury building, and the Defense Department.

By October 4, 1952, Newspaperboy Day was officially celebrated by government officials, expressing the nation's appreciation for the boys' accomplishments throughout the war years. A large banner was hung in the Franklin Institute in Philadelphia proclaiming, *Busy Boys--Better Boys*. Treasury Secretary, John W. Snyder, a former paperboy from Arkansas, congratulated the extensive efforts of the children and then unveiled an enlarged postage stamp. The three-cent postage stamp replica pictured a paperboy with his canvas bag. The usual name of a newspaper on the canvas had been replaced with the words: BUSY BOYS---BETTER BOYS. In small print on the stamp the words: IN RECOGNITION OF THE IMPORTANT SERVICE RENDERED THEIR COMMUNITIES AND THEIR NATION BY AMERICA'S NEWSPAPERBOYS

## With Other Paperboys

By October, the stifling summer temperatures receded, reducing the fear of further polio outbreaks, which in 1952 was already proclaimed the worst year for polio. The paperboys' benefit games to raise funds for the March of Dimes had been played. People had filled the March of Dimes cards they received from carriers just like they filled the Defense Bond booklets with ten-cent stamps. Carriers had collected dimes to fight a deadly war and collected dimes to fight a deadly disease. At school, paperboys continued to place dimes in their savings accounts. And now for three cents, the public could purchase a stamp that recognized the fine efforts by thousands of newspaper carriers.

Far across the nation, Bill Gamel felt the autumn sun setting earlier in Anchorage. He buttoned his jacket as the evening temperature slipped below the freezing level. He paused to place bets with his customers on the Yankees' and Brooklyn Dodgers' 1952 World Series. On October 4, the Yankees won and the teams were tied at two and two. Bill and his hearty, neighborly baseball fans were unconcerned with a new three-cent postage stamp.

In Ohio, Gary Kost, with Goofy, noticed the maple leaves showing autumn colors; John Nicon read the comics before he delivered the *Seattle*

*Times*; and Carole Bergeron made certain her *Tacoma News Tribune*. customers received their comics. Back East the "largest first-day sale of a commemorative postage stamp" was heralded. In Philadelphia, a mass mailing of the issued sheets was expected to reach a record 500,000. It topped 600,000.

## Rising Further

The number of paperboys increased and programs for recognition expanded. In Portland, Oregon, TV viewers saw Ross Webb, a local paper carrier for the *Oregon Journal*, featured in the *Journal*'s television commercials. When students at school asked him if he was the "*Journal* guy" he felt special, quite "cool."

Reaching 1960, an estimated 600,000 carriers were saluted by newspaper companies, who continued to celebrate the children with banquets, prizes, and ever more wonderful trips. And like one paperboy selected to represent all carriers as the postage stamp figure in 1952, a single boy was selected as a winner on a TV program.

In the 1960s, television entertained housewives with the popular "Queen for a Day." On Newspaperboy Day the program switched to "King for a Day" when emcee Jack Bailey selected a "Royal" paperboy to win a grand trip that included visits to America's two new states. The show passed over calling the program "Prince for a Day" or choosing a princess.

By the '70s, the number of carriers reached 700,000. The boys, and more girls, accumulated money and purchased nicer clothes, cars, and enrolled in college. However, the popular, plentiful after-school routes steadily shifted to early morning hours, as locally owned newspaper companies came under consolidated national company ownership. Convenient afternoon newspaper routes were on the decrease.

Through the decades, what other first job, as a steady part-time position before or after school, existed for hundreds of thousands of children? The youngsters overcame obstacles, acquired opportunities, soared to more advantages whether or not they were ever officially celebrated. Recognition of the American icon was secured in statues, the commemorative stamp, and in national newspaper carrier exhibits like the ones at Valley Forge, Pennsylvania, and in the Newspaper Carrier Hall of Fame in Washington D.C. The displays showed how prevalent the year-round job for America's youth really was. And commemorates just how significant newspaper carrier assignments were for legions of children.

# CHAPTER 20
## REFLECTIONS

### Energetic, Athletic

Paul Meyer, in 1951, earned essential money for a trip from Tacoma to the Derby Downs in Akron, Ohio, to compete in the All-American Soap Box Derby. He won second place in the national, competitive entries. Not the top star, nevertheless, Paul received congratulations and a hand shake from a star: Ronald Reagan. Besides Derby costs, he saved for his coming college tuition. His route, of 200 customers, kept him active. Once in college his energetic state did not subside. He qualified as a rower on the University of Washington award-winning crew team.

Several decades forward, past paperboy and University of Washington Husky, Ron Haringa, rows with Paul three or four times a week. They belong to a rowing club, founded in 1989 by senior men over age 60. The crew chose a descriptive name: The Ancient Mariners. Their strenuous, Olympic-class sport requires strength, in core muscles and the entire body. Like Paul, Ron was energetic during his paper carrier years. He pedaled his bicycle with his stuffed canvas bag up Holman Road, a long hill used for qualifying in Soap Box Derby contests. Still rowing, both men attribute their athletic prowess to physical development on the paper route.

Other former carriers attest to lifetime physical benefits. Beginning in 1945, Bruce Adams bicycled 10 miles every day for three years on dirt roads, rolling papers as he rode to serve 100 customers. With controlled muscles, he biked using no hands other than for shooting the rolled paper into the customer's delivery tube.

A small tyke, Tom Lewis pulled a wagon loaded with empty bottles he collected for deposit money. By age 10, he hefted a full canvas bag seven days a week that built strength in his shoulders, arms and wrists. When time allowed, he played tennis. Then played more often, making the varsity Garfield High School team in Seattle. Tom has now crossed the age 70 line. Slim, athletic and enthusiastic, he teaches tennis to school children, coordinates competitions, serves as co-captain for his winning team. Amidst his work, many activities and responsibilities, the "senior" paperboy plays tennis five times a week.

These robust fellows are not setting age-records as senior sportsmen, not the oldest to compete in athletic events. They do demonstrate sensible, frequent activity instilled from childhood. The excess weight in a scruffy bag that paperboys carried didn't morph into a pudgy Pillsbury dough boy, even with daily snacks and donut stops. Not slouching on the couch, the carriers scuttled outside with the bag slung on their shoulders on a strong spine.

## Physical, and the Social

In addition to physical strength, developing appropriate behavioral skills resonates with former carriers. On his seven-day route for six years, Mike Rhodes stated, "The paper route, a classroom unto itself, was more than just a business venture." In his routine, Mike had "experienced and tasted a real slice of life that would stay with me forever."

Jack Moore delivered seven days a week both morning and afternoon. From his experience, he said, "Most of my life lessons, I learned on my paper route."

Though Jim Rudy's 1964 trip to Italy re-routed him to public high school, his maturity stayed on track. "The BEST thing about my paper route: the life lessons I learned, which included self-reliance, honesty, responsibility---I never was late or skipped a day without a capable substitute." He still does not skip any rounds. With Gipper, his gentle golden retriever, Jim visits Littleton Adventist Hospital twice a week, with "heartfelt conversation and equally heartfelt tail wags" that bring smiles from the sick.

Whether it was learning from multiple mistakes, acquiring social skills with every stratum of society, coping with difficult adults, the newspaper carriers developed wisdom early in life. Dr. Reed's report in 1915 stated, "The boys ability to analyze human nature was there and later on will be a valuable asset." Children, unable to extrapolate and explain the meaning in their lessons before reaching adulthood, nevertheless, held the wisdom in their heart and head.

## Accountable

Money management had to begin the first week of the route and continue for the course of the job. In the case of Jim Rudy, this continued to his three brothers, Dale, Greg, and Tom. All four worked under the same discipline. As Jim said, "I learned self-reliance and the value of money. My parents loved me by NOT giving me an allowance. I pity kids today who have everything just given to them, and never learn or prepare themselves for adult life."

Parents did not hand out an allowance, a "foreign term" as Dale Wirsing expressed. Instead, children handed money to mother. For Jesse Montoya's fun times swimming in the Columbia River, bicycling around town, selling papers--- especially the Apple Blossom Festival editions---his good times lifted him less than his parent's pride in their son. For his sharing with family, "Mom was so grateful and Dad so proud. Their praise really kept me going."

For Harry Ansted, the best part of his morning route over five years was "feeling a part of family finances." Though Harry bought his own clothes, met any of his expenses, he "contributed most of the earnings to family support."

Even when cash wasn't handed to mother, money impacted the children beyond the tangible financial benefits. Bill Gamel understood he was, "expected to buy all my clothing, sports gear, bike. I never ever expected any help or anything from my family. The independence gave me a great feeling of strength and self-confidence that has helped in my adult life."

Tom Rockne's father planted the importance of a college education, and Tom met that goal. Saving money was key to enrolling at Iowa State University, and so was his self-confidence to pursue his degree. Bob Brink, on his route for seven years, said, "I found success in the business community. I could earn my way. I believed in myself. This confidence was jump-started as a result of my years as a news delivery boy, and that led to two law degrees."

The instilled self-reliance lasted and expanded when tackling longer jobs. A major shift in the twenty-first century to lower teen employment connects to the lack of pre-teen experiences and initiative. Until the 1990's, 70 percent of newspaper carriers were youngsters, and these carriers "gained critical skills from early work experiences." Then their numbers sharply receded. In a few years the impact was apparent. At the same time, the United States shifted from a manufacturing economy to a service industry, and the interactive social skills for service positions became ever more essential.

Expanding beyond lessons taught by parents and school teachers, paperboys honed their ability to be dependable and accountable. The daily act of plopping papers on the porch was less relevant alongside the involved process of collecting and then managing that money. Also, the subscriber-management factored in, because of those few contentious, crabby customers.

# Building

To augment their practical street knowledge, some enrolled in vocational training, which further enhanced career opportunities. Bill Ruth's wisdom was founded on his early experiences. From delivering the morning *Johnstown Democrat*, then his excellent World War II military service, and his master's degree at The Ohio State University, he developed the first adult vocational education system in Ohio. Unlike Dr. Reed's proposal in Seattle (her plan was thrust aside), Mr. Ruth implemented his education program for Ohio schools. He believed in and applied his paperboy knowledge. "I learned more about life from my paper route than I did in any college education, including my speaking and listening skills."

In the vocational program, Bill selected applicants similar to a Tom Rockne, Sam Rarig, Tom Lewis: ones who held an Eagle Scout standing and paper route experience. He knew such candidates, with their practical basic skills, were reliable and determined. They went to "the top of the application pile."

# Hired

After 10 years in *Main Street School* with the *Tacoma News Tribune*, augmented with structured classroom learning, Carole Bergeron entered college. She enrolled through her paper route savings. With graduation, leaving the University of Puget Sound to begin teaching, the experience in her first job interview was repeated in subsequent interviews. The employer was impressed and accepted her, specifically crediting her paper route years. The carriers' formal education, complemented with practical experiences produced beneficial results. These habits in an active, entry-level, daily job created an attitude plus experiences for being ready to work.

# Lasted Longer

An adolescent requested a paper route for the money. Dick Kalivoda wanted a bicycle. He earned and also learned. His maturity outlasted the bike. Later, in a full-time position, Dick "realized paperboys acquired necessary skills for working with people." Gaining tangible possessions, carriers gained more as subtle shifts in behavior broadened with intangible benefits.

Curious and humorous, carriers invariably made mistakes, adjusted, and persevered. A boy also nurtured an innate love to be competitive. He found it exhilarating to better himself. Like Jesse Montoya, paper carriers didn't dwell on appearance or socio-economic status, but worked to improve their circumstances.

Yes, the funds mattered, particularly for family food, for shoes, and school fees. The motivation mattered every bit as much and lasted longer than money. A paperboy earned his base pay, about one-quarter or one-third of the collection funds, and pocketed tips for his reliable, efficient service. Tips were not automatic. Hitting his stride, his capability opened wider. He obtained a second route, was appointed station manager, solicited new subscribers, and supplemented his earnings with extra seasonal jobs.

## ABC's

Reflecting on past decades, in their brief period as a paperboy, former carriers stated that first lessons learned in *Main Street School* continued to influence decisions and directions. These experiences affected higher education, a lucrative career, raising a family, supporting a church, strengthening community services. The carriers' basic ABC's resonate in the retained enthusiasm for their first job. A: Active, Appreciative, and Accountable. B: Belonging, Building and Balancing. C: Capable, Confident with Common sense.

Delivering newspapers was not a glorious, grand nor noble task. Still, young carriers regularly fulfilled the humble act as though it stood foremost in community service. A child stepped forward to complete the aggregate of adult efforts from journalists, editors, pressmen, photographers, salesman, deliverymen, and more. Yet, it was the paperboy who closed the clasp on a circling chain of information for the community. Entrusted to the hands of children, a multi-million dollar industry routinely reached the customers.

The daily newspapers that youth delivered were not "just about communication but also about community" as stated in *The Functions of Newspapers in Society*. This connection with citizens strengthened in the paperboys who were central in lacing the community together.

## Free to Soar

Besides the benefit of funds, before long carriers recognized freedom and friendships as primary benefits. Warren Thor, covering a seven-mile path all seven days, considered his "self-reliance" the best part of a paper route. Bill Gamel's "independence," and Vernon Franze's "self sufficiency" rated highest. Many concurred. Charlie Fry, contributing most of his money to his family in 1938, continued into the next decade delivering papers during his law school classes. His route was fun, but the most valuable element: "freedom." From the self-assurance in managing a route, managing money, he developed an independence that directed him forward.

That same importance existed for other individuals. Doug Larson, in spite of his struggles in Lincoln, Nebraska with breaking windows, being bitten by dogs, and "scared in heavy blizzards," he valued his work because it, "gave me freedom."

When Terri Hazlewood, in 1978, approached her father to ask for a bicycle, he replied the same as many parents: earn the money. And so Terri began her daily *Herald Examiner* route, seven mornings a week, in Torrance, California. Responsibly collecting each month, "though I hated it!" Terri soon proved to her father that she'd obtain her goal. And once she owned the aqua blue Schwinn Strand Cruiser with white wall tires, the bike "lived in my bedroom for three years. It was too special to be in a dirty old garage." Her determination expanded to more goals.

Further jobs, that built her savings, led to a Toyota Corolla. Her commitment to setting goals didn't stop. From her successful efforts, she soared. Through her pattern of determination, Terri became an airline pilot. Today, a wife, mother of two little charmers, she operates in a world-wide fleet. Captain Hazlewood flies the B747-400s for United Parcel Service, UPS. Reflecting on the start to her goals, she states, "I very much value my experiences as a paperboy."

As does Ron Petersen. In spite of horrific weather, his enjoyable time in Utah as a paperboy when he watched and listened to the B-36 planes zoom overhead, inspired him to enter the Air Force. Serving as navigator, Lt. Col Petersen spent 25 years on active, rewarding duty.

## Topped by the Best

*A poem the English teacher read in class, what were those lines? "No man is an island, entire of himself. Every man is a part of the mainland." Yeah, something like that.* Savoring the solitude on an early morning round, a carrier's quiet hour felt good. As John Wilson said, "the route gave me time to think." But a child balanced that freedom with lots of friends and friendly public encounters. He was part of his family and the community with an identity as a paperboy. This placed him in the best of both worlds: an independent individual and an active member.

Paperboys didn't wander down streets with no purpose, lost without direction or connection. The parameter of a carrier's route belonged to him and he belonged in his world. While his financial and educational benefits increased, so did social gains within his sphere.

Vernon Franze knew he was the oldest of six and didn't separate from responsibility as a big brother. Max Fiske was attached to his "best family" in a link with leeway. Close to the family, yet not confined, the carrier further enlarged his involvement with other carriers and customers to fill a larger place in the neighborhood. Henry Petroski, delivering the

*Long Island Press,* appreciated being involved in something bigger than the usual school boy identification.

Like a gifted sculptor, circulation manager, Mr. Francis Pike, shaped the lives of his carriers with a valuable identification. Connected to the company, which held a vital position in the core of the community, the *Columbia Daily Tribune* boys belonged to Columbia, Missouri. They possessed both freedom and attachment as a business-team member.

# Belonging

Struggling with shyness, when David Merrill picked up his bundle of papers on Main Street in John Day, a town in eastern Oregon, his pride elevated, knowing he, "held a role in the community." Sitting tall in the saddle, as his horse trotted through the snow, the school boy felt pleased with meeting his early morning assignment for residents. Seeing, hearing, smelling, really sensing what was occurring in his town, his shyness began to recede.

Bob Barr, disgusted after two years with the train arriving late from San Francisco, focused on the job advantages and switched to the local *Klamath Herald & News.* He earned money, but more importantly, he held a, "feeling of performing a needed service, of accomplishing something. Being a paperboy was one of the best growing experiences."

In the midst of World War II, Burt Wilson delivered the *Sacramento Bee.* The next year he changed to the morning *San Francisco Examiner.* Though the war raged in Europe and the Pacific, Burt was secure in Sacramento, where "everyone knew everyone." The 10-year-old enjoyed fun and camaraderie with other carriers. And for him, the best element, "having a route was like a second family." Identifying with his customers and his community, Burt belonged.

Though newspaper delivery in the early morning hours left some less personally known by their subscribers, many other carriers enjoyed recognition and appreciation by the adults. Folks in Anchorage, who scooted Bill Gamel inside to warm by the stove, gave him further attachment to his town. Bill was independent yet connected.

Earning the money, Bruce Adams purchased a new Schwinn Imperial bicycle in 1946. He won incentive trips sponsored by the *Seattle Times.* Yet, Bruce considered the "best part of his paper route: the people. Met a lot more people as a member of the community."

Don Jones' older brother passed his *Columbia Daily Tribune* route to Don. This continued the family's association with customers for another four years, 1948 to 1952. Don knew his subscribers "very well." Living in Ashland, Missouri, a small congenial place, he "knew nearly everyone in town." An established resident, "fifty years later I'm still enjoying many of those wonderful relationships." His early interaction with the newspaper customers secured an excellent feeling of belonging, right on through the decades.

After four years delivering the *Mount Vernon News*, Gary Kost changed jobs. However, he did not change his interest in one customer's daughter, Beth Banning. Gary and Beth graduated from The Ohio State University, returned to their All-American City, married, taught school in Mount Vernon and in 2012 celebrated their Golden Wedding Anniversary. From his paper route, they followed a route to the finest friendship.

Tom Skipton, in Marietta, Ohio, began at age 9, managing three papers: *Marietta Times*, the *Pittsburg Press*, and the *New York Times*. His first delivery to neighbors and friends headlined the end of World War II. For the next five years, the people relied on him, knowing "their paperboy" would be along shortly, especially after he bought a bike. Tom appreciated the "very nice people who remained friends for life."

Enjoying adult-level discussions with the manager and members of the community, the carriers saw their position as good. And friendly subscribers made the route even better. For lively children, meeting with carriers, in similar circumstances, at their drop-off spot created...

## The Best Place

The newspaper sub-station, a clubhouse or shack, was simple, scruffy, and as ordinary as the members who congregated there each day. It was a beehive of chatter, giggles, and activities. The boys played jokes, played cards, and competed with each other. Certainly the fun station, for refining real friendships with buddies, registered as the best.

Al Thurmond, after waiting for a route, joined boys in 1942 at a "paper shack located on a street at 85th NW near 15th Avenue, by the Seattle city limits. The old garage with a dirt floor" served as their clubhouse and was managed by a high school boy who "was very nice and helpful." His little brother also delivered a route, and his younger sister was in Al's class at school. The neighborhood gathering place was a center of talk and laughter as boys folded their *Seattle Times* papers, always filled with news about World War II. For Al, the best part of his route was, "the friendship of the other carriers."

## Bonds

Jim Kavanaugh, hurrying through cold Idaho mornings to reach the substation, arrived to a potbelly stove that warmed him, and so did the "camaraderie with other carriers." The jabber, laughter and competition for who folded their *Spokesman Review* papers the fastest, such good feelings stayed with him as he moved through the freezing dark, alone.

Delivering in 1942, he felt energized realizing his friends also handled the blackout conditions on empty streets.

Dale Rudy swished past the customers' homes pedaling his Schwinn Wasp. With 95 customers, and in 1963 the *Rocky Mountain News* editions were thick, he needed the heavy duty wheels with extra strong spokes. He porched his papers, as much as 90 feet from the street, trying on good days to reduce his delivery time. "If you got done with your route early, you'd find your buddies and help them. Afterwards we would go to the Dutch Boy" for those tasty donuts. His focus centered on friends rather than a monotonous task.

An exemplary station, one with sports teams, offered a dual identification as paperboy and team player. Whether they were baseball or basketball teams, a bowling league, a winning station team, carriers spent additional daily time together bonding as a unit.

Long after the throwing arm relaxed, after graduation and careers drew paperboys in various directions, the spirit held. Being a paperboy wasn't always simple. At times the route was hard, but the challenges didn't harden him. More than the funds, the friends and freedom counted the most, and often still matter. Luke Chase expressed what fellows experienced. He delivered in the 1940s. And 70 years later stated, "for each of us old paperboy grads, when we meet each other, we share a bond of fraternity that is truly unique."

Glen Carter holds the same attitude. Yes, nettlesome kids existed at the shack where Glen was station manager, but he could "count on the fellows." They've remained friends through the years. Lee Desilet met with three buddies at the bakery in Lewiston, Idaho, each morning for a Butterhorn. They still talk about those fun days, regardless of now living in different locations.

The bonds that formed at the drop-off location, at a newspaper office, the donut shop, wherever they gathered, strengthened between carriers as well as within the individual's development. An American icon grew in stature, filled out his mature status, shaped his character by the daily discipline of delivering papers. Balanced between the occasional adversities and his numerous advantages, a cheerful attitude dominated.

## Attributes

Youth requested paper routes for the money; the parents, mangers, and politicians expounded platitudes about building character. For children, character was not a concern. They wanted to finger coins in the pocket. It was later they recognized a route affected their childhood. Any number of leaders and writers certainly recognized the early influence, as is apparent in the frequency with which it is stated in autobiographies and biographies.

A voice that spoke above the others, because of his irrefutable greatness was

General George C. Marshall. The five star General served under President Roosevelt during World War II as the Chief of Staff for the United States Army. Later, he served as Secretary of State for President Truman. In 1953 General Marshall received the Nobel Peace Prize for creating the vital Marshall Plan, which rebuilt a crumbled Europe.

In reference to paperboys, General Marshall stated, "No group of boys represent more truly the typical American qualities of alertness and initiative than those youngsters who serve the public as newspaper carriers. Any boy who has mastered the many lessons to be learned in this teen-age career of newspaper work is already started towards the full manhood, which has always characterized the American soldier."

From the same era, renowned journalist Ernie Pyle, reporting one of his hundreds of valuable World War II newspaper stories, wrote a statement by a medical officer in Italy. Interviewing Captain Allamon, who told Pyle, "If he could pick a company suited best for warfare, he would choose all ex-newspaper boys, who shift for themselves so early in life they build up great initiative that helps carry them through battle."

## Strength

With hair combed and parted, shirt tucked in, not slouching, an experienced paperboy stood straight and maintained eye contact as he spoke with adults. His big-boy polished manners felt natural. Ready to move on, carriers moved forward and upward to positions as: teacher, chaplain, engineer, principal, CEO, doctor, professor, attorney, realtor, military officer, broker, salesman, contractor, airline pilot, editor, manager, writer, through every career and organization. Accomplishments written into memoirs and biographies, and a lengthy directory for the Newspaper Carrier Hall of Fame, all attest to extensive qualities in the child's first job.

Decade on decade, through the core of the American Century, millions (in total) managed paper routes. A simple appearance covers over the complex attributes that developed in their childhood with this early responsibility, which impacted their character. Legions of reliable, accountable youth serving their community impacted the American character.

Assessing a paper route as a coveted, respected position, Harve Harrison and Dick Irvine considered it a privilege to have their entry-level job. John Kearns felt proud to be a carrier. Climbing hills, slipping in the snow, assaulted by mean dogs, such challenges declined in significance for the carriers as they walked forward through reality. Granting a nostalgic pass at the era of paperboys, if people pause to peer beneath the image of a likeable icon into the substantive influence on vast numbers of youngsters, the importance is recognized. The children's paper route widened into more jobs, longer jobs. A paperboy began as a preteen, often by age 9 or 10, and worked for two or three hours a day. His fast pace did not slacken. The more he worked, the more he accomplished later.

## Balanced

Fortunately, the Child Labor Amendment of 1924 never became law. Rather than prohibiting part-time work, the newspaper industry countered with a reasonable code. At least reasonable for a child who was 12, or had a way to step around the age and hour restriction.

Learning to balance on the handlebars of his big brother's bicycle, 6-year-old Jesse soon balanced his playtime with selling *Wenatchee World* papers after school. As though a juggler, the little merchant held a steady rhythm of school, chores and jobs. If problems occurred, throwing him off, he quickly challenged himself to re-balance. His 1947 photograph with Mr. Woods instilled more enthusiasm, which grew stronger through the decades as he continued to contribute to his Wenatchee community.

And across the country, in the flat farmland of western Ohio, another lad in 1947 responsibly handled newspapers, for the daily *Bellefontaine Examiner*. Ed Boblitt had begun at age 8 as a carrier assistant. By age 9, he walked his own afternoon route, # 26. Before long, he owned a bike and sped on his way. During the 1950 Thanksgiving weekend, the Buckeye Blizzard swirled across the open fields of Logan County, around Bellefontaine. On Monday, Ed bundled up against the record cold and delivered the severe storm news. He had turned 12, of age to be assigned a route. He held to his routine through the awful polio epidemics in 1949 and 1952. The paperboy commemorative postage stamp in October, 1952, depicted ones like this busy boy. However, his interest that October centered on the local photo and news story about his mode of delivery.

Now into five years on his route and age 14, he was "tall enough to reach the pedals," he was given. His grandfather and father crafted a unicycle at the A.J. Miller plant where they worked. Staying on time for his route and doing his newspaper sales for the Mary Rutan Hospital, Ed caught time to practice hopping on the unicycle seat, pushing off with his right foot and wobbling forward. In five days he conquered the challenge. With that, he added his canvas bag slung to one side, (no handlebars, no basket, no rear fender), shifted his weight as necessary, sat erect but not stiff, and biking on the sidewalk, porched his papers. He could ride down steps maintaining his balance.

The *Bellefontaine Examiner* did a short article and photograph about their agile paper carrier. The Associated Press (AP) picked up on the story. An ordinary, reliable teenager was about to put his county seat in the national eye. At the request of LIFE magazine, photographer Joe Munroe went to Bellefontaine. Ed was excused from school for two days while Mr. Munroe photographed him riding on roads, streets, porching papers. On June 15, 1953 his story and pictures appeared in LIFE magazine, in the same issue with the special-feature, colored photos of Queen Elizabeth II's coronation. Ed knew everyone by name in his small town. For certain, they all knew him now.

He was very considerate with people who wrote from all over the country, California to New York, asking about the unicycle. He hand-drew exact blueprints and replied with the construction explanations for anyone who requested them.

Polite with the public attention, he balanced it with his private interest. From a simple, little unicycle he turned to a big, complex car. Balancing his time with extra jobs cleaning offices, pumping gas, washing cars, along with managing his paper route, he purchased a 1936 Chrysler four-door sedan. He paid $35 for his first car. By age 16 he gave up the unicycle and used his next vehicle, 1947 Studebaker. With high school graduation, he ended his paper route after eight years. He was moving on. College, career, marriage, these beckoned. However, when benefit groups wanted the novelty of a unicyclist at an event, he volunteered to ride the unicycle to help them raise money.

Though one time he fell short of helping a person. An adult driver rolling through the streets in Bellefontaine, not familiar with a unicycle and paperboy, turned his head to watch Ed. As every paperboy knows, look forward when going forward. This driver looked back to follow Ed's pedaling. Ed heard the fender crunch. He saw the crumbled hood. The stunned driver had crashed into a tree, and was left off balance.

At times, adults could be very unbalanced, whether it was trying to stop children from working, expelling a boy after visiting the Vatican, hiding behind curtains to avoid payment responsibility, placing a fresh tomato in each lunch box---well, that one might be excused.

Holding paperboys to endless rules was unnecessary, and worse, un-enjoyable, so carriers found ways to have fun, to challenge themselves, to be tested by competitive interests.

## Creating Little Merchants

Starting out with tousled hair, cold nose dripping, dirty hands, the paperboy was not polished, pretentious, or perfect, and sometimes not punctual or polite, especially if he decided, "Enough!" Unlike a Swiss train on an exact schedule, the boy's timeliness improved as his maturity expanded by having mastered multiple mistakes. His fun and freedom matched the friends he enjoyed, balancing both like a bicycle, or unicycle, rolling forward. His path across the lawn was not destructive. A broken window was bad but not devastating damage. Caught in devilment, he wasn't innocent; yet, the naive innocence of a child came through. The customers enjoyed these mere boys in men's boots who managed as productive *little merchants*—as *paperboys*—contributing to the good life in the golden era of youth delivering newspapers.

# NOTES

The abbreviation "Int" stands for interviews. Following the completion of a fact-finding questionnaire, further questions were answered through telephone interviews, personal meetings, and additional written interviews.

## Preface

The Museum of History and Industry, MOHAI, located in Seattle, Washington. Lorraine McConaghy, Ph.D. the senior historian for the Museum, conducted classes in *Nearby History A Seminar for Researchers and Writers*, designed to document ordinary neighborhood and community history. The 15 independent researchers and Dr. McConaghy were key to expanding the newspaper carrier project.

Interviews (Int) occurred with friends, neighbors, family members, church members, in the Northshore Senior Center, the Golden Kiwanis, Probus, readers of *Prime Time* (senior citizen newspaper), military reunion, community museum contributors, circulation managers' conferences, and with individuals told of the research by their friends.

## Part I Struggle

Picture of Mr. Rufus Woods, President and Publisher of *The Wenatchee Daily World*, and Jesse Montoya, photographed in the Wenatchee newspaper office, May, 1947.

Paperboy Jesse Montoya was included in *The Wenatchee World's* publication, *Buckle of the Power Belt* for the 100th anniversary of the newspaper. His chapter: "A Street Urchin's Tale, Jesse Montoya 1946-1951" p.134.

The *Wenatchee World* staff writer, Sheila Graves, featured Jesse Montoya's paperboy days in an Accent article on August 11, 1996, titled "Extra, Extra, Read All About It."

Opening chapters of *Buckle of the Power Belt* documents the story of Rufus Woods' struggles and lasting success in creating a community and the Washington North Central region.

Wenatchee, Washington, Apple Blossom Festival originated in 1920, expanded over the decades with parades, sports events, concerts, benefits, a queen and her court.

DDT is a synthetic insecticide: dichlorodiphenyltrichloroethane. Through Rachel Carson's publication of *The Silent Spring*, 1962, the use of DDT on agriculture crops ended in 1972.

On Newspaperboy Day and in the booklet, *Circulation Management Training Program*, 1974, leaders claimed more than one million youth as newspaper carriers in North America. p31. Subtracting Canadian paperboys, total was nearly one million.

Carl Lane (author's older brother) delivered the daily *Mount Vernon News* and the weekly *Fredericktown News* in central Ohio. Because of him, the paperboy project developed.

Pickenpaugh, Roger, Buckeye Blizzard, Ohio and the 1950 Thanksgiving Storm. Nov, 1950.

Goldberg, Ronald *America in the Twenties*. Urban defined as centers of 2,500 or more. Over 59 million live in communities of fewer than 8,000. Intro. p. 19.

Nasaw, David, *Children of the City*, Chap. 5 "The Newsies" collected data proving "nothing": p. 70, 71.

## Chapter 1: Wantin'

David Bowles wrote his Autobiography Journal. Widow Charlotte Bowles, excerpted the newsboy days, and further expanded on his experiences in interviews: September 7, 2005, January 16, 2006, and February 8, 2010.

R. L. Polk & Company, Ellensburg & Kittitas County Directory, 1923-1924. Ellensburg, Washington, Public Library.

R. L. Polk & Company, Bellingham and Buyers' Guide, 1918. Northwest Room, Everett, Washington, Public Library.

Editor & Publisher, January 7, 1950. p. 10.The New York *Sun* began September 4, 1833. Heralded as the first continuing successful penny paper, "N.Y. *Sun* Achieved Success Early As Penny Newspaper."

Douglas, George, *The Golden Age of the Newspaper*, "A Bright and Shining Moment" Chap. 17, p.233.

Editor & Publisher, August 11, 1951, "Circulation Gain Greater than Population Growth." p. 7.

The Child Labor Amendment, 65 Congressional Record 10142, June, 1924.

Lee ,Alfred, *The Daily Newspaper in America, from Press to People*. States that ratified. p. 293.

American Federation of Labor. University of Washington, Seattle, Suzzalo Library

Lee, Alfred, *The Daily Newspaper in America, from Press to People*. FDR signed the code; effective March 12, 1934, p. 243, 295, 296.

State by state minimum age and hour restrictions, *Circulation Management Training Program*, p. 34.

Reed, Anna Y. *Newsboy Service: A study in Educational and Vocational Guidance*. Yonkers-on Hudson: World Book Co., 1917. Preface, p. ix. University of Washington, Suzzalo Library, Seattle.

R. L. Polk & Co., Inc. Seattle City Directory, 1915, 10 dailies for sale. Special Collections Room, University of Washington Suzzalo Library.

Nasaw, David, *Children of The City: At Work and At Play*, Ch. 5, "The Newsies" p.68.

Goldberg, Ronald, *America in the Twenties*, p. 19

Editor & Publisher, June 17, 1933, *Des Moines Register* p. 34.; Stodghill, p. 9. The 588,000 is not a verified United States-only figure. University of Washington, Suzzalo.

McDaniel, Henry, *The American Newspaperboy*, Introduction p.17.

Governor Langlie salutes paperboys, 1949 *Seattle Times* published photo. Personal collection of Jack Gahan.

Editor & Publisher, January 5, 1952, Des Moines Register states 6,500 carriers; University of Washington, Suzzalo.

1962, *Tacoma News Tribune* banquet program saluting carriers locally and stating national figures. Personal collection of Kathy Grab.

1965, *Seattle Times* recognition of paperboys. The carriers' newspaper, *Young Merchant* October, 1965. Collection of Glen Carter

Editor & Publisher, July 31, 1965, *Indianapolis Star & Indianapolis News*, University of Washington, Suzzalo.

*Seattle Times*, November 11,1918, University of Washington, Suzzalo, microfiche.

Bowles, David, personal autobiography collection.

Bristow, Nancy, The deadliest of epidemics, *American Pandemic*, "Lost Worlds" p. 3

Cooper, John, Woodrow Wilson's stroke, *Woodrow Wilson*, "The League Fight" p. 533.

*Seattle Times* article reports *Union Record* paper closed, September, 1919; University of Washington, Suzzalo Library

Presbrey, Frank, *The History & Development of Advertising*, Chap.LIX "World War Demonstrates Great Power of Advertising," p.565

Lee, Alfred, *The Daily Newspaper in America*. Advertising well organized by 1920s, p. 360.

Bennett, Charles, *Integrity in a Changing World*. Opening chapter explains establishment of the ABC audits.

Postol, Todd, *Journal of Social History*. "Creating the American Newspaper Boy" Transition of hawker to carrier routes. By 1930s, paperboys are 70 percent on routes, p.328

## Chapter 2: Wishin'

Henry McDaniel, *The American Newspaperboy*. Use of contracts, "Approximately 70 per cent of all carriers work under written contracts." Of the contracts "75 per cent" require parent signature. p. 118.

Glen Carter retained his copy of the *Seattle Times* contract. Jim Leo held his copy for the *Everett Daily Herald*.

Editor & Publisher, Oct. 7, 1950, The *Journal-Times*, Wisconsin, carriers sign three-year contracts. p. 58.

Ibid., Mar. 1, 1952, "Wood Survey Details Metropolitan Techniques." Survey finds 68.1 percent have written contracts. p. 44.

## Chapter 3: Waitin'

"Brave"

Grand Coulee Dam, Washington. Information from the U.S. Department of the Interior.

Clifford Grulee, *The Child in Health and Disease*, Fig. 8 Weight and Stature development chart, p. 17. for Leroy Modine.

"Behave"

Editor & Publisher, February 2, 1952, "Dailies' Circulation exceeds 54,000,000." p.7.

George Kimball, *At the Fights, American Writers on Boxing*, the Golden Gloves, p.52.

## Chapter 4: Enclave

Int with Henry Petroski, December, 2006. Initiation details in *Paperboy: Confessions of a Future Engineer.*

Unsupervised shacks were hotbeds: John Kearns Int. Aug, 2005, "tough older boys set fire to the station"; James Grout, Int June, 2006, "rough kids, some went to jail"; Jim McArthur Int. Dec. 2005, "Boys being boys, we lost the shack" Rough damage and noise closed shacks.

Editor & Publisher, August 8, 1953, "New Bedford S-T Motto: Sports Instead Courts." p.48.

Editor & Publisher, February 14, 1953, "ICMA Carrier Training Program Is Launched, Carrier Boy Orchestra." p.49.

The federal Child Labor Amendment adopted by the Senate, June 2, 1924. 65 Congressional Record 10142. Everett Library. Submitted to the state legislatures for ratification.

Alfred Lee, *The Daily Newspaper In America*. Progress toward ratification of the Child Labor Amendment, p. 293.

## Part II Strive

Int with Doug Coleburn, November, 2006. About to collect from bootlegger named "Sea Cat" Doug had to run. "Sea Cat" was set to shoot people.

## Chapter 5: The Routine is Routine

Int with Leonard Lair, January, 2006, personal papers of Mr. Lair as Fastpitch Champion in United States Men's Major Fastpitch Championship.

*Mount Vernon News*, April 7, 1966. All-American City awarded by LOOK Magazine and National Municipal League. Mount Vernon Library, Mount Vernon, Ohio.

## Chapter 6: Morning Has Opened

Jim Kavanaugh, Walter Dreyfus, Walter Johnson, many paperboys, awakened independently with the common alarm clock, before daylight.

LIFE magazine, Jan 12, 1942: cover title, Pacific Coast Defense. The man-made night, create blackouts by burning oil, tar, wet coal, p. 10.

## Chapter 7: Main Street School

The *Columbus Dispatch*, Sunday, September 4, 1949. Photo and "Dispatch Carrier Title Goes to Station 52 Team."

Henry McDaniel, *The American Newspaperboy*. Study revealed newspaperboys are more influenced by district managers than by teachers. p130

Anna Reed, *Newsboy Service: A Study in Educational and Vocational Guidance* Prefatory Note, vii; p. 158; p.132.

Editor & Publisher, "Newspaperboy" April 14, 1956, Renowned syndicated columnist George Crane, p. 112.

Herbert Huffman, minister of music for Broad Street Presbyterian Church, Columbus, Ohio, founded the Columbus Boychoir, 1937. Howard Wagner notes.

## Chapter 8: Thank God, only 24 Hours

Russ Tobey, int. Sept 2006, shared his flight log book showing the record from his first flying lesson, to his solo flight. *Examiner-Enterprise* published a 25 Years Ago clip of Russ Tobey's solo.

David Nasaw, *Children of the City*, Chap 10, p. 145. "agents of child welfare organizations...were empowered to arrest children violating child labor laws."

Russell Baker, *Growing Up*, Chap 11, "I could balance forty pounds" p. 193.

Henry Petroski, American Scientist, May-June, 2002, "Delivering Papers", Bundles could weigh 50 pounds. p. 218.

Clifford Grulee, *Physical Growth and Development*, Table 2. Stature and Weight of Children. p.18.

Chris Harrald, *The Cigarette Book*. "First puffs" p. 95.

## Chapter 9: Aches, Ailments

Terry Graedon, *The People's Pharmacy, Home Remedies*. Remedy: sting, p. 32; toothpaste, p. 35; onion, p. 34; colds, p. 48, 49.

Mary Ruebush, *Why Dirt is Good*. The 5 rules: "Let them Eat Dirt" p. 65.

Henry Petroski, *Paperboy Confessions of a Future Engineer*. Of 3,000 carriers, *Long Island Press*, over 100 at a time had Asian flu, p. 339.

Jack Gahan int. February 8, 2007, personal notes.

Polio:

David Oshinsky, *Polio: An American Story*. By 1955, 40 million televisions in homes. p. 210.

Jeffrey Kluger, *Smithsonian* magazine. "Conquering Polio", first 60 years. p.85.

David Oshinsky, 1916, greatest number of polio cases, p. 162; Jeffrey Kluger, p.84.

Jeffrey Kluger, *Smithsonian*, "Conquering Polio", FDR lending his voice to founding the March of Dimes. p.85.

Int with Jack Gahan December 20, 2005, Jan 18 2006, February 8, 2007

Int with Roger Leed April 11, 2006; January 14, 2007

David Oshinsky, *Polio: An American Story*, 1949 epidemic, 42,000 cases, p.128.

Ibid. 1952, increase to 57,000 cases p. 161.

March of Dimes National Foundation produced annual posters to educate the public. The *1952 Polio Precautions* stated 4 instructions.

David Oshinsky, *Polio, An American Story*. Community health procedures: close theaters, swimming pools. p. 285.

Int with Nils Ladderud, December 22, 2005; October 1, 2012

Editor & Publisher, September 9, 1950, p. 62., "Play Polio Benefit."

Editor & Publisher, February 16, 1952, p.58."5th Polio Benefit Series,"

Editor & Publisher, October 18, 1952, p.46. "Aid in Iron Lung Drive,

David Oshinsky, *Polio: an American Story*. National Foundation for Infantile Paralysis, $66.9 million, highest contribution for charity, 1954 Agency table p. 239.

Jeffrey Kluger, *Smithsonian*, "Conquering Polio" By 1961 with vaccine 98 percent improvement, p.88.

## Chapter 10: Achates to Attacker

Int. and personal notes of newspaper carrier experiences with dogs.

## Chapter 11: Accidents

Seattle Times carrier newspaper, "Young Merchant" instructions. August, 1969.

Editor & Publisher, October 15, 1960, p. 53. "Boys, Prices, Rope" Rope replacing wire,

Seattle Times carrier newspaper, "Young Merchant," column "Good Deeds, Service:" John McArthur injury, August 1950.

## Chapter 12: I Can Do Better. Yes I Can

*Where Mountains Meet the Sea*, Alaska's Gulf Coast, Vo. 13, No. 1, 1986, Alaska Geographic.

Ibid. Cordova, p. 94.

Nicki Nielsen *From Fish and Copper, Cordova's Heritage and Buildings*. No. 124, 1984.

*John Glenn A Memoir*, Chap 12, p. 233. "Soviet Union shocked America."

Doris Kearns Goodwin, *Lyndon Johnson and the American Dream*. Economic

Opportunity Act, Jan. 1964.

Clifford Grulee, *The Child in Health and Disease*, Fig. 8 Weight and Stature table. p. 17.

Editor & Publisher, April 29, 1950, "Carrier Standards Urged Upon Papers," p. 28.

Todd Postol, *Journal of Social History*. "Creating the American Newspaper Boy," Vol. 31, 1997. Notes to the study, " Girls represented an insignificant proportion of route carriers." p. 341.

Alfred Lee, *The Daily Newspaper in America*. The 1934 survey included 2,520 girl carriers. p. 298.

David Nasaw, *Children of the City*. Chap 7, "The Little Mothers." Girls were present selling newspapers in the 1900-1920 study. p. 101-105.

Editor & Publisher, July 15, 1950, "Stodghill Stresses Need for Carrier PR Programs," 1949 Newspaperboy Day clippings "Cites Use of Girl Carriers" p.38.

Ibid., "ICMA to Consider Ban on Girl Carriers" June 10, 1950. Added to the ICMA 1930 resolutions, "Be it further resolved: That no girl be permitted to engage in newspaper work." p. 36.

## Chapter 13: The Raison d'etre for a Route

Seattle Times department store advertisements for children's clothes and for household wares, 1928. University of Washington, Suzzalo.

Seattle Times carrier newspaper, "Young Merchant." August, 1969. Cart and attachment cost.

Int with Ron Casto, Sept. 17, 2008, Marietta Times, Marietta, Ohio.

Editor & Publisher, May 5, 1951, "Inland Publishers Tell Ideas on Circulation," insurance policies available for carriers, p. 44.

Seattle Times carrier newspaper, "Young Merchant." October, 1952. Insurance available.

Int with Mike Hall, August 2, 2010. Spokane Daily Chronicle.

Int. with Ron Casto, Sept. 17, 2008, Marietta Times, Marietta, Ohio. Bonds assured payment of the wholesale bill if the carrier was unable to collect his total charges. The company returned bond funds when the carrier ended his route.

Editor & Publisher, May 5, 1951, "Inland Publishers Tell Ideas on Circulation" Bonds on a saving account basis, returned to carrier when he leaves. p.44.

Seattle Times carrier newspaper, "Young Merchant." July, 1969. Small claims fees.

Int with Jack Gahan, Feb. 7, 2007. Carriers use small claims court.

Robert Macklin, Circulation Management Training Program. 1974 "Those Hard-to-Collect Areas," take the matter to small claims court. p. 66.

## Chapter 14: Be

Anna Reed, Newsboy Service, A Study in Educational and Vocational Guidance. p. 132.

The Holy Bible, authorized King James version. Book of Matthew, Ch 7, versus 7, 8.

## Chapter 15: C. for Considerate, Compassionate. For Conversions, Christmas

Andy Dappen, Buckle of the Power Belt: Recollections of the Wenatchee World's First 100 Years. The publisher printed $500 in scrip to aid against the Depression. 1932. p.338.

Int with Bill Ruth, Sr. Sept. 2, 2005. Would have an "IOU from my Mother, therefore I was also a loan officer."

John Long, The Roanoke Times. Dec 27, 2007. "A tip at year's end." Newsboys Christmas card collection in the Salem Museum, Virginia.

## Chapter 16: Sensuous Sightings and Confused Silence

Andy Dappen, Buckle of the Power Belt: Recollections of the Wenatchee World's First 100 Years. 1937. p. 339.

Robert Skylar, Movie-Made America, A Culture History of American Movies. Chap. 11, p.175.

## Part III Soar

Seattle Times, Sept 28, 1924. Suzzalo Library, University of Washington. microfiche. Around the world flight.

Berg, Scott, Lindbergh. Chap. 1, "Karma" p. 5.

Dappen, Andy, Buckle of the Power Belt: Recollections of the Wenatchee World's First 100 Years. 1931. p. 337.

Int with Kent Sturgis. Sighting red Aurora Borealis, Fairbanks, Daily News-Miner, Mar. 4, 1957.

Grant, R.G., Flight: the Complete History. New York: D.K. Publishing, 2007.

Glenn, John, John Glenn, A Memoir. Part Four, Project Mercury, p. 257.

## Chapter 17: Dimes for Sweets  Dollars for Success

Int with Gene Chiodo. His brother, Don, who purchased the auto, was featured on the cover of Reminisce magazine, Aug/Sept, 2006, for promoting defense bonds.

## Chapter 18: Rewards, Prizes and Trips

Davenport Hotel, not an ordinary city hotel, was the social center of Spokane, the Inland Empire. The place to be seen for anyone of fame. Closed in 1985, reopened in 2002, more grand than ever. During World War II the sky lights were blackened with tar for blackouts.

Butte Daily Post, Dec. 15, 1930, Front page photo and column, "Wins High Honor." recognizes Jack Rodda.

Newspaper Boys of America, Inc. Headquartered in Indianapolis, Indiana. Commercial trade group for circulation supplies for paperboys and promotional material for training and retaining newsboys.

Washington Times, Dec. 24, 1930, Newsboys' Special edition. Headline: President to Meet Carriers Tomorrow. Front page: Newsboys Feast on Turkey at Hotel and Boys Visit Tomb of Unknown Soldier. Photo of Jack Rodda placing the wreath.

Postol, Todd, Journal of Social History. Vol. 31, Winter 1997, "Creating the American Newspaper Boy" In the 1930s, 70 percent are youth. p. 328.

Ibid., in 1936, 300 circulation departments conducting carrier sales programs. p. 329.

Int with Jack Gahan, Feb 7, 2007. Seattle Times carrier newspaper, Young Merchant, Oct. 1969 states, "1,300 newspaperboys visit Victoria."

Int with Joe Forsee, July 5, 2008, Washington, D.C. trip.

Seattle PI, June 4, 1961, front page, told of Seattle Times carriers stranded on Blake Island.

Goodwin, Doris Kearns, Lyndon Johnson and the American Dream. The Economic Opportunity Act for centers of economic poverty.

Editor & Publisher, June 13, 1959, Young Columbus trips. p.44.

Ibid., May 9, 1964, "U.S. Carrier Boys have Papal Blessing," p. 34.

## Chapter 19: Recognition: Statues, Salute, Stamps

Statues: Hughes, Barrie, The World Honors the News Carrier. Kingston, Ontario, Canada, "1895

Fountain and Newsboy Statue, Great Barrington," p. 16.

Alaska newsboy statue, estate of Robert Atwood, viewing arranged by Bill Gamel.

Salute: Editor & Publisher, Oct.1948, "Stodghill Is Father of Newspaperboy Day," p.10.

Ibid., Sept. 17, 1949, "Full Participation Urged on Newspaperboy Day," p.17.

Ibid., Oct. 1, 1949, "Schools, Clubs, Industry Promote Newspaper Week," p. 5.

Ibid., Aug 26, 1950, "Urge Wide Use of Radio on Newspaperboy Day," p.46.

Ibid., Oct. 3, 1953, "To the Newspaperboys of America," p.7

Ibid., Sept. 30, 1948, "Bob Hope Film Ready as Tribute to Boys," p.26.

Ibid., Sept. 17, 1949, "CNF Offers New Film for Newspaperboy Day," p.50.

Stamps: Postol, Todd, Winter 1997 Vol. 31, No. 2 "Creating the American Newspaper Boy," p. 340.

Editor & Publisher, Feb. 24, 1951, "Treasury Dept. Seeks Carrier Aid in Drive," p.48.

Ibid., Apr. 21, 1951, Carriers Congress Added to Defense Bond Drive," p. 42.

Ibid., Oct.11, 1952, "Government Big Guns Salute Newspaperboys," p. 12-13.

Ibid., Jan. 3, 1953, "Boy Stamp Sale, A Philatelic Record," p.40.

Ibid., Oct. 8, 1960, Salute to Boys in 2 TV Shows," p. 46.

Hughes, Barrie, The World Honors the News Carrier. "1974 Famous Newspaper Carriers of America Exhibit, Valley Forge, Pa." p.36.

Editor & Publisher, July 2, 1960, "ICMA Votes to Establish Newspaperboy Hall of Fame," p. 13.

Hughes, Barrie, The World Honors the News Carrier. "1974 ICMA Newspaper Carrier Hall of Fame, Reston, Virginia," p.31. (current Hall of Fame at the Newseum, Washington, D.C.)

## Chapter 20: Reflections

Jim Rudy featured in Recognition Reporter, "Jim and Gipper, Making a Difference" Littleton Adventist Hospital, April, 2011.

Reed, Anna, *Newsboy Service: A Study in Educational and Vocational Guidance*, p. 132.

Dappen, Andy, *Buckle of the Power Belt*. Jesse Montoya,"A Street Urchin's Tale" p. 136.

Knowledge @Wharton, March 7, 2007. "Why Teens Aren't Finding Jobs, and Why Employers Are Paying the Price" quoting Robert Rubrecht of Newspaper Association of America, 70 percent youth carriers. "Leveraging Early Work Experience" teens gain critical skills  Wharton School, University of Pennsylvania.

Bill Ruth, Ohio Veterans Hall of Fame, November 5, 2010 and personal papers of Bill Ruth.

Shaw, Donald and Charles McKenzie, *The Functions of Newspapers in Society*, Chap. 10, p. 139.

John Donne, 1580s Elizabethan poet and cleric in the Church of England wrote the poem, *No Man is an Island*.

Cray, Ed, *General of the Army: George C. Marshall Soldier and Statesman*.

George C. Marshall, *Newspaper Circulation*, Texas Circulation Managers' Association, The Steck Co., Austin, Texas, 1948. Quote attributed to General Marshall, p. 129

Pyle, Ernie, *Here's Your War*. Stories from the war front by renowned WW II journalist.

Ernie Pyle, *Newspaper Circulation*, Texas Circulation Managers' Association, The Steck Co., Austin, Texas, 1948. Quote attributed to Ernie Pyle. p.129.

Andrew Sum, of Northeastern University, "more you work now" Knowledge@Wharton, March 7, 2007.

Logan County Historical Society Museum in Bellefontaine, Ohio has Ed Boblitt's unicycle, photographs, letters and blueprints to construct a unicycle.

The Ohio Historical Society Archives/Library, Columbus, Ohio, has the original Joe Munroe photograph, which appeared in LIFE magazine, June 15, 1953.

# TO READ MORE

Alcabes, Philip, Dread: How Fear and Fantasy Have Fueled Epidemics From the Black Death to Avian Flu. New York: Public Affairs, 2009.

Baker, Russell, Growing Up. New York: New American Library St. Martin's Press, Inc., 1982.

Berg, A. Scott, Lindbergh. New York: Berkley Books, 1999.

Bennett, Charles O., Integrity in a Changing World, Seventy-five Years of Industry Self Regulation Through the Audit Bureau of Circulation. Chicago: The Mobium Press, 1989.

Bristow, Nancy K., American Pandemic: the Lost Worlds of the 1918 Influenza Epidemic. New York: Oxford University Press, 2012.

Burroughs, Harry E., Boys In Men's Shoes A World of Working Children. New York: The MacMillan Co.,1944.

Callahan, Patricia, "Delivering the News: Children Injured on Paper Routes Often Go Uninsured." Wall Street Journal, July 19, 2002.

Coontz, Stephanie, The Way We Never Were. New York: Harper Collins Inc., 1992.

Cooper, John Milton, Jr., Woodrow Wilson, A Biography. New York: Alfred A. Knopf, 2009.

Cray, Ed, General of the Army: George C. Marshall Soldier and Statesman. Maryland: Cooper Square Press, 2000.

Dappen, Andy, Buckle of the Power Belt: Recollections of The Wenatchee World's First 100 Years. World Publishing Co. Wenatchee, Washington, 2005.

Dolan, Michael, The American Porch: An Informal History of an Informal Place. Guilford, Ct: The Globe Pequot Press, 2002.

Douglas, George H., The Golden Age of the Newspaper. Westport, Conn: Greenwood Press, 1999.

Downie, Leonard Jr. and Robert G. Kaiser, The News About the News. New York: Alfred A. Knopf, 2002.

Emery, Edwin, The Press and America: An Interpretative History of the Mass Media. Englewood Cliffs, New Jersey: Prentice Hall Inc., 1972.

Glenn, John and Nick Taylor, John Glenn, A Memoir. New York: Bantam Books, 1999.

Goldberg, Ronald Allen, America in the Twenties. Syracuse, New York: Syracuse University Press, 2003.

Goodwin, Doris Kearns, Lyndon Johnson and the American Dream. New York: St. Martin's Press, 1991.

Graedon, Terry and Joe, The People's Pharmacy, Quick & Handy Home Remedies. Washington D.C.: National Geographic, 2011.

Grant, R. G., Flight: The Complete History. New York: D.K. Publishing, 2007.

Grulee, Clifford G. and Richard Cannon Eley, The Child in Health and Disease. Baltimore: Williams & Wilkins, 1948.

Gulley, Philip, Front Porch Tales. Sisters, Oregon: Questar Publishers, Inc., 1997.

Halberstam, David, The Fifties. New York: Fawcett Columbine, 1993.

Harrald, Chris and Fletcher Watkins, The Cigarette Book, The History and Culture of Smoking. New York: Skyhorse Publishing, 2010.

Harsanyi, David, Nanny State: How Food Fascists, Teetotaling Do-Gooders, Priggish Moralists, and Other Boneheaded Bureaucrats Are Turning America Into a Nation of Children. New York: Broadway Books, 2007.

Hughes, Barrie J. The World Honors the News Carrier. Kingston, Ontario, Canada: 1975.

Kimball, George & John Schulian, editors, At the Fights: American Writers on Boxing. New York: The Library of America, 2011.

Kluger, Jeffrey, Splendid Solution: Jonas Salk and the Conquest of Polio. New York: G.P. Putnam's Sons, 2004.

Kluger, Jeffrey, "Conquering Polio." Smithsonian magazine, April, 2005.

Lee, Alfred M., The Daily Newspaper in America: The Evolution of a Social Instrument. New York: The MacMillan Co. 1937.

Macklin, Robert A., Circulation Management Training Program. Washington, D.C. International Circulation Managers Association booklet, 1974.

Martin, Shannon E. and David A. Copeland Edited, The Functions of Newspapers in Society. Westport, Connecticut: Praeger Publishers, 2003.

McDaniel, Henry, The American Newspaperboy: A Comparative Study of His Work and School Activities. Los Angeles: Wetzel Publishing Co. Inc., 1941.

Members of the Texas Circulation Managers Association, Newspaper Circulation: Principles and Development of Modern Newspaper Circulation Methods for the Study and Training of the American Newspaper Boy. Austin, Texas: The Steck Co., 1948.

Nasaw, David, Children of the City: At Work and At Play. New York: Anchor Press /Doubleday, 1985.

Nielsen, Nicki J., From Fish and Copper, Cordova's Heritage and Buildings. Alaska Historical Commission Studies in History No. 124, 1984.

Oshinsky, David M., Polio: An American Story. New York: Oxford University Press, 2005.

Petroski, Henry, Paperboy Confessions of a Future Engineer. New York: Random House, 2002.

Petroski, Henry, "Delivering Papers." American Scientist, May-June, 2002.

Pickenpaugh, Roger, Buckeye Blizzard, Ohio and the 1950 Thanksgiving Storm. Baltimore, Md.: Gateway Press, Inc., 2001.

Postol, Todd Alexander, "Creating the American Newspaper Boy: Middle-Class Route Service and Juvenile Salesmanship in the Great Depression."Journal of Social History, Vol. 31, No. 2, Winter 1997.

Presbrey, Frank, The History and Development of Advertising. Garden City, New York: Doubleday, Doran & Co. Inc., 1929.

Pyle, Ernie, Here's Your War. New York: Black Dog & Leventhal Publishers, 2005.

Reed, Anna Y., Newsboy Service: A Study in Educational and Vocational Guidance. New York: World Book Co., 1917.

Ruebush, Mary, Ph.D., Why Dirt is Good, 5 Ways to Make Germs Your Friends. New York: Kaplan Publishing, 2009.

Simpson, Roger, "Seattle Newsboys: How Hustler Democracy Lost to the Power of Property." Journalism History, 18, 1992.

Skenazy, Lenore, Free-Range Kids: Giving Our Children the Freedom We Had Without Going Nuts with Worry. Hoboken, New Jersey: John Wiley & Sons, 2009.

Sklar, Robert, Movie-Made America, A Cultural History of American Movies. New York: Vintage Books, 1994.

Stevens, Paul and Walter Stevens, The Messenger. Ft. Dodge, Iowa: Messenger Publishing, 2006.

Von Drehle, David, "The Boys Are All Right" Time magazine, August 6, 2007. P. 38-47.

# ACKNOWLEDGEMENTS

To untangle my image of newsboys from movies and novels and to complete a record of my older brother's newspaper days, I asked a good friend, Paul Reasoner, "Were you ever a paperboy?" With boyish enthusiasm, his "Yes" reply sent me on a long route, further enlarged by help from Ernestine, his wife. They truly conveyed a community spirit.

With no hesitation, Ron Petersen completed the first questionnaire and just as quickly answered additional questions. His remarkable experiences spurred me forward.

Through Lorraine McConaghy, the historian for the Museum of History and Industry and director of the respected Nearby History, I progressed from a pilot project in the Northwest to regions throughout America. Dr. McConaghy's seminar for researchers and writers gave the structured base. I remain grateful to her and the 14 fellow researchers who offered direction, when so involved with their interesting history projects. Then Dr. McConaghy directed me to Dr. Roger Simpson, University of Washington, where he teaches journalism history, who guided me to Dr. David Nasaw's fine text, *Children of The City: At Work and At Play*. Thank you for the valuable assistance.

The libraries, archives and government reports offered by excellent librarians set the personal paperboy responses on a factual foundation. In Anchorage, Mount Vernon and Columbus, Ohio, Everett, Seattle, University of Washington Suzzalo Library, the expert librarians responded beyond my requests.

Brian Naplachowski, a conscientious circulation director, readily connected me with Dale Irvine. And Dale extended help, introducing me to Jack Gahan and to the Northwest International Circulation Executives (NICE). Because of Dale, I met Joe Forsee, retired director for the International Circulation Managers Association (ICMA), who helped immeasurably with the project. I am exceptionally grateful for this enthusiasm and warm, friendly outreach. His fellow ICMA members reflect Mr. Forsee's spirit and caring, especially: Ed Norlin, Ron

Anderson, Walter Dreyfus, Grover Friend, Paul Haygood, John Hayes and Terry DeVassie.

To those who helped, suggesting others until a newspaper carrier community stretched beyond a narrow neighborhood, thank you. Your interest and sincere involvement energized the project. Some of the key contributors: Art Armstrong connected me with his astute members of Probus; wonderful friends at the University Presbyterian Church, Paul Meyer, Tom Lewis, Ross Webb, John Rodda and sister Kathleen; Loren Day and friends with the Shoreline Museum; Jesse Montoya introduced me to the nine Grab sisters, models of family unity; journalist Jim Stingl and his enthusiastic readers of the *Milwaukee Journal Sentinel*; Bill Ruth's brothers and family, to include his family of military friends. It was a privilege to spend time with dads and sons, especially the Ed Norlins, and father Francis Walsh and Jerry Walsh. To enjoy the closeness of brothers was also delightful, in particular: the Rudy boys, McArthurs, Linnes, and Ruths. The stories, artifacts, photographs, and most of all laughter of ordinary citizens kept me probing. Growing more entertaining and informative, I watched "senior" paperboys tightly roll and tuck a newspaper faster than they could pop bubble gum. Yes, they recalled a different time, when pay phones, party phone lines and clotheslines were abundant. Fortunately, friendships have lasted. My sincere thank you to all the carriers, friends and family, newspaper personnel for their time and willingness to provide valuable input.

The paths I pursued to uncover the modern history of youth delivering newspapers led to even greater appreciation for their resilience and fortitude. The hundreds of "silver-haired" carriers spoke modestly of the experiences they endured on their first job. These people strengthened my respect for their reliability and accountability while still only children. Thank you.

To the legions of men and women who managed a route in childhood, whom I did not record, please tell your story. Share with your grandkids. They struggle to grasp how children survived covering a paper route without a cell phone, leaning down to pick up pennies, appreciating a dime, walking over a long route, walking to collect, walking to school.

The Pacific Northwest is rich with writers' organizations, conferences, and writers who first and foremost dedicate themselves to helping others. A special thank you to the Pacific Northwest Writers Association, the Whidbey Island Writers Association, the Edmonds Write on the Sound Conference, the dedicated Seattle Seven (particularly William Dietrich), and the expanding Northwest Women Writers created by the intense effort of Betsy Diedrick.

For this book to reach the important readers, it required professional handling. I'm very grateful to the guidance and patience of

Tom Masters, and for introducing me to Kathryn Gilmore, a dedicated editor. Kathryn's careful, fine editing was exceptionally valuable. Early in the project when photos arrived, Dannie Mullene efficiently computerized them. Mary Gogulski has the excellent, expert eye of a designer. And Marcia Breece with her organized professional skills pleasantly handled all the necessary eBook steps. Thank you.

I greatly appreciate the enthusiasm and assistance from our daughters, Marilyn Laura and Beth Ann. Both gave valuable input. Marilyn's professional computer skills brought me out of many technical jams. And the boundless humor, support and encouragement from my husband, Terry, as well as his patience, kept me laughing and the project moving forward.

To my teasing, devilish brother who left the house, alone, with his soiled canvas bag, stopped at the post office for his bundles, rode his used bike around the route and returned home hungry, to Carl, who in spirit led me, thank you. I persisted with the newspaper carrier project in honor of him. This book is in honor of all the youth who committed to daily rounds, so customers conveniently enjoyed their newspaper companion.

# PAPER CARRIERS

Paper Carriers who delivered more than four seasons in the 1920 to 1970 era, who shared in detail their experiences.

| | | |
|---|---|---|
| Adams, Bruce. | Seattle Times, Wa. | 1945-1948 |
| Anderson, Ron | Democrat & Chronicle, Charlotte, New York | 1951, 1952 |
| Ansted, Harry | Seattle Star, Seattle PI, Seattle Times | 1938-1943 |
| Armstrong, Art | Seattle Star, Everett Daily Herald, Seattle PI | 1940-1942 |
| Atkins, Ted | Industrial Post, Huntington Park Daily, Calif. | 1950-1955 |
| Atkinson, Joe | Idaho Evening Statesman, Boise, Idaho | 1953-1955 |
| Ausmus, James | Columbia Daily Tribune, Columbia, Mo. | 1949-1951 |
| Bailey, Robert | Appleton Post Crescent, Appleton, Wis. | 1934-1939 |
| Ballough, Ron | University District Herald, Seattle Times | 1948-1956 |
| Barnhart, Terry | Arizona Republic, Ariz. | 1950-1956 |
| Barr, Bob | San Francisco Examiner, Klamath Herald | 1936-1941 |
| | Klamath Falls, Oregon | |
| Bates, Bill | Seattle Star, Seattle PI | 1938-1941 |
| Bennett, Albert | Everett Daily Herald, Everett, Wa. | 1932-1934 |
| Bennett, Francis | Everett Daily Herald, Everett, Wa. | 1934, 1935 |
| Benson, Clifford | Everett Daily Herald, Everett, Wa. | 1951-1955 |
| Berbert, David | Columbia Tribune, Columbia, Mo. | 1941-1943 |
| Bergeron, Carole | Tacoma News Tribune, Tacoma, Wa. | 1949-1959 |
| Bingham, Don | Seattle Star, Seattle PI, Seattle Times | 1936-1942 |
| Birchman, Jim | Detroit News, Mich. | 1941-1943 |
| Bloomer, Raymond | Cincinnati Enquirer, Ohio | 1938-1941 |
| Boblitt, Ed | Bellefontaine Examiner, Ohio | 1947-1955 |
| Bolf, Ken | Albany Democrat Herald, Oregon | 1961-1964 |

| | | |
|---|---|---|
| Bowles, David | Bellingham Herald, Seattle Star, Union Record | 1917-1925 |
| | Ellensburg Evening Record, Wa. | |
| Brigham, John | Commercial Appeal, Tenn. | 1955-1959 |
| Brink, Bob | Elmira Star Gazette, New York | 1954-1961 |
| Brunner, Beverly | Syracuse Post Standard, New York | 1945, 1946 |
| Buescher, Maribeth | Columbia Daily Tribune, Mo. | 1949, 1950 |
| Burns, Ed | Seattle PI | 1942-1944 |
| Butler, Tom | Oregonian, Oregon | 1950-1954 |
| Cain, Charles Bill | Southwest American, Ariz. | 1936-1941 |
| Cameron, Ron | Seattle Times | 1953-1958 |
| Carpenter, Jim | Mount Vernon News, Ohio | 1951, 1952 |
| Carter, Glen | Seattle Times | 1963-1966 |
| Casto, Ron | Marietta Times, Ohio | 1955-1960 |
| Chase, Luke | Columbia Tribune, Mo. | 1940-1944 |
| Chiodo, Don | Des Moines Register & Tribune, Iowa | 1940-1943 |
| Clark, Harry | Indianapolis Time, Indianapolis News, Ind. | 1938-1941 |
| Coleburn, Doug | Richmond News-Leader, Virginia | 1940-1943 |
| Dailey, Marc | The Wenatchee World, Wa. | 1958-1960 |
| Dappen, John | Sioux City Journal, Des Moines Register, Iowa | 1930-1938 |
| Day, Loren | Seattle Times | 1954-1959 |
| Deirlein, Jack | Seattle Times | 1928-1931 |
| DePrez, Paul | Seattle PI, Seattle Times | 1966-1972 |
| Desilet, Leroy Lee | Spokane Chronicle, Lewiston Tribune, Id | 1937-1943 |
| DeVassie, Terry | Columbus Dispatch, Ohio | 1952-1957 |
| Dodson, Bruce | Alton Evening Telegraph, Ill. | 1951,1952 |
| Dreyfus, Walter Bud | Birmingham News, Ala. | 1932-1935 |
| | Nashville Banner, Tenn. | 1935-1939 |
| | Indianapolis Star, Ind. | 1939, 1940 |
| Dulaney, Ed | Columbia Daily Tribune | 1939-1943 |
| Dungee, John | Chicago Tribune, Ill | 1943, 1944 |
| Dunphy, Barry | Ketchikan Fishing News, Ak. | 1940-1942 |
| | Idaho Statesman | 1943-1948 |
| Dunphy, Burnie | Ketchikan Chronicle, Ak. | 1940-1946 |
| | Idaho Statesman | |
| Eagles, Bill | Seattle Star, Seattle PI | 1933-1937 |
| Eng, Pat | Des Moines Register & Tribune, Ia. | 1953-1956 |

| | | |
|---|---|---|
| Epstein, Joe | New York Times, New York Tribune | 1956-1960 |
| | Mirror, Newark Star | |
| Everett, Nathan | Mishawaka Times, Ind. | 1962-1965 |
| Fellows, Paul | Minneapolis Tribune, Minneapolis Star | 1954-1957 |
| Felzer, Clement | Seattle Star, Seattle Times | 1934-1937 |
| Fisk, Max | Seattle Star, Everett Daily Herald | 1937-1940 |
| Forsee, Joe | Columbia Daily Tribune, Mo. | 1939-1943 |
| Fraigun, Dave | Cleveland News, Ohio | 1926-1930 |
| Fraits, Don | Providence Journal, R. Island | 1940-1943 |
| Franze, Vernon | The Wenatchee World, Wa. | 1931-1934 |
| Friend, Grover | Evening Standard, Pa. | 1948-1952 |
| Fry, Charlie | Miami Daily News, Fl. | 1938-1941 |
| Fulton, Ruth | Cordova Times, Ak | 1939, 1940 |
| Furtaw, Joe | St. Louis Post Dispatch, Mo. | 1954-1956 |
| Gahan, Jack | Tacoma News Tribune, Seattle Times | 1942-1953 |
| Gamel, Bill | Anchorage Daily Times, Ak | 1949-1953 |
| Gardner, Ken | Everett Daily Herald, Wa | 1967-1972 |
| Gatterman, Eugene | Everett Daily Herald, Wa. | 1951-1955 |
| Gatto, Susan | Tacoma News Tribune, Wa. | 1962-1966 |
| Gennarelli, Frank | Binghamton Press, New York | 1947-1952 |
| Gilluly, Robert Bob | Glasgow Courier, Mont. | 1938-1944 |
| Grab sisters: | Tacoma News Tribune, Wa. | 1950-1964 |
| | Mary Ann, Phyllis, Teresa, Patricia, Frances, Josie, Kathy, Barbara, Suzie | |
| Graham, David | Columbus Citizen, Ohio | 1952, 1953 |
| Gray, Clifford | Roswell Record, New Mex. | 1937-1942 |
| Gray, John | Birmingham News, Ala. | 1939-1942 |
| Grout, James | Seattle Times | 1951-1954 |
| Guzzo, Dante | Columbus Citizen, Ohio | 1935-1937 |
| Hagen, Roger | Argus Leader, in Parker, S. Dk. | 1945-1947 |
| Hahn, Ed | Rochester Weekly, New York | 1939, 1940 |
| Hall, Mike | Spokane Daily Chronicle, Wa | 1955-1960 |
| Hamm, Shirley | Bangor Daily, Portland Press Herald | 1946-1951 |
| | Katadin Times, Penobscot Times, Maine | |
| Hammond, Charles | Seattle Star, Seattle Times, PI | 1931-1938 |
| Hancock, Preston | Omaha World Herald, Neb. | 1935-1937 |

| | | |
|---|---|---|
| Hansen, Ben | Manitown Herald Times, Wis. | 1935-1938 |
| Hanson, Dick | Everett Daily Herald, Wa | 1946-1948 |
| Hanson, Larry | Everett Daily Herald, Wa | 1948-1950 |
| Hansen, Robert | Toledo News Bee Co., Ohio | 1932-1934 |
| Haringa, Ron | Seattle PI, Seattle Times | 1952-1957 |
| Harrison, Harve | Seattle PI, Seattle Times | 1932-1935 |
| | Tacoma Tribune, Portland Oregonian | |
| Haygood, Paul | Atlanta Journal, Ga. | 1939, 1940 |
| Hazlewood, Terri | Herald Examiner, Calif. | 1978-1980 |
| Henry, Kirk | Memphis Press, Tenn. | 1953-1955 |
| Holmes, Dugg | Rocky Mountain News, Colo. | 1935-1940 |
| Horna, Gerald | Chester Times, Pa | 1949-1955 |
| | Philadelphia Bulletin & Inquirer, New York Times | |
| Houser, Tillman | News-Telegram, Oregon Statesman, Oregon | 1936-1940 |
| Hubbard, Don | Spokesman Review, Spokane Chronicle | 1948-1952 |
| | Portland Oregonian | |
| Hudson, Larry | Tribune Democrat, Pa | 1960-1963 |
| Hughes, Barrie J. | The Calgary Herald, Alberta | 1949-1954 |
| Iffrig, Bill | Seattle Star, Everett | 1943, 1944 |
| Irvin, Dick | Des Moines Register, Tribune, Ia. | 1923-1932 |
| Irvine, Dale | University District Herald, Seattle Times | 1948-1955 |
| James, John | Standard Sentinel, Hazleton, Pa. | 1923-1932 |
| Janecke, David | Seattle Star | 1937-1939 |
| Janecke, George | Seattle Star | 1938-1940 |
| Jeffery, Paul | Newark Star Ledger, Paterson Evening News | 1952-1957 |
| | and New York papers in New Jersey | |
| | In New York, The Long Island Press | |
| Johnson, Walter | Seattle PI, Seattle Star, Seattle Times | 1940-1942 |
| | Mt. Vernon Argus, Wa | |
| Johnston, Jack | Seattle PI, Everett Daily Herald, Wa | 1960-1962 |
| Jones, Don | Columbia Daily Tribune, Mo. | 1948-1952 |
| Kalivoda, Richard Dick | Seattle Times | 1950-1955 |
| Kavanaugh, Jim | Spokesmen Review, in Idaho | 1940-1942 |
| Kearns, John | Seattle Times | 1936-1942 |
| Kniest, Paul | Seattle Times | 1973,1974 |

| | | |
|---|---|---|
| Knight, John | Patriot News, Harrisburg, Pa. | 1940, 1941 |
| Knizek, Harvey | Seattle PI, Seattle Star, Seattle Times | 1949-1954 |
| Koeble, Charles | The Milwaukee Journal, Wis. | 1943-1946 |
| Kopczynski, Joan M | Lewiston Morning Tribune, Id. | 1963-1968 |
| Kost, Gary | Mount Vernon News, Ohio | 1951-1955 |
| Kress, Michael | Times Union, New York | 1960-1963 |
| Kvamme, Olaf | Tacoma News Tribune, Wa | 1938-1940 |
| Labuhn, Gordon | Detroit Times, Mich | 1941-1943 |
| Ladderud, Nils | Everett Daily Herald | 1950-1952 |
| Lair, Leonard | Seattle Times | 1950-1955 |
| Lamb, Coby | Daily Forum, Mo | 1960-1964 |
| Lane, Carl | Mount Vernon News, Ohio | 1947-1951 |
| | Fredericktown News | |
| Lane, Dwayne | Everett Daily Herald, Wa | 1947, 1948 |
| Larson, Doug | Lincoln Journal, Neb. | 1963-1966 |
| Lee, Tony | Dallas Times Herald, Tex | 1968,1969 |
| Leed, Roger | Seattle PI | 1949-1953 |
| Leo, Jim | Everett Daily Herald, Wa | 1950-1952 |
| Lewis, Tom | Seattle Times | 1947-1949 |
| Linne, John | Indianapolis Times, Ind. | 1954-1956 |
| Linne, Walter | Indianapolis Times, Ind. | 1952-1956 |
| Long, Cynthia | Seattle Times | 1971, 1972 |
| MacDonald, Cal | Boston Globe, Mass. | 1951-1955 |
| MacDonald, Chris | Everett Daily Herald | 1975-1977 |
| Mack, Jim | Detroit News, Mich. | 1943-1950 |
| Mailloux, Don | Lafayette Journal & Courier, Ind. | 1946-1949 |
| Malone, Bill | Commercial Appeal, Tenn. | 1941-1947 |
| Mast, Joel | Springfield News, Oh | 1972-1980 |
| McArthur, Ed | Seattle Times | 1948-1952 |
| McArthur, James | Seattle Star, Seattle Times | 1945-1951 |
| McArthur, John | Seattle Star, Seattle Times | 1947-1957 |
| McArthur, Tom | Seattle Times | 1949-1957 |
| McDaniel, Rudy | Memphis Commercial, Ark | 1966-1969 |
| McManus, Paul | Seattle PI, Seattle Times | 1957-1961 |
| McManus, Kirby | Seattle PI, Seattle Times | 1960-1962 |
| McManus, Stephen | Seattle PI, Seattle Times | 1960-1962 |

| | | |
|---|---|---|
| McQueen, Roy | Andrews County News, Tex | 1952-1958 |
| Merrill, David | John Day, Oregon | 1959-1961 |
| Meyer, Paul | Tacoma News Tribune, Wa | 1948-1952 |
| Miller, Bill | Manchester Evening Herald, Ct | 1943-1948 |
| Mitchell, Vyron | Cadiz Record, Ky | 1951-1960 |
| Modine, Leroy | Walla Walla Union Bulletin, Wa | 1950-1959 |
| Monsaas, Barrett | Seattle Times | 1952-1954 |
| Montoya, Jesse | Wenatchee World, Wa | 1947-1955 |
| Montoya, Lee | Wenatchee World | 1945-1952 |
| Moore, Jack | The Daily Oklahoman, The Oklahoma City Times | 1946-1949 |
| | The Sunday Oklahoman | |
| Mushen, David | Detroit News, Mich | 1959-1964 |
| Newman, Jerry | Seattle PI, Aberdeen World, Oregonian, Wa | 1950, 1951 |
| Nicon, John | Seattle Times | 1949-1953 |
| Nixon, Ron | The State Journal, Mich. | 1956, 1957 |
| Nolting, Bill | Brooklyn News, N Y | 1928-1930 |
| Norlin, Ed, Sr. | The Oklahoman Times, Oklahoma News | 1926-1931 |
| | The Sunday Oklahoman | |
| Norlin, Ed, Jr. | The Oklahoman, Daily Oklahoman | 1953-1956 |
| | The Sunday Oklahoman | |
| Noyes, Robert | Seattle Times | 1932-1934 |
| Opp, Jim | Binghamton Press, N Y | 1955-1958 |
| Overland, Norman | Yakima Daily Republic, Seattle Star, Wa. | 1932-1937 |
| Park, Ron | Daily Star, Niles, Mich. | 1943-1947 |
| Paterson, Jon Robin | Seattle Star, Seattle Times | 1944-1946 |
| Peifer, Harry | Seattle Star, Seattle Times | 1942,1943 |
| Peter, Jerry | Chronicle Telegram, Elyria, Ohio | 1957-1960 |
| Petersen, Ron | Salt Lake Tribune, Utah | 1948-1950 |
| Petroski, Henry | Long Island Press, New York | 1954-1958 |
| Plopper, Bruce | Syracuse Herald Journal, New York | 1960-1963 |
| Poletti, Ray | Seattle Times | 1961-1964 |
| Popp, Michael | The Sun Telegraph, W.Va | 1944-1946 |
| Pugh, Bob | Columbia Tribune, Mo | 1954-1956 |
| Rarig, Sam | Shamokin News Dispatch, Pa | 1935-1943 |
| Reasoner, Paul | Cleveland Press, Ohio | 1947-1949 |

| | | |
|---|---|---|
| Reed, John | San Francisco Examiner, Ca | 1938-1944 |
| Reed, Richard | Spokesman Review, Wa | 1962-1966 |
| Reiber, Gene | Tacoma News Tribune, Wa | 1942-1945 |
| Reilly, Ed | Seattle Times | 1966, 1967 |
| Rhinehart, Gary | News Chronicle, Pa | 1950-1955 |
| Rhodes, Mike | San Jose Mercury, Calif. | 1955-1962 |
| Richardson, Ron | Seattle PI | 1947, 1948 |
| Robinson, James | Seattle Star, Seattle Times | 1944-1946 |
| Roby, Joanne | New Bedford Standard Times, Mass | 1950-1954 |
| Rockne, Tom | Minneapolis Tribune, in N Dk. | 1960,1961 |
| Rodda, Jack | Butte Daily Post, Mont. | 1927-1931 |
| Rodda, John | Oregonian, in Walla Walla, Wa | 1958-1960 |
| Rodin, Glenn | Seattle Star | 1936,1937 |
| Root, Jim | Seattle PI, Seattle Times | 1945-1951 |
| Ruck, James | Tacoma News Tribune, Wa | 1942-1945 |
| Rudy, Dale | Rocky Mountain News, Colo. | 1963-1969 |
| Rudy, Greg | Rocky Mountain News | 1967-1971 |
| Rudy, Jim | Rocky Mountain News | 1959-1964 |
| Rudy, Tom | Rocky Mountain News | 1974, 1975 |
| Ruth, Bill | Johnstown Democrat, Pa | 1934-1940 |
| Ruth, Bill Jr. | Columbus Citizen, Columbus Dispatch, Oh | 1959-1965 |
| Ruth Paul | Johnstown Democrat, Pa | 1940-1945 |
| Ruth, Richard | Johnstown Democrat, Pa. | 1936-1942 |
| Ruth, Robert | Johnstown, Democrat, Pa. | 1928-1930 |
| Ruth, Stephen | Columbus Dispatch, Oh | 1965-1968 |
| Rydzak, John | Washington Reporter, Pa | 1930-1932 |
| | Pittsburgh Press | |
| Satterthwaite, John | Seattle Buyer's Guide | 1938-1940 |
| Scanlon, Robert | Chicago Tribune, Ill | 1933-1937 |
| Schneiger, Frank | Journal Sentinel, Wis. | 1953-1955 |
| Schroth, Ed | Cleveland Press, Cleveland Plain Dealer | 1948-1952 |
| | Cleveland News, Oh | |
| Schultz, Neoma | Rocky Mountain News, Denver Post, Colo. | 1954-1957 |
| Sherrill, Tom | Tampa Daily Times, Fl | 1942-1946 |
| Siegel, Ron | Dayton Daily News, Oh | 1959-1961 |
| Skipton, Tom | Pittsburg Press, Marietta Times, Ohio | 1945-1950 |

| | | |
|---|---|---|
| Smith, Orin | Spokane Daily Chronicle, in Idaho | 1948-1952 |
| Smyth, Sam | Seattle Star, Wa | 1932-1935 |
| Soriano, Dominic | Everett Daily Herald, Seattle Star | 1934-1942 |
| | Seattle PI, Seattle Times | |
| Soriano, John | Everett Daily Herald, Seattle Star | 1941-1946 |
| | Seattle PI, Seattle Times | |
| Spahr, Bob | Seattle PI | 1950-1952 |
| Stanley, Zita | Rockford Morning Star, Ill | 1952, 1953 |
| Sterling, Ed | Trenton Times, N J | 1967-1969 |
| Stevens, Jim | Seattle Times | 1942-1945 |
| Stevens, David | The Messenger, Iowa | 1963-1968 |
| Stevens, Paul | The Messenger, Iowa | 1955-1960 |
| Stevens, Walter | Sioux City Journal | 1928-1933 |
| | Omaha World Herald | |
| Stingl, Jim | Milwaukee Journal Sentinel. Wis. | 1965-1970 |
| Stoebuck, William | Wichita  Beacon, Kan. | 1941-1945 |
| Stonington, David | Rocky Mountain News, Colo. | 1955-1957 |
| Sturgis, Kent | Daily News-Miner, Ak | 1957-1960 |
| Terrell, Len | Highpoint Enterprise | 1945-1955 |
| | Greensboro Daily, N.C. | |
| Thompsen, Leo | Brooklyn Daily Eagle | 1937-1939 |
| Thor, Warren | Tacoma News Tribune, Seattle Times | 1943-1946 |
| Thorp, Cary | Columbia Daily Tribune, Mo | 1947-1953 |
| Thurmond, Al | Seattle Times | 1942,1943 |
| Tobey, Russ | Bartlesville Examiner, Okla. | 1936-1942 |
| | Tulsa Tribune, World | |
| Vannice, Cathryn | Spokesman Review | 1956-1958 |
| Wagner, Howard | Columbus Citizen Journal, Oh | 1941-1952 |
| Walsh, Francis | Columbus Citizen Journal, Oh | 1932-1935 |
| Walsh, Jerry | Columbus Dispatch, Oh | 1963-1965 |
| | Columbus Citizen Journal | |
| Walsh, John F. | New Bedford Standard Times, Mass | 1950-1952 |
| Watson, Robert | Seattle PI | 1934-1940 |
| Watt, Donald | Toledo Times, Oh | 1934-1936 |
| Webb, Ross | Oregon Journal, Portland, Or | 1952-1954 |
| West, Paul | Seattle PI | 1952-1954 |

| | | |
|---|---|---|
| White, Ed | Hudson Dispatch, N. J | 1942-1948 |
| Whitlock, Flint | Hammond Times, Ind. | 1955, 1956 |
| Wilkerson, Doug | Seattle Times | 1950-1955 |
| Wilson, Burt | Sacramento Bee, San Francisco Examiner, Ca | 1943-1945 |
| Wilson, John | Tracy Press, Stockton Record, Ca | 1960, 1961 |
| Wirsing, Dale | Tacoma Times, Tacoma News Tribune | 1944-1954 |
| Wise, Grant | Courier Journal, Louisville Times, Ky | 1960-1966 |
| Woods, Bill | Daytona Beach Courier, Fl | 1951-1954 |
| Wyatt, Robert | Kansas City Journal, Kansas City Star | 1928-1938 |
| Young, Herb | Seattle PI, Seattle Star | 1939-1942 |

# INDEX

# ABOUT THE AUTHOR

Sandra Walker began the newspaper carrier project to honor her brother's memory, since as a boy he delivered the Mount Vernon Daily News in Ohio. Discovering abundant stories, she expanded the project across America interviewing hundreds of former paperboys and girls. As a teacher and counselor, she understood the rowdiness and reliability of these energetic children. She lives by Puget Sound and is active with Northwest writers' associations.